The Book of Travels

Volume One

# Letter from the General Editor

The Library of Arabic Literature makes available Arabic editions and English translations of significant works of Arabic literature, with an emphasis on the seventh to nineteenth centuries. The Library of Arabic Literature thus includes texts from the pre-Islamic era to the cusp of the modern period, and encompasses a wide range of genres, including poetry, poetics, fiction, religion, philosophy, law, science, travel writing, history, and historiography.

Books in the series are edited and translated by internationally recognized scholars. They are published as hardcovers in parallel-text format with Arabic and English on facing pages, as English-only paperbacks, and as downloadable Arabic editions. For some texts, the series also publishes separate scholarly editions with full critical apparatus.

The Library encourages scholars to produce authoritative Arabic editions, accompanied by modern, lucid English translations, with the ultimate goal of introducing Arabic's rich literary heritage to a general audience of readers as well as to scholars and students.

The publications of the Library of Arabic Literature are generously supported by Tamkeen under the NYU Abu Dhabi Research Institute Award G1003 and are published by NYU Press.

Philip F. Kennedy
*General Editor, Library of Arabic Literature*

# كتاب السياحة

## حنّا دياب

### المجلّد الأوّل

LIBRARY OF
المكتبة
ARABIC
العربية
LITERATURE

# The Book of Travels

## Ḥannā Diyāb

## Volume One

Edited by
JOHANNES STEPHAN

Translated by
ELIAS MUHANNA

Foreword by
YASMINE SEALE

Volume editor
MICHAEL COOPERSON

NEW YORK UNIVERSITY PRESS
*New York*

NEW YORK UNIVERSITY PRESS
*New York*

Copyright © 2021 by New York University
All rights reserved

Library of Congress Cataloging-in-Publication Control Number: 2020054531

New York University Press books are printed on acid-free paper,
and their binding materials are chosen for strength and durability.

Series design by Titus Nemeth.

Typeset in Tasmeem, using DecoType Naskh and Emiri.

Typesetting and digitization by Stuart Brown.

Manufactured in the United States of America
c 10 9 8 7 6 5 4 3 2 1

# Table of Contents

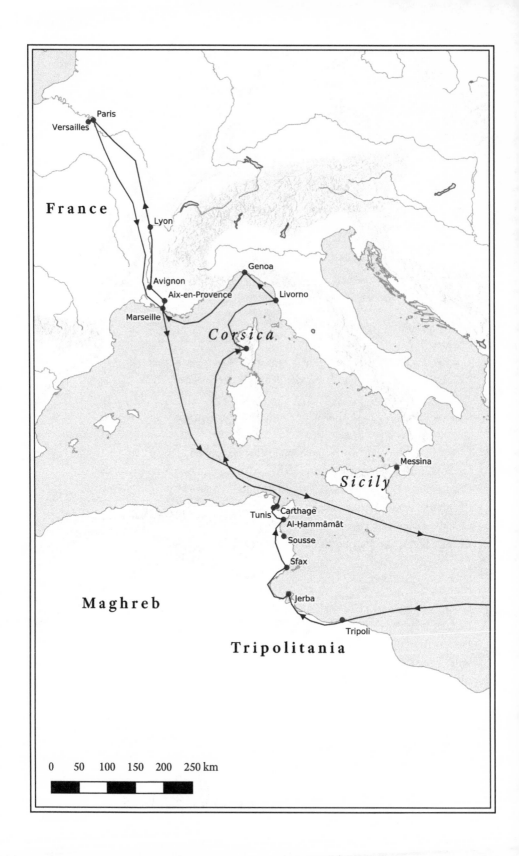

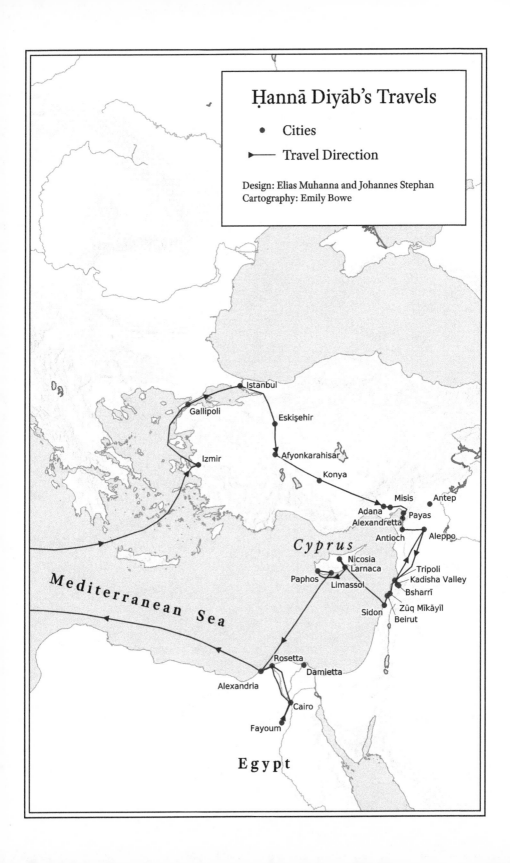

# Ḥannā Diyāb's Travels

- **Cities**
- ►— **Travel Direction**

Design: Elias Muhanna and Johannes Stephan
Cartography: Emily Bowe

Istanbul

Gallipoli

Eskişehir

Izmir

Afyonkarahisar

Konya

Misis     Antep

Adana     Payas

Alexandretta

Antioch     Aleppo

*Cyprus*

Nicosia
Larnaca

Paphos          Tripoli
          Kadisha Valley
Limassol

Bsharrī

*Mediterranean Sea*

Sidon     Zūq Mīkāyīl
          Beirut

Rosetta

Damietta

Alexandria

Cairo

Fayoum

**Egypt**

# Foreword

## Yasmine Seale

One morning in October 1708, two men walk into a room at Versailles where King Louis XIV is waiting to receive them. Between them is a cage of curious animals: a pair of honey-colored mice with giant ears and long hind legs, like miniature kangaroos. The older man, Paul Lucas, has just returned from a mission to the Ottoman Empire, where he was sent to hunt for coins, gems, and other precious things to feed the royal collection. Among the loot he has brought back are these strange, alert creatures. The king wants to know more. Lucas boasts that he "discovered" them in Upper Egypt, despite their being very difficult to catch. (He is lying: in fact, he was sold them by a Frenchman in Tunis.) And what are they called? Lucas, unable to say, turns to the young man by his side.

"I replied that, in the lands where it is found, the animal is called a *jarbū'*." Of how many people can it be said that their first words to the Sun King contained the Arabic pharyngeal '*ayn*? The pharynx, and the story, belong to Ḥannā Diyāb, a multilingual monk-in-training from Aleppo who, around the age of twenty, dropped out of the ascetic life to be Lucas's assistant on his voyage—translating, interceding and, once or twice, saving his life—in exchange for the promise of a job in Paris.

It was probably through Diyāb that *gerboise*, the desert-dwelling jerboa, entered the French lexicon. At the king's request he writes down the animals' name. At the request of the king's son ("of medium height and quite rotund"), they are painted onto an enormous illustration of wild beasts. Then Diyāb is marched around the palace to be peered at, by princess after princess, until two in the morning. He peers back.

The promise is eventually betrayed; after two years with Lucas and no job forthcoming, Diyāb returns home to Aleppo where he spends the rest of his life selling cloth—and, no doubt, telling stories of his adventure. Fifty-four years after the facts, unknowably transformed, he commits them to paper.

Time is also a translator. After telling us about his encounter with the king, Diyāb adds: "Is it possible I could have retained perfectly everything I saw and heard? Surely not." It is the only moment in the memoir when he calls his own reliability into question, pointing to the half-century that separates the tale from the event. Yet *The Book of Travels*' most astonishing scene, its perihelion, is also its most believable: the royal curiosity rushing to classify, the chubby prince, the little lie.

You are reading Diyāb's true story because of others he made up: Aladdin (spelled in Arabic as 'Alā' al-Dīn), 'Alī Bābā, a dozen more told to Antoine Galland over a handful of spring nights. These encounters, among the most consequential in literature, are recorded in a cooler key, offhand. Nothing could be more normal, less worthy of note than the telling and swapping of tales— "collaborative sessions," as the editor of this volume aptly puts it.

Aladdin, readers are sometimes surprised to learn, is a boy from China. Yet the text is ambivalent about what this means, and pokes gentle fun at the idea of cultural authenticity. Shahrazad has hardly begun her tale when she forgets quite where it is set. "Majesty, in the capital of one of China's vast and wealthy kingdoms, whose name escapes me at present, there lived a tailor named Mustafa . . . ." The story's institutions are Ottoman, the customs half-invented, the palace redolent of Versailles. It is a mishmash and knows it.

Like Aladdin, like Aleppo, Diyāb's is a story of mixture. He knows French, Turkish, Italian, even Provençal—but not Greek: in Cyprus, unable to understand the language, he feels like "a deaf man in a wedding procession." Slipping in and out of personae, he is alert to the masquerades of others. Behind the European envoy's mask we glimpse a con man: Paul Lucas travels in the guise of a doctor, prescribing remedies in exchange for treasure. He treats a stomach ache with a paste made of parsley, sugar, and crushed pearls.

To meet the king, Diyāb has been encouraged to wear his native dress: turban cloth, pantaloons, dagger. But the calpac on his head is actually Egyptian, and his trousers cut from *londrin*—London or Mocha broadcloth, a textile made of Spanish wool, manufactured in Languedoc and exported to Aleppo by merchants in Marseille. His outfit, like his mind, bears a pan-Mediterranean print.

In *The Book of Travels* he is forever drawing comparisons: between Lyon and Aleppo, Seine and Euphrates, Harlequin and Karagöz. Against the clash of cultures, here is a cradle; against the border, a lattice. Here is a Syrian's view of France, a description of Europe where Arabs circulate and thrive, a portrait of the Mediterranean as a zone of intense contact and interwoven histories.

This is also an old man's account of what it was to be twenty years old, gifted and curious, somewhere new. Time has sharpened its colors. Its thrill is picaresque:

a tale of high drama and low ebbs, the exuberant perils of early modern travel. At a Franciscan monastery in Cyprus, Diyāb is kept awake all night by the grunting of pigs. He is eaten alive by mosquitoes in Rosetta, by lice in Fayoum; ambushed on the way to Livorno by corsairs who cry *"Maina!,"* lingua franca for surrender; abandoned to the whims of muleteers. Tobacco is smuggled in a mattress, a mummy in straw. Much energy is spent evading English pirates.

In the long tradition of Arabic travel writing, Diyāb is different: he lets us in and keeps us close. Unlike Ilyās al-Mawṣilī, whose account of the Spanish conquest of America Diyāb seems to have owned, he is not a cleric seeking to secure his reputation. Nor is this a self-consciously literary document in the vein of ʿAbd al-Ghanī al-Nābulusī's descriptions of his journeys through the Muslim world. There is no poetry in this memoir, no quotation. Its cadences are those of Syrian speech, its subject everyday emotions: fear, shame, astonishment, relief.

Some of the most vivid pages concern a storm in the Gulf of Sidra, where Diyāb and his companions nearly drown. By the time the castaways reach land, their throats are so dry they cannot speak, and their food has turned soggy with seawater. For days they eat nothing but dates, then they are reduced to eating cats. When they finally reach Tripoli, after fifteen days without nourishment, and are given bread, Diyāb is unable to swallow it: "it tasted like ashes."

Then there are the fifteen icy days in December 1708, the coldest winter in five hundred years, during which tens of thousands froze to death. "Paris was a ghost town . . . The priests of the city were forced to set up braziers on the altars of their churches to prevent the sacramental wine from freezing. Many people even died while relieving themselves, because the urine froze in their urethras as it left their bodies and killed them." Diyāb has to be rubbed from head to toe with eagle fat (another of Lucas's remedies) and wrapped in blankets for twenty-four hours before he recovers sensation in his limbs. It is in these moments of plain, precise language that hunger, thirst, and cold—untranslatable pain—come through.

Unusually for a travel writer, Diyāb is a working man. For all the pomp of the French court, his attention remains trained on those who, like him, labor invisibly: hospital workers who serve soup three times a day in tin bowls; nuns who launder clothes in the river; prostitutes whose doors are marked by a large heart made of thorns. Striking, too, is the sheer violence of everyday life. In Livorno he sees a soldier punished for desertion—nostrils slashed and forehead branded with the king's seal. In Paris he goes to a courthouse to watch the trial of highway robbers, and to the public square to see them killed.

A thought recurred as I read: you couldn't make it up. While Lucas bathes rusty coins in vinegar to reveal their inscriptions, Diyāb probes the strangeness of the world. Miracles—magical causes applied to mechanical effects—jostle with the most daily phenomena. The true colors of things take on a hallucinated quality. If the Dauphin's bestiary contains no jerboa, can his own eyes be trusted? If the remedy is bogus, but you were healed, what then?

Scholars argue over how much of Diyāb is in Aladdin, where to draw the line between fiction and truth. This memoir smudges such distinctions by showing how fantasy is woven into life, how enchantment is neighbor to inquiry. At the opera, Diyāb is dazzled by stage contraptions. Knowing how they are built does nothing to lessen their magic. Mechanical causes with magical effects: this is art.

Yasmine Seale
Istanbul

# Acknowledgments

## Editor's acknowledgments

I wish to express my sincere gratitude to those colleagues who helped me during the process of preparing this edition and added to my understanding of the text and its context. Altogether, this work is the outcome of a physical and mental voyage over almost a decade. I wish to first of all thank Reinhard Schulze in Bern (Switzerland), who directed me to the scarcely studied group of texts written by Maronite travelers from Aleppo during the mid-eighteenth century. Leafing through Georg Graf's famous reference work, itself a time machine through early modern and modern Ottoman history, I noticed Ḥannā Diyāb's text, attributed to "Anonymous." That sparked my curiosity. In the years to follow and with the support of the University of Bern I was able to travel to Lebanon and to the Vatican to see *The Book of Travels*, as well as to Germany, to the Forschungsbibliothek in Gotha to consult manuscripts from Ḥannā Diyāb's time. I wish to thank the Orient-Institut Beirut for their support during my stay as a researcher there in 2013. I was able to gain insight into numerous collections of manuscripts from the early modern period in Lebanon. My stay in Lebanon brought me in touch with the Bibliothèque Orientale at the Université de Saint-Joseph in Beirut, where employees Magda Nammour and Karam El Hoyek in particular helped with the consultation of manuscripts relevant to this project.

Over the years of working on my PhD thesis on Ḥannā Diyāb and this edition I enjoyed informative conversations with Ibrahim Akel, Bernard Heyberger, Paule Fahmé-Thiéry, and Hilary Kilpatrick, among others, during my trips to Denmark, France, and Switzerland. All of them shared important perspectives on the material at hand. For help with the preparation of the edition I wish to thank Ziad Bou Akl and Enass Khansa as well as my students in Bern for sharing their impressions on the tone, style, and linguistic register of the text. Thanks also to Elias Muhanna and Michael Cooperson for the fruitful exchange and for the efficient collaborative process; the same goes for the whole Library of Arabic Literature crew for their support of this project. I also wish to express my gratitude to everyone at the Kalīla and Dimna – AnonymClassic project, where

I currently hold a research post, notably Beatrice Gründler and Isabel Toral who are interested in the continuation of my research on the Middle Arabic register. Special thanks, lastly, go to my partner Feriel who during our holidays followed my geeky attempt to find the "Tower of Skulls," without any doubt one of today's most thrilling sights in Houmt Souk (Djerba, Tunisia).

Translator's acknowledgments

*For Laila and Maya*

I wish to express my gratitude to the many individuals whose contributions have enriched this book. Johannes Stephan has been all that one could ask for in a co-author, and Michael Cooperson's erudition and wit have improved our work immeasurably. I'm grateful to Paolo Horta for helping to interest the Library of Arabic Literature in the manuscript, to Philip Kennedy and the rest of the Editorial Board for their faith in the project, and to an anonymous reviewer for many helpful suggestions. Chip Rossetti, Lucie Taylor, and the production team have taken scrupulous care of our work. I would like to thank Professors Hilary Kilpatrick and Jérôme Lentin for introducing me to Diyāb's manuscript many years ago. Finally, I thank my wife Jen, whose discernment has caught many an unmusical phrase, and my daughters Laila Rose and Maya, whose love has kept me whole when, as Diyāb would say, the world seemed to crowd in upon my miserable self.

# Introduction

## Johannes Stephan

The author of *The Book of Travels* (*Kitāb al-Siyāḥah*),[1] Ḥannā Diyāb,[2] became known to Western scholarship more than a century after his death, when his name was discovered in the diaries of Antoine Galland, the great French Orientalist and translator of the *Thousand and One Nights*.[3] Since that discovery, Diyāb, a Maronite Christian merchant and storyteller from Aleppo, has become a familiar figure to scholars interested in the textual history of the *Nights*. He has been described as Galland's muse: The informant who supplied several famous stories to the French translation of the collection, including "Aladdin" and "'Alī Bābā and the Forty Thieves."

Until the early 1990s, few scholars were aware that in 1764 Diyāb had written his own travelogue.[4] Because the first pages were missing, his work was catalogued as anonymous by the Catholic priest Paul Sbath, who came into possession of it at some point in the early twentieth century.[5] After Sbath's death in 1945, his family gave the manuscript to the Vatican Library, where it remains today. The work is an account of Diyāb's travels, mostly in the company of a Frenchman named Paul Lucas. Starting in early 1707, from the vicinity of Diyāb's hometown of Aleppo, the two journeyed through Ottoman Syria, then traveled across the Mediterranean to Paris, passing through Cyprus, Alexandria, Cairo, Fayoum, Tripoli, Djerba, Tunis, Livorno, Genoa, Marseille, Lyon, and the court of Versailles, among many other places. They arrived in Paris in September 1708 and lived there together for several months. In June 1709, Diyāb set out for home. His voyage took him first to Istanbul, where he lived for some time. After crossing Anatolia by caravan, he returned home to Aleppo in June 1710.

Ḥannā Diyāb's connection to the *Thousand and One Nights* has long tantalized scholars, and the publication of his travelogue may help shed light on that.[6] But *The Book of Travels* is also significant in its own right. Among the topics it allows us to explore are Diyāb's relationship to his French patron, Paul Lucas; different forms of oral storytelling proper to *The Book of Travels*; and the culture of Arabic writing in eighteenth-century Aleppo.

## The Aleppan Traveler and His French Patron

For the most part, *The Book of Travels* centers on the relationship between an Aleppan working man and a French antiquarian, which began as a business agreement. In exchange for serving as a translator, Diyāb was offered the chance to accompany Lucas on a journey that would span three continents. The asymmetry of this master-servant arrangement reflects, in a way, the relationship between Catholic states in the West and the Ottoman Empire during the early and mid-eighteenth century, just as it portrays an ambivalent relationship between East and West. Diyāb's relationship to his patron encompasses a combination of postures and affects, ranging from servitude, respect, and emulation to the occasional display of irony. For his part, Lucas, who also wrote an account of the voyage, does not mention Diyāb once.

Apart from a few scraps of manuscript evidence, the only available record of Diyāb's life is to be found in his travelogue, which also seems to be the only text he authored. Toward the end of the book, he indicates that he wrote it at the age of seventy-five. This means that he must have been born between 1687 and 1689, probably in the northern Aleppo suburb of al-Jdayde, a traditionally Christian quarter. The manuscript was completed in March 1764. It ends with an account of Diyāb's final adventure with Lucas after the latter's return to Aleppo in 1716. By then, Diyāb had begun a career as a textile merchant.[7] Half a century later, when he set about writing *The Book of Travels*, he enjoyed a respected social position within the Maronite community of Aleppo.[8] From the book we learn that he married a few years after his return, and fathered several children. He mentions his mother, but says nothing of his father. He does speak of his older brothers, ʿAbdallāh and Anṭūn, whose correspondence with him during his travels suggests they were responsible for him.[9]

Another detail one may infer from the book's first pages pertains to the Maronite community to which Diyāb belonged. Like other Eastern churches, it was undergoing a process of catholicization that had begun in the sixteenth century. Only a few years after the Council of Trent, in the late sixteenth century, the first Catholic missionaries established themselves in Aleppo and began to reformulate Eastern Christian rites and dogma. A decade later, the Holy See opened a Maronite college in Rome. This catholicizing of the Eastern churches, which peaked in the first decades of the eighteenth century, entailed the establishment of new teaching institutions, the proliferation of books and literacy, the introduction of a printing press, and the formation of the Melkite Greek Catholic church.[10]

It was during this time of change that Diyāb set out, in 1706, for the Monastery of Saint Elishaʿ, the main residence of the Lebanese Maronite order. The order had been established in 1694 by the young Aleppans ʿAbdallāh Qarāʿalī, Jibrīl Ḥawwā, and Yūsuf al-Baṭn, with the permission of the patriarch Isṭifān al-Duwayhī.[11] In founding the first indigenous monastic order based on a European model, these young men became important figures in the catholicization of the Maronite community.[12] Hoping to become a monk, Diyāb arrived at a moment when the community was still in the throes of an internal dispute over hierarchy and doctrinal direction.[13]

The experience at Saint Elishaʿ and his meeting with one of the founders, ʿAbdallāh Qarāʿalī (d. 1742), left a profound impression on Diyāb. He vividly portrays his reverence for the monks' "angelic conduct" (§1.17) and for the orderly rhythms of monastic life. He soon came to feel, however, that he did not belong in the community. When at one point he fell ill, he received permission from the abbot to leave the monastery, under the pretext of convalescing in his hometown. Failing to find a job in Aleppo, he resigned himself to returning to the monastery. On his way back, he met Paul Lucas, a traveler "dispatched by the sultan of France," and joined his entourage (§1.29).

The "gentleman" (khawājah) Paul Lucas, as Diyāb first calls him, was born in 1664 to a merchant family in Rouen. Two years later, after serving in the Venetian army, he embarked on his first tour to the Levant.[14] By the time he met Diyāb, he was in the midst of his third voyage to the East. Drawn by Diyāb's linguistic skills, Lucas offered him the job of personal companion and dragoman on a journey across the Mediterranean world. In exchange, Lucas promised Diyāb a position at the Royal Library in Paris. The young Aleppan was intrigued by the offer, and quickly accepted, presenting himself as a traveler interested in seeing the world rather than a humble novice returning to his monastery. After making a few discreet inquiries about the Frenchman's integrity, he agreed to accompany him on his travels.

When they arrived in Paris, Diyāb lived with Lucas, from September 1708 to June 1709, waiting patiently to be hired into the position at the Royal Library, as he had been promised. When no such job materialized, Diyāb grew frustrated. In the meantime, he had made the acquaintance of Antoine Galland, whom he describes as an "old man who was assigned to oversee the library of Arabic books and could read Arabic well" (Volume Two, §10.9). After Galland arranged for Diyāb to be hired by a member of the French court to work, like his former master, as a traveler dispatched by Louis XIV, he decided he would leave the

French capital, but the offer of employment—like the library position he coveted—never came through. On his way home to Syria, he stopped for some time in Istanbul, where he worked as a valet and a housekeeper until he was urged by a friend to accompany him to Aleppo. Right after Diyāb's return from his travels in June 1710, his brother ʿAbdallāh, with the help of an uncle, opened a textile shop for him. A few years later, Paul Lucas returned to Aleppo, sought out Diyāb, and reproached him for leaving Paris so rashly. After going on one last adventure together in the vicinity of Aleppo, the two men went their separate ways. Diyāb tells us that he worked as a textile merchant for twenty-two years, but gives no details about his life after he retired in his forties.

The encounter with Lucas had a profound influence on Diyāb. It was common for Aleppan Christians in the seventeenth and eighteenth centuries to work for (French) consuls, traders, missionaries, and travelers who formed part of the social fabric of the city. In fact, Lucas was not Diyāb's first patron; like his brothers, Diyāb had worked for a dozen years, beginning before he was ten years old, as a domestic servant in the employ of various French merchants. His contact with Europeans helped him acquire a good knowledge of French, Italian, and Turkish. His association with Lucas also helped him to attain a prestigious position within his community. In the 1760s, when he wrote *The Book of Travels*, it was important to Diyāb to assert this prestige before his extended family and larger community. Lucas is accordingly mentioned in two of the book's chapter headings. He doubtless also appeared in the now-lost first pages of the narrative, and perhaps even in the title of the book.

In the first chapters of Diyāb's travelogue, Lucas's discoveries and his acquisition of artifacts—rare precious stones, coins, books, and a mummy, among other things—are the main focus of the narrative. Diyāb describes how Lucas offered to treat people's illnesses in exchange for objects he wanted to acquire, something Lucas himself reports that he did. Diyāb mentions Lucas's expertise in astronomy, geometry, philosophy, natural history, and other disciplines. He recounts how Lucas came to his aid on more than one occasion, such as when Diyāb nearly froze to death during the icy winter in Paris, or when he was arrested by the French gendarmerie.

Given Diyāb's apparently reverential attitude toward Lucas, it is noteworthy that the latter nowhere mentions Diyāb in his own travelogue. The young Syrian cannot even be discerned among the nameless servants and dragomans that Lucas happens to mention on occasion.[15] This discrepancy between the two works can be seen in other ways. Diyāb offers a richly detailed account of the logistics of travel, of the food they consumed, and of the different types of clothing he saw. Lucas's focus is, rather, on sightseeing at ancient ruins, collecting antiquities, and describing his adventures, which include the occasional miracle.[16] He excludes from his account the countries of Catholic Europe that so fascinated Diyāb, who describes them along with the parts of the Ottoman Empire that were largely unknown to Aleppans. Thus, although the itinerary described in the two travelogues is generally the same, only a few episodes correspond well enough to be fruitfully compared.[17]

One such episode is the story of the jerboas that Lucas presented to Louis XIV and his entourage at Versailles. In his account, Lucas offers a drawing of a jerboa,[18] and claims to have witnessed a hunt for the animals in the desert in Upper Egypt.[19] In Diyāb's version of the story, we learn that Lucas had in fact acquired the jerboas at a French merchant's house in Tunis. As he reports the lie his patron told the king, Diyāb gives his readers a glimpse of his own feelings about Lucas's posturing. He also recounts how Lucas, unable to identify the exotic species for the king, turned to his companion for help. Diyāb knew the animal's name in both French and Arabic and was able to write these down at Louis XIV's request.

The jerboas—a subject of great interest to the members of the royal court—served as Diyāb's entry to the king's private chambers. As he was paraded through the palace and its various mansions, carrying the cage with the two jerboas to present them to the royal family, Diyāb, dressed in a turban, bouffant pantaloons, and a fancy striped overcoat, and wearing a silver-plated dagger in his belt, came to be regarded as a curiosity in his own right. In Diyāb's account, it is at this moment that he becomes the protagonist of his own story. By sharing with the French court his knowledge of the Orient, he outdoes his master, the supposed authority. Recollecting these events more than fifty years later, Diyāb reveals to his readers his patron's unreliability, correcting the record of what Lucas attempts to convey about his own experiences.

A further element of Diyāb's relationship with Lucas is the medical knowledge he believed he had acquired by association with him. On his journey home, Diyāb used those skills to treat people in exchange for accommodation and food. Dressed as a European, he came to be known in Anatolia as a "Frankish doctor," (Volume Two, §11.83) modeled on his master. Like Lucas, Diyāb recounts how rumors of his medical skill spread as he traveled through Anatolia, and that the masses flocked to him to receive treatment.[20] However, while Lucas regarded himself as a genuine master of various treatments and procedures, Diyāb's self-portrayal is decidedly less confident. He presents himself as overwhelmed by the difficulties of masquerading as a physician. His humility, confusion, and reliance on God's guidance stand in clear contrast to the self-confident mastery Lucas ascribes to himself. Setting these two accounts alongside each other, one might read Diyāb's description of his experience as a traveling doctor as a parody of Lucas's account. But it is unlikely that Diyāb meant it that way. Whereas Diyāb mentions Lucas's journaling and the fact that he had sent his book manuscript to the printer after arriving in Paris, it is unlikely that Diyāb read much of Lucas's book or earlier notes. That said, he would have known Lucas's perspectives on their shared adventures.

The relationship between Ḥannā Diyāb and Paul Lucas was one of mutual dependence. Lucas was an antiquarian with little knowledge of Arabic and other Southern Mediterranean languages and literary traditions. His dependence on local Eastern Christian guides who could move flexibly within a Western Christian context is indisputable, even if that dependence was not reflected in his own accounts. On the other hand, Lucas seems to have served both as a source of personal protection and, to some extent, as a model for the young man from Aleppo. Diyāb's interest in Lucas's professional activities during the long journey to the "lands of the Christians," as well as his emulation of his medical practices, mean he was not merely an "Oriental" servant to a French traveler, but also a Catholic familiar with global institutions such as the missionary movement and Mediterranean trade.

Oral Storytelling and *The Book of Travels* as a Frame Narrative

By the time Ḥannā Diyāb met Antoine Galland, the latter's translation of the *Thousand and One Nights* was already enjoying immense popularity in Parisian court society. The prospect of discovering new material to add to his translation must have excited the French Orientalist. Even so, Galland was scrupulous in his choice of what to publish, preferring to rely on written rather than oral sources whenever possible. At his disposal was a fifteenth-century manuscript of the *Nights* that he had received from Syria some time before meeting Diyāb. Using it and a few other written sources, he had completed eight volumes of his translation, at which point he ran out of stories. His first encounter with Diyāb, which took place on March 25, 1709, at the house of Paul Lucas, a colleague with whom he shared an interest in antiquity and numismatics, seemed promising.[21]

After this first meeting, Galland recorded in his journal a description of the young man from Aleppo as a learned person who spoke several languages and possessed a knowledge of "Oriental" books. Diyāb told Galland about the existence of other tales, including those collected in *The Book of the Ten Viziers*,[22] and promised to put some stories into writing. In a note written six weeks later, on May 5, Galland reports that Diyāb had "finished the story of the lamp."[23] Titled "Aladdin and His Wonderful Lamp," this would come to be the most famous story in the *Nights*. It was only in November of the following year, however, that Galland explicitly refers to a written version of the story.[24] Whether Diyāb had written it down himself while in Paris, dictated it to a commissioned scribe, or even sent it to Galland at a later stage remains an open question. Yet there is good reason to doubt that Diyāb wrote it down himself, at least during his time in Paris in 1709. He makes no mention of writing anything during his meetings with Galland, even though he stresses his ability to write single words, letters, and also, of course, his own *Book of Travels*. As for the *Nights*, he mentions only his oral contribution to the collection of stories, and that the old man was very appreciative of his service (Volume Two, §10.9).

From Galland's *Journal* we learn that after Diyāb performed or wrote down the story of "Aladdin," the two met several more times. During their meetings, Galland took notes on stories recounted for him by Diyāb. These stories would become the basis of volumes nine through twelve of the French translation (published between 1712 and 1717), marking a break with Galland's previous practice of relying exclusively on written sources. One might envision these meetings between Diyāb and Galland as collaborative sessions in which the former used both Arabic and French to convey the stories to the French Orientalist. Of these stories, only the tale of "The Ebony Horse" has an attested written origin beyond Galland's notes. All the others can be identified only to the extent that they contain well-known motifs from oral folk narratives.[25] As they do not have a written source, they have been referred to by scholars as "orphan stories."[26] Of the sixteen tales he heard from Diyāb, Galland chose to publish ten. These include "'Alā' al-Dīn," the equally famous "'Alī Bābā and the Forty Thieves," and "Prince Aḥmad and the Fairy Perī Bānū."

A further link between Diyāb's *Book of Travels* and the *Thousand and One Nights* emerges from the narrative mode Diyāb adopts in his own book, one that makes ample use of embedded narratives—the central structural paradigm of the *Nights* and *The Book of the Ten Viziers*, as well as *The Book of Sindbad the Sailor*. Diyāb's travelogue contains almost forty secondary stories, most of them diegetically independent of the main narrative. Some consist of only a few lines, whereas others extend over three or more manuscript pages. The stories are a mix of historical and hagiographical anecdotes, although they also include a few tales of crime and horror. The narratives seem to stem mainly from oral sources, but a few have well-attested written origins. Among the popular early-modern motifs that make an appearance are the figure of a person buried alive, the legend of the philosopher's stone and the water of life, and reports of wonders such as the hydraulic Machine de Marly in Versailles and the Astronomical Clock in Lyon. Many of the stories are told at the point in the journey at which they were supposed to have taken place, while others are grouped according to theme.

Diyāb uses the classical Arabic categories of *khabar* ("report" or "account") and *ḥikāyah* ("story") as generic frames to indicate independent narrative units. These units are also highlighted through the use of colored ink and textual indentions. As is typical of classical frame narratives, about one third of the inserted stories are introduced not by the primary narrator, Diyāb himself, but by the characters from the story world—that is, by the people Diyāb meets during his voyages. This telling of a secondary tale by direct quotation, though common in Diyāb's narrative, is unusual in early-modern travelogues. A skilled storyteller, Diyāb drew upon a repertoire of narratives he had probably acquired from collective reading sessions in coffeehouses and elsewhere, as well as spontaneous oral accounts, and fashioned these along recognizable plotlines. It is likely that, standing in front of Galland, he performed in a manner similar to that described by Scottish doctor Patrick Russell:

> The recitation of Eastern fables and tales, partakes somewhat of a dramatic performance. It is not merely a simple narrative; the story is animated by the manner, and action of the speaker. A variety of other story books, besides the Arabian Nights Entertainments, (which, under that title, are little known at Aleppo) furnish materials for the storyteller, who, by combining the incidents of different tales, and varying the catastrophe of such as he has related before, gives them an air of novelty even to persons who at first imagine they are listening to tales with which they are acquainted.[27]

The way Diyāb employed the skills Russell describes becomes clear when we examine how he combines plotlines and details known from other narratives.[28]

For example, in one passage in *The Book of Travels*, he enters the home of a nobleman and sees a stunning trompe l'oeil painting of a man holding a bird that seems to jut out of the wall it is painted on (Volume Two, §9.41). He proceeds to elaborate on the theme by providing a biography of the artist (who may have been a Fontainebleau painter of the Renaissance school) in three episodes. In the first episode, a shoemaker's apprentice falls in love with a princess. Her father laughs at the apprentice's proposal but says he will give him his daughter's hand in marriage if he can paint her portrait. The suitor agrees, and succeeds in painting a beautiful portrait that deeply impresses the prince. But the latter refuses to give his daughter to the apprentice, offering his second daughter instead. This breaks the young artist's heart. He leaves the prince's service, goes insane, and becomes a famous painter wandering the world. More than any other story in *The Book of Travels*, this episode exudes the spirit of the *Thousand and One Nights*.[29] The prominent role of the image recalls the motif of falling in love with a portrait, which appears in Diyāb's story of "Qamar al-Dīn and Badr al-Budūr" (omitted by Galland from his translation). Second, the motif of becoming an artist out of lovesickness appears in the *Majnūn Laylā* story cycle, which may have been familiar to Diyāb from *Khosrow and Shīrīn*, a Persian retelling popular during Ottoman times. Finally, demanding an impossible or difficult task of a suitor is a motif known from the fifth tale told during the tenth day in Boccaccio's *Decameron*, a book that itself is believed to have been inspired by "Oriental" models of frame-narrative storytelling.

In the second episode, Diyāb reports that the apprentice painter once painted on one of his master's portraits a fly so realistic that the master tries to shoo it away. Though Diyāb presents this as part of the biography of the painter whose work he had seen, the same story is told by Giorgio Vasari (d. 1574) about Giotto di Bondone (d. 1276). To this episode Diyāb adds a third episode in which the painter, now named Nīkūlā, challenges his master to a contest of realism. The master creates an image of fruits so lifelike that birds come to peck them. But Nīkūlā wins by painting a curtain so realistic that his master tries to draw it aside to see the painting behind it. This story evidently stems from the one told by Pliny the Elder (d. 79) about the contest between the painters Zeuxis and Parrhasius. Both tales include a variant of the line attributed by Pliny to Parrhasius and given by Diyāb as follows: "It doesn't take much skill to fool a few birds [...] Fooling a master painter like you? That takes some doing" (Volume Two, §9.51). Although the motif is attested in traditions other than the Greek, it may have come to Diyāb's attention in France, since it was deployed by eighteenth-century

European intellectuals in their theorizations of art.[30] In his account of Paris, Diyāb mentions in passing that he had taken painting classes there.

Diyāb produces these episodes and combines them into a whole at a moment in his travelogue when he has just narrated his confrontation with the trompe l'oeil painting in Paris. He is as amazed by this painting as he is by a realistic depiction of Jesus Christ in Livorno, and by the Paris opera stage, which is populated by real animals, convincing landscapes, and royal chambers. The common theme is art that can be easily confused with reality, but Diyāb's accounts of such works appear in different places in the travelogue. Creating his own piece of art as a narrative, both in the *Thousand and One Nights* and in his *Book of Travels*, Diyāb combines motifs and known episodes, and adds new names and details to them, giving them "an air of novelty," as Russell puts it. The orphan tales, most prominently "'Alī Bābā," are novelistic and complex. "'Alī Bābā," as Aboubakr Chraïbi has shown, consists of a parallel structure in which two plot lines converge.[31] Admittedly, as Chraïbi notes, Diyāb may have modeled the orphan tales on originals that were already complex. Still, tales like "The Two Sisters Who Envied Their Cadette" and "Prince Aḥmad and the Fairy Perī Bānū" have the additional feature of combining tales of two different types into one. The story of "Aladdin" may be the result of a similar process.[32]

The frame narrative structure, the modeling of new tales on old ones, and the compositional style are all features that Diyāb's *Book of Travels* shares with the *Thousand and One Nights*. Structurally, the parallels between the two books are grounded in the way the storyteller's memory functions and in his manner of refashioning existing narratives and motifs. Although some features may be unintended, in general Diyāb's storytelling in *The Book of Travels* reflects an oral practice mostly based on oral accounts. Yet, we know that Diyāb did not tell stories only from memory—he also owned books, and contributed to a new practice of travel writing that emerged in the 1750s and '60s.

## Writing an Autobiography in Mid-Eighteenth-Century Aleppo

Diyāb was one of several Maronites and other catholicized Christians who composed accounts of their experiences in the Western Catholic world. Though interested in travelogues, he composed his *Book of Travels* very much as a personal narrative, and it consequently exhibits, both in plot and the perspective, specific features characteristic of autobiography.

We can get some idea of the literary models available to Diyāb by looking at his library. Besides his own *Book of Travels*, written at the end of his life, Diyāb owned at least six other books. Four are handwritten copies of devotional works:

1. a *Treatise on the Seven Deadly Sins and the Seven Virtues* (*Sharḥ mukhtaṣar fī al-sabʿ al-radhāyil wa-mā yuqābiluhā aʿnī al-sabʿ faḍāyil*), translated from Latin, and bound in a volume dated July 1753;

2. *A Useful Book on Knowing One's Will* (*Kitāb Mufīd fī ʿilm al-niyyah*), another treatise on moral theology;[33]

3. *The Precious Pearl on the Holy Life of Saint Francis* (*al-Durr al-nafīs fī sīrat al-qiddīs Fransīs*),[34] a vita of Saint Francis Xavier (d. 1552), the founder of the Jesuit order, based on the account by Dominique Bouhours (d. 1702), and translated into Arabic by a Jesuit missionary in Aleppo, dated December 1753; and

4. a four-volume collection of hagiographic tales (*Kitāb Akhbār al-qiddīsīn*) translated into Arabic by Pierre Fromage (d. 1740), dated between 1755 and 1757. The owner's name, being partially struck out, is not entirely legible, but the handwriting of this codex resembles that of the works above, as well as that of *The Book of Travels*.

The two other books are travelogues, probably copied in the 1750s or '60s, and bound in a single volume:

5. a copy of *The Book of Travels* (*Kitāb al-Siyāḥah*) by Ilyās al-Mawṣilī (d. after 1692). A struck-off name deciphered by Antoine Rabbath (d. 1913) as "Ḥannā son of Diyāb" appears as a former owner.[35]

6. an Arabic translation of the Turkish *sefâretnâmeh* by Yirmisekiz Mehmed Çelebi Efendi.

From this list, and from the way Diyāb's name appears in the codices, one can draw a few inferences about his participation in the written culture of Aleppo. First, the codices establish him as an owner but not necessarily a writer of books. Second, the items in his library, which include translations from Western European languages, represent an ideological affiliation with the Catholic world and with the Western institutions of knowledge production and power he depicts in his travelogue. Finally, although Diyāb had other travelogues at his disposal, his own adopts a different and distinct mode of self-representation.

With respect to ownership, the name "Ḥannā ibn Diyāb" appears six times as the owner of a particular text. A few volumes state, using a well-known formula, that Diyāb had "obtained the book for himself from his own money."[36] A unique inscription in the copy of Saint Francis Xavier's vita implies that Diyāb had "copied," "transmitted," or even "translated" (*naqala*) the book.[37] It remains uncertain whether he copied his books himself, commissioned others to do so, or dictated them, along with *The Book of Travels*, to the same scribe.

The layout of *The Book of Travels* suggests that it may have been dictated. Although a large portion is presented as a finalized codex, with colored and centered chapter headings and the same number of lines per page, almost every folio contains words that have been crossed out and replaced with others. Also, the oral and colloquial nature of the text smacks of dictation. The language is a register of so-called Middle Arabic, containing many dialect features as well as many loanwords from Ottoman Turkish and Italian. Although typical of oral storytelling, as with the popular epic (*siyar*) tradition, Diyāb's language displays more variation than do other examples of Middle Arabic, notably the orthography, which is highly idiosyncratic: The same word might be spelled two different ways in as many lines. Such inconsistencies may well be the result of rapid writing that reflects actual pronunciation, and serves as a reminder of the story's initial orality.

Oral narrative, as Walter Ong has argued, displays greater redundancy than its written counterpart.[38] In *The Book of Travels*, redundancy is evident on different levels, from single words to entire episodes. For instance, Diyāb tells the story of his mother's recovery from melancholia no less than three times. He also recycles structural formulas such as "let me get back to what I was saying," a characteristic of oral performance, to link successive episodes.[39] In these respects, *The Book of Travels* resembles a performance by a public storyteller. Indeed, it may be the result of an extended performance that included some of the embedded stories.

As for the Catholic element, some of Diyāb's devotional books contain stories that resonate with the material found in his *Book of Travels*. *The Precious Pearl*, a multivolume collection of hagiographies, had served as a synaxarion, a collection of saints' lives read as part of the liturgy. It had been translated into Arabic from a French composition that was in turn based on a Spanish collection of vitae, one for each day of the year. Short hagiographic stories proliferated widely in the eighteenth-century Levant. Around the time Diyāb set out for the monastery, the superior of the Lebanese Maronite order, and later bishop of Aleppo, Jirmānūs Farḥāt (d. 1732), had just completed his rewriting of a Byzantine collection of hagiographic and other edifying tales from Eastern and Western Christianity. Titled *The Monks' Garden* (*Bustān al-ruhbān*), this work garnered considerable attention.[40] Diyāb repurposed the contents of *The Precious Pearl* for his own narrative, borrowing elements from the stories of Saint Genevieve of Paris and Saint Elizabeth of Hungary and merging them into one narrative. He refers to the biblical story of Saint Mary Magdalene and her fate in Marseille, and to the story of Helena of Constantinople, both of which also appear in *The Precious Pearl*.

Diyāb seems also to have drawn on accounts of missionary activities, of which he was a great admirer, as he notes in several passages of the travelogue. His library included one such account, the vita of Saint Francis Xavier. A kind of spiritual travelogue, it recounts the attempt to convert Indians and Japanese to Catholic belief. Diyāb also owned a copy of the travelogue of Ilyās al-Mawṣilī, a member of the small Catholic Chaldean community of Iraq. Al-Mawṣilī's seventeenth-century journey took him across France, Italy, and other European countries, with the aim of fostering connections and collecting money from Catholics there. After arriving at the Spanish court, al-Mawṣilī was offered the opportunity to travel to the New World, where he remained through at least 1683. Like Diyāb, he expresses awareness of being a curiosity in the territories he visits. Similarly, he presents his readers with the picture of a world divided between Catholics and native populations awaiting conversion.[41] Both authors are interested in displays of linguistic knowledge, in acts of healing, and in the workings of charitable institutions. Each describes a meeting with an Ottoman ambassador, and each declares himself a recipient of divine guidance.

Like al-Mawṣilī, Diyāb titles his account *siyāḥah*, literally "wandering" or "peregrination." This is different from *riḥlah* ("journey"), a term used by many Muslim authors, but only rarely by Diyāb. A *riḥlah* is a journey undertaken with a clear destination or defined purpose; it also denotes a written account of such a journey. *Siyāḥah*, by contrast, emphasizes the activity of moving around, and also describes the practice of wandering that formed part of Sufi and Christian piety.[42] The term *siyāḥah* may also suggest a protracted journey. The famous Ibn Baṭṭūṭah, who traveled for more than thirty years, uses the term several times. So do al-Mawṣilī, who traveled for at least fifteen years, and Evliya Çelebi, who spent his life traveling, and even seems to define himself by that activity.[43] Yet, despite the conceptual similarities, the scope of the two books, and their strong Catholic impetus, Diyāb does not model his account closely on al-Mawṣilī's.

Whereas the latter's travelogue consists of a terse listing of events and activities, Diyāb offers long descriptions and complex, embedded secondary narratives. Diyāb is a much more personal narrator who, unlike al-Mawṣilī, does not depict himself as an audacious adventurer, but rather as an inexperienced and God-fearing young man. In this respect, it is noticeable that Diyāb, especially when recounting his journey home, makes use of the relief-after-hardship motif, which is reminiscent of classical Arabic prose.

The volume containing Ilyās al-Mawṣilī's account also contains the embassy account (sefâretnâmeh) of Yirmisekiz Mehmed Çelebi Efendi, a travelogue by one of the most important Ottoman diplomats of the eighteenth century. His travelogue circulated in Aleppo, where it was copied several times.[44] It seems to have been translated into Arabic in the 1740s or '50s.[45] A copy of it exists as a standalone codex in the library of Diyāb's contemporary Ḥannā ibn Shukrī al-Ṭabīb (d. 1775), an Aleppan physician, who was himself the author of travelogues. In 1764 he turned the travel diary of his younger brother Arsāniyūs Shukrī (d. 1786) into a comprehensive travel account,[46] and in 1765 composed an ethnographic account of Istanbul, which he had visited the previous fall. It is quite likely that Diyāb's report of the Ottoman embassy is copied from that of Ḥannā al-Ṭabīb.

Diyāb thus appears to have been part of a culture of sharing and reading travelogues, something that must have informed his own writing. For example, upon reading Yirmisekiz Çelebi's account of his festive reception in Toulon, which included crowds of French people waving at him on the streets, Diyāb might have recalled being welcomed with great curiosity at the French court. Similarly, Yirmisekiz Çelebi's description of the opera and other festive events may have reminded Diyāb of his own visit to the opera in 1709 and his attendance at a banquet of statesmen in Istanbul.[47]

Although he writes from a Catholic perspective, Diyāb nevertheless emphasizes the importance of European-Ottoman relations. He discusses an Ottoman ambassador's visit to the French court, recounts his employment with the Venetian consul in Istanbul, and relates several stories about the cordial relationship between the governor of Tripoli (in North Africa) and a French deputy. His possession of the travelogues by al-Mawṣilī and Yirmisekiz Çelebi suggests an interest in the links between Istanbul, Aleppo, Paris, and other European centers of power—an interest he shares with his contemporary Ḥannā al-Ṭabīb.

*The Book of Travels* is no meticulous description of distant places. Rather, it has the character of an early-modern adventure novel with some picaresque elements. Speaking of his experiences, Diyāb often employs the term *qiṣṣah* (story). From the passages where the term appears, one can track those parts of the travelogue that relate to Diyāb's own story. These passages describe, first, the loss of his ties to his workplace in Aleppo, and his decision to travel back to the monastery; second, his encounter with Paul Lucas, who made possible the journey to Paris that takes up the bulk of the story; and third, the scheme by which Antoine Galland and a French nobleman, the Abbé de Signy, induced him to travel back to Aleppo.

These three travel episodes form the main part of Diyāb's wanderings and are encapsulated by the monastic experience at the beginning of the existing narrative and the final adventure that took place upon Lucas's return. The main episode, which fills more than two-thirds of the 174 extant folios, is the story of an unfulfilled promise. It parallels the experience that befell many other travelers from the Levant in this period, including Niqūlāwus al-Ḥalabī (d. ca. 1661) and Salomon Negri (d. 1727), who were hired by Western travelers and scholars.[48] During Diyāb's travels, he encounters several such people—that is, catholicized Christians from the Middle East who somehow ended up in Europe, working as merchants, coffeehouse owners, and practitioners of other trades. Although some of these individuals succeeded where Diyāb did not, in the sense that they managed to gain employment in Europe, they too lament the difficulties of survival in their new home. By writing about them in his travelogue, Diyāb affirms his ties to these diasporic catholicized Middle Easterners.

Throughout *The Book of Travels*, Diyāb refers to his own thoughts and emotions, though he often relies on formulaic expressions to describe his state of mind. To express despair, for example, he often uses an expression that means "the world closed up on me" (see §1.28 and Volume Two, §10.42); of interest is the fact that such moments of despair are often followed by a radical shift in the direction of the plot. And while he often expresses his delight at the beauties of nature or architecture (see §3.7 and §3.19), the emotion he experiences most often is fear, which he expresses in many different ways.[49]

Diyāb's ability to produce a work that focuses on himself suggests that he was familiar with other autobiographical narratives. Whether in oral or written form, the autobiographies of figures such as the monk and bishop ʿAbdallāh Qarāʿalī[50] and the nun and living saint Hindiyyah al-ʿUjaymī[51] were known in Aleppo during the 1740s and 1750s. Like Qarāʿalī and al-ʿUjaymī, Diyāb describes leaving his family to start a life of his own, and in doing so creates a particular perspective on the traveling younger self.

Diyāb's narrative style merges the craftsmanship expected of a *Thousand and One Nights* storyteller with the conventions of travel writing popular among the catholicized Christians of his time. By embedding and framing personal narratives, Diyāb moves between different positions of perception. As he comments on his own actions, adds illustrative stories, and reproduces dialogue, the narrator alternates between proximity and distance to the story world. In this respect, Diyāb's *Book of Travels* has much in common with the fictional narratives that appeared in Arabic during the nineteenth century.

Like other works in Middle Arabic, Diyāb's travelogue has been marginalized in the study of Arabic literary history. Works from the late-medieval and early-modern periods, especially those in what has been termed Middle Arabic, have routinely been dismissed as illustrative of decadence and decline. But the travelogues of Ḥannā ibn Shukrī al-Ṭabīb and Fatḥallāh al-Ṣāyigh (fl. 1810, an Aleppan who traveled with Lascaris de Vintimille),[52] to name but two, deserve, like Diyāb's, to be read as Arabic literature—that is, read with attention to their oral narrative style, their patchwork character, and their autobiographical conventions, as well as their connections to other travelogues from the Arabic literary tradition. Thanks to the recent revival of interest in the Arabic textual archive of the early-modern period, Middle Arabic works are, fortunately, beginning to receive more attention. Reading them as literary constructions, rather than as examples of decadence and decline, will help us rethink the ways in which we write and understand Arabic literary history.

# Note on the Text

## The Manuscript

There is only one known manuscript of Ḥannā Diyāb's *Kitāb al-Siyāḥah* (*Book of Travels*), preserved in the Vatican Apostolic Library's Sbath collection under the class mark 254. The first ten pages of the manuscript are missing, judging from the numbers handwritten in brown ink on the first forty folios. In the absence of the opening pages, both Paul Sbath in his *Catalogue* and Georg Graf in the *Geschichte der christlichen arabischen Literatur* categorized the text as anonymous. This erroneous designation may explain why the text was disregarded until the early 1990s, when Jérôme Lentin identified the author as Ḥannā Diyāb.[53]

The binding of the codex is typical of Ottoman codices. It contains some fragments, including a page in Syriac script. Aside from the missing pages, which were evidently torn out after the book was first composed,[54] and some water stains, the codex is relatively well preserved. Although it has some of the features characteristic of professionally prepared codices, it also shows signs of being a work in progress. As was typical for Diyāb's time, the text is laid out in black ink interspersed with red for decorative and structural purposes. The first six chapter headings are centered and followed by a short subtitle in red. The subsequent chapters lack rubrication. The last sections seem to have been planned as chapters but are not marked as such, nor is there any room left for large chapter headings. On nearly every page, letters and words have been struck through or replaced. Most of the strikethrough lines are colored in red ink. Red ink is also used for scribal marks, such as the pilcrows that indicate the ends of episodes. Some of the lines bearing paragraph marks at the end are indented, as can be seen frequently after folio 45 of the manuscript. Another structuring device is the use of dots to mark the end of syntactic units such as interrogative sentences and to mark a change of speakers. With its subdivision into paragraphs and its proto-punctuation, *The Book of Travels* is in some respects reminiscent of a modern book. The manuscript text, which ends on folio 174, is followed by a few names, such as the mention (given also in Roman script on the same page) of the book's owner, Anṭūn Yūsuf Ḥannā Diyāb, probably the author's son. On the bottom of the page that describes Diyāb's journey from Marseille to Paris, a great-grand-child left an ownership note: "This account of the voyage of my father's grand-father entered the possession of Jibrāyil, son of Dīdakūz Diyāb, of the Maronite community, on the 19th of April in the year 1840 of the Christian era."

## Previous Edition

*Min Ḥalab ilā Bārīs. Riḥlah ilā Balāṭ Luwīs al-Rābiʿ ʿashar.* Edited by Muḥammad Muṣṭafā al-Jārūsh and Ṣafāʾ Abū Shahlā Jubrān (Beirut: Manshūrāt al-Jamal, 2017).

This edition, the readings and annotations of which rely heavily on the pub-lished French translation (see below), follows a diplomatic standard—that is, it reproduces the original handwritten text as closely as possible. It does, however, normalize some spellings such as the *tāʾ marbūṭah* and omits some of the hyper-corrective *hamzah*s. There are some typographical errors and omissions: mis-reading *tajrīd* for *tajribeh*, for example, and sometimes leaving out the colloquial *bi-* prefix of imperfect verb forms. Some terms, rarely attested in dictionaries, are not annotated.

## Previous Translations

French translation: Hanna Dyâb, *D'Alep à Paris. Les pérégrinations d'un jeune syrien au temps de Louis XIV. Récit traduit de l'arabe (Syrie) et annoté par Paule Fahmé-Thiéry, Bernard Heyberger et Jérôme Lentin* (Paris: Actes Sud, 2015).

This meticulous rendering, on the basis of Lentin's linguistic study of the text, is the result of collaboration by three expert scholars. The extensive apparatus contains linguistic explanations and historical remarks on the early-modern Mediterranean and Middle Eastern Christianities as well as original biographical material on individuals mentioned in the text. Both the introduction and the note on the language are detailed but accessible. The translation is often literal, but captures the liveliness of the original. We record in the English endnotes those places where our translation adopts a different interpretation of the original.

German translation: Hannā Diyāb, *Von Aleppo nach Paris: Die Reise eines jungen Syrers bis an den Hof Ludwigs XIV.* Translated by Gennaro Ghirardelli (Berlin: Die andere Bibliothek, 2016).

This is based on the French translation, the introductions of which it reproduces. It emends the French rendering in a few places. The wording of the translation is occasionally archaic.

English translation: Hannâ Diyâb, *The Man Who Wrote Aladdin*. Translated by Paul Lunde (Edinburgh: Harding Simpole, 2020).

This book was published four years after the death of the translator, who apparently never planned to publish it.[55] Caroline Stone added an introduction to the volume with a focus on historical keywords. The English text, which is structured into subchapters and indented secondary narratives, is followed by an appendix containing historical information.

## This Edition

Our edition aims to preserve most of the distinctive features of Diyāb's Middle Arabic text. Though often repetitive and marked by oddities carried over from oral performance, *The Book of Travels* is remarkably rich in its vocabulary, orthography, and linguistic variety, though the manuscript is generally unvocalized. Evidently, the author was familiar with the style of the coffeehouse narrator as well as with the conventions for telling stories in written form (see the introduction to the translation).[56]

Our paragraphing largely follows the structure suggested by the manuscript text, though we have added some additional breaks for the sake of readability, notably where there is a change of speaker (for example, from the general first-person narrator to the speech of a character in the text, creating an embedded narrative), and when a transitional word such as اخيرًا or حيندٍ, or the frequently used formula فنرجع الى ما كنا في سدده indicates a break in the narration.

In dealing with the linguistic particularities of the text, we have relied on the studies of Jérôme Lentin, Elie Kallas, and Paule Fahmé-Thiéry.[57] Also useful were Adolf Wahrmund's *Handwörterbuch der neu-arabischen und deutschen Sprache*, which contains a whole range of vocabulary of Turkish origin and from Arab-Christian contexts, and Adrien Barthélemy's *Dictionnaire arabe-français*, which is especially valuable for its coverage of historical Levantine Arabic.[58] In cases where water stains and marks made by the author have left some passages difficult to decipher, we have often benefited from the reconstructions in the French translation and the previous Arabic edition.

The footnotes to the Arabic record marginal additions as well as a few significant passages crossed out in the manuscript or added to the borders of the page.
They also note cases where we have amended rare scribal peculiarities, such as
the omission or addition of consonants.

*The Book of Travels* is one of many works composed in so-called Middle
Arabic—that is, in a written form that diverges from the standard *fuṣḥā* ("pure
speech").[59] It is often imagined to be the result of a failed effort to use the formal
literary register. In reality, however, it is a semi-standardized idiom that was
used at least until the advent of print culture in the nineteenth century, and that
probably appeared along with Arabic book culture a millennium earlier. It combines elements of the standard grammar and lexicon with elements impacted
by or stemming from the Arabic dialect spoken by the given author or scribe.
It also contains hypercorrection—that is, the introduction of features mistakenly
believed to represent standard forms.[60] Middle Arabic texts vary widely, with
some containing only minor spelling variation and others diverging markedly
from normative orthography and grammar. Diyāb's work falls at the furthest end
of the spectrum from standard Arabic. A description of some of the distinctive
features of Diyāb's text follows.[61]

In the realm of orthography and phonetics, final *a* may be written with an *alif*
(ا), a dotted *alif maqṣūrah* (ى), a *tāʾ marbūṭah* (ة), or its undotted form (ه). Certain lexemes are contracted: For example, the verb قال with a personal suffix frequently loses its *alif* (if it has one) and is written as one word, as in قلي (for قال لي,
"he said to me") and قلنا (for قال لنا, "he said to us"). In other cases, verbs receive an
additional *alif* due to vocalization, as in spoken colloquial, including احكالي (for
حكى لي, "he told me") and اتفرج (for تفرج, "to look at"). Second- and third-person
plural imperfect forms appear without -*ūn* and are frequently written with an
*alif wiqāyah* as if they were subjunctive forms, e.g., بتعرفوا ("you know").

The *tāʾ marbūṭah* is used interchangeably with *tāʾ maftūḥah* in construct,
as in the Ottoman-Turkish loanword *iskele*: اسكلت صيدا ("the port of Sidon"),
and strikingly when *tāʾ marbūṭah* is used for the suffixes of third-person and
occasionally first-person perfect verb forms, e.g., استقامة for استقامت ("stayed").
In several cases, a *hamzah* appears where standard orthography does not call
for it, e.g., ابأى (for أبى, "to refuse"), and sometimes فرنسا ("France"), among other
names. As they are repeated several times, these must be hypercorrections
rather than arbitrary additions.

Another feature specific to Middle Arabic is the partial or full interchangeability of dental sounds, which may be pronounced and spelled differently from

the *fuṣḥā* standard. This interchangeability may be, but is not necessarily, the result of interference from colloquial. However, other deviations from *fuṣḥā* require writing an entirely different letter and are therefore more likely to reflect colloquial forms. For example, the letter *ṣ* (ص) is often replaced by *z* (ز), as in زغير (conforming to the Levantine pronunciation of صغير, "small").

The characters *p* (پ) and *č* (چ), used to write Ottoman Turkish, occur a few times in the text, e.g., الپاپا ("the pope") and چوخدريه ("valets" or "servants"). To spell loanwords containing those sounds, Diyāb prefers to use the characters *b* (ب) and *j* (ج); *j* (ج) is interchangeable with *z* (ز), as is the case in spoken Arabic when both sounds occur in one word, e.g., يجوزه (for يزوّجه, "he marries him off"). In any event, the spelling of loanwords and names is highly variable. For example, Diyāb renders Paris as بهريز (Bahrīz) and بهريس (Bahrīs), but rarely as the expected باريس (Bārīs).

As pronounced in Levantine dialects, imperfect verbs are often written with the prefix *b-*, as in بيدخل ("he enters") and بيرعب ("he is scared"); in some cases, *bi-* indicates the future. The particles عمال or عمالين are used to indicate simultaneous action, e.g., فرأنا عمالين منتغدا ("he saw us having lunch"). Traces of Diyāb's Aleppan dialect include *m-* instead of *b-* for the first-person plural of the imperfect, as in منتغدا ("we eat lunch"), and the replacement of the initial *yāʾ* with *bi-*, as in بقول ("he says").[62] Demonstrative pronouns (هذا, هذه, هؤلا) preceding the article contract with it to هل, which is written as an independent lexeme and is not to be confused with the interrogative هل.

Diyāb's specific lexicon includes many frequently used verbs that differ from the standard in meaning or form, including the colloquial جاب ("to bring"), انبسط ("to be or become happy"), شاف ("to see"), حط ("to put"), and the partial auxiliary استقام ("to remain or continue"). In many cases, Diyāb prefers the *fuṣḥā* standard over the colloquial form.[63] He typically uses the standard Arabic verb مضي ("to walk or go"), for instance, instead of the typical Levantine راح or the standard ذهب, though these do appear.

Most of the syntactic peculiarities in *The Book of Travels* have to do with agreement between masculine and feminine or singular and plural. These peculiarities remain within the typical range of Middle Arabic.[64] Common deviations from standard Arabic include:

- indefinite adjectives following a definite noun, as in كنيسه الكبيره (instead of الكنيسة الكبيرة, "the big church");
- genitive construction (*iḍāfah*) in which both nouns are occasionally definite, as in الربطات التتن (for ربطات التتن, "the bundles of tobacco");

- inanimate plural nouns with a masculine singular or a plural form, as in شبايك كبار (for شبايك كبيرة, "large windows");

- lack of agreement for demonstrative pronouns, such as هذه التجّار (for هؤلاء التجّار, "these merchants").

## This Translation

Our aim has been to produce an English rendering of this work that captures the voice of Ḥannā Diyāb. The author's gifts as a storyteller—only tantalizingly suggested by his famous involvement with the history of the *Thousand and One Nights*—are in evidence in *The Book of Travels*, where he documents his journey across the Mediterranean with dramatic flair. The linguistic register varies across the work between a conversational Levantine vernacular and more formal varieties of Arabic. We have attempted to approximate the vernacular quality of Diyāb's language, particularly in the dialogues, without rendering it overfamiliar.

In the interest of making the translation accessible, we avoid transliterating Arabic words. Only in rare cases do we retain a word without translating it, such as when Diyāb glosses a word he suspects might be unfamiliar to his readers. With some multivalent words, we refer readers to the Glossary while translating the term differently according to the context, for instance caravansary, hostel, inn, and market for *khān*. Indeed, we have not insisted on translating a word the same way each time it is used, for instance rendering *bustān* as garden, orchard, and meadow; *sarāya* as palace, pavilion, mansion, and embassy; and *aghā* as officer and commander. Likewise, we render the term *al-sharq* as "the Orient" when it is used by Lucas and other Frenchmen. In all other cases, we translate it as "the East." We have also taken the liberty of rendering some of Diyāb's formulas in slightly different ways, for the sake of variety. For example, his favorite narrative cue following a lengthy digression is the phrase "We now return to what we were discussing" (*wa narjiʿ ilā mā naḥnu bi-ṣadadihi*), which we render as "But let's get back to our story," "As I was saying," and the like.

We confine our endnotes to points of clarification. Readers interested in additional information are referred to the fine French translation by Paule Fahmé-Thiéry, Bernard Heyberger, and Jérôme Lentin, whose work has enriched our own.

# Notes to the Introduction

1   Since the first five folios of the MS of the work are lost, we based our choice of Kitāb al-Siyāḥah as the title on Diyāb's frequent use of the word *siyāḥah* (on which, see below).

2   His full name is Ḥannā ibn Diyāb (Ḥannā son of Diyāb), but Ḥannā Diyāb has become current in English.

3   Zotenberg, "Notice sur quelques manuscrits des *Mille et Une Nuits* et la traduction de Galland," 194.

4   The sole exception is Lentin, "Recherches sur l'histoire de la langue arabe au Proche-Orient à l'époque moderne," 1:48–49. After Lentin's discovery, the first comprehensive nonlinguistic studies of the text are Heyberger's introduction to Dyâb, *D'Alep à Paris*, and, from a literary perspective, Stephan, "Von der Bezeugung zur Narrativen Vergegenwärtigung" and "Spuren fiktionaler Vergegenwärtigung im Osmanischen Aleppo," both 2015.

5   Sbath, *Bibliothèque de manuscrits: Catalogue,* 1:122, previously published with a slightly different description in his "Les manuscrits orientaux de la bibliothèque du R.P. Paul Sbath (Suite)," 348. See also the reference to the travelogue in Graf, *Geschichte,* 3:467.

6   Notable are the recent works of Bottigheimer, "East meets West: Ḥannā Diyāb and *The Thousand and One Nights*"; Marzolph, "The Man Who Made the Nights Immortal"; and Horta, *Marvellous Thieves: Secret Authors of the Arabian Nights.*

7   Lucas, *Troisième Voyage du Sieur Paul Lucas dans le Levant,* 101–2.

8   Heyberger, introduction to Dyab, *D'Alep à Paris*, 9, uncovers a source which reveals that in 1740, Diyāb was head of a household of twelve persons. A 1748 petition to the Maronite patriarch to protect the Aleppan monks has his signature as well as those of other family members (Fahd, *Tārīkh al-rahbāniyyah*, 147).

9   See Heyberger, introduction to Dyab, *D'Alep à Paris*, 9, on the father, who probably died when Diyāb was young.

10  See the concise overviews in Raymond, "An Expanding Community: The Christians of Aleppo in the Ottoman Era," 84; Masters, *Christians and Jews in the Ottoman Arab World: The Roots of Sectarianism,* chapters 3 and 4; and Patel, *The Arab Nahḍah: The Making of the Intellectual and Humanist Movement,* chapter 2. On the proliferation of books, see Heyberger, *Hindiyya: Mystique et criminelle 1720–1798,* chapter 2.

11  Qarāʿalī, "Mudhakkirāt," 24–26.

12    Heyberger, *Les chrétiens du Proche-Orient au temps de la réforme catholique*, 110–11 and 434.

13    See the account in Qarāʿalī, "Mudhakkirāt," 32ff. on this matter; also cf. Heyberger, *Les chrétiens*, 434.

14    On Lucas's family and early travels, see Omont, *Missions archéologiques françaises en Orient aux XVIIè et XVIIIè siècles*, 317ff., and Commission des Antiquités, "Note."

15    E.g., Lucas, *Deuxième Voyage du Sieur Paul Lucas dans le Levant*, 169.

16    For examples, see Horta, *Marvellous Thieves*, chapter 2.

17    Other episodes include the account of a visit to ruins near Kaftīn and of bathing at Hammam-Lif in Tunisia (§§1.35–36 and §5.94).

18    Lucas, *Deuxième Voyage*, 53.

19    Lucas, *Deuxième Voyage*, 197–98.

20    Lucas, *Deuxième Voyage*, 117.

21    Galland, *Le journal d'Antoine Galland (1646–1715)*, 1:290.

22    Galland, *Journal*, 1:358.

23    Galland, *Journal*, 1:321.

24    Galland, *Journal*, 2:253.

25    For a comprehensive list of Diyāb's stories, see Marzolph, "The Man Who Made the Nights Immortal," 118–19.

26    Gerhardt, *The Art of Story-Telling: A Literary Study of the Thousand and One Nights*, 14–15.

27    Russell, *The Natural History of Aleppo*, 1:148–49.

28    Van Leeuwen and Marzolph, *Arabian Nights Encyclopedia*, 425.

29    Among the tales Diyāb told Galland is one about a prince who falls in love with a portrait. Here Diyāb may be reversing the motif: Instead of falling in love with the subject of a portrait, the hero paints a portrait out of love.

30    See the quotation and explanation in Görner, "Das Regulativ der Wahrscheinlichkeit: Zur Funktion literarischer Fiktionalität im 18. Jahrhundert," 92; and the study by Peucker, "The Material Image in Goethe's *Wahlverwandtschaften*," 197–98.

31    Chraïbi, "Galland's 'Ali Baba' and Other Arabic Versions," 166.

32    See Sadan, "Background, Date and Meaning of the Story of the Alexandrian Lover and the Magic Lamp."

33    Syrian Catholic Archdiocese of Aleppo, Ar 7/25.

34    Université Saint-Joseph MS BO 645. I am grateful to Ibrahim Akel, who directed my attention to this and the previous manuscript and thus helped confirm the hypothesis that Diyāb was an owner of several books.

35  See note in Université Saint-Joseph MS BO 29, fol. 2r, and in the Preface to his edition, "Riḥlat awwal sāʾiḥ sharqī ilā Amirka," 823, and further Matar, *In the Lands of the Christians: Arab Travel Writing in the Seventeenth Century*, 48. Ghobrial, "Stories Never Told: The First Arabic History of the New World," 263n8, suggests that Diyāb is the copyist of al-Mawṣilī's book.

36  E.g., Université Saint-Joseph MS BO 594, 298v.

37  Université Saint-Joseph MS BO 645, 132r.

38  Ong, *Orality and Literacy: The Technologizing of the World*, 39.

39  Ott, "From the Coffeehouse into the Manuscript," 447.

40  On the *Bustān* see Graf, *Geschichte*, 3:413.

41  Ghobrial, "The Secret Life of Elias of Babylon and the Uses of Global Microhistory," 66.

42  In the Islamic context, as shown by Touati, *Islam et voyage au Moyen Âge*, 187–91, *siyāḥah* refers to long desert journeys undertaken in order to seek mystical union with God. In the Christian context, *siyāḥah* means being a hermit—that is, a wandering monk who lives in remote places and practices piety.

43  On Evliya Çelebi and his books, see Özay, "Evliyâ Çelebi's Strange and Wondrous Europe."

44  See Krimsti, "The Lives and Afterlives of the Library of the Maronite Physician Ḥannā al-Ṭabīb (c. 1702–1775) from Aleppo," 206.

45  The Arabic manuscripts of Yirmisekiz Mehmed Çelebi's sefâretnâmeh found in the households of Diyāb and Shukrī are falsely attributed to one Saʿīd Bāshā, very likely Mehmed Çelebi's son, Mehmed Said Paşa, who returned from Paris in 1742. A list of the gifts for the French king is attached to Arsāniyūs's travelogue (MS Gotha arab. 1549, 215v).

46  Cf. Krimsti, "Arsāniyūs Shukrī al-Ḥakīm's Account of His Journey to France, the Iberian Peninsula, and Italy (1748–1757) from Travel Journal to Edition."

47  On Mehmed Çelebi's account, see Göçek, *East Encounters West: France and the Ottoman Empire in the Eighteenth Century*.

48  Ghobrial, "The Life and Hard Times of Solomon Negri: An Arabic Teacher in Early Modern Europe," 311, 331; and Kilpatrick and Toomer, "Niqūlāwus al-Ḥalabī (c.1611–c.1661): A Greek Orthodox Syrian Copyist and His Letters to Pococke and Golius," 15, 16.

49  These include *khawf* (fear), *fazʿ* (fright), and *tawahhum* (apprehension).

50  Qarāʿalī, "Mudhakkirāt."

51  See the edition in *Al-Mashriq* by Hayek, "al-Rāhibah Hindiyyah (1720–1798)," and further Heyberger, *Hindiyya*. For an English translation, see *Hindiyya, Mystic and Criminal*.

52  See the recent edition of Al-Ṣāyigh, *Riḥlat ilā bādiyat al-Shām wa-Ṣaḥārā l-ʿIrāq wa-l-ʿajam wa-l-Jazīrah al-ʿArabiyyah*.

53  The only earlier reference to the text appears in Martin's short 1979 piece "Souvenirs
    d'un compagnion de voyage de Paul Lucas en Égypte (1707)," which uses it as a source
    for contextualizing the early modern history of French archaeology.

54  See Fahmé-Thiéry, "L'arabe dialectal allepin dans le récit de voyage de Hanna Dyâb," 223.

55  Stone, "Foreword" in Diyāb, *The Man Who Wrote Aladin*, viii.

56  Cf. also Lentin, "Note sur la langue de Hanna Dyâb," on this matter.

57  Lentin, "Recherches," Kallas, "The Aleppo Dialect According to the Travel Accounts of
    Ibn Raʿd (1656) Ms. Sbath 89 and Ḥanna Dyāb (1764) Ms. Sbath 254," and Fahmé-Thiéry,
    "L'arabe dialectal."

58  Also very useful in preparing both the text and the translation were Dozy's *Supplément
    aux dictionnaires arabes*, Redhouse's *Turkish and English Lexicon*, and Graf's *Verzeichnis
    arabischer kirchlicher Termini* as well as al-Asadī's *Mawsūʿat Ḥalab al-muqāranah*.

59  This term was known to Diyāb, who speaks of "pure language" (*al-ʿarabī al-faṣīḥ*) when
    recounting one of his encounters in Paris.

60  On this tripartite division of features see Lentin, "Middle Arabic," and further Blau,
    *On Pseudo-Corrections in Some Semitic Languages*.

61  The full description of linguistic features will appear independently in a scholarly edi-
    tion with the Library of Arabic Literature.

62  See Kallas, "Aleppo Dialect," 30–31.

63  Lentin, "Note," 49.

64  See Lentin, "Recherches," vol. 2, especially chapters 12–14, 18, and 19.

كتاب السياحة

المجلّد الأوّل

# The Book of Travels

## Volume One

# الفصل الأوَّل [1]

١.١ ... مايدتهم غير الرهبان والمبتدين لا غير فاستقمنا تلك الليله في المنزول الي الصباح وبعدما حضرنا القداس فارسل الريس دعانا الي قلايته فبعدما قبلنا اياديه استرحب فينا وامرنا بالجلوس وبعده فصار يسالنا انكان لنا نية الرهبنه فقلنا له هذه نيتنا من قبل خروجنا من حلب فقلنا الله يبارك عليكم وعلى نيتكم والان لكم عندنا في الدير اربعة ايام فصار عندكم معلوم بسيرتنا وقانوننا والان يجب تعملوا رياضه ثلاثة ايام [2] وفيها تفحصوا كل واحد منكم ضميره ويهيي ذاته ليعترف اعتراف عام وتتناولوا الاسرار المقدسه. اخيرًا بتلبسوا تياب المبتدين وتمسكوا قانون الرهبنه كما هو مسطر في هل كرازه.

٢.١ واخرج واعطا لكل واحد منا كراسه حتى ندرسها وبعده دعا مدبر الدير الذي هو قس يوسف ابن البودي وامره بانه يسلم لكل واحد منا قلايه وبارك علينا واصرفنا مع المذكور فاعطا لكل واحد منا مفتاح ماطوره وقلايه وكتاب صلاوات فاستقمنا ثلاثة ايام في الرياضه وكان الريس عين لنا كاهن لاجل ارشادنا وتدبيرنا في امور الروحيه وبعد الثلاثة ايام اعترفنا اعتراف عام وتناولنا الاسرار الالهيه اعني القربان المقدس.

٣.١ وبعده ادخلنا مدبر الدير الي مكان حوايج الرهبان فقدم لي اولاً قميص ورفيق وقباز خام سميك وعبايه صوف سوده وزنار ليف وعرقيه سودا ودورين شاش من صوف مسبوغ عسلي غامق ونداس تريسي اسود. حينذٍ قلي المدبر المذكور اشلح يا اخي والبس تياب التجربه عقبال ما منلبسك الاسكيم الرهباني الملايكي. حينذٍ شلحت ثيابي الرفاع والبست ذلك القميص الخام الغليص وباقيت الحوايج المذكور

---

[1] عنوان الفصل غير معروف لأنّ الصفحات الأولى مفقودة. [2] الأصل: ايا.

# Chapter One

[1] . . . their table were only the monks and the novices. We spent that night at the inn, and after we'd attended mass the next morning, the abbot summoned us to his cell. We kissed his hands and he welcomed us, inviting us to sit. Once we were seated, he asked if we had any interest in joining the order. We confirmed that this had been our intention when we left Aleppo.

"May God bless you and your intention!" he said. "Now that you've spent four days with us at the monastery and gotten a sense of our way of life and of our rules, you'll have to complete a three-day retreat. Each of you should examine his conscience during that time, and prepare himself for a general confession. You'll then receive the holy sacrament, clothe yourself in novice's robes, and adhere to the monastic rule, as spelled out in this tract."

He gave us each a booklet to study, and asked the steward of the monastery, Father Yūsuf ibn al-Būdī, to provide us each with a cell.[2] The abbot blessed us and sent us off with Father Yūsuf, who gave us each a key for our own cubbyhole and cell, and a prayer book.

We spent three days performing our retreat. The abbot had designated a priest to offer us spiritual guidance, and when the three days had elapsed, we made our general confessions and received the holy sacrament, which is to say, Holy Communion.

The steward of the monastery then took us into a storeroom containing the vestments of the monks. He presented me with a shirt, some drawers, a thick linen tunic, a black woolen cloak, a hempen belt, a black skullcap, two rounds of woolen turban cloth dyed a dark honey color, and black sandals with plaited cords.

"Get undressed, brother, and put on these novice robes," the steward said to me. "I look forward to the day when we dress you in the habit of an angelic monk!"

ولبست فوقهم تلك العبايه الغليظه السميكه وتزنرت بذلك الزنار الليف فبقيت مثل بياعين الليمون عبابي معبيه ورفعت الشاش والقاووق من على راسي ولبست تلك العرقيه السوده ولفيت تلك الشاله العسليه الصوف ولبست ذلك النداس التريسي.

٤،١ حينٍ تاملت في حالي فرايت حالي بقيت مذهر ومن ذلك الوقت نفرقلبي من الرهبنه وندمت على ما فعلت لكن الكبريا ماسكتني ما بينت على حالي شي من هذا وبعده لبس رفيقي ايضًا مثل ما لبست انا وكان المذكور جلبي . . . .[١] اخيرًا خرجنا من هنا فاجا جميع الرهبان والمبتدين باركوا لنا في دخولنا للتجربه وفرحوا فينا قوي كثير وهنونا.

٥،١ وبعده كل منا دخل قلايته الي حين ما اندق ناقوز الغدا فنزلنا الي بيت المايده فاينا الريس وجميع الرهبان مجموعين فدخل الريس وجلس في راس المايده وتبعوا الكهنه كل من جلس في مكانه وبعدم دخلوا الرهبان وجلسوا بقيوا المبتدين واقفين وبعد هنيه اذن لهم الريس بالدخول فدخلنا وكل منا جلس في مكانه اعني الاقدم يجلس فوق الحديث وحاطين في المايده ثلاثة الوان اول لون شوربة عدس وفحيه واوقات حبوب وما يشبه ذلك من الحبوب والخضر وثاني لون لبنه وثالث لون تين مكبوس بدبس وبين كل تين سودة نبيد وبوقال وكل واحد بيشرب على قدر قوته وكيفه.

٦،١ ورايت مصفوف على رفوف المايده جماجم موته من الرهبان الذين ماتوا سابقًا وكل جمجمه مكتوب عليها اسم صاحبها وفي اخرالمايده في مكان علوه جالس راهب بيقرا اخبار الشهدا وعداباتهم الفادحه الغيرمحتمله كما هو معلوم عند الجميع فلما رايت هذا انصدمت عن الاكل والشرب وبقيت بهتان. اخيرًا لما بينضر الريس بان الجميع رفعوا ايادهم من الاكل بينهض من مكانه وبينهضوا الجميع معه وبيصلوا صلوة الشكر ويخرجوا من المايده. حينٍ يجي الطباخ والراهب الذي كان بيقرا يجلسوا بيتغدوا.

٧،١ وبعده يخرج الريس ومعه جميع الرهبان والمبتدين الي برات باب الدير الي مكان على شكل الديوان خانه منهم بيجلسوا ومنهم بيتمشوا ويتكلموا مع بعضهم بعض في مداكرات روحيه وبيستقيموا مقدار نصف ساعه. اخيرًا كل واحد منهم يمضي الي

---

[١] في الأصل مطموس: منفتا[. . .].

I took off my finery and put on that crude linen shirt and the rest of the clothes. I pulled on the heavy, coarse robe and attached the belt. With my robes all puffed up, I looked like a lemon seller.[3] Removing the turban and felt hat I'd been wearing, I put on the black skullcap, wrapped the honey-colored woolen cloth around it, and pulled the sandals on.

I studied myself. What a sight! At that moment, my heart turned from monasticism and I regretted what I'd done, but I was too proud to let my feelings show.

My friend Çelebi [. . .] and we left the vestry together.[4] All the monks and novices then came to offer their blessings upon us for beginning our initiation. They seemed delighted with us, and showered us with congratulations.

We each entered our cell and remained there until the lunch bell rang. We then went down to the refectory and found the abbot and the rest of the monks gathered outside it. The abbot entered first and sat at the head of the table, followed by all the priests, who sat at their places. Next, the monks entered and sat, while the novices remained standing outside. Finally, the abbot permitted the novices to come in. So we did, and each of us sat at his place, with the seniors sitting closer to the head of the table than the juniors.

There were three sorts of food on the table: a soup with lentils, wheat berries, grains, and other similar vegetables and pulses; some curd cheese;[5] and figs preserved in molasses. A bottle of wine and a glass were placed between each person and the next. Everyone drank to his heart's content.

Lined up along the shelves of the refectory were the skulls of dead monks, each with the name of the deceased written on it. At one end of the refectory, a monk sat on a dais, reading aloud the stories of martyrs and the torments they'd suffered, whose intolerable horrors were known to all. I was shaken by this frightful scene, and couldn't bring myself to eat or drink.

Seeing that all had finished eating, the abbot would rise to his feet and everyone would stand with him and say a prayer of thanksgiving.[6] Following that, all would leave the refectory, and the cook would sit and have lunch along with the monk who'd been reciting.

The abbot would then take the monks and novices outside, passing through the gates of the monastery into a sort of gathering space.[7] Some would sit and others would stroll, chatting about spiritual matters. They'd remain there for about half an hour, then each man would go attend to the duties appointed to him by the abbot. The tailor would go to his sewing, the cobbler to his

1.4

1.5

1.6

1.7

شغل المقلد فيه من الريس اعني الخياط الي خياطته والسكاف الي شغل السكافه والكاتب الي كتّابته والبستاني الي بستنته وما يشبه ذلك من اشغال المخصوصه بالدير وما بتعود تري احد في الدير غير المدبر لا غير .

٨،١ والمسا بعد صلوة الغروب والستار بيدق ناقوز العشا وبعد العشا يجتمعوا ايضاً في الديوان المذكور ويتمشوا كالمعداد وبعده بيدخلوا جميعهم الي الكنيسه بيصلوا كل واحد بمفرده. اخيراً بيدخل الريس الي قلايته وبيدخل عنده واحد بعد واحد بيكشف افكاره للريس ما هو اعتراف انما هو بطريق الارشاد حتي يعرف الريس انكان تلك الافكار هي من الشيطان ام من الهامات الروح القدس او من بعض ملكات سببة هل افكار . حينئذٍ الريس بيرشده وبيعلمه حيل ابليس المحال وانكان را فيه خطيه بيامره بالاعتراف قبل النوم وبهذه الطريقه بينام الراهب والمبتدي بغاية الراحه والسلام.

٩،١ وبعدما بيدخلوا عند الريس ويخرجوا بيسكتوا وما بيبقاء احد يتكلم مع رفيقه الي ثاني يوم بكره. اخيراً الذي بيريد يدخل الي قلايته والذي بيريد يتمشا في الدير بيتمشا وبعده كل من بيدخل الي قلايته وبينام ونصف الليل محكم بيخرج القندلفت بيدور علي القلالي وفي يده الجرس بينبه الرهبان والمبتديين الي صلوة نصف الليل فيجتمعوا جميع الرهبان والريس والمبتديين في الكنيسه وبيصلوا صلوة نصف الليله التي بيستقيم مقدار ساعه او اقل وبعده برجعوا الي قلاليهم وبيناموا الي محل الفجر بيدق ناقوز الكبير الي صلوه الصبح وبعد خلوص الصلوه بتبدا القداس وكل واحد منهم بيحضر القداس ويروح الي شغله الموكل فيه بغير فتور الي حد قبل الظهر بساعة بيصلوا صلوه السادسه وبعده بيدق ناقوز الغدا كما ذكرنا كل راهب ومبتدي مفروض عليه في كل سبعه بيلتزم بانه يعترف ويتقرب.

١٠،١ وكان بين المبتديين رجل اختيار طويل القامه شايب بلحيه بيضه مهيب فسالت بعض من الرهبان عن هل رجل كيف انه مسن في العمر ووصل لهل شيخوخه بيدخل للرهبنه وبيقف مع المبتدين فقلي الراهب ان سالت يا اخي عن هل رجل هذا كان شيخ ضيعه ورجل طعام عيش كل ليله بيلتقي في مايدته عشرين نفر واكثر وله من اولاد

shoemaking, the scribe to his writing, the gardener to his gardening, and so on. Only the steward was left inside the monastery.

In the evening, following vespers and compline,[8] the bell would ring for dinner, following which all would meet again in the same gathering place and go for a walk. Then they would make their way to church, where each person would pray on his own. Finally, the abbot would repair to his cell. Each resident of the monastery would come to visit him, one at a time, to reveal his thoughts. This wasn't so much a confession as a form of guidance, so that the abbot might discern whether a person's thoughts had come from Satan or were, rather, inspirations from the Holy Ghost or one of the angels. The abbot would offer his guidance and instruct the man about Satan's devious tricks. If he perceived any sin in the man's thoughts, he would order him to perform a confession before going to sleep. That way, every monk and novice slept peacefully each night.

1.8

After visiting the abbot, each man departed in silence, forbidden from speaking to his companions until the following day. Some would go to their cells, and others, if they wished, would go for a walk in the monastery. Finally, each retired to his cell and went to sleep. At midnight, the sacristan would go around to all the cells carrying a bell. He'd rouse the monks and novices, and all would gather together with the abbot to pray the nocturne, which lasted an hour or less. Then all returned to sleep until dawn.

1.9

Each day, the large bell would ring for the morning prayer, and the mass would begin. Everyone attended mass, then went off to their designated work without any breakfast, until an hour before noon. Next they'd pray the sext prayer.[9] Afterward, the bell would ring for lunch (as described earlier). It was incumbent upon every monk and novice to confess his sins and receive communion every day of the week.

There was among the novices a tall, dignified elderly man, with gray hair and a white beard. I asked one of the monks about him. Why would a man enter the order at such an advanced age and join the ranks of the novices?

1.10

"You're interested in his story, are you now, brother?" the monk said. "Well, it seems that the old man was once a village elder, and a generous one at that. Each night, he'd welcome twenty people or more to his dinner table. Seven sons he had, all married! And married daughters too. Now, this fellow and wife had made an agreement to give up worldly things and spend the rest of their lives in orders. His wife joined a convent, and he came to this monastery.

سبعة شباب مزوجين وبنات مزوجات ايضاً فهذا اتفق هو وامراته بانهم ينبذوا العالم ويكملوا حياتهم الباقيه في الرهبنه فراحت امراته ودخلت في دير راهبات وهو اجا الي هذا الدير من مدة ثلاث سنوات ولما واجه ابونا الريس جرمانوس وطلب منه بانه بيريد يدخل للرهبنه فلما الريس سمع منه هل كلام تعجب.

١١،١ وقله يا اخي اعطيت زهرت عمرك للعالم والان عند اخر عمرك بتريد تعطي شيخوختك للرهبنه وقال هذا ابونا الريس ليمتحن عزمه فاجابه الشيخ الاختيار لعل الله بيقبلني مع الفعله الاحد عشر ساعه يا ابونا فلا زال بليح علي الريس ويتوسل اليه حتي حن عليه وقله يا اخي ما يمكني ادخلك للدير واجملك مع الرهبان الا بعد ما امتحن عزمك فقله الشيخ افعل بي كما تريد. حيندِ قله الريس انكان ولا بد بتستقيم برات الدير من غير شركه مع الرهبان الي حين ما يشا ربنا فاجابه الشيخ فقله الشيخ امرني يا ابونا وانا بطيع امرك.

١٢،١ فلما راء الريس هل عزم الذي له امره بانه يستقيم داخل باب الدير التحتاني بواب وكان ورا الباب بيت زغير مثل الكوخ فقله سمعاً وطاعه فاستقام ثلاثة سنين في ذلك البيت الزغير يحتمل برد الشتا وحر الصيف وهو صابر من غير شكوي ويقتنع بقليل من الماكل الذي يفضل من مايدة الدير فلما الرهبان والكهنه راو صبر هل رجل وثباته توسلوا الي ابونا الريس حتي يدخله للدير ويقبله من جمله المبتدين. حيندِ قبل الريس طلبتهم ودخله ولبسوه توب المبتدين والان له ثلاثة اشهر في التجربه وهذه حكايته والسبب.

١٣،١ فلما سمعت من الراهب خبر هل رجل اعتجبت وانخزلت في ذاتي والاغرب فيوم من ذات الايام دخلنا الي بيت المايده حتي نتغدي كالمعتاد فبعد ما دخل الريس والرهبان للمايده وجلسوا الجميع حيندِ اذن الريس للمبتدين حتي يدخلوا فدخلوا فلما راد يدخل هل رجل الاختيار فزجره الريس ومنعه عن الدخول فارتد الي الورا مكتف الايدين ومحني الراس واستقام هكذا الي حين ما خلصوا الرهبان الغدا وخرج الريس من المايده واتي الي قربه بوجه عبوس مغضب فاكع الشيخ عند اقدام الريس وهو طارق في الارض وبدي الريس يزجره ويوبخه بقوله له يا شيخ الخرفان قليل الاحتشام

That was three years ago. He met with the abbot, Father Jirmānūs, and asked him if he could become a monk.[10] The abbot was incredulous.

"'Brother, you gave the bloom of your life to the world. And now, in old age, you choose to give the rest to monasticism?' the abbot said, trying to test the old man's resolve.

1.11

"'Yes, Father,' the old man replied. 'And perhaps God will accept me among the laborers of the eleventh hour.'[11]

"He continued to beg and plead, and finally the abbot took pity on him, but insisted that he wouldn't admit the old man to the monastery and let him join the monks until he tested his resolve.

"'Do with me what you will,' the old man replied.

"'In that case, you'll live outside the monastery without mingling with the monks, until such time as our Lord sees fit.'

"'As you wish, Father,' he said.

"Confronted with the old man's determination, the abbot ordered him to serve as a gatekeeper, and lodged him in a little hut just inside the lower gate to the monastery. He spent the next three years living in that hut, enduring the cold of winter and the heat of summer without complaint, and contenting himself with the meager scraps he received from the monastery's table. Seeing his steadfastness and perseverance, the monks and priests begged the abbot to admit the old man to the monastery and accept him among the novices.

1.12

"The abbot agreed, and they brought him in and clothed him as a novice. That was three months ago," the monk concluded. "And that's his story."

The man's story left me astonished. And yet, an even stranger thing happened some days later, when we went to the refectory to have lunch. After the abbot and monks entered the hall and everyone had sat down, the abbot admitted the novices. But when the old man walked in, the abbot rebuked him and forbade him from taking his place. The old man retreated, his arms folded and his head bowed, and remained in that posture until the monks finished lunch. The abbot, his face twisted into a furious scowl, got up from the table and strode over to him. The old man knelt prostrate at the feet of the abbot, who launched into a tirade.

1.13

"You shameless, senile old man!" he shouted, giving him a tongue-lashing as severe as any lampoon a poet ever dished out. When the torrent of abuse finally stopped, the abbot kicked him and said, "Get up, you wretch, and eat with the cook!"

وصار يهجيه وناهيك عن رجل شاعر اذا راد يهجي انسان فبعدما هجاه وبخه بكلام منكي مر رفسه برجله وقله يا شقي اتعدا مع الطباخ في الحال نهض وقبل يد الريس وطلب منه العفو والمسامحه امام جميع الرهبان والمبتدين ودخل للمايده حتي يتغدا مع الطباخ وخرجنا جميعنا الي مكان المعتاد نتنشا فالفقير لما رايت هل مدهر شربت الشربه وقلت في بالي ان كان رجل اختيار مثل هذا عامله الريس بهذه الصرامه كيف حالي انا اذا وقعت في زله بابنا صرامه يعاملني.

١،١٤ واستقمت في هذه الفكره الي المساء وانا موهوم فلما حان وقت كشف الافكار دخلت الفقير حتي اكشف افكاري كالمعتاد وكان اول كلامي للريس باني هذا اليوم كله بفتكر فيك يا ابونا كيف انك عاملت بصرامه هل رجل الاختيار ولمتك في فكري فتبسم الريس وقلي يا اخي حقاً هل رجل ما رايت عليه دنب ابداً ولكن وظيفتي بتقضي باني افعل هكذا مع المبتدين حتي امرنهم[1] علي التواضع وكسر الذات حتي ينموا في الفضيله وهذا الرجل انا قوي بحبه لان فيه قداسه وهذا فعلته لتوبيخ بعض متكبرين حتي يستفيدوا من تواضعه[2] وصبره وطاعته لان مفهوم عند الجميع باني وبخته بغير دنب. المراد لا زال يوعظ عليّ ويسليني حتي برد قلبي وخرجت من عنده وانا مريض ومبسوط فرايت حينئذٍ بان كشف الافكار لها فايده عظيمه.

١،١٥ ويوم اخر خرجنا من المايده بعد الغدا وطلعنا برات باب الدير لاجل التنزه كالمعتاد كما ذكرنا فدعا الريس الي راهب كان يسمي موسا وكان هل راهب مخصص لقضي حوايج الدير وكان الريس يرسله الي طرابلس لقضي اشغال الدير والي غير اماكن ايضاً فهذا لما حضر امامه امره بان ياخد الاخ ارسانيوس معه ولما يصل الي طيعة بشره يركبه علي البغله ويوصله الي ضيعة سيدة زغرتا ويسلمه بيد خوري الضيعه ويدير باله عليه ويداريه في الدرب واعطاه مكتوب للخوري توصاي فيه ويحكمه.

١،١٦ اخيراً ارسل احد الرهبان يدعي الي عنده الاخ المذكور اعني ارسانيوس وكان ذلك مريض وما له قوه يمشي في الدير الا بالجهد[3] فلما حضر امام الريس ركع وباس يده.

---

١ الأصل: امرنهم. ٢ الأصل: تواضه. ٣ الأصل: بالجهدد.

The man rose to his feet, kissed the abbot's hand, and begged his forgiveness as all the monks and novices looked on. He then went into the hall to have lunch with the cook while we all filed out for our usual walk.

Witnessing this spectacle was a bitter pill to swallow. If the abbot could treat an old man so harshly, I wondered, what would happen to me if I ever crossed him? What sort of rebuke might I face?

The incident stayed with me all day, until I felt it was time to reveal my    1.14
thoughts to the abbot. I went in to see him.

"Father," I blurted out, "I've spent all day thinking about what you did, and how you treated that old man so harshly! I've reproached you in my thoughts, Father!"

The abbot smiled.

"To be candid, brother, I knew he'd done nothing wrong," he said. "But my position demands that I treat the novices harshly. It trains them to be humble and it breaks down their sense of self. When it works, they grow in virtue.

"I love that man," the abbot continued. "There's something saintly about him. In fact, that's why I treated him the way I did. We have certain novices here who are too full of themselves. It'll do them good to see what real humility and resignation look like, especially since everyone knows the man had done nothing wrong."

He continued to counsel and comfort me until my nerves had steadied, and I left feeling better. I realized then that the exercise of revealing one's thoughts to the abbot was profoundly beneficial.

Another day, we got up from lunch and went out the gate of the monastery    1.15
to go for our usual walk. The abbot called for a monk named Mūsā, who was in charge of procuring the monastery's provisions. The abbot would occasionally send him to Tripoli, among other places, to take care of the monastery's affairs.

When Brother Mūsā appeared, the abbot ordered him to take Brother Arsāniyūs to the village of Bsharrī and put him on a mule. He was to convey him to the village of Saydat Zgharta, where he'd hand him over to the village priest. The abbot told him to take care of Arsāniyūs and protect him along the way, and gave him a letter recommending Mūsā to the priest, asking him to treat Arsāniyūs.

The abbot sent another monk to fetch Arsāniyūs, who was ill, and hardly    1.16
had the strength to walk through the monastery. He dragged himself before the abbot and knelt to kiss his hand.

حينذٍ صار يتكلم معه الريس بهذا الكلام فقله انا امرك يا اخي بامر الطاعه بانك تروح مع اخينا موسا الي عند خوري سيدت زغرتا وتكون تحت طاعته في جميع ما بيامرك فيه وانك ان بيامرك باكل الظفر تكون تاكل وتقبل الادوية التي يقدمها لك من غير انك تنقص عنها[1] وفي خلوص كلام الريس معه نهض في الحال وباس يد الريس وتوجه ونزل في الدرج وانتهره الريس ودعاه الي قدامه فلما رجع امام الريس ركع وقله اغفر لي يا ابانا وباس الارض بعداً والريس يوبخه ويقله يا قليل العقل والتمييز لين رايح هل انك بتقدر تمشي حسب قانونا من هاهنا الي ضيعة زغرتا هل فيك هل قوي لكن الكبريا غالبه عليك يا شقي انهض واسمع ما بقوله لك ولا تخالف فنهض الاخ الوديع وهو محني هامه للارض ويقول اغفر لي يا ابانا فقله حينذٍ لما بتصل الي بشره اركب البغله ولا تمشي ابداً وامر احد الرهبان بان ياتيه بكتاب صلواته وعكازته وعبايته الفوقانيه فاعطاهم الي الاخ موسا المذكور وبارك عليه واصرفه. حينذٍ التفت الريس الينا وتهد قايلاً كت بشتهي[2] يا اولادي بان تكون هل طاعة العميا التي هي في هل اخ تكون في جميعكم هل نضرتم كيف انه ما اعتدر لي بقوله يا ابانا ما لي قوه لكي امشي بل انه توجه حالاً بطاعته الي كلامي من غير ارتياب بانه بيقدر يمشي واستقام الريس في تلك النصف ساعة التي هي للتنزه يوعض علينا في هل معنا.

١٧،١ والفقير رايت اشيا كثيره في هل رهبنة المقدسه ومن الرهبان الذين سيرتهم سيره ملايكيه وهذا دكرته وهو القليل من الكثير بل انما ذكرته خجلاً لي وتنبيه لغيري ليلا يروح الي الرهبنه بغير استعداد لهذه الدرجة المقدسه وخصوصاً وقبل كل شي يستقيم مده مديده يطلب من الله بان يرويه دعوته ويتدبر علي يد مرشد فهيم عامل ومعلم. حينذٍ بيكون بامان من قبل دعوته.

١٨،١ اخيراً بعد دخولي للتجربه بقليل من الزمان وقعت في مرض ثقيل واستقمت مريض مدة شهرين وشهر اخر ما بين مريض وطيب وفي ذلك الشهر رفع عني الريس قانون

---

1 بعد «عنها» جملة مشطوبة في الأصل: «وانا امرت الي اخي موسا بانه في بشره يركبك علي البغله فاركب وتكون مطيعه في الدرب». 2 الأصل: بشتهتي.

"Brother, I order you to go with our brother Mūsā to see the priest of Saydat Zgharta. Obey his every word! If he orders you to eat fatty food, then do so, and accept without question the medicine he gives you."[12] When the abbot finished speaking, the monk rose and kissed his hand. He turned and started down the stairs, but the abbot shouted after him, calling him back. The man returned and knelt before the abbot.

"Forgive me, Father," he said, kissing the ground.

"Where are you going, you senseless dolt?" the abbot shouted. "Are you going to walk all the way to Zgharta just because our Rule says you should? You don't have the strength! Pride has overcome you, you wretch! Now stand up and listen carefully, and don't disobey me."

"Forgive me, Father," the monk said meekly as he stood up, head bowed.

"When you arrive in Bsharrī, get on the mule and don't go another step on foot," said the abbot, and ordered one of the monks to fetch the man's prayer book, walking stick, and outer robe. He gave them to Brother Mūsā, blessed him, and sent him off. The abbot turned to us and sighed.

"My sons, I yearn to see the blind obedience of this monk in all of you," he said. "Did you notice that he made not a single excuse? He didn't say, 'Oh Father, I don't have the strength to walk!' No, he set off immediately, obeying my orders without any doubt that he was able to walk."

The abbot continued to preach to us on this subject for the next half hour, which was supposed to be spent strolling outdoors.

I saw quite a few things in this sacred order and among the monks, whose   1.17 conduct is truly angelic. What I've recounted here are just a few stories. Even though they may reflect poorly on me, I've told these stories in order to warn others not to pursue the path of monasticism without being prepared for such a saintly vocation. Specifically, before doing anything else, you should spend a good long while asking God to reveal His calling to you. And you should train at the hand of a learned and practical guide. Then and only then will you be certain that you have indeed been called.

Shortly after I began my novitiate, I became very ill. I was ill for two months,   1.18 and spent another month recuperating. During that month, the abbot freed me from the monastic rule and would send me out with the monks whenever

الرهبنه وصار يرسلني مع الرهبان برات الدير لما يخرجوا في اشغال الدير فكنت اروح اتنزه صحبتهم.

١٩،١ فيوم من ذات الايام راحوا اثنين من الرهبان الي الطاحون حتي يطحنوا قمح للدير فامرهم الريس بان ياخدوني معهم للطاحون حتي اتنزه فمضيت معهم الي مكان يسما راس النهر حيث كانت الطاحون فلما وصلنا ونزلوا القمح عن ظهر الحمير فاء وا بان ما لهم ضور للطحن لان كان قبلهم وصلوا كثيرين حتي يطحنوا فالتزموا بانهم يناموا هناك الي ان يجيهم دور. حينذٍ قالوا لي الرهبان قوم يا روح يا اخونا للدير وخد معك الاتان واحكي للريس سبب رقادنا في الطاحون حتي لا يبقا باله.

٢٠،١ فنهضت وسقت الاتان امامي وسرت حتي وصلت الي الوادي وبدينا في النزول من ذلك العلو فنزل الاتان امامي وفي نزوله رايت كانه تهور الي الاسفل فلحقت ومسكت ديله ليلا يتهور فنترني معه وانا ماسك ديله. اخيرًا فلت مني وطلع وانا صرت اتدركل من فوق الي تحت حتي اتكسرت اضلاعي وبعد قليل فقت من غموتي واوعيت علي حالي فما رايت الاتان. وقتيذٍ قلت في بالي بان احد الحميديه اخد الاتان وراح فيه وايش عدت ارد جواب للريس في فكارات وصرت ونسيت اوجاعي وصرت ادور في الوادي وافتش علي الاتان فما رايت له خبر ولا جنيت اثر فخزنت وبقيت في حيره وقطعت[1] الاياس من الاتان. اخيرًا توجهت الي الدير وانا ماشي رويدًا رويدًا الي ان وصلت الي الدير.

٢١،١ فاتفق ذلك اليوم بان كام واحد من المبتدين الحلبيه الذي مر ذكرهم كانوا متقلقلين وطلبوا الخروج من الدير وبهذا صعب علي الريس كثير فزعًا علي غيرهم من المبتدين ليلا يرتجي عزمهم فصار يدعي واحد بعد واحد ويفحصه هل هو ثابت ام لا. اخيرًا ارسل دعاني فقالوا له الرهبان بان اخونا راح مع الرهبان للطاحون كما امرت فقلهم لما بيرجع من الطاحون ارسلوه الي عندي وكان وصولي للدير في تلك الساعه

---

١ الأصل: قطت.

they went to take care of the monastery's business. I'd join them and take in a walk.

One day, two monks set off for the flour mill to grind some wheat for the monastery. The abbot ordered them to take me along so I could have a walk. We headed out to a place called Rās al-Nahr, where the mill was located.[13] When we arrived and unloaded the wheat from the donkeys, the monks realized that they wouldn't be able to grind the wheat right away, as many other people had arrived ahead of them. They'd be compelled to spend the night there, waiting their turn.

"Brother, go back to the monastery and take the donkey with you," the monks told me. "Explain to the abbot why we've stayed over at the mill, so he won't be worried."

I headed out, driving the donkey ahead of me. We began to descend when we reached the valley, the donkey leading the way. As it clambered down the slope, it seemed to me as though the beast was about to slide down to the bottom! So I raced after it, grasping its tail to hold it back, but it yanked me forward, slipped loose, and galloped off while I tumbled all the way down, battering my ribs. As I recovered from my daze a moment later, I looked around. The donkey was nowhere to be seen.

My first thought was that a member of the Ḥamādah tribe must have taken the donkey and made off with it.[14] What was I going to tell the abbot? In my desperation, I forgot my aches and pains and set about searching for the donkey in the valley, but it had vanished without a trace! My heart sank. Unsure what to do next, I gave up the search and trudged all the way back to the monastery.

As it happened, on that very day, a few of the Aleppan novices I mentioned earlier had grown restless and were asking to quit the monastery. The abbot was upset about this, worried that the other novices would lose their resolve. So he summoned all the novices to him, one by one, and examined each to ascertain whether he was firmly committed or not.

When it was my turn to be summoned by the abbot, some monks reminded him that I'd gone off to the mill with the other monks, as he'd ordered.

"When he returns from the mill, send him to me," the abbot replied.

Not long afterward, I happened to arrive at the monastery, and as I came inside—feeling ashamed and frightened after the loss of the donkey—I found the monks waiting for me.

1.19

1.20

1.21

فلما صعدت الي الدير وانا في تلك الحاله موهوج ومرعوب من فقدي الاتان قالوا لي
الرهبان كلف خاطرك يا اخي الي عند الريس بيدعوك.

٢٢،١ فلما سمعت منهم هل كلام تحققت بان الريس سمع في فقد الاتان فزاد رعبي رعب
فلما امتثلت امام الريس وبست يده امرني بالجلوس فجلست فقلي يا اخي بوجه
عابس اتعرف ليش دعيتك لعندي قلتله لا يا ابونا. حينذٍ قلي بان كام واحد من المبتدين
طالبين الخروج من الدير ولاجل ان هذا يضر غيرهم من المبتدين فصرت الفحص
واحد بعد واحد منهم واختبر هل هو ثابت ام لا ليلا كل مده يخرج واحد وبيصير
سبب تجربه لغيره.

٢٣،١ اخيراً بعد كلام مستطيل قلي هل انك ثابت ام لا فاجبته علي الفور لا يا ابانا بروح
بتحكم في حلب ولما بطيب مليح برجع الي الدير. حينذٍ بش وجهه في وصار يوعضني
باناسه ويقلي لا تخلي التجربه تغلبك يا اخي وترجعك الي العالم مغلوب يا ابني ولا زال
يلاطفني بالكلام ويريني محبه الي حين ما قلته دعني يا ابانا افتكر اليوم وانضر كيف
الله بيوجهني.

٢٤،١ فرضي الريس وباركني ثم اصرفني حتي اروح افتكر ولما خرجت من عنده فايت
بعض من الرهبان واقفين باستنضاري حتي يتلافوني ليلا اغير عزمي عن الرهبنه.
حينذٍ سالتهم عن الاتان هل وجدوه ام لا فبهتوا من كلامي وقالولي ما هذا الاتان
الذي بتقول عنه فحكيت لهم بالمجراويه كما تمت فصاروا يبتسموا بقولهم لي ان هذا
الاتان الرهبان استعاروه من بشره ولما رجع معك ما هرب بل راح الي مكانه للضيعه
لا تخف يا اخي هذا ما ضاع والاتن رجعوا الي مكانهم ايضاً الذين كانوا
معك وهذا بيفعلوه دايماً.

٢٥،١ حينذٍ ركن قلبي ومضيت الي قلايتي افتكر ماذا اعمل واستقمت ذلك النهار
وتلك الليله في تلك الافكار الي ان اصبح الصباح وبعد كالت القداديس بجمعنا الريس
وسالنا انكان استقمنا عن نيت الخروج من الدير فقلنا له نعم. حينذٍ امر بان يحضروا

"Brother, if you will, go to the abbot," they said. "He's calling for you."

At the sound of these words, I was certain the abbot had heard about the   **1.22** donkey's disappearance. My terror mounted. I presented myself before the abbot and kissed his hand, and he ordered me to sit down.

"Brother, do you know why I summoned you?" he asked, frowning.

"No, Father."

"A few of the novices have asked to leave the monastery," he said. "Such an event would be harmful to the other novices, so I've been questioning each man to establish whether he's firm in his resolve or not. I do this to avoid having novices trickling out periodically, which is difficult for the others to bear."[15]

After going on at some length in this way, he finally asked if I was deter-   **1.23** mined to stay or not.

"No, Father," I replied without hesitation. "I need to leave and seek medical treatment in Aleppo. When I'm well again, I'll return to the monastery."

He smiled and began to exhort me gently.

"Don't let the novitiate make you give up and return you to the world a defeated man, my son," he said. He went on speaking in the same kindly manner until at last I spoke.

"Father, let me think on it today, and see how God guides me."

The abbot was satisfied with this response, and he blessed me and sent me   **1.24** on my way to do some thinking. As I emerged from his quarters, I saw some of the monks waiting for me, hoping to convince me to change my mind about leaving the order.

I asked them whether they'd found the donkey.

"What donkey?" they asked, confused.

I told them what had happened, and they broke into grins.

"The monks rented that donkey in Bsharrī," they replied. "When it came back with you, it didn't run away—it just went home to its village! Don't worry, brother, it's not lost. All the donkeys returned to their stables, including the ones you took to the mill. That's what they always do."

Relieved, I went to my cell to think about what I would do. I spent all day   **1.25** and night until morning lost in thought. After the masses were over, the abbot gathered us all together and asked if we still intended to leave the monastery.

"Yes," we replied.

لنا حوايجنا وشلحونا ثياب التجربه ولبسنا ثيابنا وكا اربعه الفقير وداود ابن جبور الكويس ويوسف ابن شاهين جلبي وميخاييل بن توما حوا فبعدما لبسنا ثيابنا ودعنا الريس والرهبان وخرجنا من الدير.

١،٢٦ وفي ذلك الوقت وصل الي الدير ريس الدير العام وهو القس عبد الله ابن قري علي فهذا لما رانا خارجين حزن من جري طلوعنا من الدير فصلي علينا ودعاني الي جانبه واحكي معي سرًا قايلًا اعتقد يا ابني ان كل الذين خرجوا من المبتدين ما عدت اقبل منهم ولا واحد ولكن ان انت رجعت بقبلك وباركني وقلي امضي بسلام.

١،٢٧ ثم مضينا جميعنا ولا زلنا سايرين حتي وصلنا الي طرابلس فاينا¹ قفل مسافر الي حلب فاستكرينا معه وجينا الي حلب وكل منا راح الي محله فاستقمت ذلك اليوم في البيت حتي استرحت وثاني يوم رحت سلمت علي معلمي المذكور خواجه رمزات فلما راني وبخني وذكرني بكلامه لي سابقًا وما عاد اعطاني التفاته ولا عاد يقبل بان اعاود الي عنده لانه كان انحصر مني كثير.

١،٢٨ فاستقمت مقدار ثلاثه اشهر وانا داير بغير شغل ولا عمل فداقت الدنيا في ونويت علي الرجوع للدير فاصطبرت حتي تهيا قفل رايح الي طربلس فرحت استكريت دبه من القاطرجي واريته بان واحد من اصحابي بدي ارسله معه وهذا فعلته حتي لا حد يعرف في خروجي حلب ليلا يمنعوني ايضًا عن الرواح.

١،٢٩ فتاني يوم استيقظت حكم السلام واخدت بعض حوايج الذي بيلزموني من رفايق وقصان وما يشبه ذلك وعبيت الجميع في خرج الذي كان عندي من اول سفره وخرجت من البيت وتوجهت الي خان الزيت حيث مكان النازل فيه القاطرجي فلما وصلت وسالت عن القاطرجي قالوا لي بانه راح يحمل الي واحد وفيجي الذي هو نازل في بيت خواجه سيريون خواجة اخي. حينذٍ عرفته وهذا كان رجل سايح من سواح سلطان فرنسا وكان جايي من بلاد الارمنيه وساح في تلك البلاد بصفت حكيم عابر طريق ومن حلب قصده يسوح في بلاد الشرقيه اعني العربه² وكان اسمه بول لوكا.

---

١ الأصل: فاربنا.  ٢ «اعني العربه» في الهامش.

So the abbot ordered that our personal effects be returned to us. The monks had us remove our initiation robes and we put on our own clothes again. There were four of us: myself, Dāwūd ibn Jabbūr al-Kwayyis, Yūsuf ibn Shāhīn Çelebi, and Mikhā'īl ibn Tūmā Ḥawā. Once we were dressed, we said goodbye to the abbot and the monks, and left the monastery.

At that precise moment, the superior general, Father 'Abdallāh ibn Qarā'alī, happened to arrive at the monastery.[16] He was saddened to see us leaving, and began to pray for us. He called me over to his side.

1.26

"Know this, my son," he said to me privately. "I've never allowed a single novice who left the monastery to return. But if you come back, I'll accept you."

He blessed me and told me to go in peace.

We set off, and made our way to Tripoli, without stopping on the road once. In Tripoli, we found a caravan traveling to Aleppo, so we booked passage and returned home. When we arrived, each of us went to his own house; I spent the remainder of the day resting.

1.27

The next day I went to pay respects to my master, the aforementioned *khawājah* Rémuzat.[17] As soon as he saw me, he set about scolding me, reminding me of what he'd told me earlier.[18] He was so upset he could scarcely look my way, and refused to let me visit him again.

I spent three months searching fruitlessly for work. Finding myself in dire straits, I decided I would return to the monastery and wait till a caravan was set to travel to Tripoli. When one was preparing to leave, I rented a horse from the muleteer, telling him it was for a friend. I did this so no one would find out I was leaving Aleppo and try to stop me.

1.28

The next day, I rose just before the call to the dawn prayer and gathered the clothes I'd need: underpants, shirts, and so on.[19] I stuffed them into a satchel I'd used on my first trip and left the house for Khān al-Zayt, where the muleteer was staying. When I arrived and asked after him, I was told he'd gone to handle the luggage of a Frank who was staying at the home of *khawājah* Sauron, my brother's master.

1.29

I knew who the Frank was. He was a traveler dispatched by the sultan of France, and had arrived from Armenia, which he'd toured as a traveling doctor.[20] From Aleppo, his plan was to travel through the East—that is, Arab lands. His name was Paul Lucas.

٣٠،١ اخيرًا حمّلت خرجي علي الكديش وكان موجود هناك كام واحد من الحلبيه مسافرين مع القفل فقلتلهم قوموا بنا نتمشي الي حين ما يجي القاطرجي. حيندٍ سحبنا كدشنا وسرنا حتي وصلنا الي القبه والعامود وما اجا القاطرجي فجلسنا هناك نستنضره وفي ذلك الوقت انا غيرت حلاسي ولفيت شاشي الابيض ولبست الجزمه وصلحت تنبليتي كما يجب وبقيت علي هيبة السفر وبعد هنيهه وصل القاطرجي وبعده وصل ذلك الفرنجي المذكور ومعه اربع خمس خواجكيه وكلهم يعرفوني في الحال ركبت دبتي وسرت وحدي قبلما يصلوا الينا وغبت عن نضرهم.

٣١،١ اخيرًا دعوه ورجعوا ونحن مشينا والحال كانت سبقت قبل بيوم الي كتين لا زلنا سايرين والمطر يصب علينا حتي وصلنا الي كتين ونحن غرقانين من تلك الامطار فدخلنا الي بيت القاطرجي وفي الحال اوقد لنا نار في الاوجاق. حيندٍ شلحنا ما علينا وصرنا ننشف ثيابنا والفرنجي نزل في تلك الناحيه هو وخدامه رجل من بلاد الارمنيه مسيحي كاتوليكي قصده كان يقدس فلما استرحنا شويه سمعت الفرنجي والقاطرجي عمالين يدابلوا لكن الواحد ما يفهم من الاخر. حيندٍ زعقلي القاطرجي بما انه يعرفني بفهم في لسان الفرنجي وقلي بحياتك قول لهذا الخواجه ماذا يريد وما هو مطلوبه فسالت المذكور بلسان الفرنساوي ماذا يريد فقلي انا سلمته في حلب بعض حوايج وما رايتهم الان فلما فهمت القاطرجي قلي ها هن موجودات عندي موضوعات في الخرج. حيندٍ انبسط الفرنجي واستكتر بخيري. اخيرًا سالني هل انت مسيحي فقلته نعم بنعمة الله تعالى قلي لا تواخدني لاني رايتك لافف شاش ابيض خمنت انك مسلم.

٣٢،١ فكلفني باني اجلس عنده واتعشي معه فابيت. اخيرًا لج عليّ بالجلوس فجلست فامر لخادمه بان يحضر العشا وكان معه من حلب زواده وافره ونبيذ طيب فاتعشيت انا واياه وبعد خلوصنا من العشا شربنا القهوه وجاب لنا الغلام غلايين التتن واستقمنا

At last I was able to load my satchel onto the packhorse. There were a few      1.30
Aleppans traveling with the caravan.

"Come on," I told them, "let's start walking while we wait for the muleteer
to arrive." We set off, tugging our horses along, and soon arrived at the dome
and column.[21] The muleteer still hadn't appeared, so we sat and waited.

Meanwhile, I changed my clothes and wrapped a white turban cloth around
my head. I put on my boots and adjusted my satchel properly. I was ready to
go. After a short while, the caravan driver arrived, followed by the aforementioned Frank. He had four or five *khawājah*s with him, each of whom would
have recognized me! So I jumped on my horse in a flash and rode off alone,
disappearing from view before they arrived.

The *khawājah*s finally bid farewell to the Frank, and our caravan set off. Our      1.31
baggage had been sent the day before to Kaftīn. We made our way there, riding
without rest even as the rain poured down. We reached Kaftīn half-drowned,
and went to the muleteer's house. He quickly lit a fire for us in the stove, and
we stripped off what we were wearing and set about drying our clothes.

The Frank came in with his servant, a Catholic man from Armenia, on pilgrimage to Jerusalem. After we'd rested awhile, I heard the Frank and the muleteer speaking, but neither could make sense of what the other was saying. The
muleteer called for me because he knew I understood the Frankish language.

"Hey, do me a favor and ask the *khawājah* what he's after," the driver said.

I put this to the fellow in French.

"I entrusted some things to the muleteer when we were in Aleppo," the
Frank explained. "And now they've vanished!"

When I explained this to the muleteer, he replied that he had the things in
question tucked away in one of his bags. The Frank was pleased to hear this,
and thanked me profusely.

"Are you a Christian?" he asked.

"I am, by the grace of God."

"Forgive me," he said. "I'd seen you wearing a white turban and mistook
you for a Muslim."

He asked me to sit and dine with him. I declined, but he insisted, so I joined      1.32
him. He ordered his servant to prepare dinner. They'd brought plenty of provisions with them from Aleppo, along with some good wine. We had dinner,
followed by coffee, and the young servant then brought us a pair of tobacco
pipes to smoke. We stayed up, chatting into the night.

نتصامر انا واياه فسالني قايلاً لي انت من اينا طايفه قلته انا من طايفة الموارنه وانا بعرفك لما كنت في حلب وكنت نازل في بيت خواجه سيرون الفرنساوي واخي عنده مخزنجي فقلي مخزنجيه هو واخوك قلته نعم فتعجب بانه كيف ما قلي بانك مسافر معنا. حينئذٍ قلته بان اخي ما صار له خبر في طلوعي من حلب قلي لاي سبب ما صار له خبر قلته لو يصير له خبر لما اطلقني اسافر .

٣٣،١ حينئذٍ قلي الي اين انت مسافر فاستحيت اخبره بقصتي انما قلته انا رايح بسوح في الدنيا و بتفرج وهذا قلته حتي اضيع عليه فهو قطع عقله باني رايح بسوح وهكذا دبرالله فقلي انكان بتريد تسوح ما بتقدر تقشع احسن مني واحكالي بانه مرسل من سلطان فرنسا حتي ادور البلاد واكتب ما اراه وافتش علي تواريخ قدم وعلي مداليا اعني معاملة ملوك القدم وعلي بعض حشايش موجوده في هل بلاد ثم ساليني هل بتعرف تقرا بلسان العربي قلته نعم وبالفرنجي ايضاً قلي ان رحت معي انا بجلسك في خزانت الكتب العربيه ويصير لك علوفه من الملك وبتعيش طول عمرك تحت نام الملك وانا موصي من الوزير باني اخذ رجل يعرف يقرا بالعربي من هل بلاد وهذا بيصير لك منه خير عظيم ابتريد تروح معي قلته نعم ثم قلي بتعطيني قرار بتبت بانك بتروح معي الي بهريز . حينئذٍ قلته ما بعطيك قرار ثابت الا في طرابلس وقلت في بالي حتي استخبر عنه هل هو صادق في هل كلام ام لا . اخيراً قلي لا تفارقني في هل درب حتي نصل الي طرابلس وكان قصده حتي اترجمله لان الذي كان معه ما بيفهم بالعربي انما كان يفهم قليلاً بلسان التلياني فاجبته علي الراس والعين. اخيراً استازنت منه ورحت عند رفقاتي وبتنا تلك الليله الي الصباح فلما اصبحنا قلنا القاطرجي بانه بيريد يكسر ذلك اليوم في الضيعه كعادتهم .

"Which community are you from?" he asked.

"I'm a Maronite," I replied. "I heard of you when you were living in Aleppo. You were staying in the home of the Frenchman, *khawājah* Sauron. My brother works for him as a warehouseman."

"The warehouseman was your brother?" he asked me.

"Yes."

"Why didn't he tell me that you were traveling with us?" he asked in surprise.

"Because he didn't know I was leaving Aleppo."

"Why ever not?"

"If he'd known, he wouldn't have let me go," I replied.

At this, the Frank asked me where I was headed. I was too embarrassed to 1.33 tell him the real story, so I merely said I was on a voyage to explore the world. This was a ruse meant to throw him off the scent, but as a result, he was convinced that I was indeed setting off on a voyage. Such was God's plan!

"If you're interested in travel, you won't find a better companion than me," he said, and explained that he'd been sent by the sultan of France to tour these lands and to write an account of what he saw. He was in search of old chronicles and of medallions—coins struck by kings of old—as well as particular plants to be found in this part of the world.

"Do you know how to read Arabic?" he asked.

"Yes, and French as well," I replied.

"If you come with me, I'll arrange a position for you at the Arabic Library," he offered.[22] "The king will pay you a salary and you'll spend your whole life under his protection. The king's minister has charged me to bring home a man from this part of the world who knows how to read Arabic. You'd benefit greatly from the minister's good graces. Will you come with me?"

"Yes," I said.

"Do I have your word that you'll come to Paris with me?"

"Not until we reach Tripoli," I said, thinking I should look into whether he was being truthful or not.

"In that case, while we're on the road to Tripoli, don't leave my side," he said, as he intended to have me serve as a translator. The fellow who was traveling with him didn't understand Arabic, only a little Italian.

"Happily," I replied.

I took my leave and rejoined my companions. I spent the night with them, and in the morning when we awoke, the muleteer said that he wanted to spend the day in the village, as he usually did.

٣٤.١ فلما سمع الخواجه المذكور بان القفل يستقيم ذلك اليوم في الضيعه فصار يسال الكهّانته انكان موجود قريب منهم عماره قديمه من ايام ملوك النصارا فدلوه علي جبل قريب من الضيعه مسافة درب ساعه وقالوله بان هناك موجود عماير نصاري ودير وكيسه لكنهم خراب انما مكتوب علي بعض حجاره احرف فنجيبه فلما سمع منهم هل كلام دعي القاطرجي وقله اريد بريد اروح الي هل جبل واتفرج فاجابه القاطرجي بان هل مكان بيلتقا من اللصوص والعرب بخاف عليك ليلا يشلحوك فقله هذا ما شغلك انما احضر لي دواب حتي نركب.

٣٥.١ فاستكري له كدش من الضيعه لان دوابه تعابا بده يريحهم حتي يسافروا ثاني يوم فلما حضروا الكدش فاخدنا معنا زواده اكل وشرب واستكرينا اربع خمس قواسه حتي يروحوا معنا صيانة من اللصوص وسافرنا وصعدنا لذلك الجبل فمشينا في الجبل قليلاً فاينا تلك العماير التي احكوا لنا عنها الكهّانته فنزلنا هناك فصار الخواجه يدور في تلك الاماكن وينسخ الكتابات المكتوبه علي بعض من تلك الحجاره فلما انتهي من تلك الكتابات فرحنا الي مكان وجدنا فيه قبر يعلوه حجر قطعة جبل. حينذٍ دار ما يدور القبر لعله يجد مكان يدخل اليه فما راء غير خراقه داخله للقبر فراد بان واحد من القواسه ينزل في هل خراق ما احد نزل منهم وقالوله يمكن هذا يكون وكر وحش ام ضبع ام نمر او غير ذلك من الوحوش الضاريه من له جرعه ينزل.

٣٦.١ ونحن في كلام مر علينا راعي معري فقالوله القواسه حتي ينزل فقال لهم ايش بتعطوني حتي انزل فاعطاه الخواجه ثلث ابوكلب فلما راء الثلث في كفه فري فوقانيه ونزل في الحال وكان غمق ذلك القبر قامه ومدة يد. حينذٍ قال الخواجه للراعي دور في القبر وايش ما شفت اعطيني اياه فدار الراعي في داخل القبر فشاف جمجمة انسان فاعطانا اياها لكن جمجمه بقدر جبسه كبيره فقلنا الخواجه هذه جمجمة رجل فرد

When the *khawājah* heard that the caravan would be spending the day in the village, he asked the residents of Kaftīn if there were any buildings nearby dating to the period of the ancient Christian kings. They pointed out a mountain, about an hour's journey from the village, and told him there were some Christian buildings there, as well as a monastery and church: They were in ruins, but there was some Frankish writing on some of the stones. On hearing this, he called for the muleteer.

"I wish to go see that mountain," he said.

"That area is full of bandits and Bedouins," the muleteer replied. "I worry that you'll be robbed."

"That's none of your concern," the Frank replied. "Bring me some mounts."

The muleteer hired some packhorses from the village, as his own animals were tired and he wanted to rest them so they could travel the next day. They brought us the horses, and we packed some food and drink to bring along, hired four or five guards to protect us from thieves, and set off to climb the mountain.

After going a little way, we came upon the structures the villagers of Kaftīn had told us about and stopped to dismount. The *khawājah* began walking around the buildings, copying the inscriptions on some of the stones. When he finished with the inscriptions, we walked over to a tomb covered by a boulder.[23] The *khawājah* circled the tomb, looking for a place where he might enter, but all he could find was a narrow gap that opened onto the interior.

He asked for a volunteer from the guards to go down into the hole, but not a single one would dare. They told him that it might be the lair of some wild beast, perhaps a hyena or a panther, or some other ferocious beast. Who would possibly venture to go in?

While we were talking, a goatherd passed by, and the guards asked him to go into the tomb.

"What will you give me if I do?" he asked.

The *khawājah* handed him a third of an *abū kalb*. Once the goatherd had the coin in his hand, he threw off his coat and clambered down immediately.[24] The tomb was as deep as the height of a man with outstretched arms.

The *khawājah* called down to the goatherd. "Walk around the tomb and hand me whatever you see inside."

The goatherd did as he was told, and found a human skull. He handed it to us. It was the size of a large watermelon.

"This is the skull of a man," the *khawājah* told us.

1.34

1.35

1.36

اعطانا جمجمة اخرى اصغر من تلك فقال لنا هذه جمجمة امراه فخمّن الخواجه بان ذلك
القبر هو قبر حاكم تلك الاراضي والبلاد. حينذٍ ارما له محزم وقله قش ما تجده في
ارضيت القبر واعطيني هو فجمع الذي وجده واعطانا هو فوجدنا بين الذي قشه
خاتم كبير سبط فتامل الخواجه في الخاتم فراه مصدي وما مبين له كبّه ولا عرف
معدنه انكان هو فضه ام ذهب او غير معدن فابقاه معه. اخيرًا قال للراعي جس
حيطان القبر فراء طاقه وداخلها سراج شبه جيرون السمان وما عرف معدنه
فاخده ايضًا وشاله وما عاد راء شي فخرج من القبر وراح في حال سبيله ونحن
رجعنا الي الضيعه بسلام.

وثاني يوم سافرنا من كفتين الي جسر الشغور[1] ومن هناك لا زلنا سايرين حتي ٣٧،١
وصلنا الي مدينة طرابلس بالسلام فنزل الخواجه المذكور في بيت خواجه بلان
الفرنساوي وانا نزلت في خان الغميضا في بيت رهبان الحلابيه اعني بهم رهبان مار
يشع ومفتاح البيت دايمًا مودوع عند اوضاباشي الخان فاخذت المفتاح منه ودخلت
حوايجي وكان الاوداباشي يعرفني لما رجعنا من الديرانا ورفقاتي فنزلنا هناك.

فاستقمت ذلك النهار وثاني يوم رحت سلمت علي خواجه رومان الذي كت ٣٨،١
جبته معي مكتوب توصاي في من معلمي خواجه رمزات في اول مره جيت الي
طرابلس حتي اترهب فبعدما سلمت عليه اوردته قضيت خواجه بول لوكا وسالته
هل هو صحيح بانه مرسل من سلطان فرنسا لاجل السياحه فقلي نعم صحيح فاستشرته
ايضًا هل بتشور عليّ باني اروح الي باريس معه قلي بتكون سعادتك روح لا تخف
هذا رجل ناس ملاح.

حينذٍ طلعت من عنده ومضيت الي عند البادره الياس الكرملتاني وهذا البادره ٣٩،١
كان لي معه معرفه لما كت في دير مار يشع عليه فسلمت عليه وقصيت له قصتي بالتمام

---

١ الأصل: الشغل.

The goatherd handed us another skull, smaller than the first, and the *kha-wājah* said it was a woman's. He supposed that the tomb belonged to the ruler of these lands.

He threw a piece of sturdy cloth down to the goatherd. "Collect everything you find on the floor of the tomb and hand it to me."

The goatherd gathered what he found and handed it all over. Among the objects was a large, plain ring. The *khawājah* studied it and saw that it was rusty. There wasn't an inscription that he could see, nor could he tell whether it was made of gold, silver, or some other metal. He kept it.

"Feel around along the walls of the tomb," he called out to the goatherd, who did as he was instructed, and found a niche. Inside the niche was a lamp, similar to those used by the butter merchants. He didn't know what sort of metal it was made of, but he took it anyway. There was nothing left to find, so the goatherd climbed out and went on his way, and we all returned safely to the village.[25]

The next day, we left Kaftīn for Jisr al-Shughūr, and continued from there till we arrived safely in Tripoli. The *khawājah* lodged at the home of *khawājah* Blanc, the Frenchman. I stayed at the Khān al-Ghummaydā, in the quarters of the Aleppan monks of Saint Elishaʿ. The keeper of the hostel always held a key to their quarters, so I took it from him and brought my things in. He knew me from the time my friends and I had returned from the monastery, for we'd lodged there.

1.37

I spent the rest of the day at the hostel. The next day I went to see *khawājah* Roman, whom I'd met the first time I passed through Tripoli on my way to the monastery, when I'd brought him a letter of recommendation from my master, *khawājah* Rémuzat. After greeting him, I told him all about Paul Lucas.

1.38

"Is it true that he was dispatched on his voyage by the sultan of France?" I asked.

"Yes," he replied. "It's true."

I also asked his advice. "Would you counsel me to go to Paris with him?"

"This is your chance—take it!" he said. "Go with him and don't worry; he's a good man."

I left him and went to see Father Ilyās the Carmelite. He knew me from the time I'd spent at the Monastery of Saint Elishaʿ. After greeting him, I told him all about my time with Paul Lucas. The priest listened to my tale from start to finish, then spoke.

1.39

مع المذكور اعني به بول لوكا فلما سمع البادري مني كلام قلي ان سالت عن هل رجل انا اخدت خبره بانه سايح من سواح سلطان فرنسا وان ردت تروح معه ما عليك باس روح لا تخف وانا بوصيه فيك.

حينذٍ صممت النيه بالرواح ورحت الي عنده واعطيته قرار ثابت بان اروح معه فلما اعطيته هل قرار فسالني هل معك هل حوايج غير الذي لابسهم؟ فقتله لا لكن لي غير هل حوايج في حلب قوي مكلفات فقلي انكان عندك حوايج مكلفات اكتب الي اخوك يرسلهم لك الي مدينة صيدا لان ان وصلنا الي باريس بالسلامه بريد ادخلك معي امام حضره سلطان فرنسا ولاجل هل سبب تكون لابس ثياب زي بلادكم يكونوا ملاح.

فامتثلت امره وفي الحال كتبت الي اخي مكتوب واعلمته بقصتي ودكرت له بان يرسلي حوايجي بالعجل مع اين من توجه الي طرابلس ومن هناك توصي بان يرسلوهم الي صيدا تحت يد واحد من خواجكيت صيدا وترسل ايضاً وتذكر لذلك الخواجه انكان اعتزت منه خرجيه يعطيني والسلام وفي البخت كان ذلك اليوم طالع ساعي الي حلب فارسلت المكتوب معه واحكيت للخواجه باني ارسلت المكتوب الي حلب كما امرتني.

"Well, since you ask," the priest said, "I can tell you that I've learned that this man is indeed one of the voyagers dispatched by the sultan of France. Don't be afraid to go with him, if that's what you want to do. I'll vouch for you."

So I made up my mind to go, and went to see the *khawājah* to give him my word that I'd accompany him. 1.40

"Do you have any clothes besides those you are wearing?" he asked after I'd presented him with my decision.

"No, but I do have some other clothes in Aleppo," I said. "Some very fine clothes indeed."

"In that case, write to your brother and have him send your clothes to Sidon," he said. "If we get to Paris safely, I should like to take you with me before His Majesty, the sultan of France. You'll need to wear your native dress, and it should be elegant."

I obeyed his instructions and immediately wrote a letter to my brother, letting him know my story. 1.41

"Send my clothes right away with anyone heading to Tripoli," I wrote. "And from Tripoli, have them send the clothes on to Sidon, in the care of one of its merchants. Be sure to write to the merchant and ask him to provide me with some money, should I need it. Farewell."

As luck would have it, a messenger was departing for Aleppo that very day! I gave him the letter and told the *khawājah* that I'd sent it off to Aleppo, as he had instructed.

# الفصل الثاني

## في خروجي من طرابلس صحبة خواجه بول لوكا السايح في شهر شباط ١٧٠٧ مسيحيه

فبعد كام يوم خرجنا من مدينة طرابلس صحبة رجل نسيب من بيت الخازن يسما
كوالير حنا وهذا كان اجتمع مع الخواجه في بيت قنصر الفرنساويه وصار بينهم محبه
وصحبه فلما وصلنا الي جبل كسروان الي مكان يسما زوق ميكاييل حيث بيت
الكوالير المذكور . حينذٍ كلف الخواجه الى بيته حتى يتغدا هو واياه .

ونحن اعني الفقير والخادم الذى معنا نزلنا في ساحت الزوق وربطنا خيلنا وجمعنا
اخراجنا ولبشنا واستقمنا نستنا الغدا من عند الكوالير لانه عزمنا ايضاً حتي نتغدا
عنده فلما راينا ما جانا غدا ونحن مضنا الجوع لاننا مشينا طول الليل حينذٍ اخرجنا من
عندنا¹ سمك بحري مقلي وخبز ونبيد وجلسنا نتغدا فما راينا الا صار حولنا جمله من
الاوادم وصاروا يسالونا هل انتم مسيحيه قلنا نعم فقالوا كيف انكم بتفتروا قبل الوقت
فقلنا لهم نحن مسافرين وطول الليل ماشيين ما علينا صوم وكان ذلك في اول جمعه
من صوم الكبير واهل تلك البلاد منهم بيصوم الي الدهر ومنهم بيصوم الي التاسعه
وما احد منهم بيقدر يتظاهر بالفتور قبل الوقت .

وهذا صار في خواجتنا ايضاً لان الكوالير صار يشغله حتي يسير وقت الدهر
ثم يغديه فلما تعوق عليه بالغدا غافله واجا لعندنا فراءنا عمالين منتغدا فجلس حتي يتغدا

---

١ الأصل: عندا.

# Chapter Two

## My Departure from Tripoli in the Company of the Traveler Paul Lucas, in the Month of February 1707 of the Christian Era[26]

After a few days, we left Tripoli in the company of a kinsman of the al-Khāzin family known as the chevalier Ḥannā.[27] He had met Paul Lucas in the home of the French consul, and they'd taken a liking to one another. In the mountains of Kisrawān we came to a place named Zūq Mīkāyīl, where the chevalier lived. He invited the *khawājah* for lunch.

Meanwhile, I went off to the town square along with the servant who was accompanying us. We tied up our horses, piled up our bags, and sat waiting for some lunch to be brought to us from the chevalier's house, for he'd invited us as well. We'd walked all night and were famished! But no lunch arrived, so we took out our own food—fried fish, bread, and wine—and settled in to eat. All of a sudden, a crowd of people formed around us!

"Are you Christians?" they demanded.

"Yes."

"Then what do you think you're doing, breaking the fast before it's time?" they asked.

"We're travelers, and we've been walking all night," we said. "We're not required to fast."

It was the first week of Lent. In those parts, some people would fast until noon and others until nine o'clock, and no one was allowed to break their fast publicly before the appointed time.

The same thing happened with our *khawājah*. The chevalier had tried to distract him until noon when he could serve lunch, but after a while, the

2.1

2.2

2.3

معنا وهو محصور من الكولير وفي ذلك الوقت اجا الكولير حنا وصار يتعذر منه في تعويقة الغدا عليه وانه يروح معه ويتغدي في الحال بغير عوقه. حينذِ استحي منه و راح معه وارسل لنا طبق تنسيف وفيه صحن عسل وزيت ورغيفين خبز حتي نتغدي فاكلنا منهم لقمتين ورجعناهم فاستقمنا ذلك اليوم في الزوق الي باكر.

٤،٢ فودعنا الكولير وسافرنا في ذلك الجبل من مكان الي مكان ومن ضيعه الي ضيعه والخواجه يفتش علي حشايش في تلك الجبال العاليه. اخيرًا وصلنا الي مدينة بيروت ونزلنا في دير بادري كبوجي فاسترحب فينا واعطا الي خواجتنا اوضه مفروشه اعني بتخت وفرشه وكراسي وما يشبه ذلك.

٥،٢ وفي ذلك اليوم اجا للدير واحد من جماعتنا حلبي يسما يوسف ابن المخل وهذا كان صاحبي في حلب فلما راني استرحب في قوي كثير وسالني عن سبب مجي الي بيروت فاحكيته في مجراويتي وكيف اني انشبكت مع هل سايح. اخيرًا استمنيته بان يدوريني في مدينة بيروت حتي اتفرج قبل ما نسافر فقلي تكرم قوم اتمشي معي حتي افرجك علي كل المدينه مكان بمكان. حينذِ ارت اغير شاش الابيض والف شاش الازرق فمنعني عن تغيير الشاش وقلي انكان بتريد لف شال اخضر في هل بلد ما في قيد علي النصراني ايش ما لبس. اخيرًا ما امكن حتي لفيت شاشي الازرق.

٦،٢ وخرجت معه ندور في المدينه ولا زلنا دايرين حتي وصلنا الي مكان كانه صرايه لكن صغير بالقد وله ليوان وجالس هناك ثلاث اربع اغاوات كاسم عصملي لافين بروسهم شاشات يانس باطراف قصب وعلي اكتافهم مشالح صوف انكلي شاككين خناجر بجوهر وامامهم عشر خمسة عشر شبب بسربندات قرمز ومنهم اخدر وشاككين كذالك فضه وسيوف سقطه فلما رايتهم تململت ورجعت الي الوراء فقلي ذلك الشاب اعني به يوسف الحلبي ما بالك يا اخي فزعان اتعرف هل اغاوات من هم

*khawājah* abandoned him and joined us. Seeing us in the midst of lunch, he sat down to eat, annoyed with his host.

Eventually the chevalier appeared, apologizing for delaying our lunch. He begged the *khawājah* to return to have lunch right away, with no further delay. The *khawājah* was embarrassed, so he went with the chevalier, who sent us on a large straw tray a plate of honey and oil and two loaves of bread for our lunch. We had a few bites and sent them back. We spent the rest of the day in al-Zūq.

The next morning, we bid farewell to the chevalier and journeyed through the mountains, from village to village, as the *khawājah* foraged for plants around those lofty peaks. Eventually we arrived in Beirut, and lodged at the monastery of a Capuchin friar. He welcomed us and gave our *khawājah* a room with a bed, chairs, and other furnishings.

That same day, a fellow named Yūsuf ibn al-Mukaḥḥal, who was from our community in Aleppo, turned up at the monastery. He was a friend of mine from back home and greeted me warmly when he saw me, asking why I'd come to Beirut. I told Yūsuf the story of how I'd gotten caught up with the French traveler and asked if he would show me around, so that I might see the sights before we set off.

"Of course," he said. "Come along, and I'll take you on a tour of the whole city."

I started to swap my white turban for a blue one, but he stopped me.

"If you wanted to, you could even wrap a green turban around your head," he said. "In this town, there's no restriction on what Christians can wear."[28] But even with his reassurance, I couldn't bring myself to wear any turban but my blue one.

We set off to tour the city. After a little while, we arrived at a small palace containing an *īwān*.[29] Seated there were three or four officers dressed in the Ottoman style. On their heads were turbans of crimped silk, the edges brocaded with gold thread. They wore long cloaks of angora wool over their shoulders, and sported jeweled daggers. Ten or fifteen young men stood before them, some wearing crimson turbans and others green ones. They too were armed with silver daggers and damascened swords.

I stopped short and took a step backward when I saw them, but Yūsuf, the young man from Aleppo, said to me, "Why are you afraid, brother? Don't you know who these officers are?"

2.4

2.5

2.6

قلته لا لكن بظن انهم حكام البلد قلي نعم انهم حكام البلاد كلها اعني بلاد كسروان وهل مكان هو الكرك الذي هن ظابطينه وهن موارنه من بيت الخازن واخدين ميري البلاد عليهم ومن هناك اخدني فرجني علي الاسكله وعلي مغارة التنين الذي قتله ماري جرجس ومن هناك رجعنا الي الدير .

٧.٢ وتاني يوم ما سافرنا فؤاد الخواجه يستقيم كام يوم في بيروت حتي يتفرج لاني كنت احكيت له علي فرجتي في يوم الاول فلما طلعت انا واياه من الدير فقلي من الان وصاعد ان احد سالك عني اقول باني حكيم وهوكان لابس ثياب بلادنا وفي راسه قلبق فطلعنا ندور في المدينه من مكان الي مكان وهو يفتش علي فلوس قدم اعني معاملة ملوك الاقدمين فاشترينا في ذلك اليوم مقدار اربعين خمسين واحد ورجعنا للدير .

٨.٢ وتاني يوم ايضاً نزلنا للمدينه ورحنا الي سوق السياغه فصار يفتش علي جار وخواتم مصورات فوجدنا كام واحد ومن الفلوس وجدنا ايضاً كام واحد ونحن راجعين للدير فصاحنا واحد مسلم معصارني فقلي عندي فلوس بتشتروهم فقلته هاتهم لنراهم فدخل الي مكانه وجاب لنا اربعين فلس كل واحد بقد ثلث لكن سميك فوضعهم امامنا فلما راهم الخواجه وهم مصديين وما مبين لهم ما كبه من كثره الصدا فابا عن اخدهم وقلي بلسان الفرنجي اشتريهم منه وجاز عنا وراح فلما راح رحت انا ايضاً .

٩.٢ فقلي ذلك الرجل ما بالك ما بتشتريهم قلته لاجل صداهم وغيابة كتابتهم ما عادوا بينفعوا شي فعاد قلي خدهم بكام ما بتريد. حينذٍ قلته الحكيم ما بيريدهم لكن كرمالك انا بشتريهم بكام بتبيعهم لي قلي بغرس كل واحد بمصري فدفعت له نصف غرش فما راد يعطيهم لي فجزت عنه ورحت في طريقي فعاد صاحني وارواني جحر خاتم سليماني مصور فيه راس جميل وتحته مكتوب احرف ما بتتعرف باينا لسان فلما رايته

"No," I said. "But I did think they might be the rulers of the town."

"Indeed," he said. "They're the rulers of the whole country, which is to say all of Kisrawān. This here is the customhouse, which they control. They're Maronites from the al-Khāzin family, and they've taken over the collection of the *mīrī* tax in the country."[30]

From there, he took me to see the seaport and the cave of the dragon slain by Saint George. We then returned to the monastery.

We didn't travel the next day. The *khawājah* decided to spend a few days touring Beirut, as I'd told him about all the things I'd seen the first day. When we left the monastery together, he said to me, "From now on, if anyone asks you about me, tell them I'm a doctor."

He was wearing our native dress and a calpac on his head. We went to tour the city, and he searched for old coins, the kind struck by ancient kings. We bought forty or fifty coins that day and returned to the monastery.

The next day, we set off again into the city, headed for the jewelry souk. He hunted for precious stones and engraved rings, and we found a few, along with some more coins. On our way back to the monastery, a Muslim oil presser called out to us.[31]

"I have some coins," he said. "Want to buy them?"

"Let's have a look," I said.

He went into his shop and brought out forty coins, each the size of a *thulth*, but thicker.[32] He placed them before us, and when the *khawājah* saw that they were so rusty that no writing could be made out on them, he declined to buy any. Before leaving, though, he said a few words to me in Frankish.

"Buy them from him."

After the *khawājah* left, I turned to leave as well.

"What's the matter? Aren't you interested?" the man asked.

"They're so rusty you can't read what's written on them," I said. "They're worthless."

"Name your price," he insisted.

"The doctor doesn't want them," I said. "But as a favor to you, I'll buy them myself. What do you want for them?"

"One piaster for the lot," he said. "That's one *miṣriyyah* each."[33]

I offered him half a piaster, but he wouldn't agree. So I walked out and started on my way. He called out to me again, showing me the stone from a Seal of Solomon.[34] On it was engraved a beautiful head, with some letters beneath

2.7

2.8

2.9

رجعت وصحة الخواجه فلما رأء جحر الخاتم رماه ورجع وقلي بلسانه اشتريه بكم ما قلك. حينذٍ قلت للرجل انا بشتري الجميع الجحر والفلوس.

٢٠،١٠ اخيراً بعد الجهد حتي الجميع وصلته بحق غرس وقلته ما في زود فاعطاني الفلوس وجحر الخاتم فاعطيته الغرش واخدتهم وسرت وكان الخواجه واقف بيستاني في عوجه فلما وصلت لعنده سالني هل اشتريتهم قلته نعم وما اعطاهم لي الا بغرش قلي عفاك سير بنا الي الدير.

٢٠،١١ وفي وصولنا الي محلنا قلي جيب لي في فراغ شويت خل وحط تلك الفلوس في ذلك الخل وصار يتامل في ذلك الجحر وفي تلك الاحرف المكتوبه وهو فرحان وقلي صدق لو يطلب هل رجل حق هل جحر وحده ماية غرش لعطيته لان هل جحر له خواص عظيم وما راد يقلي عن خواصه بل قلي بان هذا راس ملك من ملوك القدم وسوف بنحص عن اسمه في التواريخ. [١]

٢٠،١٢ وثاني يوم باكر دخلت الي عنده فرايته عمال بيمسح الفلوس من الصدا فرايت جميعهم فضه خالصه وبانت كتاباتهم مسرجه بينه فقلي الخواجه بان هذه معامله هل ملك الذي رايت صورته في جحر الخاتم الذي اشتريناه من ذاك الرجل المصراني والشاهد بذلك كا سالنا ذلك الرجل من اين حصل علي هل فلوس والجحر فقلنا بانه راكثير منهم في اساس حيط قديم لما خرب وراد يعمره فواهم مضمورين في الارض.

٢٠،١٣ وذلك اليوم خرجنا ايضاً ندور في المدينه ونفتش علي فلوس قدم وكان ذلك الوقت شاع خبر الخواجه بانه حكيم فصاروا يتهادونا من مكان الي مكان وهو يحكم البعض منهم والبعض يوصف لهم وصفات ويطلب حق لهم فلوس قدم فلمينا مشوار من تلك الفلوس وراينا بعضهم فضه ونحاس وكام واحد دهب نشتريهم بثمنهم.

٢٠،١٤ وبعد كام يوم خرجنا من بيروت وطلعنا الي جبل الدروز ودرنا في تلك الاماكن نفتش ايضاً علي فلوس والخواجه يحكم وبواسطة الحكمه كانوا يفتشوله علي فلوس فحصلنا

---

[١] الأصل: التواريخ.

it in some indistinguishable language. When I saw it, I turned and called after the *khawājah*. He looked at the stone and tossed it aside.

"Buy it for whatever price he asks," he said to me as he left.

"I'll take it all," I said to the man. "The stone and the coins."

After a lengthy negotiation, I brought him down to a single piaster for          2.10
everything, saying I could go no higher. He handed over the coins and the stone, and I gave him the piaster. I gathered everything, left, and found the *khawājah* waiting for me around the corner.

"Did you buy it all?"

"Yes, but he wouldn't sell for less than a piaster."

"Bravo!" he said. "Let's go back to the monastery."

When we arrived, he said, "Bring me a little bit of vinegar in a bowl." He          2.11
put the coins in the vinegar, and studied the stone and its engraved letters with great delight.

"Believe me, if that man had asked for a hundred piasters for the stone alone, I would have given it to him, because this stone has tremendous magical properties," he said, but he wouldn't tell me what they were. "This is the head of an ancient king," he continued. "I'll look for his name in the chronicles."

The next day when I went in to see him, he was wiping the rust off the coins.          2.12
I could see that they were all pure silver, and the inscriptions were clearly visible.

"These coins were struck by the king whose image was on the gemstone we bought from that oil presser," he said.

It was evident that they were ancient coins, because when we'd asked the man where he found the coins and the stone, he said he'd discovered many of them at the base of an old crumbled wall. When he set about rebuilding it, he found them buried in the ground.

That same day, we went again to tour the city in search of old coins. Mean-          2.13
while, news had spread that the *khawājah* was a doctor, and people sent us from one place to another. He would treat some people and prescribe medicines to others, asking everyone for his fee in the form of old coins. We amassed an assortment of coins, some of silver, some of brass. A few were made of gold, which we bought, paying what they were worth.

After a few days, we left Beirut and went up to the Mountain of the Druze          2.14
and roamed about looking for coins.[35] The *khawājah* would dispense medical treatment, using it as a means to have people hunt for coins on his behalf.

علي كام واحد منهم وايضاً علي بعض حشايش التي وجدناها في تلك الجبال ومن هناك توجهنا الي مدينة صيدا ونزلنا في بيت القنصر الذي هو داخل خان واوض البازركانة ايضاً داخل ذلك الخان وصار للخواجه من القنصر والبازركان أكرام جزيل .

٢،١٥ وفي ذلك الوقت انوجد كام راهب من رهبان السكلنت ماضيين الي القدس فهم الخواجه في السفر معهم وبما انه كان اوعد خزمتكاره الذي كان معه يخدمه بانه يرسله الي القدس فالتزم بان ياخده معه وابقاني انا في بيت القنصر وسافر مع الرهبان وما صار لي نصيب اروح معه من قلت بختي .

٢،١٦ فاستقمت هناك الي يوم من ذات الايام وانا جالس في باب الخان فدعاني واحد من البازركان القاطنين هناك وسالني عن اسمي فاجبته عن اسمي وعن كنيتي فقلي جاني مكتوب من حلب منشانك ودخلني الي مخزنه واخرج اعطاني المكتوب ففتحت المكتوب وقراته وهوكان من عند اخي وباعت يوبخني كثير كيف اني خرجت من حلب من غير علمه واني اقوم ارجع الي حلب من كل بد مع اول قفل الذي بيتوجه الي طرفنا وداكر لي باني استقيم عند ذلك الخواجه الي حين ما بيتوجه احدا الي طرابلس تكون تسافر معهم من كل بد وسبب ولا تخالف .

٢،١٧ فلما كملت قراات المكتوب صار عندي حزن عظيم كيف انه ما ارسلي الحوايج التي ذكرت له عنها. حينذٍ الفت الي ذلك الخواجه وقلي انا وصلني مكتوب من عند معلمك خواجه رمزات باني ارسلك الي حلب ان ردت وما ردت فقتله انا ما ني الان تحت حكم خواجه رمزات ولا انت بتقدر تلزمني بالرواح انا رجل مرشد طريقي وانا الان خادم عند خواجه بول لوكا سايح سلطان فرنسا لما بيرجع من القدس هو بيرد لك عني جواب .

٢،١٨ اخيراً من بعد مناهده عظيمه واخد ورد فراء ما مني جاره. حينذٍ اعطاني مكتوب ثاني من اخي وداكر لي انكان ما بتريد ترجع الله يسهل طريقك واصلك تحت يد ذلك الخواجه ببقية الحوايج التي ذكرت لي عنها بتكون تاخدها من عنده وايش ما اعترت من المرجيه ايضاً خد منه وانا ذكرت له بانه يوصلك مهما اعترت من الدراهم وترسلي

We turned up a few, along with some mountain plants. From there, we headed to Sidon and lodged at the home of the consul, which was in a caravansary where all the foreign merchants had their quarters. The *khawājah* was treated very honorably by the consul and the merchants.

At that same time, some Franciscan friars happened to be traveling to Jeru-    2.15
salem.[36] The *khawājah* decided to travel with them, as he'd promised the servant who attended him during his travels that he would take him to Jerusalem. So he was obliged to accompany him, and to leave me at the consul's home while he traveled with the friars. Unluckily for me, I didn't get to go along.[37]

So I remained in Sidon. One day, while sitting by the gate of the caravan-    2.16
sary, one of the foreign merchants who lived there called me over and asked my name. When I told him my given name and family name, he said he'd received a letter for me from Aleppo! He took me into his store, took out the letter, and handed it over.

I opened it. It was from my brother, who'd written to admonish me furiously for leaving Aleppo without telling him, and to demand that I return with the first caravan headed his way. Until then, I was to stay put, with the merchant.

"I want you on the next caravan to Tripoli, no ifs, ands, or buts!" he wrote.

As I came to the end of the letter, I welled up with sadness. How could he    2.17
have refused to send me the clothes I'd asked for?

The merchant turned to me and said, "I also received a letter from your master, *khawājah* Rémuzat. He told me to send you back to Aleppo whether you liked it or not."

"I'm not under the authority of *khawājah* Rémuzat anymore," I said, "and you can't make me go anywhere! I'll decide where I go all on my own! I now serve *khawājah* Paul Lucas, a traveler on the sultan of France's business! As soon as he returns from Jerusalem, he'll speak for me."

After much argument and back-and-forth, the merchant saw that I wouldn't    2.18
budge. So he took out a second letter from my brother, and handed it to me.

"If you don't wish to return, God grant you a smooth journey," my brother had written. "I've sent you the bundle of clothes you'd requested, in the care of this merchant. Take the clothes from him, along with as much money as you'll need. I've told him to advance you whatever you ask for. Send me receipts for the clothes and the money you've taken. Godspeed."

وصول في الحوايج والخرجيه التي بتاخدها منه والسلام فلما قرات ثاني مكتوب فصار
عندي فرح عظيم في وصول الحوايج. حينذٍ اخرج اعطاني بقجة الحوايج وسالني ايش
قدر بريد من الخرجيه فاخدت منه كام غرش واعطيته وصول من يدي بالجميع
ورجعت الي بيت القنصر وانا مبسوط في غاية ما يكون.

١٩٠٢   واستقمت في صيده ادور واتفرج من مكان الي مكان وكان حكم عندنا عيد
الكبير وعند طايفة الموارنه طريقه ما احد منهم بيقدر يعترف ويتناول الاسرار الا
في كنيسته عند الخوري لاجل بعض اسباب فعزمني واحد صاحب ليلة العيد الي
بيته حتي نبكر ونروح نعترف عند الخوري ونحدر القداس ونتناول وبعدما قضينا
فرضنا اخدني ايضاً الي بيته وضيفني ووقف في واجي.

٢٠٠٢   اخيراً استقمت في صيدا الي حين ما رجع معلمي من القدس فاحكيته بان
وصلتني الحوايج مع مكتوب من اخي وكيف انه كاتب لذلك الخواجه بانه يرجعني الي
حلب طيبه غصيبه والان انا ثابت بقراري معك فقلي وانا ايضاً بكل وعدي معك
ان وصلنا بالسلامه الي مدينة بهريس والخزمتكار الذي راح معه للقدس ما عاد
رجع فاستقام هناك حتي يروح الي بلاده فاستقمت انا وحدي في خدمة هل
خواجه وبعده همينا بالسفر الي جزيرة قبرس.

After reading the second letter, I was overjoyed to learn of the arrival of the clothes! The merchant took out the bundle, handed it to me, and asked how much money I wanted. I took a few piasters and wrote out receipts for everything and returned to the consul's home, as happy as could be.

I stayed on in Sidon, touring and seeing the sights. It was Easter time, and 2.19 according to the custom of the Maronites, for some reason or other, one could only attend confession and receive communion from one's own church and priest. A friend of mine invited me to spend the evening of the feast at his home so that we might rise early and go to confession with the priest, attend mass, and receive communion. After fulfilling our obligation, he invited me back to his house as his guest and treated me with due regard.

I remained in Sidon until my master returned from Jerusalem, whereupon 2.20 I informed him that my clothes had arrived with a letter from my brother.[38] I told him all about how my brother had instructed the merchant to send me back to Aleppo by hook or by crook.

"I'm fully committed to joining you on your voyage," I said.

"And I promise to do right by you, if we get to Paris in one piece," he replied.

The servant who'd gone with him to Jerusalem hadn't returned, remaining there so he could continue on to his own country. So it was that only I remained in the service of this *khawājah*.

We made ready to travel to the island of Cyprus.

# الفصـل الثالـث

## في اول نـزولي للبحـر مع خواجة بول لوكا
## وكان ذلك في شهر ايار سنة ١٧٠٧

ولما كان اليوم الخامس من شهر ايار خرجنا من مدينة صيدا صبحة شيطيه روم ٣.١
قاصده جزيرة قبرس فسافرت الشيطيه من اسكلت صيدا في ثاني ساعه من الليل
وانا من حين نزولي في الشيطيه دخت ونمت في جانب الصاري وكان الريح طيب
معنا وقبل ما يصبح الصباح وصلنا الي اسكلت الملاحه اعني الي جزيرة قبرس.

فلما انتبهت من رقادي وانا دايخ فرأيت القلعه والاوادم الذين في الاسكله فما ٣.٢
صدقت باننا وصلنا الي قبرس بل خمنت باننا لا زال نحن في اسكلت صيدا الي حين
ما اصبح الصباح مليح فتحققت حينذٍ باننا وصلنا الي قبرس واستهونت سفر البحر كيف
اننا في ليله وصلنا من صيدا الي قبرس.

اخيراً خرجنا من الشيطيه الي الاسكله ومن الاسكله حملنا حوايجنا ورحنا الي ٣.٣
بيت قنصر الفرنساويه فلما دخلنا وراءنا القنصر فاسترحب في معلمي قوي كثير وهيا له
اوضه مفروشه اعني بخت مجلل وكراسي وما يشبه ذلك من لوازم المنامه ونقلوا
حوايجنا ايضاً الي اوضة منامتي.

وبعد يوم طلعنا ندور ونتفرج وصاروا يعزمونا تجار الفرنساويه القاطنين في ذلك ٣.٤
المكان وكل خزمتكاريتهم روم كريكيه وكلهم ما بيلقشوا الا بالرومي وانا كت بينهم
كالاطرش في الزفه ما بفهم في لسانهم ولا هن بيفهموا بلساني ولماكت القش معهم

# Chapter Three

## My First Time at Sea with Paul Lucas, in the Month of May 1707 [39]

On the fifth of May, we left Sidon on a Greek ship headed for the island of    3.1
Cyprus. The ship sailed from Sidon at two o'clock in the morning. I felt seasick
from the moment I set foot on board, so I lay down to sleep by the mast. The
winds were favorable and, before dawn broke, we arrived at the port of Larnaca, on the island of Cyprus.

When I awoke from my slumber—still feeling seasick—and saw the fort    3.2
and all the people on the wharf, I could scarcely believe we'd arrived in
Cyprus. I had assumed we were still in the port of Sidon! By the time day
had fully broken, I realized we were indeed in Cyprus, and I marveled at how
easy it was to travel by sea. We'd made the journey from Sidon to Cyprus in a
single night!

We disembarked onto the dock, gathered our baggage, and went to the    3.3
home of the French consul. When we walked in, the consul greeted my master
warmly and had a furnished room prepared for him, with an ornate bed,
chairs, and other necessary comforts. All of our things were brought up to
my bedroom.

The next day, we toured and saw the sights. The French merchants who    3.4
lived in Larnaca began to invite us over. Their servants were all Greeks, and of
the Orthodox faith. I felt like a deaf man in a wedding procession: I couldn't
understand their language, they couldn't understand mine. When I spoke to
them in French, they understood but would only respond in Greek, mocking

بلسان الفرنجي بما انهم بيفهموا لكن ما يريدوا على الا بالرومي استهزا في لانهم بيبغضوا قسم الكاثوليكي على خطًا مستقيم فكنت ممرر بينهم.

٣.٥ وبعد كام يوم راد معلي يروح الي المدينه التي هي بعيده عن الملاحه حكم مسافة اربعة عشر ساعه او اقل وهل مدينه تسما نيكوسيا وهي مدينة الكبرا في جزيرة قبرس وكان قاطنها رجل بادري من رهبنة مار فرنسيس فلما هينا بالرواح الي تلك المدينه فاعطانا القنصر مكتوب للبادري المذكور توصاي فينا وانه يقبلنا عنده في الدير فاستكرينا مع رجل قاطرجي وسافرنا ذلك اليوم الي المسا فوصلنا الي ضيعه حيث كان بيت القاطرجي فنزلنا في بيته.

٣.٦ وبعد ساعه فسمعت حس غاوش وضوضه عظيمه مقبله من البر فخرجت لشاهد ما الخبر فرايت مقبلين قطعان خنازير راجعين من المرعا وقطيع الواحد اجا الي بيت القاطرجي الذي كنا نازلين فيه وكان برات البيت سياج فدخلوا تلك الخنازير داخل ذلك السياج وما قدرنا نقدر نرقد تلك الليله من تشخرتلك الخنازير.

٣.٧ فلما اصبح الصباح سافرنا وكان سفرنا كنا ماشيين في روضه من كثرة الاشجار والمياة الجاري والارض كلها خدراء حتي الدروسه النابته من الارض كلها مليح جحر ابيض ازرق خلقه شريفه ولا تسال عن الكروم الموجوده في تلك الجبال شي كثير وما لهم اصحاب. حينٍ تحققت ما سمعته عن هذه الجزيره بانها جزيرة الخضره.

٣.٨ اخيرًا وصلنا حكم العصر الي المدينه ونزلنا في دير ذلك البادري المذكور فاسترحب فينا قوي كثير واعطانا مفاتيح القلالي الموجوده في الدير وقلنا انزلوا في اي مكان الذي بتريدوه علي خاطركم فاستقمنا تلك الليله وتاني يوم حضرنا قداسه وبعد هنيهه وصل ساعي الي البادري من عند الريس الذي هو قاطن في الملاحه وامره بانه في حال وصول المكتوب اليه يقوم يروح الي عنده من كل بد وسبب من غير تاخير. حينٍ استعدر البادري من معلي واراه المكتوب وانه التزم في الرواح لان امر الريس مطاع غير انه اعطانا مفتاح الكلار وقلنا بان كل شي موجود في ذلك الكلار من سمن وزيت ونبيد عتيق وجديد ولحم خنزير مكبوس مملح وجنبون وزيتون وجبن وما يشبه ذلك ما عدا الخبز وخبز قبرس ما له شبيه في الطعم واللذه كنا نشتريه كل يوم طري.

me, as they harbored a deep loathing for Catholics. I endured their company with much bitterness.

After a few days, my master decided to visit Nicosia, the largest city in 3.5 Cyprus, just under fourteen hours from Larnaca. A priest belonging to the order of Saint Francis lived there. As we were about to set off for Nicosia, the consul gave us a letter of recommendation to present to the priest, asking him to accept us at the monastery. We hired some mounts from a muleteer, traveled all day, and arrived at the muleteer's village in the evening. We lodged at his house.

An hour after our arrival, I heard a great racket coming from the surround- 3.6 ing countryside. I went outside to find out what was going on and saw several herds of swine returning from the pasture. One herd came to the muleteer's home, where we were staying. The pigs went into a corral by the house, and we couldn't sleep a wink all night because of their grunting and snorting.

In the morning, we set off again. The abundance of trees and the water 3.7 coursing everywhere made it seem as though we were strolling through a garden! Everything was green, even the ears of grain shooting up out of the earth. All the stone was white and blue and of fine quality. To say nothing of the lush vineyards found in those mountains, with no owners to tend them! That's when I knew that everything I'd heard about Cyprus was true. It was indeed the Green Island!

In the afternoon, we arrived at the city and lodged at the priest's monastery. 3.8 He welcomed us most generously and gave us keys to the cells, telling us to settle in anywhere we liked. We spent the night there and attended his mass the next day. A little while later, a messenger arrived from the abbot who lived in Larnaca. The priest was ordered to go see the abbot as soon as he received the message, and not delay for an instant. The priest showed my master the letter, apologized, and explained that he had no choice but to set off right away, as the abbot's orders had to be obeyed. He did, however, give us the key to the cellar and told us it was fully stocked with butter, oil, old and new wine, salted pork and ham, olives, cheese, and so on. The only thing missing was bread. The bread of Cyprus, by the way, is delicious and has no equal. We bought it fresh each day.

٩.٣ اخيرًا ودعنا وسافر الي عند ريسه فاستقمنا ذلك اليوم ايضاً في الدير لان ما راينا احد يدلنا علي الدروب. اخيرًا اخذ خبرنا رجل فرنجي مولود في تلك المدينه يسما كاليميره فاجا الي عندنا وسلم علي معلمي واسترحب فيه ففرح معلمي في قدوم هل رجل الي عنده لاجل انه ابن البلاد ويعرف الطرق فجلسوا يتسامروا معاً . حيندٍ قله معلمي بطلب من فضلك بانك نهار غدي تكلف خاطرك بان تاخذني معك حتي اتفرج علي هذه مدينه فاجابه تكرم علي راسي وعيني. حينذٍ مسكه معلمي حتي يتعشا عندنا فاستقام واتعشا وبعد العشا فساله معلمي عن كاره فقله كاري حكيم فصار يساله هل يوجد في جبالكم حشايش وارواه كتاب مرسوم فيه بعض حشايش الذي كان دايماً يفتش عليها في الجبال فاجابه بينوجد في فلان جبل الذي هو بعيد سفر يوم وفيه عماير قديمه خرابه مثل كنايس وديوره وضيع لكن كلها خراب فان شئت تروح الي تلك الاماكن انا بروح معك.

١٠.٣ فارتضي معلي في الرواح واوصاه بان تلك الليله يربط علي مكاري حتي من باكر يسافروا وثاني يوم بعت اشتري ما يلزمهم من الصخيره واخذوا معهم خادم من اولاد البلد واوصاني باني استقيم في الدير لان البادري جعله في تسليمنا وراح ولاجل هذا ما يجوز لنا بان نترك الدير فاضي ليلا يصدر امرٍ من الامور يصير منه ضرر للبادري.¹

١١.٣ فحينذٍ التزمت باني استقيم في الدير وحدي وبعده سافروا وطلعت انا ادور في المدينه اتفرج ولكن ما ابعدت ليلا اضيع فرجعت الي الدير وكان في الدير رجل اختيار كبير في العمر ما فيه يتحرك وكان البادري اوصانا فيه حتي نطعمه من غدانا ومن عشانا وكان له بيت زغير في حوش الدير فوديت له غدا وعبيت له كوز الماء وانسته فصار يحاكيني بلسان الرومي فلما راني ما بفهم بالرومي فحاكاني بالتركي وسالني عن بلدي وجنسي.

١٢.٣ فاجبته انا حلبي من طايفة الموارنه فرد علي بلسان العربي وقلي السلامه في ابن جماعتي فقلته هل انك ماروني قلي نعم انا بقيت من سلالة الموارنه الذين كانوا قاطنين

---
¹ الأصل: للبادي.

The priest bid us farewell and went to see his abbot. We remained at the 3.9
monastery that day, as we couldn't find anyone to guide us on the roads.
A Frankish man named Callimeri, born in Nicosia, heard we were in town and
came by to offer his greetings to my master and to welcome him.[40] My master
was pleased by the arrival of this fellow, as he was a local who knew his way
around. They sat and chatted.

"Would you be kind enough to take me around the city tomorrow to see the
sights?" asked my master.

"It would be my pleasure," Callimeri replied.

My master took him by the arm and insisted he stay for dinner, which he
did. Afterward, the *khawājah* asked him what his occupation was.

"I'm a doctor," he replied.

"Are herbs to be found in your mountains?" the *khawājah* asked, showing
him a book illustrated with various herbs that he was always on the lookout for
in the mountains.

"You can find them on a certain mountain, about a day's journey away,"
Callimeri replied. "There are some ancient buildings there—churches, monas-
teries, and settlements, all of them in ruins. If you're eager to visit these places,
I'll go with you."

My master agreed, and advised him to hire a muleteer that night so they 3.10
could set off early in the morning. The next day, he sent for the supplies they
needed, and enlisted a local fellow to work as a servant. My master directed me
to remain at the monastery, since the priest had left it in our care.

"It wouldn't be right for us to leave the monastery untended," he said. "We
wouldn't want anything to happen that might cause the priest any trouble."

So I alone had to stay behind in the monastery. After they left, I too went 3.11
out, to tour the city and see the sights, but I didn't stray far so as not to get
lost, and soon returned. There was an elderly man there. He was too old to
move about anymore. The priest had entrusted him to our care, and asked us
to share with him our lunch and dinner. He had a small house in the monastery
courtyard. I took him some lunch, filled his tankard of water, and kept him
company. He started to address me in Greek, but when he saw that I didn't
understand him he switched to Turkish and asked me where I was from.

"I'm Aleppan, from the Maronite community," I said. 3.12

"Ah, a fellow Maronite! Welcome!" he responded in Arabic.

في هذه الجزيره لما كانت ملك البنادقه وكانوا اكثر من خمسماية عيله وللان موجود ناس منهم لكن ما هن معروفين خيفة من الكريكيه الهراطقه وانا ملتجي عند هل بادري بيتصدق عليّ بلقمت طعام لاجل قيام حياتي وانا لي زمان بخدم هل دير والان ما بقا في قوه للخدمه.

٣،١٣ فسليته واستقمت عنده الاقشه ويلاقشني الي حين ما امسا الوقت. حينذِ قمت من عنده وطبخت لي شي اتعشاه فعدما اتعشيت وعشيته عبيت غليوني وصرت اتمشي في حوش الدير فايت درج من بحر فصعدت في الدرج الي صطوح[١] الدير ولما انتهيت الي اخر الصطوح[٢] فايت ستاره فودت اعرف ما في ورا الستاره فايت حوش داخلها حريم ورجل كانه صاحب المكان فلما راني فصار يشتمني في لسان الرومي وبالتركي وانا لما رايت حريم عاوت في الحال وذاك الرجل لا زال يعيط ويشتم فنزلت من الدرج الي حوش الدير اتمشا فما رايت والا باب الدير بيندق بجر فمشيت الي باب الدير وسالت من هو الطارق.

٣،١٤ بجاوبني بلسان التركي بقوله افتح يا كلب افتح وصار يشتمني ويتهددني بان كان ما بتفتح بروح بجيبلك مباشر من عند الباشه حتى اقشع كيف انك بتشرف على حريم الناس فلما سمعت منه هل كلام توهمت قوي كثير وصرت اقله يا سيدي لا تواخذني انا رجل غريب وامس دخلت لهل مكان وما عرفت بان خلف الستاره موجود حريم. المراد كلما املقه واحد بخاطره كان يزداد بالشتم والعياط وفي دق الباب بالجر.

٣،١٥ وفي ذلك المحل جاز رجل كريكي انه مسيحي كاتوليكي كان الله ارسله لخلاصي من هل ردي فصار يلاقشه بالرومي ويملقه ولا زال ياخد بخاطره حتى اصرفه من على الباب ولما انصرف فصار يلقش معي بلسان التلياني بقوله لي افتح لا تخف انا صاحب وذاك اصرفته وراح وانا من فزعي ما رت افتح الباب فعاد عليّ بالكلام وقلي افتح لا تخف انا متلك مسيحي كاتوليكي فلما سمعت منه هل كلام في الحال فتحت

"Are you a Maronite?" I asked.

"Yes, I'm one of the last remaining descendants of the Maronites who lived on this island when it was under Venetian rule," he said. "There used to be more than five hundred families here. Some of their descendants remain to this day, but they don't make their presence known because they're afraid of the heretic Greeks. I've taken refuge with this priest. He's shown me charity, and provided me with a little food so I can live out my days. I worked at the monastery a long time, but I don't have the strength for service anymore."

I stayed around to chat with him and raise his spirits till evening came, when I left to cook some dinner. After I ate and brought him his food, I packed my pipe and went for a walk in the courtyard. Coming upon some stone steps, I climbed up to the terrace. When I reached the far end of it, I came to a parapet. Curious to know what was beyond, I peered over and saw a courtyard. In it were some women, along with a man who seemed to be the owner of the house. 3.13

When he saw me, he began to curse in Greek and Turkish! I immediately turned away the moment I saw the women, even as the man continued to shout and curse, and I retreated downstairs to the monastery courtyard to resume my stroll. Suddenly, I heard someone hammering on the monastery door with a rock! I walked over to the door and asked who it was.

"Open the door, you son of a bitch!" he replied in Turkish, cursing me. "If you don't open up, I'll fetch one of the pasha's magistrates. Then we'll find out why you're spying on people's women!" 3.14

"Please forgive me, my lord!" I called out, terrified. "I'm a stranger here, and only arrived yesterday. I didn't know there were women behind that wall!"

But the more I begged his pardon and tried to mollify him, the more he cursed and shouted and hammered on the door with the rock.

It so happened that a Greek man was passing by at that time—a Catholic—whom God sent to save me from the nasty neighbor. He began to converse with the neighbor in Greek, sweet-talking and soothing him until he managed to send him away. After the man left, the Catholic fellow spoke to me in Italian. 3.15

"Open up," he said. "There's no need to be afraid; I'm a friend. And I've gotten rid of that other man. He's gone now."

Still terrified, I didn't dare open the door.

"Go on, open up," he repeated. "Never fear, I'm a Catholic like you."

له الباب حتي دخل وفي الحال اغلقت الباب فزعاً من هل ردي ليلا يعاود. اخيراً
اوصاني بان لا عدت اطلع الي السطوح ولا اروح صوب الستاره.

٣،١٦ وقلي لو ترجع ثاني مره وتشرف عليه لكان ضربك برصاصه قتلك علي ما حلفلي
هل ردي ولا نخمن من اجل غيرته ليلا تنضر حريمه بل لاجل بغضه لهل بادري والدير
بغضه شيطانيه وعاملين هل كريكيه كل جهدهم حتي يبطلوا هل ديرمن فزعاً
علي اولادهم ليلا يحدبوهم للايمان الكاتوليكي الروماني لانهم يقولوا دايماً مسلمان ولا
رومان ولا بيت من بيوتهم خالي من مسلم وتنين واحيان ثلاثه لانهم يجوزوا بناتهم
للانجكاريه حتي يكونوا لهم حمايه عند الحكام وما يشبه ذلك لان ما لهم لا عرض
ولا دين.

٣،١٧ فلما رايت منه هل اناسيه والمحبه توسلت اليه بانه كل يوم يبقايزوريني الي حين
ما يجي معلي فقلي تكرم ومساني وراح وانا بقيت في فكارات ليلا ينزل هل ردي علي
في الليل ويقتلني فدخلت الي قلايتي ودرست الباب من بعد ما قفلت واستقمت
تلك الليله موهوم وما قدرت انام من فزعي الي الصباح.

٣،١٨ ولما اتضي النهار اجا زارني ذلك الشاب المذكور واخد بخاطري وسلاني ولما
رايت منه هل محبة حينةٍ طلبت منه انكان بريد يكلف خاطره ياخدني معه حتي
اتفرج علي المدينه قبل اني اسافر فضي بطلبتي فخرجنا من الديرمعاً.

٣،١٩ وصار يدوريني في شوارع المدينه وكانت مدينه عظيمه لكن اكثر اماكنها خراب فرينا
في مكان متسع فرايت جامع عالي البنا وسيع الاركان وله مادنه عاليه وقبه كبيره
عظيمه ولكن طوق القبه معمر فيها تماتيل ملايكه من الرخام وباب الجامع معمر من
رخام ابيض واسود شي قوي كلف ومن جانبي الباب معمرتمتالين من الرخام الابيض
الواحد ماري بطرس وجنب الثاني ماري بولص ايضاً من رخام الابيض فلما تاملت
في هذه العمارة المكلفه تعجبت وسالت ذلك الشاب ما هذا المكان قلي هذا جامع
فقلته كيف يمكن يكون جامع ومبنيه فيه هل تماتيل من ملايكه وقديسين وهذا شي
محرم عند المسلمين فاجابني بان داخل هل مكان ايضاً في تماتيل كثيره معمره في البنا

When I heard this, I opened the door right away to let him in and slammed it shut immediately, for fear that the short-tempered neighbor would return. My Catholic friend counseled me not to go up to the roof or near the wall.

"If you go back a second time and peep in on him, he'll shoot you," the man said. "That's what he swore he'd do. And don't think that this is all about him jealously guarding his wives from your sight! No, it's because he hates the priest and the monastery like the very Devil. The Greeks, you see, are working like mad to abolish the monastery, because they're afraid it'll draw their children to the Roman Catholic faith. They always say, 'Better Muslims than Romans!' There isn't a family here that doesn't have a Muslim or two in it, sometimes even three. They marry their girls off to the janissaries, you know. That way, they're protected from the authorities. They have no honor! And no religion either."[41]

3.16

Struck by the man's friendly demeanor, I begged him to visit me each day until my master returned. He politely consented and said goodnight. Left alone, I was terrified that my irate neighbor would set upon me in the night and kill me. I retreated to my cell, locked and bolted the door, and spent the whole night lying awake in fear.

3.17

When morning came, the young man came by for a visit. He was kind enough to keep me company and chat with me to take my mind off my predicament, and his affectionate manner led me to ask if he'd be willing to take me out to see the city before I traveled away. He agreed, and we left the monastery together.

3.18

As he guided me through the streets, I could see that Nicosia was a grand city but that most of its buildings were in ruins. We passed by a vast open space surrounding a tall mosque with broad columns, a towering minaret, and a large, magnificent dome. Around the base of the dome were statues of angels in white marble. The portal of the mosque was made of precious white and black marble, and alongside it were two statues carved from white marble. One was Saint Peter and the second—also in white marble—was Saint Paul. I contemplated the splendid building in amazement.[42]

3.19

"What is this place?" I asked the young man.

"A mosque."

"But how can it be a mosque, with statues of angels and saints?" I asked him. "That's forbidden to the Muslims."

وكلها مشتبكه في بعضها البعض ان رادوا يشيلوها بيتلزموا بانهم يخربوا الكنيسه كلها ولاجل هل سبب ابقوهم ليلا تخرب كلها.

٣.٢٠ اخيراً اخذني وصرنا ندور في البلد فرايت في السقاقات نسا بيبيعوا خمر وكل واحده وقبالها زق من الخمر وبتنادي عليه بانه طيب وعتيق وكل شفشق بعثماني وبعضهم بيبيعوا لحم خنزير وبعضهم محله علي جحش الضرف النبيد دايره بتبيع بين البيوت وكلهم اوجاههم كشف من غير ستار فلما رايت هذا المنضر القليل الاحتشام فقلت لذلك الشاب الذي كان معي فين كلام ذلك الرجل الذي وبخني بان شرفت علي حريمه ها الان بجد حريمهم مكشوفين الوجوه بغير استحيا ولا احتشام جالسين في الازقا امام الجايه والرايح قلي صدقت لكن كنت سبقت واحكيتلك ان الذي فعله هل ردي ما هو من جهة اجل انك طلعت علي حريمه بل من اجل بغضه للبادري ولذلك الدير .

٣.٢١ فعدت سالته كيف ان المسلمين الذين هم قاطنين في هل مدينه بيرضوا بان ينباع الخمر ولحم الخنزير في الشوارع والازقا فاجابني بانهم مازونين من حكام البلد لاجل وفا مال الميري الذي عليهم لان استقام ذلك الميري الذي كان يعطوه والبلاد عامره والان خربت فلا زال بياخدوا منهم نفس ذلك الميري القديم وهذا الذي اوجب ان كثير من اهل هل جزيره بانهم يهربوا من زود الظلم الذي صاير عليهم .

٣.٢٢ اخيراً انتهينا من الدوره ورجعنا الي الدير واستقمت تلك الليله وثاني يوم اجا معلمي وذلك الحكيم الذي كان معه وجابوا معهم من تلك الحشايش المصوره في الكتاب المذكور . حينذٍ احكيت الي الخواجه بالذي جري علي في غيابه من ذلك الردي كم ذكرنا فلما سمع معلمي مني هل كلام احتد بالغضب وفي الحال كتب مكتوب الي القنصر بصوره الواقعه وذكر له بانه في الحال يرسل له من عنده ترجمان حتي يشتكي علي ذلك الرجل المذكور للباشه وينتقم منه حتي يتادب غيره ولا يعود احد يتجرهم علي الدير ولا علي البادري .

٣.٢٣ واستكري ذلك الرجل الذي سافر معهم واعطاه المكتوب حتي يوصله الي حضرة القنصر في الملاحه وفي ذلك الوقت حضر ذلك الحكيم وعرف مقصود الخواجه

"There are many more statues inside the building, which are part of the structure itself," he said. "If they wanted to remove them, they'd have to destroy the whole church. So they've left them in place to prevent the whole thing from collapsing."

We left and he took me on a tour of the town. I saw women selling wine in the streets, each with a wineskin in front of her. They extolled the wine they were hawking as delicious and well-aged. A draft cost a single *'uthmānī*. Some women sold pork, and one had loaded a wineskin onto a donkey, and would go around to people's houses, selling it. None wore veils, so all had their faces exposed.[43]     **3.20**

"What about all that talk from the fellow who scolded me for spying on his women?" I said to the young man, when I saw such immodesty on display. "Just look at all their women, shamelessly exposing their faces! And sitting in the street in front of all the passersby!"

"You're right," he said, "but as I explained before, what that bully did had nothing to do with you looking at his wives. It was because of his hatred for the priest and the monastery."

"Why do the Muslims who live in this city allow people to sell wine and pork in the streets?"     **3.21**

"The people have permission from the governors of the country, so they can pay the *mīrī* tax they owe," the man explained. "They continue to pay the same tax they did when the country was prosperous. It's ruined now, and yet the governors continue to levy the same old tax. These oppressive conditions are worsening, which is why so many on the island have fled."[44]

We finished the tour and returned to the monastery, where I spent the night. The next day, my master arrived with the doctor who'd accompanied him on his trip. They'd brought back some of the herbs that were illustrated in my master's book. I told the *khawājah* about what had happened with the nasty man during his absence. When he heard the story, he was furious and immediately dashed off a letter to the consul, informing him of the situation and asking him to send a dragoman right away so that he could lodge a complaint with the pasha, seeking restitution against that man. His intention was to make an example out of him so people would stop threatening the monastery and the priest.     **3.22**

He hired the muleteer they'd taken on their excursion to the mountain and gave him the letter to deliver to His Excellency the consul in Larnaca. But then     **3.23**

فصار يصده عن تكميل هل الامر الذي بيريد يفعله لان بينتج منه ضرر للبادري وللدير من الروم القاطنين في تلك المدينه والبادري ما هو عايش معهم الا بالملق والملاطفه وبالهدايا والا ماكان بيقدر يستقيم في هل دير ولا يوم فلما سمع الخواجه منه هل كلام تغيرت نيته ورجع المكتوب .

٢٤،٣ واستقمنا في الدير الي ان اجا البادري فسلمناه ديره وودعناه وسافرنا الي الملاحه الي بيت القنصر فاستقمنا الي حين ما تهيا مركب فنساوي مسافر الي مدينة اسكندريه فاستكرينا وسافرنا في ذلك المركب قاصدين الرواح الي بلاد مصـر .

the doctor came forward and, having learned of my master's intentions, tried to dissuade him from following through with the whole affair, as it would just lead to trouble for the priest and the monastery at the hands of the Greeks living in the city. It was only through flattery, civility, and charity that the priest had managed to live among these people. Otherwise, he wouldn't have lasted a single day in the monastery! When the *khawājah* heard this, he changed his mind and took back the letter.

We stayed at the monastery until the priest returned, at which time we returned it to his care, bid him farewell, and traveled back to the home of the consul in Larnaca, where we remained until a French ship bound for Alexandria was ready to depart. We booked passage, boarded the ship, and set sail for Egypt.

3.24

في سفرنا الي بلاد مصر وما جري لنا
في شهر حزيران سنة ١٧٠٧[١]

٤،١ فطلعنا من اسكلت الملاحه وبعد يوم وصلنا الي اسكلت بافا التي هي في جزيره قبرص فرسي المركب هناك وكان قصد القبطان يوسق من تلك الاسكله زفت وقطرن لان في تلك الجبال موجود نبوعه يخرج منها[٢] الزفت واهل تلك الجبال بيلموه وبينباع علي كيس الميري وجماعته وقليل من الفلاحين الذين بيلموا الزفت والقطران.

٤،٢ حينذٍ طلعوا البحريه يتصيدوا من ذلك الجبل الي حين المسا فجابوا للمركب معهم ثلاث روس معزي وراس بقر مقتولين بالرساس فصرت انا الفقير الوهم علي هذا الفعل كيف انهم بيستحلوا مال القريب وهذا شي ما بيجوز. حينذٍ واحد من البحريه اكد لي بان هل معزا والبقر ما لهم اصحاب لان اصحابهم هربوا من الظلم وتركوا بوشهم في هل جبال وموجود كثير من معزا وبقر وخنازير داشرين في هل جبال وكنت تري كرومهم بيستقيم العنب فيهم سنه علي سنه وما في احد يقطفه وما صاير فيهم هكذا الا من قلة محبتهم للقريب.

٤،٣ اخيرًا بعدما وسق القبطان الزفت سافرنا من هناك الي اسكلت ليماصون فلما وصلنا ورسي المركب طلعنا الي تلك الاسكله[٣] وهي عامره اعني موجود فيها اوادم وبيع وشري وكل شي الموجود عندهم للبيع هو الخمر لان قنطار الخمر بخمسة غروش والخمر

---
١ ورد: التاريخ في الهامش.  ٢ الأصل: من.  ٣ الأصل: الاسكله.

# Chapter Four

## Our Voyage to Egypt and What Happened to Us in the Month of June 1707 [45]

A day after leaving Larnaca, we arrived at the port of Paphos, which is also on the island of Cyprus. The ship laid anchor there, as the captain aimed to load the ship with bitumen and tar from the port. There was a bitumen deposit in the mountains, which the mountain folk would gather and sell, using the revenue to pay the *mīrī* tax. We went ashore and found the port in ruins. There was no one to be seen except for the tax official and his men, and a few peasants harvesting the bitumen and tar.

The sailors went off to hunt in the mountains, and returned to the ship in the evening with three goats and a cow, which they'd shot with a rifle. I rebuked them for doing this. Hunting other people's livestock was wrong; how could they do that? In response, one of the sailors insisted that the goats and cow didn't belong to anyone, as their owners had left them in the mountains when they had fled their oppressors. Many goats, cows, and pigs had been abandoned, and the grapes remained on the vines year after year, with no one around to harvest them. All because of how badly they'd been treated by their own neighbors.[46]

Once the captain had loaded the bitumen, we set off for the port of Limassol. We arrived, laid anchor, and went ashore. We found a prosperous port city, full of people and commerce. The main thing for sale was wine, five piasters for a *qinṭār*.[47] They stored the wine in cisterns, each of which held twenty *qinṭār*s or more. This abundance was on account of the many vineyards in the

4.1

4.2

4.3

حاطينه في حواصل وكل حاصل بيسع عشرين قنطار وازود وهذا من كثرة الكروم التي في جبالهم فاتسوق القبطان من هل خمر خمسين فوجيه وكل فوجيه بتسع قطار حلب وكما ذكرنا الفوجيه بخمسة غروس حتي يبيعه في اسكندريه ومنه يروح الي بلاد مصر .

٤،٤ فبعدما خلص المسواق والوسق تهيا القبطان للسفر في اول ريح الذي بيناسب للسفر في تلك الليله في حكم ساعتين من الليل ونحن نتمشا علي صطح المركب فما راينا الا رجل عايم في البحر واجا الي طرف المركب وهو لافف قميصه علي هامه . اخيرًا لبس قميصه وتستر وخرج الي عندنا وصار يسالنا عن القبطان فخرج القبطان اليه وساله من تكون وايش هو مرادك . حينٍ ارتي علي رجليه وصار يتوسل اليه بان ياخذه معه الي اسكندريه فاجابه القبطان هل معك طسكره من اغة الميري فقله لا يا سيدي وانا هربان منه فقله القبطان ما بتعرف بان علينا قيدكلي بان لا ننزل احد للمركب بغير يكون معه طسكره من اغة الميري قله نم فقله بعد الذي بتعرف كيف يمكني ان اخذك في مركبي .

٥،٤ وامر البحريه بان ينزلوه في القارب ويرموه في الاسكله فلما مسكوه البحريه حتي ينزلوه في القارب فصار ييكي ويتدخل علينا حتي نشفع فيه عند القبطان فوق قلب معلي عليه واستمن القبطان بان ياخذه معه فالتزم القبطان لاجل خاطر معلي بان ياخذه معه لكن شرط عليه شرط بان يحلقوا دقنه ويلبسه من حوايج البحريه ويلبسه شعر وبرنيطه حتي لا يعرف انه كريكي فرضي الرجل بذلك الشرط في الحال حلقوا دقنه وشواربه واعطوه البحريه بعض حوايج رثه ولبسوه شعر وبرنيطه واستقام في المركب مع البحريه يخدم.

٦،٤ وبعد يومين طاب الهوا فسافونا قاصدين مينة اسكندريه فوصلنا الي المينا في اربعة وعشرين ساعه ولما ردنا ندخل الي الاسكله فخرج في ذلك الوقت ريح عاصف من البر فالتزمنا في الرجوع الي البحر واستقمنا نضرب ولطه في البحر اثني عشر يوم حتي اتانا ريح طيب من البحر فدخلنا للاسكله بالسلامه .

mountains. The captain loaded fifty casks of wine—each the size of an Aleppan *qinṭār*, costing, as I said, five piasters—to sell in Alexandria. From there, the wine would find its way to the rest of Egypt.

After the loading was complete, the captain prepared to sail with the 4.4 first favorable wind. That evening, two hours after nightfall, we were strolling along the deck of the ship when we spotted a man swimming in the sea! He approached the side of the ship with his tunic wrapped around his head. As he climbed aboard, he put it on, covering himself up, and came over to us. He asked to see the captain.

"Who are you? What's your business here?" the captain demanded as he strode toward the man.

The fellow threw himself at the captain's feet and begged to be taken to Alexandria.

"Where are your travel papers?" the captain asked.

"I don't have any travel papers," said the man. "I'm on the run from the tax official."

"You know I'm not allowed to let you board without clearance from the tax office, don't you?" the captain asked.

"Yes."

"Well then, how am I supposed to let you onto my ship?"

He ordered the sailors to put the man into a rowboat and drop him off at 4.5 the port. When the sailors seized him he began to weep, imploring us to intercede on his behalf with the captain. My master took pity on him and prevailed on the captain to bring him along. Out of respect for my master's wishes, the captain was bound to take the man, but on condition that they shave the man's beard, dress him in sailor's clothes, and give him a wig and a hat so that he wouldn't be recognized as a Greek.

The man agreed to the terms, so they shaved his beard and mustache on the spot. The sailors gave him threadbare clothes, a wig, and a cap, and he stayed on the ship, working alongside the sailors.

After two days, fair winds began to blow and we sailed for the port of Alex- 4.6 andria, reaching it in twenty-four hours. Just as we were about to enter the harbor, though, a gale blew out from the land, and we had to retreat to sea. Twelve days of tacking later, a favorable wind blew out from the sea and we managed to enter the harbor safely.

٤،٧ وخرجنا من المركب وتوجهنا الي بيت القنصر فاسترحب القنصر في معلي قوي كثير وامر الخدام بان يروحوا للمركب ويجيبوا حوايجنا وهيوا لنا اوض مفروشات ونقلنا كلما لنا من الحوايج بغير ان يكشف عليهم الكركي واستقمنا في بيت القنصر بغاية العز والاكرام وصاروا خواجكيت الفرنساويه يعزمونا الي عندهم ويقفوا في واجب معلي قوي كثير.

٤،٨ وبعد كام يوم اخدوا معلي الي برات المدينه وفرجوه علي عامود عالي بعلو مادنه بقرب البحر ومنقوش علي ذلك العامود شكل طيور ودبابات وغزلان وما يشبه ذلك الحيوانات والعامود علي راي المعلمين بانه طبخ لانه غير ممكن بانه يكون صخر لان في تلك البلاد ما في جبال ولا صخر ابدا وثانيا بان غلض هل عامود وكبره بانه ما يمكن ينسحب في عجله او ينقام او احد يقدر يحركه لانه مدفون في الارض بقدر طوله القايم برات الارض وبهذا اتضح بانه طبخ من المعادن.

٤،٩ واخيرا استقام معلي عند ذلك العامود ونسخ جميع تلك التصاوير المنقوشه عليه فلما سالوه لاي سبب نسخ تلك التصاوير وما هو المعني فقال بان هل تصاوير بيرمزوا عن احرف وكلام تحت الفاظ سريه كانوا يعتنوا بها الفلاسفه اليونانيين في ذلك الزمان.

٤،١٠ وبجانب العامود مغاره تسما مغارة العبد وهي منقوره من صخر والبحر داخل فيها ولها ضوضا عظيمه من شده الامواه التي داخلها وقليل من العوامين يقدر يدخل اليها والذين دخلوا احكوا بانها مغاره متتسعة ما احد قدر يصل الي اخرها من شده اتساعها وتلاطم الامواه التي داخلها.

٤،١١ اخيرا مضينا الي مكان الذي معمرين فيه اربعين بير منشان الماء ليشربوا منها اهل تلك المدينه لما كانت تنفسد ينابيع ميامها من تاثيرات بعض كواكب علي راي معلمين[١] الفلك الذين كانوا في ذلك العصر بقولهم بان تلك الامياه المفسوده بتاثر جنون للذين بيشربوا منها ولاجل هل سبب عمروا تلك البياره وكانوا الفلاكيه يرصدوا قبل ورود تلك الكواكب بحين فيديروا ينابيع ميامها علي تلك الايار ويعبوها من ذلك الماء حتي

---

١ الأصل: معلملين.

Once we disembarked, we headed for the residence of the consul, who wel-  4.7
comed my master warmly and ordered his servants to bring our things from
the ship. They prepared some furnished rooms for us and brought over all our
bags without the customs official inspecting them. There we stayed, treated in
the most honorable fashion, and the French merchants began inviting us to
their homes, displaying their due regard for my master.

A few days later, the merchants escorted him outside the city to show him  4.8
a column as tall as a minaret standing by the sea.[48] On it were carved birds,
reptiles, gazelles, and other animals. According to those informed about the
subject, the column was made of baked brick. It couldn't possibly have been
made of rock, as there were no mountains in those parts, nor any kind of rock
to speak of. What's more, the column's thickness and immense size meant it
couldn't have been dragged on a cart or carried. No one could have budged it!
The length of column buried in the ground was as great as its height above
ground. It was clear, for all of these reasons, that it was made of brick.

My master stood by the column, copying all the images inscribed on it.  4.9
When they asked him why he was copying the images and what they meant,
he replied, "These pictures represent letters and words—secret signs containing mysteries that engaged the Greek philosophers long ago."

Beside the pillar was a cave known as the Cave of the Slave.[49] It was a hollow  4.10
in the rock, and open to the sea, so it roared with the pounding of the waves.
Very few swimmers could reach the cave; those who had managed to do so
said it was huge. It was so vast and the waves so turbulent that no one had ever
reached the end of it.

Next, we went to see the forty cisterns the people of the city had once built  4.11
to store their drinking water.[50] According to the astrologers of the time, the
appearance of certain stars had a polluting effect on the spring water. They
believed that the polluted water caused those who drank it to go mad; that
was the reason they built the cisterns. The astrologers would observe the
skies shortly before the appearance of those stars, then divert the water of the
springs toward the cisterns and fill them. They drank the cistern water until the

اذا حكم الوقت يبدوا يستقوا من تلك البياره الي حين ما تجوز تاثيرات تلك الكواكب وهذا الذي سمعناه عن سبب عماره هذه البياري والله اعلم.

٤،١٢ اخيرًا تفرجنا علي اماكن وعماير قدم شي كثير لان مدينة اسكندريه هي من مدن الكبار التي كانت في زمان القديم علي ما بتني التواريخ. اخيرًا رجعنا الي محلنا واستقمنا في تلك المدينه برهة ايام بغاية العز والاكرام.

٤،١٣ وكنت اروح كل يوم الي الاسكله واتفرج علي السموكات التي بتخرج من ذلك البحر المخلوط مع بحر النيل شي بيفوق الوصف ومن جهت طعمه ما رايت ولا استلذيت في طعم سمك مثله في جميع البلاد الذي درتها وعاملين في تلك الاسكله داخل البحر سياجات منشان صيد السمك وعاملين في تلك السياجات حركه حتي اذا دخل السمك داخلهم ما بيعود بيقدر يخرج. اخيرًا بيصطاداوه من داخل تلك السياجات بغير تعب وتراه مكوم علي حفة الاسكله كوم كوم ومنه يخرجوا البطارخ ومنه يملحوه وبيقددوه وبيروح منه الي ساير البلاد شي بالكبيري. المراد اكثر معيشة اهل تلك البلد الرجبال من ذلك السمك وشغل الاصيوطي اعني الكتان.

٤،١٤ اخيرًا تهيا معلمي حتي يروح الي مدينة مصر يتفرج علي تلك الاماكن فاستكرينا مع معاش اعني قارب كبير الذي بيسافروا في بحر النيل فخرجنا من بيت القنصر سلام الصبح ونزلنا في ذلك المعاش المذكور وسافرنا في بحر المالح الي ان وصلنا الي بوغاز بحر النيل وهناك موجود دايمًا اناس لاجل المعاشات الذين بيدخلوا في البوغاز حتي يدلوهم من اي جانب يجب ان يدخلوا لان كل مده بيتكوم الرمل في ناحيه في البوغاز وبيصير حاجز عن الدخول.

٤،١٥ وفي ذلك الوقت تفرست في دخول بحر النيل في بحر المالح شي عجيب لانه بيدخل في بحر المالح بغير انهم يختلطوا ابدًا وكنت اري صاير خط ما بين البحرين لان بحر النيل طالب الوطاه في بحر المالح وهذا شي رايته في سفري في بحر المالح وكنت اري في قاع البحر خطوط بيض في وقت الغلينه فسالت ما هي هل خطوط فاجابوني بانها الانهر الحلوه التي بتدخل في البحرين غير انها تختلط بما المالح وعلي قول البعض منهم بان السحاب بيشرب من هل الانهر.

effects of the stars passed. At least, this is what we heard about the construction of the cisterns, but God knows best.[51]

We toured many other ancient sites and buildings. The city of Alexandria    4.12
is one of the world's great ancient cities, just as the chronicles record. We
returned to our house and stayed in the city a few more days, and were treated
honorably and hospitably.

Each day, I'd go down to the harbor and gaze at the fish caught in the sea,    4.13
whose waters mixed with the waters of the Nile. It was something amazing to
see! I'd never seen or tasted such delicious fish in all the lands I'd toured.

In the harbor, they'd built some corrals in the water to catch fish. Inside
each corral was a device that prevented the fish from leaving once they'd
entered. In that way, they could be caught in the corrals without any effort
at all. You'd see the fish piled up in heaps along the edge of the harbor. From
some fish, they'd harvest the roe; others would be salted and dried. A great
quantity was exported to many countries. All this is to say that the livelihood
of the working people in that country came mostly from those fish and Asyūṭī
fabric, meaning linen.

My master prepared to travel to Cairo and see its sites. We booked passage    4.14
on a *maʿāsh*—which is a large riverboat that travels along the Nile.[52] We left
the consul's home in the morning, went down to the riverboat, and sailed
in the sea till we arrived at the straits of the Nile. Every now and then the
sand would pile up on one side of the straits, blocking the entrance, so there
were always people there to guide riverboats in, pointing out which side to
enter through.

As we passed through, I studied the way the Nile flowed into the sea. It    4.15
was something wondrous! It poured into the sea, but didn't mix with it at
all: I could see a line between the two bodies of water, as the Nile waters
headed to the seabed. This was something I'd observe again during my voyages at sea. I saw white lines on the seabed when the waters were calm, and
when I inquired about them, I was told they were the freshwater rivers that
entered the sea without mixing with the salt water. Some people claimed that
the clouds would absorb water from these rivers.

١٦٬٤ وهذا ايضاً رايته في البحر في ايام الشتي لما بينزل سحاب من الغيم الي البحر يصير في ذلك المكان طغره عظيم بيشق البحر اعني ويتصل الي تلك الانهر وبيشرب منها الماء الحلو والشاهد علي هذا هو ان في بحر المحيط اعني بحر الهند لما يفرغ الماء من المركب مستقبزين سطل من نحاس بيدلوه الي نهر الذي بيكون جاري في ذلك المكان وبيتعبا عبا من ذلك الماء الحلو وله حركه اذا تعبا بيطبق غطاه عليه طبق محكم بغير ان يدخله ماء مالح وبيستقوا منه ما حلو كما سمعنا من الذين سافروا في بحر المحيط المذكور .

١٧٬٤ ونرجع ما نحن في صدده. اخيراً دخلنا في بحر النيل بذلك المعاش المذكور وسافرنا ذلك النهار الي ان وصلنا الي مينة رشيد التي هي اسكلت مصر الواحده والثانيه مينة دمياط فلما انتهينا الي الاسكله خرجنا من ذلك المعاش ورحنا الي بيت رجل تاجر وفنساوي يسمي خواجه دوران فلما دخلنا في منزله صعدنا في درج من حجر متسع واخر الدرج انتهينا الي رصيف متسع مرصوف ببلاط واخر الرصيف ديوانخانه بتشرف علي بحر النيل واراضي الرز الخضره البهيه كانها زمرد شي بيشرح الخاطر .

١٨٬٤ اخيراً طلع الي لقانا خواجه دوران واسترحب في معلمي بغاية الاكرام والتحيي وامر الخدام حتي ينقلوا حوايجنا الي فوق وهيا الي معلمي اوضه مفروشه بجميع لوازمها فاستقمنا كامل ذلك النهار الي ان حل وقت العشا فبعدما تعشوا وتعشينا نحن ايضاً مع جملة الخدام فاستقمت اتصامر مع الخدام الي ما حان وقت المنام. حينذٍ واحد من الخدام دعاني حتي يروني اوضه التي كانوا هيوها لي للمنامه فابايت وقلت له انا بنام في هل نصيف من بيقدر ينام داخل اوضه في هل ايام الصيف والحر الشديد فنصحني اول وثاني فما سمعت كلامه. اخيراً تركني ومضي فبقيت وحدي في ذلك النصيف اتمشا. اخيراً فرشت فرشت الدرب التي كانت معنا واتكيت حتي انام وما بعرف ايش بده يجري عليّ في تلك الليله.

١٩٬٤ فما لحقت توست في الفراش والا سمعت حس وزيز عظيم واتلبس وجهي وهو الناموس اعني البق الذي بيتكون في مياة الرز المقيله في تلك الاراضي فلما تلبس وجهي ذلك الناموس نهضت من الفراش كالمجنون وصرت اكشه عن وجهي وعن

I also witnessed this at sea on rainy days, when a rain cloud would descend    4.16
to the sea and the water would churn and boil beneath it. It would split the
sea open and reach down to those rivers, soaking up the fresh water. Here's
one proof of this: When a ship's fresh water runs out while sailing on the
ocean—the Indian Ocean, I mean—the sailors lower a copper bucket into an
undersea river that flows below. The bucket fills with fresh water, and a mechanism inside the bucket closes the lid tightly so no salt water can get in. And
that's how they get their fresh water, according to those who've traveled the
Indian Ocean.

Let me return to my account. We entered the Nile on that riverboat and    4.17
traveled the whole day before arriving at Rosetta, one of the two access ports
to Cairo; the other is Damietta.[53] When we arrived, we disembarked and went
to the home of a French merchant named *khawājah* Durand.[54] We entered
his house, ascended some wide stone stairs, and arrived at a spacious, paved
walkway. At the end of it was a salon overlooking the Nile and the surrounding
emerald-green fields of rice. It was a sight that truly warmed the heart!

*Khawājah* Durand came up to meet us and greeted my master most effu-    4.18
sively. He ordered the servants to carry our things upstairs and had a room
prepared for my master with all the necessities. We remained there the rest of
the day, till it was time for dinner. They dined together while I ate with the rest
of the servants, staying up late to chat with them until it was time to sleep. One
of the servants offered to show me the room they'd prepared for me to sleep
in, but I declined.

"I'll sleep here, on this walkway," I said. "Who could possibly sleep inside in
summertime? In this scorching heat?"

He advised against it, and tried to insist, but I wouldn't listen, so he left me
to my own devices. There I stayed, all by myself on that walkway, strolling back
and forth. I set up the camp bed we had brought with us and lay down to sleep.
I had no sense of what was about to happen to me that night.

As I lay down on the bed, I heard a loud buzzing noise and my face was sud-    4.19
denly covered with mosquitoes—the insect found in the stagnant waters of the
rice fields in that region. My face swarming with them, I jumped up from the
bed like a madman and tried, unsuccessfully, to bat them away from my face,
arms, and legs. In the end, I lit my pipe and the smoke of the tobacco drove

سواعدي ورجلي برهه من الزمان وما امكن انه يعتقني حتي ولعت غليون التتن ودخنت فم دخنت التتن تركني ومضي فسرت اتمشا في ذلك النصيف والغليون في في. اخيرًا تعبت وغلب عليّ النوم فرجعت الي الفراش حتي انام فصابني مثل ما صابني في الاول فنهضت ايضًا اتمشي واشرب تتن حتي لا يقرب اليّ الناموس.

٢٠،٤ فاستقمت علي هذا الحال الي حكم سلام الصبح. حينذٍ خطر في بالي بان الخادم قلي بانه هياء لي ناموسيه في الاوضه فصرت اجس البواب واحد بعد واحد الي ان انتهيت الي باب اوضه فلما جسيته فتح الباب فدخلت داخل المكان فرايت وله ناموسيه اعني جلال رفيع وداخله مفروش فرشه بجرجفين١ كان علي غاية ما يكون فعرفت حينذٍ بان هل فرشه كانت منشاني فما كدبت خبر فللوقت انطرحت علي ذلك الفراش الناعم ورقدت الي حين ما جاوا نبهوني حتي اتعدا.

٢١،٤ فلما انتبهت ولبست ثيابي فرايت ذاتي دايخ وما لي نجل ولا قابليه للاكل فاصرفت للي اجا نبهني واستقمت في الاوضه وانا مخبل وما اقدر افتح نواضري وانا في ذلك الحال رايت مرايه معلقه في جانب الاوضه فلما نضرت الي وجهي في تلك المرايه فرايت انقلبت صحنتي الي بشاعه هذا عظم مقدارها حتي ما عدت اعرف داتي وهو ان وجهي انتفخ حتي صار فوق خدودي خدود وفوق جفون عيوني جفون وسمكت شفتي وغاص في وبقيت في حاله زريه وهذا كله كان من قرص الناموس.

٢٢،٤ حينذٍ استقمت في تلك الاوضه بغير اكل المساء من حيابي من الناس. اخيرًا استفقدني معلمي وسال عني فقالوله بانه مخبا في الاوضا وما بيريد يخرج فظمن باني مريض فاجا الي عندي حتي يراني فلما راني في هل حاله فسالني ما لي اراك في هل حاله. فاحكيته بالذي جرا لي في ذلك الليل من الناموس وكيف اني ما قبلت نصيحه من ذلك الخادم فقلي لا تاخد علي خاطرك وفي الحال جاب لي دهون ودهن وجهي وفي ذلك اليوم فش ذلك الورم ورجع وجهي كما كان سابقًا وهذا كتبته نصيحه للذي بيروح الي رشيد لا ينام بغير ناموسيه.

---

them away, so I strolled for a while along the walkway with the pipe in my mouth. Eventually I felt sleepy, and went back to my bed. But the mosquitoes came for me again, just as they had the first time! So I got up again and walked and smoked so that the mosquitoes wouldn't come near me.

I did this until just before daybreak. Then I remembered that the servant had told me he'd set up a mosquito net for me in the room. I went around, quietly trying the doors one by one till I found a door that opened. Inside, I came upon a bed with a mosquito net—a light drapery covering a bed dressed with two sheets of the finest linen. I was certain that this was the bed intended for me and, unwilling to look a gift horse in the mouth any longer, I threw myself down on the soft mattress and slept until they came and roused me for lunch.     4.20

When I got up and put on my clothes, I felt dizzy and weak, and had no appetite. So I sent away the person who'd come to wake me, and stayed in the room feeling all muddled, and unable to open my eyes properly. I saw a mirror hanging on one side of the room, so I went over to look at myself. My complexion was hideous, and my proportions so exaggerated that I didn't even recognize myself. My face had swollen up, and it appeared as though I had cheeks on top of my cheeks, and eyelids over my eyelids! My lips had swollen, my mouth was engorged, and I felt terrible. All thanks to those mosquitoes!     4.21

I stayed in the room all afternoon without eating, too ashamed to let myself be seen by others. Finally, my master noticed I was absent and asked where I was. They told him I was hiding in my room and wouldn't come out, so he assumed I was ill.     4.22

He came by to visit me.

"Whatever happened to you?" he asked, when he found me in that sorry state.

I told him what had transpired overnight with the mosquitoes, and how I'd not taken the advice of the servant.

"Don't you worry," he said, and brought me some ointments right away, daubing my face with them. The swelling subsided that same day and my face returned to normal. Let this be a warning to anyone who might go to Rosetta. Don't sleep without a mosquito net!

وبعد ذلك اليوم خرجت انا ومعلمي ودرنا في تلك البلده وتفرجنا علي اماكنها
وشوارعها وخاناتها فاينا خان ساكنين فيه يهود هن وعيالهم ونشاهم جالسين في
رواقات الخان بيشتغلوا من غير ستار ولا غطي ولا بيتحجبوا من احد كانهم في
بلاد الفرنج وهذا ما رايته في غير اماكن من اعمال مصر وقهواتهم علي حفت بحر
النيل ودائماً فاتحين ليل مع نهار وكل انسان مباح له بان يدور بالليل من غير ان احد
يتعارضه لا من حاكم ولا من غيره خلاف عن غير اماكن من بلاد مصر . المراد بلد
شرحه وامينه في غاية ما يكون وما رايت فيها عيب غير الناموس فقط فمن شده ما
انبسطنا وانشرحنا في هذه البلده استقمنا اثني عشر يوم كانها يوم واحد .

وبعده استكرينا مع المعاش وسافرنا الي مدينة مصر علي بحر النيل الي ان وصلنا
الي بولاق التي هي اسكلت مصر فنزلنا حوايجنا مع الحماره وركبنا من تلك الحمير الرهاونه
ودخلنا مدينة مصر وامرنا الحماره بان يوصلونا الي حارة الموسكي التي هي مقر تجار
الفرنساويه وداخل تلك الحاره بيت قنصر الفرنساويه فلما دخلنا الي تلك الحاره راح
خبر للقنصر في وصولنا من عنده خدام فارسل بنا الي بيت المذكور فلما وقع
نضره علي معلمي فعانقه واسترحب فيه بغاية العز والاكرام لانه كان سمع في قدومه الي
مدينة اسكندريه وانه مرسل من حضرة سلطان فرنسا لاجل السياحه ولاجل ذلك
عمل له اكرام زايد وفرش له اوضه مكلفه من خاص اوضه وامر الخدام بانهم يقفوا
في خدمته خلاف عن غير قناصر .

فاستقمنا في بيت القنصر ثلاثة ايام الي حين ما كملت مسالمته مع التجار وبعد
الثلاثة ايام استازن الخواجه من حضرة القنصر بانه بيريد يدور يتفرج في مدينة
مصر . حينذٍ عين القنصر واحد من الغز الذين في بابه بانه يروح معنا ويدورنا في
مدينة مصر فصار ذلك الرجل كل يوم يدورنا في صايح من صوايح مصر ويفرجنا
علي الاماكن اعني علي قصر فرعون وعلي القلعه والرمليه¹ وعلي بيوت السناجق وما

---
¹ الأصل: والرميله.

The next day, my master and I toured the town, observing its buildings, streets, and caravansary. We passed by a tenement inhabited by Jews and their families. Their women sat working in the covered arcades, without veils or scarves. They didn't withdraw from anyone's sight—it was as though they were living in the land of the Franks! I saw similar things in other parts of the countryside around Cairo.

4.23

The coffee shops were on the banks of the Nile, and they'd remain open all day and night. One was free to walk around at night without being stopped by the authorities or anyone else—unlike other parts of Egypt. It was a wonderfully pleasant and safe town. There wasn't a single thing wrong with it, except for the mosquitoes. We were so happy and relaxed in Rosetta that we spent twelve days there, but it felt as though only a single day had passed.

We booked passage on the riverboat and traveled to Cairo along the Nile.[55] We arrived at Būlāq, the port in Cairo, and had some donkey drivers load up our bags. We straddled a pair of trotting donkeys and rode into Cairo, having ordered the drivers to take us to the Mouski quarter, where all the French merchants lived. The French consul's house was in that quarter, and news of our arrival sped ahead to the consul as soon as we reached it. He sent some servants, who brought us to his home.

4.24

When the consul set eyes upon my master, he embraced him and greeted him most cordially and honorably. He'd heard about my master's arrival in Alexandria, and knew he'd been dispatched on a voyage of exploration by His Majesty the sultan of France, so he treated him with great deference and prepared one of his finest rooms, going so far as to order his domestics to put themselves at my master's service—something that other consuls had not done.

We remained in the consul's home for three days, receiving all the merchants and paying our respects. Then the *khawājah* asked the consul's permission to let him tour Cairo and see the sights, and the latter appointed a *ghuzzī* in his service to accompany us and take us around the city. The man came along each day and gave us a tour of a different quarter of Cairo, showing us the

4.25

يشبه ذلك من المفترجات فاستقمنا ندور مع هل رجل الغزي ثلاثة ايام نتفرج فتعلمنا مسالك الدروب والازقا والشوارع.

٢٦.٤ اخيراً راد معلي بان ندور وحدنا من غير ذلك الرجل لان كان قصده بانه يفتش على اشيا الذي كان دائماً يفتش عليها في كل بلد الذي يدخلها مثل مداليات قدم وكتب تواريخ قديمه وقطع حجار ثمينه مثل الماس وياقوت وزمرد وزفرجل وما يشبه ذلك من الحجار الكريمه وبعض حجار لها خواصات وما هي معروفه في بلاد الشرق الا من قليلين وكان معلي له معرفه بليغه في الجواهر الثمينه والمعادن المجهوله في بلادنا سوف ندكر خواصها في محلها.

٢٧.٤ وعلى ما رايت من هل رجل اعني معلي عنده من كل خبر اعني في علم الطب كان ماهر في الغايه لانه اذا طلع في سحنة الانسان يعرف مرضه من غير ان يساله عن مرضه وكان ماهر في علم الفلك وعلم الهندزه والفلسفه وعلم الطبيعيات وعلم السحنه وكان يعرف جميع خواص الحشايش والنباتات والعقاير المتنوعه وما يشبه ذلك من امور الطب ورايت كثيره من براهين سوف ندكرها في محلها.

٢٨.٤ اخيراً بعد دورتنا مع ذلك الرجل الغزي المذكور قصد معلي بانه يزور بيت سيدتنا مريم العذري الذي هو في مصر القديمه وهو بعيد عن مصر الحديثه مسافة ثلاث اميال اقل او اكثر فلما وصلنا نزلنا في دير ريحان القديس ومن هناك اخدنا البادري الي ذلك المكان الذي فيه بيت العذري وهو الان داخل كنيسة القبطي فدخلنا الي ذلك المحل الشريف الذي تسكت فيه البتول وماري يوسف والطفل يسوع سبع سناوات كما يذكر الانجيل الشريف.

٢٩.٤ وبعده حضرنا قداس ذلك البادري علي هيكل العذري الذي هو داخل البيت المذكور وبعد حضورنا القداس عزمنا البادري حتي نتغدا عنده في الدير فبعدما تغدينا فاخدنا البادري وصار يدورنا ويفرجنا علي تلك الاماكن القديمه الخرابه ومن جملتهم فجنا علي عنابر القمح الذي كان عمرهم يوسف الحسن كما يذكر الكتاب المقدس وكان عددهم اربعين عنبر الذي مبين اثرهم من غير الذين انهدموا بالكليه ولا عاد يرالهم اثر.

pharaoh's palace, the Citadel, Ramliyyah Square, the residences of the *sanjak*s, and other sites. We toured with the *ghuzzī* for three days, and learned our way around all the lanes and alleys and avenues.

My master wished us to tour on our own, without a guide, as he wanted    4.26
to hunt for the things he typically sought out in every town: old medallions, old chronicles, diamonds, rubies, emeralds, peridots, and other such precious stones. He was also on the lookout for stones with medicinal properties, which few people knew about in the lands of the East. My master had a vast knowledge of the region's valuable stones and obscure minerals, whose properties I will discuss in the appropriate place.

As far as I could tell, this man was familiar with just about every science. He    4.27
was especially skilled in medicine. Just by looking at a person's face, he'd know what his illness was, without asking about it! He was proficient in astronomy, geometry, philosophy, natural history, and physiognomy, and knew all the medicinal properties of the different herbs and plants, and other such things related to medicine. I witnessed many proofs of his skill, which I will recount in the appropriate place.

After our tour with the aforementioned *ghuzzī*, my master decided to visit    4.28
the home of Our Lady the Virgin Mary in Old Cairo. It was three miles from New Cairo, more or less. When we arrived, we stopped at the Monastery of the Holy Basil.[56] From there, the priest took us to the Virgin's house, which is now surrounded by a Coptic church. We entered that noble place, where the Virgin and Saint Joseph and the baby Jesus lived for seven years, as the Holy Gospel recounts.[57]

We attended that priest's mass at the temple of the Virgin, inside the    4.29
house. Following the mass, the priest invited us to have lunch with him at the monastery, after which he took us out and gave us a tour, showing us all the ancient sites and ruins, including the storehouses of grain Joseph the Fair had built, as the Holy Book recounts.[58] There were forty storehouses whose traces could still be seen. Those that had been completely demolished had left no trace.

٣٠،٤ وبعد ما درنا وتفرجنا رجعنا الي محلنا الي بيت القنصر وبعده سرنا ندور وحدنا بغير
دليل ونعدي الي الاسواق والقهاوي ونجالس اصحاب الدكاكين حتي انعرف معلي بانه
حكيم وكان كثير من ناس تقصدنا لاجل الحكمه وكان يحكمهم بلاش انما يطلب منهم
يفتشوا له علي مداليات اعني فلوس قدم وكانوا يجيبوله كثير منهم.

٣١،٤ واحد الايام رجل قبطي جاب لنا توراه مكتوبه علي رق وملفوفه بلسان السرنيكي
الذي هو منشق من لسان السرياني بقوله لنا بان هل توراه مكتوبه من زمان بني
اسرايل لما كانوا قاطنين في مدينة مصر في ايام الفراعنه وان في تلك الايام الورق
ماكان له وجود فكانوا يكتبوا علي رق` فلما نضرها معلي راد يشتريها منه لكن بشرط
انه يختبرها بعد كم يوم فرضي ذلك الرجل فاعطانا هي فاخدناها وفصلنا ثمنها اربعين
غرش اريال ان كانت صحيحه توراه.

٣٢،٤ فلما اخدها معلي فاروها الي البادريه حتي يفحصوا عنها هل هي توراه ام لا فبعد
ما فحصوا علي حقيقتها فوجدوها بانها توراه ومكتوب فيها سفر الخليقه من اناس ذو
معرفه في هل لسان. اخيرا تحقق عند معلي بانها توراه صحيحه فقبض حقها لذلك
الرجل كما قلنا اربعين اريال. حيندٍ قلي معلي بان هذه التوراه بتسوا عندي اربعة الف
غرش وفرح فرحاً شديد في مشتراتها.

٣٣،٤ واشترينا كتب تواريخ قدم من ساير الالسن من هل بلاد ومن غير بلاد ايضاً
وبعده نزلنا ندور في شوارع مصرحتي دخلنا الي سوق السياغه فاشتري معلي
من دلك السوق اشيا كثيره من الحجار المثمنات وخصوصاً من حجر الزفرجل شي
بكثره ومن كثرته اشتريناه بالميزان بثمن رخيص وهذا الحجر في بلاد الفرنجيه ثمنه
بثمن الزمرد.

٣٤،٤ ويوم اخرا اجانا رجل يهودي وسالني انكان منزيد نشتري حجار ثمينه فقلتله نعم
فقلي الحقوني فمشينا معه الي ان دخلنا الي وكاله اعني خان وقيصريه فصعدنا معه
الي اعلي مكان ودخلنا الي اوضه وسكر الباب علينا. اخيرا فتح سندوق محدد فرجي

---

١ «وان في تلك ... علي رق» في الهامش.

We toured and saw the sights, and returned to our lodgings at the consul's    4.30
home. From then on, we began to tour on our own, with no guide. We'd go
through the souks and coffeehouses, and sit and chat with the shopkeepers.
It soon became common knowledge that my master was a doctor, and many
people would come to see us to be treated. He'd see them for free, asking only
that they hunt for medallions—that is to say, ancient coins—and they'd bring
great quantities to him.

One day, a Coptic man brought us a Torah on a roll of parchment. It was    4.31
written in Estrangelo, which is derived from the Syriac language.[59] He claimed
that this Torah had been copied during the time the Israelites lived in Cairo,
in the days of the pharaohs. Paper didn't exist at that time, he explained, and
people wrote on parchment. When my master saw it, he wanted to buy it from
the man, but on condition that he could first study it for a few days. The man
agreed, and gave it to us. We settled on a price of forty *riyāl* piasters, if it was
indeed a genuine Torah.

My master showed it to the priests, who examined it to determine whether    4.32
it was in fact a copy of the Torah. After studying it, some people with a knowledge of the language concluded that it was truly a Torah, and that it contained
the Book of Genesis. Convinced of its authenticity, my master paid the man
the forty *riyāl* piasters for it, as we'd agreed.

"To me, that Torah is worth four thousand piasters," he said, and was very
pleased with his purchase.

We bought old chronicles written in the various languages from those and    4.33
other lands. We continued to tour the streets of Cairo, and at the jewelry souk
my master bought many valuable stones, and an especially large quantity of
peridots. Because of the abundance of this stone, we bought it cheap in bulk.
In Frankish lands, this stone is worth as much as an emerald!

One day, a Jewish man came to see us and asked me if we wanted to buy    4.34
valuable stones.

"Yes," I replied.

"Follow me," he said.

We followed him to a *wikālah*, a sort of guesthouse or caravansary, and
went up to the top floor with him, where he took us into a room and shut the

وصار يخرج لنا من الحجار المتمنه مثل الماص وياقوت وزمرد وما يشبه ذلك من الجواهر المتمنه فبقي منهم معلمي كام حجر وبعدما فصلهم معه قله الحقني الي بيت القنصرحتي اقبضك الدرامه وكان مع المذكور امرمن السلطنه الي جميع القناصر الذين موجودين في بلاد الشرق بان مهما طلب الخواجه بول لوكا من الدرامه فليعطوه .

٣٥،٤ اخيرًا ردنا نخرج من ذلك المكان فقلنا اليهودي بريد اروپكم شي الا بشرط انكم بتحلفولي بانكم ما بتبيحوا بالسر . حينٍ اكد له معلمي بانه بيحفظ السرلا يخاف فبعده اخرج لنا زنار مجوهر بيساوي خزنت من المال وقال لنا بان هل زنار زنار ملك من ملوك الترك فلما تامل فيه معلمي راه بيساوي مال كثير فما راد يشتريه انما قله انكان بتقلع لي من هل زنار بعض حجار بشتريهم .

٣٦،٤ فابا اليهودي من ذلك وبعده اخرج من السندوق علبه داخلها حجر الماس اسود وزنه اربعة وعشرين قيراط ناذره من النوادر شي فزيد فتعلق قلب معلمي في ذلك الحجر لكن صار يقول لليهودي بان هذا الحجر مسبوغ ما هو خلقه فوقع الجدال ما بينهم حكم ساعه . اخيرًا اسبت اليهودي بانه خلقه فكان قصد معلمي بانه يشتري ذلك الحجر لكن فزعًا ليلا يطمع ذلك اليهودي وما يعود يسير بازار معه فاحتال عليه بانه جاهل ثمنه وما بيعرف فيه انكان هو الماس صحيح فقله روح معي الي بيت القنصر وهناك بنختبر هل حجر وبفصله معك .

٣٧،٤ فابا اليهودي فزعًا ليلا يظهر خبر الحجر وياخدوه منه بالزور احد السناجق . اخيرًا حققنا له بان ما ندع احد يعرف فيه ولا يخاف من هل جيهه . اخيرًا بالجهد الجهيد حتي انطلق معنا الي بيت القنصر وهناك دخلناه الي اوضه القنصر فاجتمع معه القنصر والترجمان ومعلمي واستقاموا وحدهم حكم ثلاث ساعات وبعده خرج اليهودي وراح في حال سبيله وما قدرت اعرف بكام اشتراه معلمي وتم الامر بخفي ما بينهم .

٣٨،٤ فاتفق ايضًا بان واحد من تجار الفرنساويه اشتري حجر مصور من واحد فلاح بماية مصريه فارواه الي معلمي فلما نضره راد يشتريه منه فما راد يبيعه فطمعه في الثمن

door behind us. He opened a Frankish steel trunk, and began taking out valuable stones: diamonds, rubies, emeralds, and other precious jewels.

My master selected a few stones and, after they had settled on a price, said to the man, "Follow me to the home of the consul, so I can pay you." My master had an order from the French realm to all the consuls in the lands of the East, stipulating that they were to grant the *khawājah* Paul Lucas all the money he asked for.

As we prepared to leave, the Jew said, "I'd like to show you something, on 4.35 condition that you swear to keep it a secret." My master assured him that he would keep the secret safe, and that he had no reason to worry. The man took out a bejeweled belt worth a fortune, and told us that it had once belonged to a Turkish king.

My master studied it and saw that it was worth a great deal of money. Although he wasn't interested in buying it, he made the fellow an offer.

"If you pry some of those stones out of the belt for me, I'll buy them."

The Jew refused. He took a box out of the trunk. Inside was a black diamond 4.36 weighing twenty-four carats, a true rarity. My master set his heart on acquiring it.

"This stone has been dyed," he said to the Jew. "This is not its natural color."

They disputed over it for about an hour. The Jew swore it was authentic. My master had every intention of buying the stone, but was afraid the Jew would become greedy and refuse to strike a deal with him. So he pretended he was ignorant of the stone's value and had no knowledge that it was a real diamond.

"Come with me to the consul's home," he said to the man. "I'll examine the stone there and settle on a price with you."

The Jew refused, fearing that if people found out about the stone, one of the 4.37 *sanjak*s would seize it. We promised him that we wouldn't tell anyone about it and that he had no reason to be afraid. After much back-and-forth, we convinced him to come with us to the house. Inside the consul's chambers, he met privately with the consul, a translator, and my master for three hours. Finally, the Jew emerged and went on his way. I had no clue how much my master paid for the stone, and the matter remained between them.

On another occasion, it happened that one of the French merchants had 4.38 bought an engraved stone for one hundred *miṣriyyah*s from a peasant. The merchant showed it to my master, who, upon seeing it, wanted to buy it.

فما امكن. اخيراً وصل معه في الثمن الي مايتين وخمسين غرش فما راد يبيعه فانحصرمنه واشتكي عليه للقنصر حتي يلزمه في بيعه بقوله له بان جميع ما بشتريه من تجاره وغير اشيا جميعها هي لخزانة سلطان فرنسا. حينٍذ القنصر دعا ذلك الخواجه والزمه في بيعها فما قدر يخالف الجر فاعطاه الجر واخد حقها كما ذكرنا.

٣٩٫٤ وفي تلك الايام اجا واحد فلاح من فلاحين الريف الي حارة الموسكي اعني حارة تجار الفرنج واعطي سره الي واحد من خدام القنصر بانه وجد جسد موميه خوفاً ليلا تسمع فيه الحكام بياخدوه ويرسلوه للسلطنه لان عليه قيد كلي ولا احد يقدر يشتريه ولاجل ذلك لما بينوجد واحد يخفوه الفلاحين حتي يبيعوه للتجار بثمن غالي وهذا بينوجد قرب الهرامات¹ اعني قبور ملوك مصر الفراعنه لكن وجوده نادر لان تلك القبور مردومه تحت تلال رمل وبعد ميات سنين بيتفق بان بيصدر ريح عاصف بيكشف الرمل عن تلك القبور وتلك الاراضي فتطلعوا الفلاحين المختبرين تلك الاراضي بيفتشوا وبالنادر حتي يروا قبر فيه جسد مصبر واذا راوا واحد يخفوه وبعد حين بيبيعوه للتجار.

٤٠٫٤ فلما معلي اخد خبر هل موميه من ذالك الخادم فللوقت اخبر القنصر والزمه بان يبدل جهده في تحصيل هل موميه لانه نادر وقوعه وانه قوي مقبول عند سلطان فرنسا. حينٍذ ارسل القنصر واحضر ذلك الفلاح الي عنده سراً واستخبر منه حقيقة الامر هل هو موجود عنده هل جسد المصبر فاجابه الفلاح بانه صحيح موجود عنده ففصل ثمنه معه بمايتين وخمسين غرش بشرط بانه يجيبه بالخفي بغير ان احد يعرف فيه فاتفقوا علي ذلك الامر وبعده مضي الفلاح في حال سبيله.

٤١٫٤ وبعد كام يوم اجا الفلاح ومعه كام حمل من التبن ودخلهم الي اخور القنصر حتي يبيعهم للسايس وطلب بتمنهم بزود ما بيسوا خيفتاً ليلا يفرغهم السايس ويجد ذلك الجسد المصبر فابقاهم في الاخور وخرج فوجد ذلك الخادم الذي كان سابقاً احكي معه من جهة تلك الموميه وقله بان يخبر القنصر في مجيه فلما سمع القنصر في

---

¹ الأصل: المرامات.

But the man didn't want to sell. My master tried to tempt him by raising the price, to no avail. He offered him 250 piasters, and the man still didn't want to sell! Exasperated, he complained to the consul, insisting that he force the man to sell the stone.

"Everything I buy, gemstones or otherwise, is for the treasury of the sultan of France!" he told him. So the consul sent for that *khawājah* and forced him to sell the stone. Powerless to refuse, he handed over the stone and accepted the money.

Around that time, a peasant from the countryside came to the Mouski quarter, where the Frankish merchants lived. Speaking in confidence to one of the consul's servants, he told him that he'd found a mummy. There was a ban on selling mummies, and he was afraid that if the authorities found out about it, they would confiscate it for the royal treasury. 4.39

Whenever a mummy was discovered, the peasants would hide it away so they could sell it to a trader for a high price. Mummies could be found near the pyramids—the tombs of the pharaohs of Egypt—but they were rare, as the tombs were covered by sand dunes. Only after a few hundred years might it come to pass that a windstorm would blow away the sand, revealing the tombs, and the sharecroppers would go looking. On rare occasions, they might find a tomb containing a preserved body. When they did, they'd hide it, selling it to the merchants a while later.

When my master learned about the mummy from the servant, he immediately relayed the news to the consul and insisted that no effort be spared to obtain it. A mummy turned up so rarely, and the sultan of France would be enormously pleased to receive one. 4.40

The consul had the peasant brought to him in secret, and interrogated him to determine whether he had indeed found an embalmed body. The peasant replied that he had. They settled on a price of 250 piasters, on condition that the peasant bring the mummy to him without anyone seeing it. Once they had agreed, the peasant went on his way.

A few days later, the peasant returned with some loads of straw. He brought them into the consul's stable to sell to the stableman, asking a higher price for the straw than it was worth; that way, there would be no risk of the stableman unloading it and accidentally discovering the preserved body. Leaving the straw in the stable, the peasant went outside and found the servant with 4.41

وصول الفلاح ارسل فاحضره وساله هل جاب معه ذلك المذكور فنكر وقال بان الذين قالولي عنه بانه موجود عندهم الان نكروا ورفعوا القواعد فلما خاب املي منهم فعييت كم حمل تبن وجهتهم الي اخورك حتي ابيعهم الي السايس فكاسرني في ثمنهم بطلب من فضلك بان ترسل تامره بان يشتريهم مني بثمن ماكذا.

٤٢.٤ وقرب الي عند القنصر حتي يبوس يده حتي ياذن للسايس بانه يشتريهم بذلك الثمن وفي ذلك المحل اعطي اشاره للقنصر بان المومية موجوده داخل ذلك التبن واعطاه علامة الخيشه الموجود فيها ذلك الجسد ففهم القنصر بالذي قاله له الفلاح. حينذٍ قال للفلاح اذهب انا بامر السايس بان يشتري منك هل تبن وبعطيك حقه فذهب الفلاح الي الاخور وجلس عند التبن وفي ذلك الوقت ارسل القنصر ودعي السايس الي عنده وارسله في سعايه الي رشيد وامره بان يعطي الي ذلك الفلاح حق التبن المذكور وفي غيابه ببقوا يفرغوا التبن ففعل السايس كما امره القنصر واعطي للفلاح حق تبنه وامر خدامه بانهم يفرغوا التبن في غيابه وسافر.

٤٣.٤ فبعد ما سافر ارسل القنصر احد خدامه وامره بان يسكر باب الاخور ويجيب له المفتاح ولا يفرغوا التبن الي حين ما يجي السايس ففعل ذلك الخادم كما امره القنصر وجاب له المفتاح واوعد الفلاح بانه في الغد يجي ياخد اكياسه متوع التبن. اخيراً اصطبر القنصر الي ان مضي نصفه من الليل ونامت الخدام. حينذٍ نزل للاخور هو ومعلي فقط وفتحوا تلك الخيشه التي اشرله عنها الفلاح فراو ذلك الجسد ملفوف بقطع كان مصري فاصعدوه الي بيت القنصر وتركوه في اوضه من اوض القنصر وقفلوا الباب واخد القنصر المفتاح.

٤٤.٤ وكل هذا صار وانا ما معي خبر في شي من هذا الا بعد خروجنا من مدينة مصر. حينذٍ احكالي معلي في جميع ما ذكرناه في خصوص هل مومية وكيف انهم اخفوها وما احد عرف فيها ولا ذلك الخادم الذي كان معه خبر ذلك الفلاح.

٤٥.٤ اخيراً بعد كام يوم ارسل القنصر واحضر الي عنده نجار واعطاه قياس سندوق طوله وعرضه وامره بانه يجعل قاطع في نصف السندوق من دف متين ويجعل له

whom he'd first shared the news about the mummy, and told him to inform the consul of his arrival.

When the consul heard that the peasant had arrived, he sent for him and asked if he'd brought the object of interest. But the peasant apparently had bad news.

"The people who told me they had it went back on their word and canceled the deal," he said. "So I gave up. I did bring some loads of straw to sell you, but now your stableman wants to bargain me down. Could you please tell him to pay what I ask?"

As the peasant approached the consul to kiss his hand—imploring him to permit the stableman to buy the straw for that price—he signaled that the mummy was inside the straw, and made a gesture indicating which sack it was in! Catching his meaning, the consul dismissed him.     4.42

"Off you go," he said. "I'll tell the stableman to pay your asking price for the straw."

The peasant went out to the stable and sat by the straw. Meanwhile, the consul summoned the stableman and ordered him to deliver a message to Rosetta, but to pay the peasant first and have the straw unloaded while he was away. The stableman did as the consul bade him: He paid the peasant for his straw and ordered a servant to unload it during his absence, and left.

After the stableman departed, the consul sent one of his servants to lock the     4.43
stable door and bring him the key, telling him to unload the straw only after the stableman returned from Rosetta. The servant did as he was told and brought the consul the key, promising the peasant that he could return the next day to get his empty sacks.

The consul waited until midnight, when all the servants were asleep. He and my master then went down to the stable and opened the sack the peasant had indicated. In it they found a body wrapped in strips of Egyptian linen. They brought it up to the consul's house, left it in a room, and locked the door, the consul pocketing the key.

This all happened without me knowing a thing about it! It wasn't until after     4.44
we'd left Cairo that my master told me the whole story about the mummy and how they'd hidden it without anyone finding out—not even the servant who'd first heard from the peasant.

A few days later, the consul sent for a carpenter and gave him the dimen-     4.45
sions for a trunk. He ordered him to make a partition in the middle using a

سفلين غيرمبصرين[1] انما ينقب مكان البصامير لا غير فبعديوم جاب النجار السندوق مشغول كما امره القنصر علي غاية ما يكون وبعده دخل ذلك الجسد المذكور داخل السندوق في الوسط وجعل فوقه من اخز قماشات الحله اعني جراجف ومحازم وكان رفيع وما يشبه ذلك من التحف الثمينه حتي امتلي وجه الواحد وبصمر عليه اول غطي وقلب السندوق وعبى من تلك القماشات المذكوره وجه الثاني وبصمر غطاه ايضاً كما فعل في الاول.

٤٦،٤ وهذا فعله القنصر حتي اذا فتحوا السندوق في الكمرك من اينا وجه كان يروا داخله من تلك القماشات المذكوره وبقي ذلك السندوق وجميع الذي اشتريناه من اراضي مصر من فلوس وجواهر وكتب وغير اشيا كثيره عند القنصر حتي يرسله فيما بعد الي مرسيليا اسكلت فرنسا واخد معلمي من القنصر سند وجريده في جميع الذي تسلمه منه وكتبه في الكنسليره اعني محكمة القنصر في مدينه مصر علي جاري عوايدهم وكذلك فعل هذا مع جميع القناصر الذي مرينا عليهم حتي اذا وصلنا الي مرسيليا نجد كل شي الذي اشتريناه من تلك النواحي والبلاد.

٤٧،٤ فبعدما درنا مدينة مصر باسرها وتفرجنا علي جميع الاماكن والخانات والاسواق وبيوت السناجق والقلعه وباب الانجكاريه وباب العرب وما يشبه ذلك وكان سبب دخولنا الي هذه الاماكن كلها بواسطة الحكمه التي كان معلمي يحكمها لاجل الفرجه فقط من غير انه ياخد شي من احد ولاجل هل سبب كان مقبول عند الجميع.

٤٨،٤ اخيراً راد معلمي بانه يروح يزور جبل تور سينا وباشر في السفر الي ذلك الجبل المقدس فلما سمع القنصر ما هان عليه في ذلك وصار يرويه صعوبة السفر الي ذلك الجبل واخطار الطريق بقوله له بانه بيلتزم انه يركب هجين عشراوي ولاجل سرعت مشوه بيربطوا الراكب عليه ليلا يتهور من علي ظهره ويقتل وفي الطريق ما بينوجد ما للشرب ولا شي للاكل بل بياخدوا معهم زواده من الماء والماكل شي يكفاهم اربعة او خمسة ايام حسب مشو الهجين لانه بيقطع مسافة سبعة ايام بيوم ولاجل هذا ما بتقدر تضاين علي هذا السفر وانا ناصحك.

---

١ الأصل: مبصرمرين.

strong board, and to leave off the top and bottom, only marking the spots for the nails. The next day, the carpenter brought the trunk, fashioned precisely as the consul had ordered. The body was placed in the middle of the trunk, and various fine fabrics—sheets, handkerchiefs, fine linen, and other expensive goods—were laid on top of it, until one side was full, and the first cover was nailed down over it. The trunk was flipped over, some more fabrics were placed inside, and the cover was nailed down just like the first one.

The consul did this so that if the trunk was opened from either side in the customhouse, they would only find the fabrics. The trunk, along with all of the things we'd bought in Egypt—including coins and jewels and books, and many other things besides—were to remain with the consul until he forwarded them to the French port of Marseille.   **4.46**

My master secured a receipt and an inventory from the consul for everything he'd handed over to him, and registered them in the chancellery (that is, the consul's court in Cairo). This was in accordance with their customary practice. This is what the *khawājah* did with every consul we visited. That way, when we arrived in Marseille, we'd find everything we'd purchased from those places.

We toured all of Cairo and saw everything: caravansaries, markets, the homes of the *sanjak*s, the Citadel, the Gate of the Janissaries, al-ʿAzab Gate, and other places too. What got us in everywhere was the medical treatment my master provided. Instead of asking for money, he treated people in exchange for the opportunity to look around. By doing this, he made himself welcome everywhere.   **4.47**

My master decided to visit Mount Sinai, and began preparing for a trip to the holy mountain. When the consul learned of the plan, he didn't look kindly upon it. He related to my master all the difficulties of the journey to the mountain and the perils on the road.   **4.48**

"You'll have to ride an *ʿashrāwī* camel,[60] which is so fast that a rider has to be tied onto its back to keep from falling off and getting killed," he said. "There's no water along the way, and nothing to eat. You'll have to bring enough food and water for four or five days, depending on the camel's pace, because it travels seven or eight days' distance in a single day. Trust me, you won't last long traveling like that!"

فلما سمع معلمي من القنصر هذا الكلام تغيرت نيته عن السفر الي ذلك الجبل ٤.٤٩
المقدس خوفًا من العطب . اخيرًا راد بانه يسافر الي ارادي الصعيد والي نبع بحر النيل
والي بلاد الحبشه والسودان واستشار بذلك الي بعض من الناس الذين راحوا الي تلك
الاراضي والقيعان فخبروه عن ذلك ايضاً وقالوا له يا خواجه انت ما بتقدر تسلك في
تلك الاراضي لان اهلها ارديا وسحارين واطباعهم وحشيه والمسير الي تلك البلاد
كثير الخطر وما هو معلوم بانك ترجع طيب من تلك البلاد وهذا شي قد اختبرناه
بانفسنا وان كان بتريد تتفرج علي تلك الاراضي ولابد امضي الي مدينة الفيوم ومن
هناك بتختبر تلك الاراضي واوادمها من غير انك تخاطر بنفسك .

حينذٍ صمم النيه علي السفر الي مدينة الفيوم واستشار بذلك القنصر فرضي بذلك ٤.٥٠
وقله بان موجود في تلك المدينه بادري حنا لا غير وانا بعطيك مكتوب حتي تنزل عنده
في ديره وتكون في امان لانه رجل حكيم ومقبول عند حاكم البلد الذي هو الصنجق .

اخيرًا تهيينا للسفر ونزلنا في معاش مسافر الي الفيوم وفي تلك الايام كان بنك ٤.٥١
زود بحر النيل فلما خرجنا من مصر القديمه مع ذلك المعاش المذكور فاينا البحر فايض
ومتصل الي اواخر تلك الاراضي والبلاد التي هي سفره اربعة ايام طول مع عرض
والضيع الموجودين في تلك الاراضي جميعهم داخل الماء كانهم ضيعات وما يدورهم
الماء لان الماء بتعلوا عن الارض حكم شبر لا غير ولما يرونا اهل تلك الضيع مارين يجوا
الينا عراه بالزلط صبيان مع بنات لاجل الشحاده حتي زميلهم كسر خبز او بقصمات
وكان ساحبين معاشنا اربع زلام لان سفرنا ضد جريان الماء وكثير اوقات يتوه الريس
عن الدرب ينشب١ المعاش في الرمل وبعد جهد جهيد حتي يرجعوه الي وسط البحر
الجاري وكان كل ليله يربطوا المعاش في جانب البر وكا جميعنا نخرج الي البر ونبات
الي الصباح ونعود نسافر .

فاستقمنا اربعة ايام ويوم الخامس وصلنا الي جسر يوسف الحسن الذي لما ٤.٥٢
ارسل وجاب ابيه يعقوب الي مصر في زمان سلطنته فعمر له مدينة الفيوم لاجل

---

١ الأصل: ينشكب.

Hearing this, my master changed his mind about traveling to the holy    4.49
mountain, afraid he might perish. He decided instead to travel to Upper Egypt,
to the headwaters of the Nile and into Abyssinian and Sudanese lands. He consulted some people who had traveled there and they, similarly, discouraged
him from going.

"*Khawājah*, you can't travel through those parts," they said. "The natives
are nasty brutes who cast spells, the trip is dangerous, and there's no guarantee
that you'd return alive. People have disappeared before, mark our words! But
if you insist, then go to the city of Fayoum. From there, you'll be able to learn
about those places and people without putting yourself in danger."

My master resolved to go to Fayoum. He asked the consul for approval, and    4.50
received it.

"Father Ḥannā is the only priest there," the consul said. "I'll give you a letter
of introduction so that you can lodge with him at his monastery. You'll be safe
in his hands: He's a physician who gets along well with the city governor."[61]

We prepared for the journey and embarked on a riverboat bound for    4.51
Fayoum. It was the flood season then. When we left Old Cairo, we saw that
the Nile waters had reached towns and territories four days' journey away.
The villages within those areas were little hamlets surrounded by water not
more than a handspan deep. When the villagers would see us pass by, they'd
come out stark naked—both boys and girls—to beg for a scrap of bread or
some hardtack.

Since we were traveling against the current, four men hauled the boat
forward. Often the riverboat captain would lose his way and the boat would
become mired in sand. With great effort, they'd manage to push the boat
back into the current. Every evening, we would tie up on the side of the river,
and go onto dry land to spend the night. In the morning, we'd return and set
off again.

We traveled for four days, arriving on the fifth at the dam of Joseph the Fair,    4.52
who summoned his father Jacob to Egypt during the days of his rule and built
the city of Fayoum for him, as the Holy Book recounts. Joseph built the dam in

سكاه كما هو محرر في كتاب المقدس وعمر هل جسر لاجل دخول الماء واجري حصه من النيل داخل هل جسرحتي تسقي تلك الاراضي ولاجل هذا سمي جسر يوسف كما هو مكتوب في حجر تاريخه.

٥٣،٤ فلما وصلنا الي ذلك المكان ربطوا معاش الذي كنا فيه في البر ونقلوا جميع وسقه الي ثاني معاش الذي هو قاطع الجسر فاستقمنا يوم علي ذلك الجسرحتي كملة النقله وفي ذلك اليوم اكلنا سمك من صيد الذي بيستاضوه من فوق اعلي الجسر وهو ان الصيادين يدلوا شباكهم من غير ان تصل الي الماء النازل من ذلك الجسرلان من عزم نزول الماء في الجسر يقدف السمك الي العلو فيقع داخل الشبك وفي هل طريقه يمسكوه وبيبيعوه كل ثلاث اربع فروخ بنصف فضه اعني بمصريه والقلايين جالسين بيقلواكل فرخ بجديد اعني بفلس.

٥٤،٤ وثاني يوم سافرنا في ذلك المعاش الثاني الذي هو قاطع الجسر المذكور الي حين المساء فوصلنا الي مدينة الفيوم واستدلينا علي بيت الباذري حنا المذكور فلما وصلنا الي بيته وراينا واعطاه معلمي مكتوب القنصر الذي ارسله له في انه ينزل معلمي عنده ويقف في واجبه ويفرجه علي تلك المدينه فلما الباذري قري المكتوب وفهم معناه حينذِ استرحب في معلمي قوي كثير وهيا له مكان للمنامه علي قدر مكنته لان بيته قوي زغير ديق.

٥٥،٤ فاستقمنا تلك الليله الي الصباح وبعدما حضرنا القداس الالهي وشربنا القهوه حينذِ وصانا الباذري بالا نخرج من بيته الي حين ما يواجهنا بحضرة السنجق الذي هو حاكم تلك البلاد وما يليها من اماكن وضيع والاراضي الي حد الصعيد وكان هل بادري قوي مقبول عند السنجق وهوحكيمه ولولاه ما قدر الباذري يسكن تلك المدينه لان اهل تلك البلاد ارديا وحشيين منهم قبط ومنهم ريفيين ولبسهم الجبه لا غير علي اللحم حافين الاقدام بالقرع واوجاههم مقلوبه بشعه وما بينفرق القبطي من الريفي وحريمهم بيغزلوا الكتان ورجالهم بيحيكوا المقاطع الاسيوطي وبينسجوا الحصر الساماني وما يشبه ذلك من تلك الاشغال.

order to channel some of the Nile waters to irrigate those territories. For that reason, it was named Joseph's Dam, as recorded on a stone that marked the date of its foundation.

When we arrived, they tied the riverboat to a mooring and transferred its freight to a second boat on the other side of the dam. We spent the day there, waiting for the freight to be loaded, eating fish caught from the top of the dam. The fishermen would dangle their nets without letting them touch the water that flowed down. The water fell with such force that it would hurl the fish into the air, and they'd fall into the nets! In that way, the fishermen would catch them and sell every three or four for half a piece of silver, which is to say a single *miṣriyyah*. The fish fryers seated there would fry a fish for a *jadīd*, in other words for a *fils*. 4.53

The next day, we traveled on the second riverboat (the one on the other side of the dam). We reached Fayoum in the evening and asked for directions to the home of Father Ḥannā. 4.54

When we arrived, my master presented him with the consul's letter, which asked the priest to lodge its bearer with him, put himself at his service, and show him around the city. After reading the letter, the priest welcomed my master warmly and prepared a place for him to sleep. He did the best he could, as his home was very small and cramped.

We spent the night. The next morning, after we attended mass and had some coffee, the priest urged us not to leave his home before he could introduce us to the *sanjak*, who was the governor of the town and the surrounding villages and countryside up to the frontier of Upper Egypt. The priest was very well liked by the governor and served as his personal physician. Were this not the case, he wouldn't have been able to live in Fayoum, as the residents in those parts were wicked and wild. Some were Copts and others were country peasants.[62] They wore nothing but tunics over their naked flesh and went barefoot and bareheaded. Their faces were misshapen and ugly, and one couldn't tell a Copt apart from a peasant! The women spun flax, and the men wove Asyūṭī fabrics. They made *samānī* straw mats and other such handicrafts.[63] 4.55

٥٦،٤ ونرجع ما كنا في صدده فلما راح البادري الي عند السنجق فاحكاه بان وافاني رجل حكم ماهر وتاقن جميع العلوم والفنون هل لك خاطر بان نواجهه مع حضرتك فاجابه السنجق علي الفور ايتيني به حتي انضره فقله البادري علي الراس والعين والان حل وقت خروجك الي دار الحكم لكن نهار غدي من الصباح بجيبه معي الي عند حضرتك حتي تراه.

٥٧،٤ وخرج البادري واجا الي بيته واحكي الي معلمي بجميع الخطاب الذي صار بينهم ولما كان الغد رحنا مع البادري الي سرايت ذلك السنجق ودخلونا الي مكان هو ما بين الحرم وسرايت الحكم فاستقمنا فيه وبعده خرج السنجق من صراية حرمه فنهضنا علي الاقدام وقبلنا اياديه . حينذ جلس وامرنا بالجلوس حداه وامر الخادم فجابوا لنا ضطلي وقهوه وبعده بديوا في المسامره والبادري يترجملهم واستمروا حكم ساعتين من النهار . اخيرا اخذنا اذن بالمسير فعند ذلك قال السنجق للبادري بانه يكلف الي معلمي بانه كل يوم صبي يجي يشرب قهوه عنده من غير تلكيف فقله سمعا وطاعه.

٥٨،٤ وكان السبب هو ان السنجق كان اهل معرفه في علم الفلك والهندزه فلما كان يسال معلمي عن هل قضايا كان يجيبه باجوبه قانعه مسدده فلاجل هل سبب انبسط منه وصار معلمي والفقير نزوح كل يوم من باكر الي عنده ونشرب قهوه ويجلس السنجق ومعلمي يتصامروا والفقير اترجم بينهم الي ان يحكم وقت خروجه الي دار الحكم نسير من عنده وندور في المدينه من غير خوف وفزع ونفتش علي فلوس قديمه فاينا منهم شي كثير واشترينا اصنام بعضهم من فضه وبعضهم من نحاس وبعض كتب مكتوبين علي رق بالعبراني وبعضهم بالسرنكالي من ايام بني اسرايل .

٥٩،٤ فيوم من بعض الايام ونحن مارين فاينا رجل مبسط في جانب الطريق وحاطط في البسطه شقف حدايد وبصامير وخرز ملون وبعض جار خواتم منهم عقيق ومنهم قزاز مسبوغ وما يشبه ذلك من القراقيع فتشخص معلمي في تلك البسط وامرني بلسانه اني اشتري من ذلك الرجل البسطه باجمعها فاستخفيت في عقله في بالي وقلتله ما

As I was saying, the priest went off to see the governor and told him that a    4.56
doctor had arrived who was deeply skilled in all the sciences and arts.

"Would it please Your Excellency to be introduced to him?" he asked.

"Bring him here, so I may see him," the governor replied right away.

"With pleasure," the priest said. "But seeing as how you're about to head off
to the Palace of Justice, why don't I bring him with me tomorrow morning for
Your Excellency to meet him?"

The priest returned to his house, where he told my master about the con-    4.57
versation he'd had. The next morning, we went with the priest to the governor's palace, and were ushered into a place between his private chambers and
the government house. The governor emerged from his private chambers.
We rose to our feet and kissed his hands. He sat down and invited us to have
a seat on either side of him. He ordered a servant to bring us marmalade and
coffee. The governor and my master began to converse, with the priest acting
as translator. Things continued in this fashion for two hours. Finally, we asked
permission to take our leave, and the governor told the priest to ask my master
to come by for coffee every morning, with no obligation or fuss.

"It would be my pleasure," my master replied.

The governor, you see, was well-versed in astronomy and geometry. When    4.58
he asked questions about these subjects, my master would reply with convincing and pertinent responses. The governor was eager to converse with
him, so we'd visit each morning and have coffee together. The two men would
converse and I translated, until the time came for the governor to depart
for the Palace of Justice. Then we'd take our leave and proceed to tour the
city fearlessly, hunting for old coins. We found a great many of them, and
also bought statues of idols (some made of silver and some of copper) and
books on parchment written in Hebrew and Estrangelo, dating to the days of
the Israelites.

One day, while we were out on a walk, we passed a man selling wares by    4.59
the side of the road. He'd laid out some pieces of iron, some nails, colored
beads, ring stones—agate, or perhaps tinted glass—and other odds and ends.
My master inspected the wares and told me, in his own tongue, to buy the
whole lot from the man. Personally, I questioned the wisdom of this proposal,
so I spoke up.

حاجتك في هل قراقيع بتخلي الناس يتضحكوا علينا فعاد علي الكلام باني اشتريها ومضي فلما رايته انحصر مني ومضي فالتزمت اني اشتريها ففصلتها مع ذلك الرجل بثلاثين فضه وفتحت منديلي واخدتها وتبعت معلمي الي بيت البادري.

<sup></sup>٦٠٬٤ فسالني هل اشتريت البسطه قلته نعم فقلي بكام اشتريتها قلته بثلاثين مصريه فاتضحك وقلي اشتريتها غالي واخد المنديل من يدي ودخل الي مكانه وبعد هنيهه اعطاني المنديل وما فيه وقلي خدكبه برا فاعتجبت من هذا الفعل لكن هو عرف ما في تلك البسطه وهوكان موجود فيها فرخ معدن خامي بيساوي برهة من المال لاني فيما بعد اتطلعت علي ذلك الحجر الكريم لانه كبه في يوميته في يوم تاريخه وذاكر اسم ذلك الحجر باسم مالوف من الجواهر الكريم القليل وجودها وهذا الرجل كان له معرفه بالجواهر وهي خاميه وربما اشترا جحاره كريمه غير معروفه من الغير وانا ما لي علم فيهم ولا انطعلت عليهم في سياحتنا هذه.

<sup></sup>٦١٬٤ والاغرب كان يعرف خواص الحجاره لان مره كت احكيت له من والدتي بان فيها دا قديم منذ عشرين سنه وهو بخار سوداوي فاشترا من سوق السياغه جحر بمصريتين كمثل جحر العقيق وهو متقوب واعطاني اياه وقلي حتي اضمه في خيط واعلقه في رقبتها وانه يصل الي صدرها فلما رجعت الي حلب وعلقت ذلك الحجر في رقبت والدتي في الحال طابت من ذلك الدا القديم بعدما كانت ما تقدر تنام ولا تلقش ولا تاكل مثل عادتها فلما وضعت هل جحر علي صدرها رجعت كما كانت¹ وهي طيبه بعدما اصرفنا عليها للحكما والوصفات شي كثير وما استفاده بشي الا من هل جحر الذي اشتراها بمصريتين.

<sup></sup>٦٢٬٤ ونرجع ما كنا في صدده فاستقمناكل يوم نروح عند ذلك السنجق حتي يتصاروا مع بعضهم فيوم من الايام قلي السنجق قول للمعلم بانه الليله يجي يتعشا عندي فلما قلت للمذكور ما قاله حضرة السنجق دق وما راد يرد جواب فقله السنجق مالك يا معلم اما تريد تاكل من اكلنا. حينذٍ قلي معلمي قول لحضرة السنجق هذا شرف لي لكن نحن

---

<sup></sup>١ الأصل: كانت.

"What do you want these odds and ends for?" I asked. "They'll make us a laughingstock."

He repeated his request and departed, annoyed with me. Left with no choice, I negotiated a price of thirty pieces of silver with the man, unfurled a handkerchief, and gathered everything up. I followed my master back to the priest's house.

"Did you buy it all?" he asked.                                                     4.60

"Yes."

"For how much?"

"Thirty *miṣriyyah*s."

He laughed and said, "You paid too much."

He took the handkerchief from my hand and went into his room. After a few moments, he returned the handkerchief and some of its contents.

"Throw it out," he said.

Now, I was bewildered by all this, but my master knew what he was doing. Among the odds and ends we'd purchased was a rough stone worth a tidy sum. Later on, I'd learn exactly what it was, as he registered it in his diary on that date, referring to it by name as a certain type of rare and precious gem. My master was knowledgeable about rough stones. In this case, he may have bought a stone unknown to anyone else! (I was personally ignorant of this subject, and wouldn't learn about it during our travels.)[64]

Strangest of all, he knew all about the medicinal properties of stones. I'd      4.61
once told him that my mother had been suffering from melancholy for the past twenty years.[65] So, he went to the jewelry souk and purchased a certain stone for two *miṣriyyah*s. It looked like a piece of agate, and was pierced. Handing it over, he explained that I was to thread the stone and put it around my mother's neck, letting it hang down to her chest. When I returned to Aleppo and placed the stone around her neck, she immediately recovered from her long illness. Before that, she hadn't been able to sleep, speak, or eat in her usual fashion, but when she put the stone on her chest, she returned to her usual healthy self. We'd spent a lot of money on doctors and medicine, but nothing helped except this stone that my master bought for two *miṣriyyah*s!

But let me get back to what I was saying. Each day, we visited the governor     4.62
so that he and my master could chat together. One day, the governor said to me, "Ask the good doctor to come dine with me this evening."

ما منقدر ناكل من غير شرب فلما ترجمت للسنجق هل كلام من عدم المواخده فقلي ما شي باس يا معلم قله مطلوبه موجود عندي وكان السنجق بيشرب.

٦٣،٤ حينذٍ اتضحكوا اثنينهم واتفقوا بانهم يتعشوا جمله وبعده دخل السنجق الي دار الحكم ونحن سرنا الي محلنا الي ان صار وقت العصر ارسل السنجق اثنين من تباعه الي عندنا وكلفوا معلي بانه يروح الي عند السنجق فسرنا معهم الي ان دخلنا سراية المذكور وجلسنا في ذلك المكان الذي هو ما بين الحرم ودار الحكم فاستقمنا هناك الي ان دخل السنجق فنهضنا علي الاقدام احترامًا له. حينذٍ اذن لنا في الدخول معه الي سرايت الحرم فدخلنا الي مكان.

٦٤،٤ وهو الديوان خانه مفروشه بفرش مكلف ومقابيلها بستان جميع اشجاره ترنج وليمون وكباد وغير اشجار فواكه[1] علي ما تمد عينك والنضرشي بيشرح الخاطر. حينذٍ امرنا بالجلوس فلما جلسنا خرج من داخل الحرم ولد محسن جميل وفي يده فنجان قهوه فاعطاه للسنجق وبعده اعطي الي معلي ايضًا فنجان[2] وللفقير فنجان[2] قهوه. اخيرًا جاب لنا غلاين تتن بالعود القاقون. حينذٍ استقاموا يتصامروا كالمعتاد حكم ساعه وبعده امر السنجق لذلك الغلام المذكور بانه يهيي المايده فبعدما فرش الغلام المايده اتي بصينيه فضه ملتوخه بذهب ودورا البشكير حولها ووضع ارغفت الزاد وبعده جاب لنا[3] من الخمر الجيد وكاسه من ذهب وبدا ينقل صحون الاكل من الحرم ويضعهم بجانب ذلك المكان وكان عدد صحون الاكل عشرين من غير المحلي.

٦٥،٤ اخيرًا صار يقدم لنا صحن بعد صحن من المواكل الطيبه اللذيذه. حينذٍ السنجق سمي باسم لله ومد يده واكل من ذلك الصحن لقمتين ومد يده معلي ايضًا والفقير اكلنا كل واحد لقمتين فشال الغلام ذلك الصحن وجاب غير واستمروا هكذا ياكلوا لقمتين من الصحن ويرفعه الغلام ويجيب غيره فاتفق بان جاب صحن دجاج وخرج منه رايحه بتشق القلب شي مفتح ريسما في لسان الترك قطان كبابي فلما معلي اكل منه استطيبه فزاد الغلام يرفعه ويجيب غيره علي حسب عوايدهم

---

١ الأصل: فوآكه. ٢ الأصل: فنجاه. ٣ الأصل: انا.

When I relayed what His Excellency the governor had proposed, my master looked pained and said nothing.

"What's wrong, doctor? You don't want to eat my food?" the governor asked.

"Tell His Excellency that I would be honored to do so," my master told me, "but we can't eat without having a proper drink."

I translated this response for the governor, and begged him not to take offense.

"Not to worry, doctor!" said the governor, who was himself a drinker. Turning to me, he said, "Tell him that I have what he wants."

They laughed and agreed to have dinner together. The governor went to the 4.63 Palace of Justice and we returned home. In the afternoon, he sent two of his attendants to escort my master over. We went with them to the palace, where we took our seats in the area between the private chambers and the government house. When the governor entered, we rose to our feet out of respect and he invited us to join him in the harem.

A salon with sumptuous furnishings awaited us. Delightfully sprawled out 4.64 before it, extending as far as the eye could see, was an orchard full of orange, lemon, and citron trees, and other trees besides. The governor invited us to be seated, and a handsome and elegant young servant boy emerged from the harem bearing a cup of coffee, which he presented to the governor. He brought some coffee for my master and me, as well as some pipes packed with agarwood-scented tobacco. They sat and conversed for an hour, then the governor ordered the servant to prepare dinner.

The boy set the table, placing on it a silver platter ornamented with gold. 4.65 He wrapped a cloth napkin around it, on which he laid some loaves of bread. He brought some good wine and a gold cup, and began to carry in plates of food from the harem, placing them off to the side. There were twenty plates of food in all, not counting the desserts.

The boy set about serving us one delicious plate after another. The governor pronounced the name of God and reached forward with his hand, eating a couple of morsels from the plate. My master and I did the same, each of us taking a couple of bites. The servant boy took away one dish and presented the next, and we continued in this way, eating a couple of bites from each dish before the boy served the next one.

فمسك معلي الصحن وصار يدم هل طريقه في لسانه لان هذا خلاف عوايد الفرنج فمن هذا المدهر غلب علي الضحك وما عدت اتكم لما كان السنجق يسالني ما لك يا معلم.

٦٦،٤ حينذٍ بست ديل السنجق وقلتله يا سيدي لا يحصل منك مواخد من قلة الادب حتي اخبر جنابك بان قسم هل فرنج عوايدهم بانهم يضعوا جميع الاكل في المايده وكل منهم يباكل من صحن الذي بيجيبه وهذا الرجل بعجبه صحن الدجاج الموضوع الان في المايده ولاجل هل سبب مسكه ومنع الغلام عن اخده.

٦٧،٤ فتحك السنجق وامر الغلام بان لا يعود يرفع صحون من المايده الي ما تكمل باقيت الصحون واستقاموا ياكلوا ويشربوا من ذلك الخمر الجيد الي ان كمت باقيت الصحون واكلوا المحلي والفواكي التي ما لها مثيل في كل اراضي مصر . اخيرًا شربوا القهوه ونزلوا الي ذلك البستان المذكور وهناك صار لنا انشراح عظيم علي تلك المروج والميات الجاريه في تلك السواقي والغدران فاستقمنا الي ان امسا المسا وان الوقت.

٦٨،٤ اخيرًا خرجنا من ذلك البستان الي المكان الذي كا فيه . حينذٍ امر السنجق اثنين من خدامه بان يصلوا معنا الي بيت البادري. وقتيدٍ معلي استكتر بخير السنجق وشكر فضله وبعده مضينا الي محلنا صحبة تينك الاثنين.

٦٩،٤ واستقمنا كل يوم نمضي الي عند السنجق حتي انعرفنا من الجميع بان السنجق له نضر علينا وما عاد علينا باس من اهل تلك البلد فاتفق يوم بان واحد قبطي احكا لنا بان قريب من مدينة الفيوم سفر ساعه موجود عامود اسود غليظ عالي ومصور عليه تصاوير وما احد قدر يعرف ايش هو هل عامود الموجود في هل اراضي الرمل الذي ما بينوجد فيها حصوه فضلاً عن حجر فلما سمع معلي من ذلك الرجل خبر ذلك العامود وهذا كان غاية اربه في الحال باشر في المسير اليه ومن غير انه يشاور البادري امرني بان استكري حمار حتي نركب ونروح ننضر هل عامود وما افتكر في الخطر الموجود في تلك الاماكن بل كان مامن بانه مقبول عند السنجق وما احد بيقدر يتنجم.

He presented us with a dish of chicken, from which wafted a ravishing aroma. Its Turkish name was *kazan kebabı*.[66] My master tasted it and found it delicious. The boy was about to remove the dish and bring another as he had been doing, but my master held on to the platter, complaining in French about this manner of eating, which was contrary to the customs of the Franks. I burst out laughing at this sight, and could hardly speak as the governor asked what was the matter.

"My lord, please don't hold this poor etiquette against him," I said, kissing the hem of the governor's robes. "These Franks have the custom of placing all the food on the table at the same time, and each person eats from the dish that he likes. My master enjoyed the chicken dish that was just brought to the table. That's why he grabbed it and stopped the servant from taking it away."

4.66

The governor laughed, and ordered the servant boy not to take away the dishes from the table until they were finished. So they sat eating and drinking that good wine until all the dishes were finished. They had dessert and fruit— which had no parallel in all of Egypt—and finally some coffee. We strolled out into the orchard, whose meadows, streams, and brooks filled us with a great sense of contentment. We remained there until evening fell and the time came for us to go.

4.67

We left the orchard and went back to where we'd been sitting. The governor ordered two of his servants to accompany us to the home of the priest, and my master heaped praise on the governor, thanking him profusely, and we headed home with the two servants.

4.68

We continued to visit the governor every day. Soon enough, everyone knew we were under his protection, and we no longer felt threatened by the townspeople.

4.69

One day, we were told by a Copt that an hour from Fayoum there was a tall, stout black column with images drawn on it.[67] No one knew how such a column had come to be built in this sandy region, where there wasn't a single pebble to be found, let alone any large stones. When my master heard about this column (such things were of great interest to him), he immediately set about preparing for the trip. Without consulting the priest, he ordered me to rent a donkey so he could go see the column. He paid no mind to the dangers in those places, secure in the thought that he was in the good graces of the governor and that no one would harass him.

٤.٧٠ فبعدما اخذنا معنا زخيرتنا اعني اكلنا وشربنا وما نحتاج اليه ركبنا وسرنا مع ذلك الحمار الي ان وصلنا الي عند ذلك العامود المذكور فنزلنا هناك فإذا عامود شامخ عالي وغليظ كمثل العامود الذي رايناه في مدينة الاسكندريه بل اغلظ واعلي ومنقوش عليه ايضًا مثل طيور ودبابات اعني غزلان ونموره وكلاب وسباع وما يشبه بذلك من الوحوش وهذا كله الغاظ وتحت معاني علي ما احكي لي معلي لان موجود عندهم كتب تواريخ بتنبي عن هل الغاظ.

٤.٧١ اخيرًا بعدما استرحنا هنينه وفترنا اخد في ذلك الوقت ينسخ هل منقوش علي العامود فما درينا والا صار حولنا بمقدار مايتين رجل من اهل تلك الاراضي حفاه مكشوفين الروس بشعين المنضر وصاروا يحدقوا فينا ويقولوا لبعضهم بعض بان كان في هل مكان عامودين علي زمان اجدادنا وكانوا يحكوا لابهاتنا بان اجا الي هذا المكان واحد روبي ودمدم علي العامود الواحد فطيره واخد الدهب الذي تحته وغاب وهذا قبل ما يغيب وياخد الدهب دعونا نقتله وناخد الدهب الموجود تحت العامود وغيرهم بيقولوا دعونا ناخد الدهب منه اولاً واخيرًا نقتله وصاروا يجبوا واحد بعد واحد ويفتحوا افزاجهم ويقولوا الي معلي اعطينا من هل دهب الذي هو تحت العامود والا منقتلك.

٤.٧٢ ومعلي ما كان يفهم قولهم. حينذٍ تقدمت وقلته بالذي احكوه وانا مرتجف وغايب عن صوابي من الرعب الذي شملني من اوليك الارديا بل الوحوش العتاه فلما سمع معلي مني هل كلام ايقن بالموت وصار يقلي كيف نعمل ومنين المهرب وكيف بيصير فينا فقلتله دعني القش معهم وصرت اقلهم اصبروا حتي يطيلع الذهب ويعطي الي كلكم وانا خدولي حصه معكم لكن دعوه يخرج الدهب اولاً وناخذه منه الذي منزيده وفي هل كلام طمنتهم وهمت فورتهم.

٤.٧٣ وفي ذلك الوقت وفي تلك الضيقه اتانا الله بالفرج وتبين من كبد البر غبار عظيم وانكشف من خيال راكب جواد وقاصدنا فلما تفرسوا تلك الاوادم في ذلك الخيال هربوا جميعهم كما يهرب النحل من الدخان وما عدت ترا منهم احد وبعد هنيهه وصل ذلك الخيال الي عندنا فلما رانا نزل عن جواده وسلم علي معلي بمعرفته فيه في سرايه

We gathered some food, drink, and other necessary provisions, and set off    4.70
with the donkey, eventually arriving at a towering column, which was both
tall and stout—like the column we'd seen in Alexandria, but even taller and
thicker. It also had birds and other animals inscribed on it: gazelles, panthers,
dogs, lions, and other such wild beasts. According to my master, these images
were all secret signs that contained meanings, which were explained in chronicles held by the Franks.

After we'd rested for a while and had some breakfast, my master set about    4.71
copying the inscriptions on the column. All of a sudden, we were surrounded
by a crowd of two hundred men! They were locals—barefoot, bareheaded, and
ugly—and they began to talk among themselves as they glared at us.

In the days of their ancestors, I heard them say, there had been two columns
in this spot. Their fathers had been told a story about a European who turned
up, muttered a spell over one of the columns, and made it vanish. He took the
gold that was buried under it and disappeared.

"Let's kill this one and get the gold that's under the column before he disap-
pears with it!" they shouted.

"No, let's take the gold from him first, and then kill him!" others retorted,
and began, mouths agape, to stride up to my master one by one to address
him.[68]

"Give us the gold under that column, or we'll kill you!"

My master couldn't understand what they were saying. Trembling and near    4.72
senseless with terror because of those savage brutes, I rushed over and told
him what they'd said. My master was certain we were going to die.

"What shall we do? How can we escape? What will happen to us?" he cried.

"Let me talk to them," I said, turning to speak to the men.

"Be patient so that he can extract the gold and give it to you—and save a
share for me while you're at it," I said. "Let's have him bring the gold out, then
we can take whatever we like." Hearing this, they settled down and stopped
shouting.

Just then, God saved us from our predicament! Out of the bowels of the    4.73
earth a great dust cloud rose, then lifted to reveal a horse and rider heading
toward us. The men saw him and fled like bees from smoke, disappearing without a trace. A few moments later, the horseman arrived and, when he saw us,

السنجق وصار يسالنا ما لكم باهتين مرعوبين. هل احد شوش عليكم. حينذٍ احكينا له بالذي جرا علينا من تلك الاوادم الوحشيه وكيف انهم تهدونا بالقتل ولو ما الله سبحانه ارسلك الينا لكانوا فتكوا فينا لا محاله.

٧٤،٤ حينذٍ طمن خاطرنا واحكالنا سبب مجيه الي عندنا كان بانه كان في ضيعت الذي هو حاكمها وكان جالس في مكان عالي وذلك المكان بيشرف علي العامود فقال رايت حول العامود جمع غفير فتعجبت ورت اعرف ما هو هذا الجمع فركبت جوادي واتيت الي هاهنا فرايتكم والان كونوا بامان ولا بقيتوا تخافوا من احد.

٧٥،٤ حينذٍ راق خاطرنا وهدي ارتياعنا ورعبنا واستقام معلمي ينسخ تلك المنقوشات التي علي ذلك العامود واستقام ذلك الجندي عندنا الي ما خلص معلمي نسخه. اخيراً ركبنا والجندي معنا الي ان وصلنا الي قرب تلك الضيعه فكلفنا الجندي باننا نروح معه الي ضيعته فسرنا معه الي ان وصلنا الي تلك الضيعه ودخلنا الي منزول الجندي فاسعدنا الي ذلك المكان العالي المذكور وهو مفروش وله شبابيك بتشرف علي ذلك البر من اربع اقطاره. اخيراً امر خادمه بانه بهيي لنا غدا وهو بيض مقلي وجبن ونحن ايضاً اخرجنا من الذي معنا من الزواد ومشروب من الخمر وبعدما تغدينا وشربنا القهوه فردنا نمضي فمنعنا الجندي وقال لنا استقيموا هنا الي حين الي ما يبرد الوقت وانا بروح معكم بوصلكم.

٧٦،٤ فاستقمنا الي ان فات العصر ساعه. اخيراً ركبنا وركب ذلك الجندي معنا ووصلنا الي بيت البادري ومضي في حال سبيله ونحن شكرنا الله تعالى الذي نجانا من اوليك الارديا العتاه وفي ذلك الوقت تغيرت نية معلمي في انه يروح الي ارادي السعيد الذي قد كان حرسوه بانه لا يروح الي تلك النواحي الخطره كما ذكرنا في سابق الخطاب عنها.

٧٧،٤ اخيراً استقمنا عند البادري من غير اننا نطرف برات المدينه ولا قدم واحد انما ندور ونتنزه داخلها وهل مدينه كانها روضه من الرياض من كثرة بساتينها واموها الكثيره وفواكيها اللذيذه وشراحية نسيمها لكن اوادمها كانهم وحوش كما ذكرنا والقمل

dismounted from his steed and came over to greet my master, whom he recognized from the governor's palace.

"What's wrong? The two of you look terrified!" he said. "Did someone harass you?"

We told him what had happened with the wild men, and how they'd threatened to kill us.

"They'd have put us to death, no doubt about it, had God Almighty not sent you!" I said.

He reassured us that we were safe, and explained why he'd come. It seemed    4.74
that he'd been in the nearby village where he served as magistrate, and was sitting on top of a hill with a view of the column.

"I was surprised to see a large crowd gathered around the column, and I wanted to know what was going on," he said. "So I got on my horse and rode here, and found you. You can relax now. No one will trouble you again."

We calmed down, our fright subsiding. My master went back to copying    4.75
the inscriptions on the column. The soldier stayed with us until my master had finished his work, and then we set off all together. As we drew close to the soldier's village, he invited us to visit it. Soon afterwards, we arrived at the soldier's house, and climbed up to the spot he'd mentioned. It was furnished, and had windows that looked out over the countryside in every direction.

He ordered his servant to prepare some fried eggs and cheese for lunch, and we also took out our own provisions and wine. After we'd had lunch and some coffee, we got up to leave, but the soldier protested.

"Stay a little longer until the weather cools off, then I'll take you back," he said.

So we stayed until the afternoon, then rode off together. The soldier delivered    4.76
us to the priest's house, went on his way, and we thanked God Most High for saving us from those savages!

That's when my master decided against going to Upper Egypt, what with its dangerous territories that he'd been urged not to visit, as I've already mentioned.

We stayed with the priest and never set foot outside the city, touring and    4.77
enjoying ourselves within its confines instead. The city was like a garden, full of orchards, abundant water, delicious fruits, and flowing breezes, but the people were like wild animals, as I've said.

يسري فيها مثل الدود لاني كنت اراه يسري علي الحيطان من كثرته شي ما رايته قط
في غير بلادكانه خلقه مثل النمل وفي بيت البادري شي بيفوق الوصف لاني كنت
اغير قميصي في النهار ثلاث اربع مرات في مبتدا دخلنا الي بيت الباذري وما اخلص
منه فقوي انحصرت واتضجرت منه.

٧٨،٤ فيوم قلت الي معلمي يا يسدي دعنا نسافر من هل بلاد لان القمل قد اكلني
واضعفني.[١] حينذٍ قلي هل قد نضرت علي فرد قمله فقلتله هذا هو العجب كيف ان
القمل ما يمسوك وانا قد اكلوني واهروا جسمي فقلي الان بخلصك منهم وفي الحال فتح
سندوقه وصر داخل كانه شي ما بعرفه وربطها بخيط وثم قلي علق هذه في رقبتك
ودخلها داخل قميصك علي اللحم فا بتعود تنضر ولا قمله ففعلت كما امرني وما عدت
شفت علي قمل طول مده سفري معه.

٧٩،٤ وهل باذري كما قاطنين عنده كان بالظاهر يحكم الاجساد وفي الباطن يحكم
الارواح لان كان يقصدوه كثير من رجال ونساء واولاد منهم قبط ومنهم فلاحين
وكان يعلمهم طريقة الايمان وكان يحكم مرضاهم بحكمه غريه وهوان كان واضع في
كانون نار وداخل مكاوي من حديد زغار وكان يكوي تلك المرضي ناس منهم في
جباههم وناس في رقابهم وناس في صدورهم ومنهم في فخاضهم وما يشبه ذلك
فيوم من الايام قلته يا ابانا اما يوجعك قلبك علي هذه الاوادم الذي بتعدبهم في هل
مكاوي النار الغير مطاق المه فاجابني بان يا ولدي هل اوادم الذي تراهم طبعهم طبع
وحوش الادوية الاعتياديه ما بتاثر في اجسادهم ولا بتنفعهم فالتزمت باني اعالجهم
مثل هذا العلاج الذي بيعالجوا فيه الحيوانات وهذا الذي رايناه في مدينة الفيوم وكتبنا
القليل[٢] من الكثير خوفاً من كثرة الكلام وليلا يضجر القاري.

٨٠،٤ وبعده همينا في الرجوع الي مدينة مصرحيث كما فعدما ودعنا السنجق والباذري
نزلنا في المعاش وسافرنا الي ان وصلنا الي جسر يوسف وانتقلنا من ذلك المعاش الي
غيره الذي هو في بحر النيل قاطع الجسر وسافرنا في بحر النيل وكان سفرنا اهون من

١ الأصل: اضعفي.  ٢ الأصل: القيل.

Lice teemed in the city like maggots.[69] There were so many that they even scaled the walls, something I've never seen in any other country! They seemed to be a species of ant, and had completely infested the priest's house. My description doesn't do it justice—I had to change my shirt three or four times a day when we first arrived, and I'd still be covered with them. Soon enough, I couldn't bear it any longer.

"My lord, let's get out of this place!" I said to my master one day. "The lice are eating me alive! I'm on my last legs!"   4.78

"Have you ever seen a single louse on me?" he asked.

"That's the strange thing," I said. "They never touch you, but they've feasted on me."

"I'll get rid of them for you," he replied, opening his trunk. He took out something I couldn't identify, wrapped it in a piece of linen, and tied it up with string.

"Hang this around your neck, and put it under your shirt against the skin," he said. "You won't see any more lice." I did as he told me, and not one louse came near me for the rest of the trip.

The priest with whom we were staying claimed to be a healer of bodies, but his real purpose was to treat the soul. Men, women, and children would seek him out—Copts and peasants too—and he would teach them the correct path to faith. He treated their illnesses in a strange manner. He'd build a fire in a stove and place some irons inside, and use them to cauterize the patient— some on their foreheads, some on their necks, others on their chests, thighs, and elsewhere.   4.79

"Father, doesn't your heart break for these people?" I asked him one day. "You torture them with hot irons and inflict such pain on them!"

"My son, these people have the nature of wild animals," he replied. "Ordinary medicines have no effect on their bodies, and provide no benefit. I've been compelled to treat them in this way, with the methods used on animals."

This is what I saw in Fayoum, of which I've related only a small portion, so as not to go on too long and bore my reader.

We decided to return to Cairo. Saying our goodbyes to the governor and the priest, we boarded a riverboat and traveled to Joseph's Dam. There we transferred to a second boat on the Nile side of dam. Now we were sailing   4.80

السابق لان سيرنا مع سبلة الماء وفي اقل ما يكون وصلنا الي مصر القديمه ثم حملنا
حوايجنا علي الحمير ودخلنا الي مدينة مصر الي حارة الموسكي ومنها الي بيت القنصر
حيث كنا نازلين وبعدما استقمنا في مصر ايضاً برهة ايام ثم سافرنا مع المعاش الي
مينة رشيد ومن رشيد رجعنا ايضاً الي مدينة الاسكندريه ونزلنا في بيت القنصر
حيث كنا نازلين سابقاً فاستقمنا في اسكندريه برهة ايام حين ما تهيا مركب مسافر
الي مدينة طرابلس الغرب.

وكان هذا المركب فرنساوي فاستكراه رجل جندي من جنود مدينة المذكورة ٨١،٤
واوسقه من بن وقماش مصري وغير بضايع التي تسلك في تلك البلاد حتي انتلا
العنبر من الرزق الموسوق فيه ثم ختمه ووضع علي بابه شمع مقير حتي لا يدخله ماء
والمركب بيسما في لسان الفرنجي بينكه اعني شيطيه زغيره بفرد عنبر واكري من
باطنه ذلك الجندي الي ناس راجعين من الحج وقاصدين طرابلس الغرب المذكوره ومن
جملتهم حرمتين مغربيات مع رجالهم وكنا بالكميه مقدار اربعين نفرما عدا البحريه.

فراد الخواجه اعني معلمي انه يسافر مع تلك الشيطيه فمنعه القنصر والبازركان ٨٢،٤
بقولهم له بان هل شطيه زغيره والركيه كثيرين والمكان ديق والركيه كلهم برابره
ورفقتهم قوي صعبه لرجل مثلك فاجابهم معلمي قايلاً بان هل ايام كون والقرصان
كثيرين في البحر واذا سافرت مع هل شيطيه صحبتة هل مسلمين ما علينا فزع من
قرصان الانكليز وثانيا هل شيطيه .بتمشي قريب من البر ما احد يراها من القرصان.
حينذٍ قالوا له افعل كما تشا.

down the Nile—an easier ride than the first journey, as we were traveling with the current. In no time at all we arrived in Old Cairo, loaded up our things on donkeys, and went off to the consul's house in the Mouski quarter, where we'd previously stayed. A few days later, we traveled by boat to the port of Rosetta, and from there back to Alexandria, where we lodged at the consul's house again. We remained there a few days until a ship bound for Tripoli of the West was ready to sail.[70]

It was a French ship. A soldier from Tripoli had hired it and loaded it up with coffee, Egyptian fabrics, and other commodities much in demand in the Maghreb. When the hold was packed to the gunwales with goods, the soldier sealed over the entrance with wax to keep the water out. In the Frankish tongue, this sort of vessel was known as a *pinco*, a small coastal boat with a single hold. The soldier rented out space inside to people returning from the hajj, heading for Tripoli. Among them were two Maghrebi women and their husbands. There were forty of us, not including the sailors.    4.81

My master had decided we would travel with the ship. The consul and the foreign merchants, however, declared this to be out of the question.    4.82

"It's a small ship, there are many passengers, and space is tight," they said. "The other passengers are all from Barbary, and a man like you wouldn't be able to abide their company."

"This is a time of war, and there are many pirates on the seas," my master replied.[71] "If we travel with this ship, in the company of Muslims, we'll have no reason to fear any English pirates. Plus, this kind of ship sails close to the coast, so the pirates won't spy it."

"Do as you wish," they said.

# الفصل الخامس

## ـفي سفرنا الي بلاد المغاربه في سنة ١٧٠٨

فنزلنا في تلك الشيطيه قاصدين مدينة طرابلس الغرب وكان ذلك في شهر شباط ١،٥
فسرنا في البحر لكن بغاية الضيقه صحبة تلك الاوادم البرابره الي ان وصلنا الي مكان
يسما كوفه دسيدره اعني البحر داخل في البر حكم مايتين ميل وعرضه مايتين ميل ايضاً
وهذا يسما ديل في لسان الترك ولاجل ان الشايقه ما يمكنها تفارق البر دخلت في
هذا الديل .

وتاني ليله من دخولنا كان مضي من الليل ساعتين حين ناموا البحريه نصفهم ٢،٥
ونصف الاخر متيقزين للنظاره حسب عوايدهم وفي ذلك الوقت كنت انا الفقير
ويازجي القبطان نتمشا في صحن المركب فما راينا والا شي يخرج من البحر مثل الطيور
فسقط منهم في المركب كام واحد فاسرعنا انا واليازجي والبحريه فمسكنا منهم كام
واحد فاينا هم سمك باجنحه مثل الطيور فتعجبنا من هذه الخلقه الغريه وعلي حس عياطنا
فاق الريس والقبطان وكل من كان في المركب فلما الريس الذي هو مدبر الشيطيه[1]
وكان رجل اختيار وقديم في كار النوتيه فلما نضر الي هذا السمك في الحال امر البحريه
بانهم يلفوا قلع الكبير ويبقوا نصف قلع الزغير الذي يسما الترنكيت ويشدوا الحبال
المعلقه فيهم القلاع وما يشبه ذلك من ترتيب المراكب في البحر .

فلما رايت هذا المنضر وما في شي بيوجب هل حرس لان الوقت كان صاحي ٣،٥
والبحر هادي والهوي معنا طيب فتعجبت وسالت ذلك اليازجي عن السبب الذي

---

١ الأصل: الشطيه.

# Chapter Five

## Our Travels to the Maghreb in the Year 1708[72]

We boarded the ship headed for Tripoli. It was the month of February, and    5.1
we sailed in painfully cramped conditions in the company of those Barbary
natives. Eventually, we arrived at a place called the Gulf of Sidra, where the
sea extends inland, forming a gulf about two hundred miles in both length and
width.[73] This is called a *dīl* in Turkish. Because our boat couldn't stray from the
coastline, it entered the gulf.

On our second night in the gulf, two hours after sundown, half of the sailors    5.2
went to sleep. The other half stayed awake to stand watch, as was their custom.
I was strolling along the deck of the ship with the captain's first mate when,
lo and behold, we saw what looked like birds flying out of the sea! Some of
them landed in the ship, and I dashed over with the first mate and some sailors
to pick up a few. They were fish with wings like birds! We were amazed by this
strange creature, and our shouts woke up the *rayyis*, the captain, and everyone
else on the ship. The *rayyis* was the overseer of the ship, an old man who'd
been a sailor for many years. When he saw the fish, he immediately ordered
the sailors to haul in the large sail and to keep the small one (which was called
the trinket) at half-mast. He also ordered them to tighten the lines attached to
the sails, and to carry out all manner of other procedures that take place on
ships at sea.

I was surprised to see all this activity, because there didn't seem to be any    5.3
reason to take such precautions. The weather was serene, the sea was calm, and
we were sailing with a good wind. I asked the first mate why they'd brought

لأجله لفوا القلوع وشدوا الحبال ومكنوا رباط المراسي وربطوا برباط متين القايق الذي هو داخل الشيطيه مع ان النوطيب والبحر هادي فاجابني ذلك اليازجي بان هل رجل الريس هو قديم هجره في كار النوتيه ويعرف نوايب البحر فيقول بان هل سمك بيدل علي فزتونه عظيمه لان من عظم هيجان البحر وكثرة ارتفاع الامواج الي العلو فطير هل سمك من عزم اختباط الامواج ويهيج وهذا هو السبب فلما سمعت منه هل كلام استخفيت في عقل الريس وما اخدت في كلامه وانتكيت ورقدت في القايق المذكور وهذا كان مكان منامتي الي حين نصف الليل وفي ذلك الوقت انتبهت فرايت البحر هايج والامواج تراكمت علي بعضها البعض وبعض موجات تكسر داخل الشيطيه حتي تعلي المياه داخل صحن الشيطيه حكم نصف دراع وما عادت المزاريب تلحق باخراج الماء وصاروا البحريه يكبوا بالمجاريف الي حين ما اصبح الصباح وكلما له الشي يزيد عن ماكان وكت تراء الامواج يعلوا الجبال الشامخه وترفع الشيطيه الي علوها. اخيرًا اتهبط الي قاع البحر وكل واحد منا متقربط وهو في مكانه في الحبال او في الصواري او في حبال المراسي خوفًا ليلا عزم الرياح والامواج تلقيه في البحر وزاد علينا البلا بكثرة الامطار والرعود والصواحق والغيوم المتكاثفه.

٤،٥ فاستمرينا في ذلك الحال والنكال يومين وليلتين ونحن مشرفين علي العطب والغرق من غير اكل ولا شرب ولا منام انما نتضرع الي الله تعالي بانه ينجينا من الغرق والهلاك وثالث يوم راينا انحدر عامود غليظ من الغيوم الي البحر وفي نزوله انشق البحر وصار وسطه تغره عظيمه وهذا هو السحاب الذي يشرب من ماء الانهار الجاريه في قاع البحر كما ذكرنا سابقاً عنه وماكت اصدق حتي نضرته بعيني.

٥،٥ فلما نضره الريس والقبطان فارتاعوا وخافا عظيما لمعرفتهم اذا سقط المركب في هل تغره بيغرق لا محاله لان في ارتفاع السحاب الي الجو يطبق البحر كما كان والمركب الذي يكون داخله بيغط في قاع البحر وما بيبقا له رجا في الخروج الا بالغرق. حينذٍ امر القبطان الي اليازجي بانه يقول طلبة العذري وطلبت جميع القديسين وايسوا من النجاه ولما كانوا البحريه يقولوا هل طلبات فاتكد عند اوليك المغاربه القاطنين في

down the sails, pulled the ropes tight, and secured all of the fastenings on the anchors. They'd even lashed down the rowboat inside the ship, though the weather was pleasant and the sea was peaceful.

"The *rayyis* has been a sailor for a long time," the first mate replied. "He knows all about the sea and its fickle ways, and he says these fish are a sign of a big storm. Apparently, when the sea becomes agitated and the waves get bigger and more turbulent, the fish start flying."

When I heard this, I thought the *rayyis* was being foolish. Paying no heed to the mate's words, I lay down to sleep in the rowboat. There I remained until midnight, when I woke to find the sea rolling and the waves rising higher and higher. There were waves breaking over the ship, and the water on deck was half an arm deep! The drains couldn't keep up, so the sailors had to bail using pails. They kept this up until morning, but the situation worsened, the waves swelling like towering mountains and raising the ship up on the crests, then sending it plummeting toward the ocean floor!

Every man clung to his spot—some at the ropes, some at the masts, some by the anchor chains—each afraid that the might of the wind and the waves would throw him into the sea. The thunder, lightning, heavy clouds, and heavy rains only added to our despair!

We endured that punishing ordeal for two days and two nights, with no     5.4
food, drink, or sleep. We were on the verge of being capsized and sunk, and we begged God Most High to save us from drowning. On the third day, we saw a great column descending from the clouds to the sea. As it descended, the sea split open and a great chasm formed within. As I recounted earlier, this was the sort of cloud that soaks up water from the rivers flowing along the ocean floor. I didn't believe such a thing could be until I saw it with my own eyes.[74]

When the *rayyis* and the captain spotted the cloud, they were terrified. If the     5.5
ship fell into the chasm, they knew it would certainly sink, because the sea would close in again when the cloud rose back up to the sky. Any ship trapped inside would be pulled down to the seabed, with no possibility of escape.

The captain ordered the first mate to pray to the Virgin Mary and to all the saints, for they'd lost hope of being saved. As the sailors fell to praying, the

الشيطيه بان غرقهم قرب لما راوا البحريه والجميع يصلوا فصاروا يتباكوا بضجيج عظم ويتودعوا من بعضهم البعض وكل منهم يقول لرفيقه ويامنه بانه اذا خلص يسلم علي اولاده واعياله واهاليه.

وانا الفقير كت ارا الموت اعيانا وغبت عن رشدي لاني رايت البحريه كل منهم مسكه برمير ومنهم مسك لوح دف وما يشبه ذلك مستحضرين للغرق وفي ذلك الوقت وانا متقربط في القايق الذي جالس فيه سمعت صوت طفل زغير ببعق فاندهلت من ذلك وايقنت بان ذلك الطفل خرج من البحر او سقط من الغيوم وبعده غبت عن صوابي كاني في سبات ثقيل وما فقت من ذلك السبات الي ان طن في داني صوت الموج واعني الولد الذي هو خادم البحريه يقول وبيشير بانه راء البر. وقتيدٍ فقت ووعيت علي حالي وايضاً فاقوا جميع المغاربه الركاب وصار عندنا فرح عظيم من هل خبر وكان صدور هل خبر المفرح بان القبطان لما راء السحاب وتلك التغره وايس من النجاه امر الماسك دفت المركب بان يدير الدفه ويقصد البر وقال في باله دع الشيطيه تنشب في البر ولا فغرق داخل البحر.

وكان ذلك الهام من الله حتي نخلص من الغريق الذي كا حاصلين فيه فلما الشيطيه توجهة علي البر صار القبطان يرسل ذلك الغلام الي قمة الصاري ويشرف علي البر فلما قربت الشيطيه الي ساحل البر بكام ميل وكان وقت وقت غروب الشمس والبحر هدي عن ما كان فءاء الغلام البر ونزل في الحال يبشر القبطان والركيه وفي هل بشاره رجعت ارواحنا الينا وصار عندنا فرح عظيم وشكرنا الله تعالي علي ما احسن الينا فما استقمنا نصف ساعه حتي راينا البر عيانا وبعد هنيهه رموا المراسي في البحر وهدي المركب فينا. حينذٍ نهضوا الركيه من مكانهم بل الموتي من قبورهم وكت تراهم كانهم خارجين من سراب او من بلوعه كل ثيابهم ملطخه بالنجس والصيان لان في تلك الثلاثة ايام كانوا يقضوا حاجة الطبيعه في سراويلهم وقصانهم وصارت حالتهم زوعه مكروهة. اخيرًا اغتسلوا وغيروا ثيابهم ولبسوا ثيابهم النضاف.

١ الأصل: القبطا.

Maghrebis on the ship, now certain that they would soon drown, began to wail and bid each other farewell, promising to pass on their goodbyes to each other's children and families if they were saved.

Seeing the sailors take hold of barrels, planks, and so on, waiting for the ship to sink, I stared death in the eye and lost my senses. 5.6

As I clung to the rowboat where I sat, I heard a small child crying out. I was bewildered to hear such a sound, and felt sure the child had emerged from the sea or fallen from the clouds. That's when I fainted, tumbling into what seemed like a deep slumber.

Suddenly, I was roused again by the child's voice ringing in my ears. It was the ship's cabin boy, calling out and waving that he could see land!

At that point I came to my senses, and all the Maghrebi passengers did too. Overjoyed, we learned that after the captain saw the cloud and the chasm, he had lost hope of being saved and ordered the helmsman to turn the wheel and make for land.

"Better we wreck on land than sink at sea," he'd told himself.

That was an inspiration from God, and it saved us from sinking. When the ship turned landward, the captain sent the cabin boy to the top of the mast to keep a lookout. When the ship was a few miles off the coast, the sun began to set and the sea had subsided a bit. And the cabin boy spotted land! He came down immediately to tell the captain and passengers. With this good news, we were ourselves again and were overcome with happiness. We thanked God Almighty for the grace He'd bestowed on us! In less than half an hour, we saw land with our own eyes, and after a short time, the anchors were lowered and the ship moored. 5.7

The passengers rose from their places like the dead from their graves. They looked like they'd emerged from a hole in the ground or a cesspit, their clothes soiled with filth. Over the course of those three days, they'd answered the call of nature in their own pants and shirts, making them filthy and miserable. They washed themselves and changed into clean clothes.

وفي ذلك الوقت كان مضنا الجوع والعطش بهذا المقدار حتي ما عدنا نقدر نتكلم مع
بعضنا لان زلاعيمنا يبسة. اخيرًا فصار كل واحد منا يفتش علي زواته فلما استفقدوا
زوادهم فواو البقصمات الذي كان معهم تشتتش من ما البحر مع الرز والسمن وكل شي
للاكل دخله ما البحر وما عاد يتتاكل من مرارة ماء البحر فاستقمنا الي الصباح بغير
اكل ولا شرب.

فلما اصبح الصبح فراينا[1] كل شي الذي كان في صحن المركب رموه في البحر حتي
براميل الماء ووجاق المطبخ والحطب وكل زخيره المركب الموجوده في الشيطيه لاجل
معيشة البحريه والقبطان ونحنا ايضًا الذي كان معنا من الزواد. حيندٍ التجوا الركبه الي
القبطان بان يعطيهم من زواده ان كان بقي عنده شي للاكل نحن القبطان عليهم وطيلع
من مكان منامته كيس بقصمات داخله مقدار اربع او خمس ارطال من البقصمات
لاجل فطوره ونصف برميل ماء صافي لاجل مشروبه.

فلما شاهد ذلك الجندي الذي كان اوسق الشيطيه كيس البقصمات ونصف
برميل الماء ظبتهم قوة والاقتدار وامر واحد من خدامه بان يستل سيفه ويقف
حدا برميل الماء حدرًا ليلا يشربوه بدفعه واحده. اخيرًا اعطي لكل واحد منا فقص[2]
بقصمات قوة لا يموت وكاس زغير من الماء حتي يبل حلقه فلما راوا هل مصيبه الركاب
ايسوا من الحياه بقولهم الله خلصنا من الغريق والان نموت بالجوع والعطش فحاروا
في امرهم كيف يعملوا لان ذلك البر الذي كشفنا عليه هو جول ما موجود فيه لا انسان
ولا وحش حتي ولا طير من قلة وجود الماء والماكل انما كله رمل مثل البحر.

اخيرًا واحد اختيار من الركبه قال لنا بان هل بر بينوجد فيه ناس لاجل قش
الطمر اعني القصب يبسطوه وبياخدوه وبيبيعوه في اراضي السودان. حيندٍ تشاورنا
بان تروح منا ناس تكشف لعل نرا احد ونشتري منهم زاد حتي نقتات فاتفقنا علي
هذا الراي مع القبطان والركبه. حيندٍ نزلوا القايق للبحر ونزل يازجي المركب والفقير
وكام زله من اوليك الركاب فطلعنا الي البر وبدينا في المسير الي ان راينا اشجار النخل

---

١ الأصل: فوارينا. ٢ الأصل: نقص.

By then we were suffering from hunger and thirst, and our throats were so 5.8
dry we couldn't even speak. When we managed to find our provisions, we discovered that the hardtack, rice, and butter were all soggy with seawater. Seawater had, in fact, gotten into all of the food, and the brine had made everything inedible. We went without food or drink till morning.

Come morning, we learned that the sailors had thrown overboard every- 5.9
thing that had been on deck. The barrels of fresh water, the cooking stove,
and the firewood were gone, along with all the supplies belonging to the
sailors and the captain. Our provisions, too, had been lost. The passengers
appealed to the captain, asking him to give them some of his own stores, if
there was anything left. He took pity on them and brought out a sack from
his cabin, containing about four or five *raṭl*s of hardtack, meant for his breakfast, and half a barrel of fresh water, which had been set aside for his own
consumption.

When the soldier who had stocked the ship saw the captain's sack and half 5.10
barrel of water, he commandeered them and ordered one of his servants to
draw his sword and stand guard next to the barrel of water to prevent anyone
from drinking it all at one go. He gave each of us part of a hardtack biscuit to
stave off certain death, and a small cup of water to wet our throats. When the
full extent of this predicament dawned on the passengers, we lost all hope of
survival.

"God saved us from drowning; now we'll die of hunger and thirst instead!"
we all cried.

We were at a loss for what to do, because the land that lay before us was a
deserted wasteland. There was neither man nor beast nor bird to be seen, as
there was no water to drink and nothing to eat there. It was nothing but a sea
of sand.

An old man among the ship's passengers spoke up. "This country is inhab- 5.11
ited," he said. "The people here harvest *qaṣab* dates. They dry them and sell
them in the Sudan."[75] We agreed that a group of us should form a search party,
in hopes of finding someone to sell us enough food to keep us alive.

The captain and passengers agreed. They lowered the rowboat into the
water, and the first mate and I boarded it along with some passengers. Once

فاستبشرنا بان موجود اوادم في ذلك الجول فلما وصلنا عند تلك الاشجار فاينا من بعد بيوت شعر مثل بيوت العرب ففرحنا وجدينا في المسير من فرحنا واستقمنا نمشي حكم نصف ساعه في ذلك الرمل حتي انقطعت انفاسنا وعيينا من التعب لان ارجلنا كانت تغوص في الرمل للخلخال.

١٢،٥ اخيرًا بعد تعب وعنا شديد وصلنا الي تلك البيوت وكل منا دخل الي بيت والفقير والياسجي ومعنا رجل مغربي دخلنا الي بيت من تلك البيوت فاينا جالس داخله رجل كانه شيطان وعيونه كانها عيون السعدان ملفح بحرام اسود وهو اسود ورويته بتفزع فسالناه انكان عنده زاد يبيعناه فاجابنا بنزه قايلًا يا مسكين ايش هو[1] الخبز فقلنا له ايش بتاكلوا انتم فقال لنا نحن ماكل البسيسه والثمر فسالنا ذلك المغربي الذي هو معنا ما هي البسيسه فاجابنا بان البسيسه هي طحين ضره فلما بيجوا الي هذه الاراضي حتي يسطحوا الثمر كل واحد منهم بيجيب معه جراب دقيق وحق سمن فيضع في كفه قليل من الدقيق ومن السمن بيسهم في كفه وبياكله وهذا هو قوتهم مع اكلهم الثمر.

١٣،٥ حينذٍ تشاورنا مع بعضنا البعض واتقفنا باننا نشتري منهم من ذلك الطمر المسطوح حتي نقتات به. اخيرًا فصلنا معهم زنبيلين من ذلك الطمر بغرش واحد فحملناهم علي جمل وارسلناهم الي المركب صحبة واحد من رفقانا وقلنا له يحمل الجمل برميلين حتي نعبيهم من الماء الموجود عندهم فلما جابوا البرميلين قلنا لتلك العربان بانهم يعبوا لنا البرميلين من الماء الموجود عندهم فابوا لنا عن ذلك وقالوا لنا ما عندنا ماء يكفي لنا ولكم وارونا مكان حافرينه داخل الرمل وفيه قليل من الماء فلما شربنا منه رايناه ماء مالح بيفرق قليل عن ماء البحر ولكن الجتنا الضروره[2] بان ناخد معنا هذا الماء المالح. اخيرًا بالجهد الجهيد حتي سمحوا لنا بان نعبي برميل الواحد بغرش فبعدما عبوه فوضعوا في البرميل الثاني شويه من الرمل حتي يوازن مع برميل الماء ثم حملوهم علي ذلك الجمل وسرنا الي المركب.

---

١ الأصل: هر. ٢ الأصل: الضروه.

ashore, we started walking and soon spotted some palm trees, which augured that there were indeed people living in the desert. When we reached the trees, we spied in the distance some tents that looked like Bedouin dwellings. In our excitement, we quickened our pace. After a half hour of marching through the sand, we were gasping and stumbling from exhaustion, our legs sinking ankle-deep into the sand with every step.

After much effort and toil, we arrived at the tents, and split up to check them all. The first mate, a Maghrebi man, and I went into a tent together. Seated inside was a man who looked like a demon: He was black-skinned, with eyes like a monkey's, and he had wrapped himself in a dark blanket. The sight of him was terrifying!    5.12

We asked if he had any bread to sell us.

"Bread? What's that, you wretches?" he sneered, and we told him our story.

"What do you eat?" we asked.

"*Bsīsa* and dates."

We asked the Maghrebi with us what *bsīsa* was, and he explained that it was millet flour.

"When they come to these parts to dry the dates, each person brings along a sack of flour and a jar of butter," the Maghrebi explained. "He puts a little flour in his palm and some butter, and mixes them together. That's what they eat, along with the dates."

After conferring with each other, we agreed to buy some dried dates. Nego-    5.13
tiating a price of one piaster for two baskets of dates, we loaded them onto a camel and sent them back to the ship with one of our companions, telling him to bring back a couple of barrels on the camel, which we'd fill with water from the camp's supply. When the two barrels arrived, we told the Bedouins to fill them with water but they refused.[76]

"We don't have enough water for you and us both," they said, and showed us the spot they'd dug in the sand, which contained a little bit of water. When we drank some of it, we found it brackish, hardly distinguishable from seawater. But we had no choice but to bring some back. Only after strenuous bargaining did they let us fill one barrel for a piaster. They filled a second barrel with some sand to act as a counterweight, loaded them onto the camel, and we headed back to the ship.

٥،١٤ فلما وصلنا ونزلنا البرميلين في القايق نزلنا نحن ايضاً وصعدنا الي المركب فصرنا
ناكل من ذلك الطمر ونشرب من ذلك الماء المالح وما نروي فاستقمنا ثلاثة ايام
ونحن مرسيين في ذلك المكان الي ان راق البحر وهديت تلك الامواج. اخيراً سحبوا
المراسي وفتحوا القلوع وسافرنا اول يوم وثاني يوم وقت الظهر فطلع علينا ريح عاصف
ايضاً. حينذٍ القبطان امر بان يقصدوا البر ايضاً ليلا يصيبنا ما صابنا في الاول فلما
قربنا الي البر وكان ذلك المكان والساحل ما فيه غمق فالتزموا يرموا المراسي بعيد عن
البر بثلاثة اميال فارموا المراسي واستقمنا تلك الليله في ذلك المكان الي الصباح
فلما اصبحنا راينا الشايقه مرسيه وغاطسه في الرمل فبهتنا جميعنا من هذا المنضر
وهذه المصيبه فسالنا الريس ما هو السبب حتي رست الشايقه علي الرمل وانسحبت
مياة البحر الي الورا بعد ميل وازود فاجابنا بان في هل مكان يصير في البحر مد وزجر
وهذا شي مفهوم عند البحريه شي طبيعي ما منه باس. المراد استقمنا ذلك اليوم
مركبنا مرسي علي الرمل وتلك الليله الي ان اصبح الصباح فاينا رجع ماء البحر كما كان
واستقامة الشيطيه مرسيه فاعتجب الريس والقبطان من ذلك وفي الحين امروا
البحريه بانهم ينزلوا الي البحر ويغوصوا تحت الشيطيه ليروا ما هو السبب.[١]

٥،١٥ فراوا الشيطيه غارزه في شعب من شعوب البحر فصاروا يدفعوها للغمق بكل
قوتهم ودربتهم فما امكنهم ان يقدروا يزنحوها من مكانها ولا شبر ولما كنا في تلك
الديقه والعتب اتانا الله بالفرج وهو ان جاز من امامنا شيطيه فصرنا ندعيها بانها
تقرب الي عندنا فلما قربت الينا فصار القبطان والريكبه يتوسلوا الي قبطان تلك
الشيطيه بان يامر بحريته بانهم ينزلوا الي البحر ويساعدوا بحريتنا حتي يدفعوا شيطيتنا
الي الغمق. حينذٍ نزلوا تلك البحريه واجتهدوا مع بحريتنا حتي يدفعوا الشيطيه الي الغمق
فما امكنهم ان يزعزعوها واستقاموا ذلك اليوم في هل معركه فما نالوا مرامهم.

٥،١٦ وقالوا بالتخمين بان انكسرت الشيطيه فزاد حينذٍ حزننا ورعبنا وايَاسنا من الحيوة
ولكن بتدبير الله تعالي وحسن توفيقه تشاوروا الريسين بان ينقلونا جميعنا الي تلك
الشيطيه حتي يخف المركب وينهض من ذلك المكان فامرونا بالنزول ناس بعد ناس

---

١ الأصل: السب.

We arrived at the dinghy and unloaded the two barrels, got in ourselves, and rowed out to the ship. We all dug in to the dates and drank that brackish water, which did nothing to quench our thirst. We lay anchored in that spot for three days until, finally, the sea grew calm and the waves subsided. The crew weighed anchor and unfurled the sails, and we set off. But on the second day, a strong gale picked up around noon, and the captain ordered the sailors to turn landward so we wouldn't be battered again. As we approached the shore, it became apparent that the water off the coast was shallow, so we had to drop anchor three miles from land. We spent the night there. 5.14

When morning came, we awoke to find our ship mired entirely in sand! We couldn't believe our eyes. What a calamity! How had the ship come to be beached on the sand, we asked the *rayyis*, with the sea now a mile or more away?

"It's just the tide," he explained. "It's a natural thing, which you'd know about if you were sailors. No reason to worry."

We spent the day and night with our ship anchored in the sand, and the next morning the sea had risen again. But the ship remained lodged in the sand. The *rayyis* and the captain were surprised. They promptly ordered the sailors to dive into the water and swim under the ship and have a look.

It turned out that the ship was caught on a reef. Using all of their strength and skill, the sailors tried to push the ship to deeper water, but it wouldn't budge an inch. As we stood on the brink of disaster yet again, God delivered us from our predicament. Another ship appeared, which we hailed as it passed. When it drew near, our captain and the passengers begged the other captain to order his men to jump in and help our crew push us out to deeper water. The sailors jumped down from their ship and added their efforts to those of our crew, but weren't able to wiggle it loose. We spent the whole day locked in a fruitless contest. 5.15

Perhaps the ship was damaged, they suggested, only adding to our sorrow, fear, and despair. But by God's providence and inspiration, the two *rayyis*es held a consultation and decided to transfer us all to the other ship so ours 5.16

في القارب ونصعد الي تلك السفينه فبعدما نزلنا جميعنا فاتبقوا تلك النسا الذين كانوا معنا وهن في كامرة القبطان فلما راونا نزلنا جميعنا فخافوا وصاروا يبكوا ويتوسلوا باننا ناخدهم معنا.

١٧،٥ وفي ذلك الوقت سمعت بكاء طفل فاتذكرت لما كنا مضنوكين في تلك الفرتونه وهياجان البحر بكا طفل وكنت متعجب من ذلك غاية العجب وماكنت علمت بان حرمة الواحده وضعة في ذلك الوقت والله تعالى خلصها وعاش ذلك الطفل ورايته في طرابلس الغرب في احد الحارات محمول من ابيه وكناه بالغريق.

١٨،٥ فنرجع الي ما كنا في صدده فبعدما انتها نزولنا وركبنا في تلك الشيطيه نزلوا جميع بحريت سفينتنا وبحريت تلك السفينه حتي يدفعوا سفينتنا الي العمق ونحن صرنا نساعدهم بالدعا والطلبات حكم ساعه من الزمان الي ان خرجت سفينتنا من ذلك الشعب[1] وشافت علي الماء من غير عطب ولا ضرر البته. حينذٍ شكرنا الله تعالي علي احسانه الينا وبعده فتحوا قلوع الشيطيه وسافرنا.

١٩،٥ وبعد يومين من مسيرنا وجد الريس اسكله الا انها قديمه نحيد ورسي في تلك الاسكله بضنه بربما نجد ناس في تلك الاسكله ونجد عندهم شي للاكل والشرب فلما دخلنا فما راينا احد الا هي اسكله قديمه خرابانه مهجوره مند سنين عديده فاستقمنا ذلك اليوم ايضاً ناكل الثمر ونشرب ذلك الماء المالح حتي يبست زلاعيمنا ونحلت قوانا واتصلوا البحريه حتي انهم اكلوا قطات الذين كانوا في الشيطيه ولو ما يوجد عندنا من ذلك الثمر لالتزمنا ناكل بعضنا البعض ولا تسال عن الحكاك الذي صرنا من اكل ذلك الثمر ونحن صابرين علي احكام الله تعالي الي ان ياتينا بالفرج.

٢٠،٥ اخيرًا بتنا في تلك الاسكله ونمنا جميعنا حتي حصت البحريه الذي عليهم ضور النظاره فلما حان وقت نصف الليل فانتبهنا علي حس ضوضوه عظيمه وهي قبطان الشيطيه انتبه من رقاده فراء الشيطيه وصلت الي قرب البر واشرفت علي التلف والانكسار اربًا اربًا فلما راء القبطان هل حاله وجميع البحريه نايمين غاب عن رشده

---

١ الأصل: العشب.

would become lighter and rise up from where it had settled. They ordered us to take turns crossing over to the other ship in the rowboat. After we'd all disembarked, the women, who had been kept behind in the captain's chambers, began to cry and beg us to take them along as well.

Suddenly, I heard a baby crying, and I remembered that when we were 5.17 stuck in the maelstrom I had heard the same thing. At the time, I was utterly mystified, ignorant as I was that someone's wife had given birth during the storm. She delivered it safely, thanks to Almighty God, and the child lived! I later saw him in the arms of his father, in one of the quarters of Tripoli. They'd nicknamed him "Man Overboard."

But back to our story. After we'd all disembarked and boarded the other 5.18 ship, our sailors and their sailors went in to push our ship toward deeper water. We aided them with our prayers for an hour or so, until the ship was finally clear of the reef and bobbed up to the surface of the water, with no damage anywhere! We thanked God Most High for His beneficence, unfurled our sails, and set off.

After two days, the *rayyis* discovered an old moorage and dropped anchor, 5.19 hoping we might find people there who had food and drink. But the place was deserted. It was an old quay that had been abandoned years before and was now in ruins. We remained there that day, eating dates and drinking brackish water until our throats were dry and our strength sapped. The sailors went so far as to eat the cats that were on the ship. Were it not for the dates, we would have been forced to eat each other. This is to say nothing of the itch we got from eating all those dates! We patiently endured God's will, waiting for Him to deliver us.

We spent the night on that quay. Everyone fell asleep, including the party 5.20 of sailors whose turn it was to keep watch. At midnight, a loud noise jolted us awake. It was the captain, who'd woken and seen that the ship had drifted close to the shore and was about to be smashed to bits! Seeing the sailors still asleep, the captain lost his mind. Seizing his cane, he began to beat them mercilessly.

وصوابه فاخد بيده عصاه وصار يضرب البحريه بغير رحمه بقوله لهم الحقوا عاجلاً
والا انكسرت الشيطيه.

٢١،٥ فهضوا جميع البحريه كانهم مجانين وصاروا يسحبوا حبل مرسيت البرانيه حتي
يرجعوا الشيطيه الي الغمق فراوا الحبل فالت من المرسايه البرانيه وما عاد يمكن بان
يرجعواها الي الغمق والمرسيت المذكوره هي ان جميع المراكب والسفن قبل دخولهم الي
اسكلت ما بنصف ميل بيرمواها في البحر وبيستقيم المركب ماشي وحبلها بينكر الي
ما يدخل الي الاسكله. وقتيدٍ بيربطوا الحبل حتي لا يعود ينكر فبستقيم المركب في ذلك
المكان لان مرسيت البرانيه بتمسكه وما بيعود يتقدم الي قدام ابداً بل بيقف في ذلك
المكان ولما بيريدوا يسافروا بيسحبوا حبل مرسيت البرانيه الي ما يصل المركب فوق
منها لان لها شوافه وهي برميل فاضي مربوط بحبل بيشوف فوق منها حتي يستدلوا
البحريه علي مكان الساقطه فيه ويسحبوها من ذلك الحبل حتي تصل الي جانب المركب
اليمين ويربطوها رباط متين ولما بيصلوا الي اسكله بيرخوها قبل دخولهم للاسكله
بنصف ميل كما ذكرنا وهذا كان سبب قرب شايقتنا الي البر لان حبل مرسيت البرانيه
انقطع وانفرد من تلك الصخور الدين في قاع ذلك المكان.

٢٢،٥ ونرجع في ما كا. حينٍ امر الريس للبحريه بانهم ينزلوا للقارب ويربطوا حبل من
الشيطيه الي القارب ويقدفوا بالمقاديف حتي يسحبوها للغمق فعملوا كما امرهم الريس
وبمعونة الله تعالي انسحبت معهم الي العمق. حينٍ فتحوا القلاع وطلبوا دهر البحر حتي
انهم بعدوا عن الاسكله مقدار عشرين ميل وامنوا علي حالهم من ذلك العطب.

٢٣،٥ فلما كان الصباح رجع مركبنا الي ذلك المكان حيث كان البرميل شايف علي
وجه الماء كما ذكرنا فسحبوا المرسييه من قاع البحر وربطوها¹ في جانب المركب ثم سافرنا
وكان الهوا والبحر معنا طيب بهذا المقدار حتي قطعنا مسافة سفر ثمانيت ايام بيوم
واحد علي ما تاكد لنا من قول الريس بان في تلك الليله منصل الي اسكلت طرابلس
الغرب المذكوره. حينٍ صار عندنا فرح عظيم وهنينا بعضنا بعض بالسلامه ونسينا
كل شي الذي جرا لنا من المخاطر والجوع وما يشبه ذلك وكان مركبنا كانه طير طاير علي

¹ الأصل: وربوطوها.

"Get up! Hurry! She's running aground!"

The sailors all jumped up like madmen and began hauling on the line tied to    5.21
the outer anchor, in order to pull the ship out to deeper water. But the rope had
come loose from the anchor, so they had no way to pull us to safety!

All ships, you see, drop an outer anchor half a mile from a harbor. As the
anchor line plays out, the ship advances into the harbor. The rope is then tied
down so that it can't unravel further. That's how the ship remains in place,
with the outer anchor holding it fast so it can't go any closer to land. When it's
time to sail again, the sailors pull on the outer anchor line until the ship returns
to the spot where the anchor was dropped. The spot is marked by a buoy—
an empty barrel tied to the anchor by a rope. The sailors heave it up with the
rope and tie it securely to the starboard side of the ship. When they arrive at
another harbor, as I've said, they drop it half a mile out again.

This was why our ship had drawn so close to land: The rope of the outer
anchor had been severed by the rocks on the seabed!

Back to the story. The *rayyis* ordered the sailors to get into the rowboat,    5.22
rig a towline, and row toward deeper water. They did as he ordered, and with
the help of God Most High, pulled the ship clear. They raised the sails and
made for the open sea, reaching a point about twenty miles from the harbor.
We'd been saved.

In the morning, the ship returned to where the buoy was floating on the    5.23
surface of the water, as I described, and we pulled up the anchor from the
seabed. After tying it to the side of the ship, we sailed off. The sea and wind
were fair, and we were able to make up eight days' journey in a single day.
According to the *rayyis*, we were to arrive in Tripoli that very evening. We
were overjoyed and congratulated each other on our safe arrival, forgetting the
perils that had befallen us, the hunger, and all the other tribulations. Our ship
was like a bird, flying over the surface of the water. We sailed all day and half
the night, lit brightly by the full moon.

"Are we approaching the harbor?" we asked the *rayyis* (this is what he'd told
us, after all).

وجه الماء فاستقمنا مسافرين ذلك النهار وتلك الليله الي ان مضي من الليل نصفه وكانت ليله مضيه لان القمر كان بدر فسالنا الريس هل قربنا الي الاسكله كما قال لنا وكان الريس في ذلك الوقت مدهول كيف انه خرم حسابه في الوصول الي الاسكله فصار يقيس عمق ذلك المكان فلما قاسه فاء ما هو بحر طرابلس كما انه مفهوم عنده في الحال امر البحريه بانهم يلفوا قلع الكبير يبقوا من قلع الترنكيت نصفه الي ان يصبح الصبح ويرا هل انه تايه ام لا فصار مركبنا يمشي قليلا كمشوة طفل زغير الي ان اصبح الصباح فاينا البر من بعد وجبل عالي.

٢٤.٥ حينٍ قالوا المغاربه الذين معنا للريس بان هل بر هو بر طرابلس القديمه وهي بعيده عن طرابلس الحديثه بستين ميل. وقيدٍ تحقق عند الريس باننا فتنا اسكلت طرابلس وسببه كان من زياده الريح الذي كان معنا وكان نحمن بان المركب بياخد ثمانيت ساعات بساعه فاخد اكثر من ذلك اعني سفر عشر ساعات بساعه. اخيراً دار المركب الي الرجوع حين كان الهوا معنا صار ضدنا حتي كان المركب يمشي سفر ساعه بعشر ساعات واستقمنا علي هذا المنوال ثلاثة ايام بلياليها راجعين حتي وصلنا الي اسكلت طرابلس.

٢٥.٥ وفي حال دخولنا خرج ريح عاصف من البر منعنا عن الدخول الا بالجهد الجهيد حتي خرج من الاسكله قايقين وسحبوا الشيطيه الي داخل الاسكله فرموا المراسي ولفوا القلوع مثل عوايدهم وكل منا هم في الطلوع الي البر.

٢٦.٥ وفي ذلك الوقت جانا قايق وفيه من العيش اعني فواكي وفرش ارغفة خبز كمج فاشتري القبطان ذلك الفرش جميعه واعطاه للبحريه حتي ياكلوا ومن الجمله الفقير اخدت رغيف من ذلك الخبز الكماج واكلت منه لقمه فما قدرت ابلعها ورايت طم ذلك الخبز كانه طم رماد فطرحت الرغيف من يدي ولعنت تلك البلاد التي خبزها ما بيتاكل فلما راني معلمي ممرر قال لي ما بالك بعد كل هل عنا والتعب حتي وصلنا الي هاهنا بالسلامه وبرا خبز هل بلد ما بيتاكل طعمه كطعم التراب فلما سمع مني هل كلام اتضحك عليّ وقلي الخبز قوي طيب لكن طم فمك تغير لان لك زمان ما اكلت الخبز.

He seemed perplexed, trying to work out how his calculations about our arrival had been wrong. Checking the water's depth, he found that it was not, in fact, the Sea of Tripoli, as he'd thought! Immediately, he ordered the sailors to take down the mainsail and leave the trinket sail at half-mast until morning. He'd then be able to see whether he had taken us off course or not.

Our ship slowed to the pace of a small child. When morning broke, we spotted land in the distance, and a towering mountain.

"That's Old Tripoli," the Maghrebis said to the *rayyis*. "It's sixty miles from New Tripoli." 5.24

The *rayyis* realized we'd sailed right past Tripoli harbor on account of those high winds. He'd thought that in the course of a single hour the ship would cover an eight-hour journey, but it was even faster than that, covering a ten-hour span in just one hour! So he had to turn the ship around and go back the way we'd come.

But now the winds were against us, and it took ten hours to cover a single hour's journey. We continued in this manner for three days and nights before finally arriving at the harbor of Tripoli.

As we were entering the harbor, a great gale rose up from the land and pre- 5.25 vented us from advancing. It was only with great effort and the help of two dinghies that came out to pull us in that we were able to gain the harbor, where the crew dropped anchor and furled the sails as usual. We couldn't wait to reach dry land.

A rowboat appeared carrying food—fruits, and a round wooden platter 5.26 bearing loaves of bread. The captain bought the whole platter and gave it to the sailors. I took a loaf myself and bit into it. I wasn't able to swallow it—it tasted like ashes! I threw it aside and cursed this place and its inedible bread!

"What's the matter?" my master said when he saw me toss the bread aside.

"We've finally arrived safely, after all that suffering and exhaustion, only to find that the bread here is disgusting!" I complained. "It tastes like dirt!"

"The bread is delicious," he said, laughing at me. "Your sense of taste has changed because you haven't eaten bread in a long time."

٢٧٫٥ اخيرًا نزلنا حوائجنا في القارب وطلعنا الي البر وقصدنا نروح الي بيت القنصر
الفرنساويه القاطن في تلك المدينه وهو يسما لميروا وله بيت مكلف فلما دخلنا الي
عنده وإياناه علي المايده يتغدا فلما راء الي معلي نهض له علي الاقدام واسترحب فيه
واكرمه غاية الاكرام وكلفه حتي يتغدا معه فامتنع عن ذلك واحكاله بالذي جرا علينا
من خروجنا من اسكندريه الي حين ما وصلنا الي طرابلس وكيف لنا خمسة عشر
يوم ما دقنا الزاد ومنها عشرة ايام كان اكلنا الطمر ونشرب ماء المالح فلما سمع القنصر
من معلي هل كلام في الحال امر الطباخ بانه يسلق اربعة تجاج سمان ويخرج امراقهم
وقال لمعلي بانه يستقيم ياكل من امراق الدجاج الي كام حتي يوم حتي تلين حلوقنا وتتفتح
امعانا فاستقمنا ثمانية ايام ناكل من تلك الامراق ونشرب نبيد قبرصي عتيق سبعة
سنين حتي رجعة قوانا الينا ولانت حلوقنا كا كانت سابقًا.

٢٨٫٥ وصرنا ندور في مدينة طرابلس بغير فسع من احد لان القنصر كان قوي مقبول
عند البيك الذي هو متملك علي تلك الاراضي والبلاد وكان القنصر عنده بمقام
اخيه والسبب لذلك هو ان البيك كان اتاخد يسير في مالطه في ايام صبوته
فاشتراه كوالير فرنساوي واخده معه الي مرسيليا فاستقام عنده مدة ايام يخدمه
فصادفه في تلك الايام مرض شديد فارسله اسداده الي المارستان فاتفق يوم
من الايام دخل خواجه لميروا القنصر المذكور الي المارستان حتي يزور المرضي
كوايدهم الحميده فرعا علي ذلك اليسير وهو ملقي علي الفراش فجلس عند فراشه
وصار يعزيه ويسليه ويحثه علي الصبر علي تلك الشده وان عقباها فرج وعافيه من
هل كلام وما منه.

٢٩٫٥ اخيرًا ساله عن بلاده وعن ملته فاجابه بانه مغربي وبلدته طرابلس الغرب وانه ابن
قوم واهله اكابر في تلك البلاد. حينٍ خواجه لميروا المذكور رق قلبه عليه وامر
ريس المارستان بان يحمله في كرسي واخده الي منزله وامر خدامه بان يهيوا له فرشه
وغيروا ثيابه ويخدموه نظير خدمتهم له و في الحال ارسل احضر طبيب واوصاه فيه
بان يعالجه كا يجب ولا يخلي ناقصه شي من الادويه والمستقطرات المكلفه.

We brought our baggage down into the rowboat and went ashore, head-  5.27
ing for the house of the French consul in the city. His name was Lemaire, and
he had a splendid house. We arrived as he was having lunch. When he saw
my master, he leapt up to greet him most graciously and insisted that he join
him for lunch. My master demurred, and told him the story of everything that
had happened to us, from the moment we left Alexandria until our arrival
in Tripoli.

"We spent fifteen days without proper food," he said. "And for ten of those
days, we ate only dates and drank only brackish water."[77]

When the consul heard this, he immediately ordered his cook to boil four
fat chickens and prepare a broth, advising my master to have only chicken
broth for a few days, until our throats had relaxed and our intestines opened up
again. We spent eight days consuming only broth and Cypriot wine that had
been aged seven years, until our strength returned and our throats returned to
their former state.

We began to tour Tripoli, with no need to worry about our own safety,  5.28
since the consul was in the good graces of the bey, the ruler of the city and the
surrounding countryside. He was, in fact, like a brother to him. It seems that
during his youth, the bey had been taken prisoner in Malta. A French cavalier
bought him and took him to Marseille, where he began working as the cavalier's servant. At some point, he became severely ill, and his master sent him
to the hospital.

One day, the consul *khawājah* Lemaire went to the hospital to visit the inva-
lids, in keeping with the laudable custom of his people. As he passed by this
particular prisoner, who was lying in a bed, he stopped to sit with him and
chat. The consul comforted him, raising his spirits and encouraging him to be
steadfast in the face of his adversity, for recovery would surely come.

He asked him which country he was from, and who his people were. The  5.29
prisoner replied that he was a Maghrebi from Tripoli, that he was from a good
family, and that his relatives were among the country's notables. Lemaire felt
sorry for him, and ordered the director of the hospital to put the prisoner in
a chair and carry him to his house, where he had his own servants prepare a
bed and change the young man's clothes, telling them to serve him just as they
served their master. Lemaire sent for a doctor and engaged him to treat the
prisoner as he saw fit, without sparing a single medicine or distillate, no matter
the cost.

٣٠.٥ فاستقام هل رجل وهو مخدوم من الخدام والحكيم الي حين ما رجعت عافيته اليه وزال عنه ذلك المرض الشديد الذي كان معتريه . اخيراً نهض من الفراش وهو معافا كمثل ما كان. حينئذٍ شكر فضله واستأزن منه حتي يروح عند اسداده. اخيراً فؤاد خواجه ليميرو ان يكمل معه الجميل فاشتراه ونزله في مركب كان مسافر الي طرابلس الغرب واعطا للقبطان كروته وحق اكله واوصاه فيه قوي كثير . اخيراً ودعه وانصرف عنه والمركب سافر ووصل بالسلامه الي تلك المدينه .

٣١.٥ واستقام مدة سنين في خدامة البيك الذي كان موجود في تلك الايام وكان ذلك البيك قربه اليه لاجل حسن خدمته له واقامه في وظيفة عاليه وهي يكون مدبرا لتلك البلاد التي هي تحت حكمه فاستقام يدبرها باستقامه وحسن سياسه وكانت كل البلاد راضيه منه ويحبوه زود المحبة فاتفق بان البيك مرض مرض شديد وبعد كام يوم مات. حينئذٍ اهل الدوله والبلاد انتخبوه بكاً عليهم واعطوه الطاعه كالمالوف عوايدهم القديمه.

٣٢.٥ وفي ذلك الزمان فاتفق بان خواجه ليميرو المذكور انتخبوه قنصر علي طرابلس الغرب من غير انه يعرف بان ذاك اليسير الذي اشتراه من اسداده وارسله الي بلاده صار بيك وتولي الحكم فلما وصل المذكور ليميرو الي مدينة طربلس وبعد كام يوم راح حتي يقابل البيك كمعداد القناصر فلما دخل الي وراءه البيك وعرفه نهض من مكانه وعانقه وقبله واسترحب فيه واكرمه غاية الاكرام بقوله للحاضرين ارباب دولته بان هل رجل خلصني من اليسر ومن الموت ايضاً والذي بيكرمه يكون اكرمني ولما خرج من صرايته ارسل معه جميع الذين واقفين في بابه وخدمته وهذا زود اكرام له عن غير قناصر الذين مروا قبله وكان دايماً يسميه اخي لشده محبته فيه.

٣٣.٥ وهذا الذي سمعنا من ناس صادقين عن خبر هل بيك وهل قنصر والذي رايته الفقير من هل قنصر المبارك شي عجيب من حسن اخلاقه وتواضعه ومحبته للفقرا واليسره الموجودين في تلك المدينه وكان جنب باب بيته اوضه مخصصها لتوزيع الصدقه للفقرا والمساكين وكان مامر واحد من خدامه يكون دايماً واقف لتوزيع الخبز والبقصمات الذي لم يدعه ينقص ابداً.

The man remained at Lemaire's home, attended by servants and the doctor    5.30
until his health returned and the severe illness that afflicted him had abated.
Eventually, he rose from his bed in perfect health, thanked the consul, and
asked his permission to return to his owner. Lemaire, however, decided to see
his act of charity through to the end. So he bought him from his master and
put him on a ship bound for Tripoli. He paid the captain for his passage and
meals, and entrusted the man to his care. He bid him farewell and sent him off
to Tripoli, where he arrived safely.

The young man remained there for many years, serving the bey at the time.    5.31
Because of his excellent service, he became one of the bey's close advisors,
and was placed in a high-ranking position as governor of the lands under his
rule. He governed righteously, and the whole country rejoiced in his rule and
loved him dearly. Eventually, after a short illness, the bey died, whereupon the
nobles and the generals chose his servant to be their bey, pledging allegiance
to him in accordance with their ancient customs.

It was around that time that *khawājah* Lemaire happened to be appointed    5.32
consul of Tripoli. He had no idea that the prisoner he'd bought and sent home
had become a bey and assumed power. When Lemaire arrived in Tripoli, he
went to meet with the bey after a few days, in keeping with the customary
practice of consuls. When the bey recognized Lemaire, he rose from his seat,
embraced him, and kissed him, doing him the greatest possible honor.

"This man saved me from captivity and death," he said to all the nobles present. "Honor him as you honor me!"

When the consul left the palace, the bey had surrounded him with all the
members of his court and his servants. He heaped more honors on Lemaire
than he had on any previous consul, and always referred to him as "my brother,"
for he loved him deeply.

This is the story of the bey and the consul, which I heard from trustwor-    5.33
thy sources. And I myself can testify to the many wonderful attributes of this
blessed consul: his cordial manners, his modesty, and his love for the poor
and the prisoners of that city. Just inside the door of his house was a room set
aside for distributing alms to the poor and the wretched. He appointed one of
his servants to stand there at all times, handing out bread and biscuits, which
never ran out.

٣٤،٥ وكان ذو عباده عظيمه وكان كل ليله قبل المنام يجمع اولاده الثلاثة صبيين وبنت وجميع خدامه الي كنيسته ويدير وجهه اليهم الي حين ما يكمبوا وما يبقا احد. حينٍ يبدوا الصلوه وطلبة العذري وبعد انتها الصلوه كلّ منهم يمضي الي منامته وبعد الجميع يدخل هو ايضاً الي منامته وكذلك باكر يحضروا جميعهم القداس معه وكان يبذل جهده في مشترات اليسرا ويرسلهم الي بلادهم لان كان يجيله صدقات من بلاد المسيحيه لاجل مشترا اليسرا. المراد كل حياته يصرفها بالفضيله.

٣٥،٥ فاتفق يوم من الايام ونحن في طرابلس اجا خبر للبيك مع عربان تلك الاراضي بان مركب بندقي كبير نشب في ساحل بعيد عن طرابلس ثلاثة ايام في البر وبما ان البنادقه دايماً هن حرب مع المغاربه فارسل البيك خمسماية جندي وامرهم يمضوا يضبطوا المركب وما فيه من المال ويسوقوا كل الاوادم الموجوده فيه الي طرابلس لكي يكونوا يساره فلما ارسلهم وبعده دعي اخوه القنصر ليمروا الي عنده واستمته بانه يرسل مركب من المراكب الموجودين في الاسكله حتي يوسق الرزق الموجود في المركب والطواب وباقيت الجباخانه الموجوده في ذلك المركب فاجابه القنصر سمعاً وطاعه.

٣٦،٥ وفي الحال مضي من عند البيك وارسل دعي الي عنده واحد من تلك القباطين المرسيه مراكبهم في الاسكله[١] وامره بانه يروح لذلك الساحل ويوسق جميع الموجود فيه من مال وطواب واوادم ويجيبهم الي اسكلت طرابلس في الظاهر ولكن في الباطن الله بيعلم كيف وجهه فسافر المركب وقصد تلك الاراضي وقبل وصوله كان وصل عسكر البيك لكن كانوا اهل المركب فرغوا جميع ما فيه ما عدا العنبر لان العنبر كان ملان من القمح الذي كانوا وسقوه من الاضات فلما كمل وسقه قصدوا بلاد البندقيه.

٣٧،٥ ولما كانوا مسافرين في البحر ندي المركب ودخل الماء فيه الي انه تقل واشرف المركب علي الغرق. حينٍ القبطان قصد البر وكان المركب قريب الي بر المغاربه وخوفاً ليلا يغرق المركب ويغرقوا هن ايضاً فترك المركب ينشب في الرمل واخرجوا ما فيه للبر

---

١ الأصل: الاسكل.

He was very pious. Each night, before going to sleep, he would gather in his    5.34
chapel his three children—two boys and a girl—and all his servants. He would
turn to face them as we waited for everyone to arrive. They would then say
their prayers and the Litany of the Virgin. After all the prayers were complete,
each person would go to his bed, and the consul would follow them to his own
bed. Similarly, all would attend mass with him early in the morning.

The consul made a great effort to buy back prisoners and send them home
to their countries, using the alms he received from Christian countries for this
purpose. In short, he devoted his whole life to virtuous acts.

One day, while we were in Tripoli, the bey received news from the Bed-    5.35
ouins that a large Venetian ship had run aground on the shore, three days'
journey from Tripoli by land. The Venetians were always at war with the
Maghrebis, so the bey sent five hundred soldiers on the march to seize the
ship and all its property, and to bring the passengers to Tripoli to be imprisoned. He summoned his "brother," the consul Lemaire, and asked him to
send a vessel from the harbor to load up the goods carried by the Venetian
ship, along with the cannons and the munitions. The consul acceded immediately to his request.

He left the bey and sent for a captain whose ship was moored in the harbor,    5.36
ordering him to sail to that spot and load up everything on board the Venetian
ship—money, cannons, and people—and bring it all back to Tripoli harbor.
This, at least, was the apparent nature of the consul's order; God only knows
what he secretly told him to do! The ship sailed, headed for the Maghreb, and
the bey's soldiers arrived first. In the meantime, however, those on the Venetian ship had emptied the vessel of all that was on board, except for the contents of the hold. It was full of wheat, which they'd loaded in the Province of
the Islands[78] before sailing for Venice.

While they were on their way, however, the ship began to take on water.    5.37
It grew so heavy that it began listing dangerously, so the captain made for land.
They happened to be near the North African coast. Afraid the ship would sink,
the captain ran it aground on the sand. They unloaded everything on board
except for the wheat and left the ship stricken at sea. Meanwhile, the bey's

وتركوا المركب غرقان في البحر والقمح الذي فيه ايضاً وفي ذلك الوقت وصل عسكر البيك صحبة اغا من اغاوات البيك فرادوا يظبطوهم ويمسكوهم مسك اليد فما سلموا عسكر المركب وفي الحال داروا عليهم الطواب والتفنك فهزموهم وفروا هاربين من امام المدافع.

٣٨،٥ الى حين ما وصل المركب المرسل من قنصر طرابلس فلما رسي وخرج القبطان للبر والتقى مع عسكر المركب المذكور وراء بانهم ما يريدوا يسلموا انفسهم حينذٍ تشاور قبطان الفرنساوي مع قبطان مركب البندقي وقال لهم انا مرسل من قبل قنصر الفرنساويه الذي هو وقتيدٍ في مدينة طرابلس وامرني بان اوسق جميع ما في مركبكم من مال واوادم وامضي فيهم الي طرابلس حسب امر البيك والقنصر . حينذٍ قالوا له نحن ما منسلم انفسنا لليسر اخير لنا باننا نموت في هذا البر من ان نسلم انفسنا.

٣٩،٥ فلما راء القبطان بان عسكر البيك ما له قدره عليهم ولا هو ايضاً لان عسكر المركب مايتين جندي ما عدا البحريه والركيه حينذٍ قلهم طاعوني وانا بنجيكم من هولاي القوم وبسافر فيكم الي البندقيه بشرط ان تعطوني خطوط اياديكم بان اذا وصلنا للبندقيه بالسلامه تحموني من الفرنساويه ليلا يرسلوا ياخدوني وينتقموا مني وتانياً تقيموا في معيشتي الي الممات فاجابوه علي الفور علي كلامه وكتبوا له وسيقه بالذي طلبه منهم وكان موجود في ذلك المركب الذي هو مركب البكليك ناس امائل ومنهم كواليريه اعني صباهيه وقباطين عسكر وما يشبه ذلك من المتقدمين للدوله.

٤٠،٥ فلما تم الامر بينهم وفي ذلك الوقت ذهب القبطان المرسل المذكور الي عند قايد ذلك العسكر المرسل من عند البيك وطيب خاطرهم قايلاً لهم بان اهل المركب والعسكر جميعهم صاروا طايعين لان ما لهم مهرب من اياديكم. حينذٍ رجع ذلك الاغا وجميع الجنود الذين اتوا معه ولما وصلوا فامر ذلك الاغا بان يوسقوا جميع الذي كان موجود في المركب البندقي فلما كملوا الوسق امر للقبطان بانه ينزل في مركبه جميع الاوادم الذين كانوا دخل ذلك المركب ما عدا المايتين جندي الذين كانوا في المركب ففعل القبطان كما امره ذلك الاغا.

soldiers arrived, led by of one of his commanders. They tried to seize the Venetians, but the ship's guards wouldn't surrender. Instead, they turned their cannons and rifles on the bey's men, putting them to flight.

Soon after, the ship sent by the consul of Tripoli arrived. Its captain dropped anchor and went ashore to meet with the soldiers from the Venetian ship. It soon became clear to him that they weren't willing to surrender.

"I've been sent on behalf of the French consul in Tripoli," he told the captain of the Venetian ship. "I have orders from the bey and the consul to transfer all the goods and people on your ship to my own, and to bring you to Tripoli."

"We won't be taken prisoner," they replied. "We'd rather die here than surrender."

The captain recognized that neither he nor the bey's soldiers had enough men to subdue them, as the Venetian ship had two hundred soldiers in addition to its sailors and passengers.

"If you do what I say, I can save you from these people," the captain urged. "I'll take you back to Venice, on the following conditions. You must swear to me, in writing, that if we reach Venice safely, you'll protect me from the French. I don't want them coming after me to take revenge. Also, you'll have to provide for my livelihood until I die."

They immediately agreed and wrote out a contract, guaranteeing his demands. You see, the ship was a vessel of the Venetian Republic, and there were important people on board, including some cavaliers, by which I mean spahis, along with some army officers and other similar high-ranking officials.[79]

After settling matters with the Venetians, the captain went to find the commander of the bey's soldiers, and reassured him that the ship's passengers and soldiers had surrendered, as they had no means of escape. The commander and his soldiers returned to the scene, and the commander ordered them to load the Venetian ship's goods onto the bey's ship. When all was complete, he told the captain to transfer the Venetian passengers to his ship, with the exception of the two hundred soldiers. The captain obeyed.

5.38

5.39

5.40

٤١،٥ اخيرًا امر الي الخمسماية جندي الذين كانوا معه بانهم يوثقوا تلك المايتين جندي الذين كانوا في المركب ويسوقوهم امامهم الي مدينة طرابلس ويعرضوهم علي حضرة البيك وبعدما اطلقهم فاد انه ينزل في المركب الفرنساوي المذكور فمنعه القبطان بقوله له ادعني اولًا اروح الي المركب وانزل الماخودين معنا للعنبر لاني بخاف ليلا يتمردوا[1] علينا في الدرب. اخيرًا برسل القايق ياخدك مع جملة خدامك لاني بريد اهيي لك مكان لايق بشانك فرضي ذلك الاغا وانطلق القبطان الي مركبه وكان هذا بحكمه ليلا يصير لوم من البيك علي القنصر باخد الاغا وجماعته معه لليسر.

٤٢،٥ فلما وصل القبطان الي المركب في الحال امرالبحريه بانهم يسحبوا المراسي من البحر وبعده يسحبوا مرسيت البرانيه فلما وصل المركب الي فوق تلك المرسيه سحبوها وفتحوا قلوعهم وسافروا فلما راء الاغا المذكور بان المركب سافر فاق حينًدٍ علي الملعوب فالتزم ذلك الوقت بانه يلحق جماعته ويسافر معهم الي طرابلس واما ذلك المركب الفرنساوي المذكور توجه الي البندقيه صحبة تلك الجماعه المذكورين ونجاهم من اليسر.

٤٣،٥ وبعد كام يوم وصل الاغا الي طرابلس صحبة تلك العسكر والمايتين جندي البنادقه الذي استيسرهم وصار ذلك النهار مفترج عظيم في دخولهم الي المدينه وهن موثوقين بالحبال واعرضوهم علي حضرة البيك فلما حضروا امامه[2] فامر في حبسهم وارسل فدعي القنصر الي عنده واحكي له بما سمعه من ذلك الاغا المرسول من قبله وكيف ان القبطان ابقاه في البر وسافر والي الان ما وصل الي عندنا العله سافر فيهم الي بلادهم وخلصهم لكن يكون عندك محقق انكان الامر تم هكذا لاقتل هل مايتين جندي علي اخرهم ولو ما المحبة التي بينا لكنت ضبطت المراكب الفرنساويه الذين في الاسكله الي حين ما يرتد لي ذلك المركب.

٤٤،٥ فلما سمع القنصر من البيك ذلك الكلام فاروي علي حاله بانه قوي اغتاض من هذا الفعل انكان هو صحيح وصار ياخد خاطر البيك ويهدي غضبه واوعده في رجوع المركب اليه وانه يكتب الي سلطان فرنسا وانه يرسل من قبله ايجي فيلزمهم في

---

The commander ordered his five hundred soldiers to shackle the two hundred, and march them to Tripoli to be paraded before the bey. After sending them off, the commander tried to board the French ship but the captain stopped him.    5.41

"Let me go and put the passengers in the hold first, as I'm worried that they'll raise a mutiny against us while we're at sea," the captain said. "Once I've prepared a decent room for you, I'll send the dinghy back for you and your servants."

The commander agreed, and the captain hurried off to his ship. This was a wise move on the captain's part; he did it so the bey wouldn't blame the consul for the capture of the commander and his coterie.

When the captain arrived at the ship, he quickly ordered the sailors to    5.42
weigh anchor and pull the ship to the outer mooring. Finally, they were able to unfurl their sails and head out to sea. As he watched the ship sail away, the commander suddenly realized he'd been tricked! He was forced to chase after his soldiers and make the journey with them back to Tripoli. As for the French ship, it sailed for Venice carrying all of those passengers, saving them from captivity.

After a few days, the commander arrived in Tripoli with the two hundred    5.43
Venetian prisoners. They made quite a spectacle as they entered the city, all bound in ropes. They were paraded before His Excellency the bey, who had them imprisoned. He then sent for the consul and told him what he'd heard from his commander, about how the captain had left him behind and sailed off.

"He still hasn't come back to Tripoli," the bey said to the consul. "Do you think he took them back to their country? Believe you me, if that's what happened, I'll kill every last one of these two hundred soldiers! And if it weren't for my friendship with you, I'd sequester every French ship in my harbor until my own ship was returned to me!"

At this, the consul made a show of insisting that he too would be furious if    5.44
that were the case, and set about trying to placate the bey. He promised that the ship would return, adding that he'd write to the king of France asking him to dispatch some envoys who'd be responsible for bringing the ship back to Tripoli. The consul also beseeched the bey, for the sake of their own friendship, to free the prisoners without harming them, for they'd done nothing

رجوع المركب انكان هل امر صحيح . اخيرًا توسل اليه بالمحبة التي بينهم بانه يطلق المسجونين ولا ياسي عليهم لان ما لهم دنب الدنب لاوليك الذين اغتصبوا القبطان في الهرب وهذا كان قلة افراز من ذلك الاغا الذي سمح بان يدخل جميع تلك الاوادم للمركب حتي قويوا علي القبطان وجماعته واستملكوا المركب .

٤٥،٥ فلما سمع البيك هل كلام من القنصر قله صدقت يا اخي كل الدنب للاغا وانا سوف بنتقم منه وفي الحال امر بان يطلقوا تلك المايتين جندي المسجونين اكرامًا لخاطر اخي اعني القنصر ويحضروهم امامي فلما احضروهم قلهم انا عفيت عنكم لاجل خاطر اخي القنصر قبلوا اياديه وامضوا بسلام وبعد ما انتهى الامر نهض القنصر وشكر فضل البيك ومضي الي بيته والفقير كت حاضر هل دعوه من اولها .

٤٦،٥ واحكوا لنا ايضًا خبرًا عن محبة هل بيك للقنصر المذكور هو انه اتفق لما كانوا مراكب بكليك طرابلس الغرب دايرين في البحر يقرسنوا كوايدهم فصدفوا في مسيرهم مركب بكليك جنوازي فتبعوه ودايقوه . اخيرًا قدروا عليه واسروه وجاوا به الي طرابلس الغرب وبعدما رسوا المراكب في المينا حيندٍ اخبروا البيك في احيدة المركب المذكور .

٤٧،٥ فامر البيك بان يحضروا تلك الرجال الموجودين في المركب امامه فلما اتوا بهم اعني بالقبطان والجنود والبحريه وباقيت الركيبه وكانوا ينوف عن مايتين فاتقرس البيك فيهم فراء بينهم غلام حديث السن حسن الصوره بهي المنضر لايح عليه امارات النعمه والاحتشام بثياب فاخره وكان هل غلام ابن امير من امرات روميه ارسله والده حتي يزور عمته في بلاد مسينا ويتنزه في مسيره الي عندها فمال قلب البيك اليه ووقعت محبته في احشاه بهذا المقدار الي ان قربه اليه وانسه وامر الترجمان بان يسكن خوفه ورعبه بقوله له لا تخف لان حضرة البيك حبك ويريد يجعلك ابنه وحبيب قلبه .

٤٨،٥ ولكن الغلام ما كان يتسلا بل يبكي فلما راء البيك بان الغلام ما بيتسلا ويزيد البكاء فما قدر يراه بتلك الحالة المحزنه فارسله الي عند حرمه حتي يانسوه ويسلوه وبعده

wrong: "The ones to blame are the ones who kidnapped the captain!" he said. "And it was the commander who showed a lapse in judgment by letting all those people board the ship. They must have overpowered the captain and crew, and taken control of the ship."

"You're right, brother," the bey agreed. "It's all the commander's fault. I'll 5.45 take my revenge on him instead!" And he ordered that the two hundred soldiers be freed.

"Set the prisoners free, as a favor to my brother the consul, and bring them before me!" he commanded.

When they were brought before the bey, he declared, "I've pardoned you for the sake of my brother the consul." They kissed his hands and left in peace. The consul rose, thanked the bey, and returned home. As it happens, I was present at the time and witnessed this whole scene from start to finish.

Here's another story we heard about the bey's affection for the consul. 5.46 It so happened that when the ships of the principality of Tripoli were plying the seas and marauding in their usual way, they came upon a ship belonging to the principality of Genoa. They followed the ship, harassing it, and eventually managed to lay hold of it and its crew. They brought it back to Tripoli, and, after anchoring in the harbor, informed the bey about the ship they'd captured.

The bey ordered them to parade before him the men who'd been aboard. 5.47 There were more than two hundred in all, including the captain, his guards, the sailors, and the passengers. Studying the prisoners, the bey saw that there was a young boy among them. He was radiantly beautiful, and wore fine clothes that were a testament to his wealth and good breeding. The boy was the son of a prince of Rome, and his father had sent him to visit his aunt in the town of Messina, by way of a pleasure cruise.

The bey was drawn to him, and felt such strong feelings of affection welling up deep within that he called him over to put him at ease, and ordered his dragoman to calm the frightened boy.

"Tell him this," the bey said to the dragoman. "'His Excellency the Bey has taken a liking to you and would like to make you his beloved son.'"

The boy wasn't put at ease at all, and instead began to cry. As his crying 5.48 grew louder, the bey realized that the child was inconsolable, so he sent him to the harem, where the women could try to soothe and distract him. He selected

انتخب اتنين من تلك اليسره حديثي السن وامرهم في خدمة ذلك الغلام حتي يتونس معهم وصرف باقي الرجال الي مكان اليسرا واما الغلام يوماً بعد يوم كان ايستانس وصار يخرج من الحرم ويتمثل امام البيك بكل احتشام وادب وكانت تزيد محبة الغلام في قلب البيك وكثير اوقات يضمه الي صدره ويقبله وجميع اهل بلاطه كانوا يكرموا هل غلام لاجل خاطر البيك.

٤٩.٥ فمضي عليه مده من الزمان وهو مكرم من الجميع الي ان وصل مركب فرنساوي الي الاسكله وفي حال وصوله خرج القبطان من المركب واتي الي عند القنصر واعطاه مكتوب مرسل من دوك من دوكوات فرنسا وداكر له فيه بان الغلام الذي وقع في اليسر عندكم في مدينة طرابلس الذي يسما فلان ارسل والده الينا رساله وداكر لنا بان نرسل نحثك بان تبدل جهدك وتستفك ابنه من اليسر باي ثمن كان وترسله الي طرفنا وواصلك صحبة القبطان القادم اليكم سندوقين من التحف المتمنات لعلهم ما يطلقوه بالدراهم تكون تقدم هل تحف الي بيك المتسلطن في تلك المدينه وانكان بيلزم تعطي فوق هل تحف دراهم فاعطي ولا تتوقف وانت مفوض الامر في هل خدمه. المراد لا يكون جوابك لنا الا بارسال الغلام الي طرفنا وباقي والسلام.

٥٠.٥ فلما قراء القنصر ذلك المكتوب وقع في حيره عظيمه بعلمه محبة البيك الي ذلك الغلام وانه من المممتنع انه يطلقه. اخيراً مضي الي عند البيك بجاري عادته بطلب وبغير طلب فلما امتثل امامه فكلفه للجلوس وبعده صار يتسامر معه كالوف عادتهم فاعرض القنصر علي البيك بان كان يعطيه قرار انه يقبل رجاه والا ما بيترجاه فالبيك ما ضن بان القنصر بده يترجا في الغلام فاجابه علي الفور قول يا اخي حاشاي بان ارد رجاك ولو مهما طلبت فاتدق القنصر عن طلبه فعاد عليه البيك قول يا اخي مهما تريد اما تعلم بان رجاك عندي ما بيرتد ولو كان علي ذاتي. حينئذٍ القنصر اعلم البيك بالمكتوب الذي وصله من ذلك الدوك.

٥١.٥ وانه ترجاني حتي اترجاك وارسل هل غلام الي عند والده ووالدته وانهم ارسلوا الي حضرتك هدايا بتليق بشانك وارسل في الحال واحضر الهدايا امامه فما التفت

two other young prisoners and ordered them to serve the boy and keep him company, and sent the rest of the men off to prison.

With each passing day, the boy felt increasingly at ease. He began to come out of the harem and appear before the bey, comporting himself most courteously. The bey's love for him grew more intense, and he would often hug him to his chest and kiss him. Out of regard for the bey, all the members of his court showed the boy every possible favor.

Time passed, and the boy continued to be held in high esteem. One day, a 5.49 French ship arrived in the harbor. The captain went to see Lemaire, the consul. He gave him a letter from one of the dukes of France.

"This concerns the boy taken captive in Tripoli—whose name is such and such," the letter read. "The boy's father has written to us, begging us to urge you to spare no effort to liberate his son from captivity, whatever the price may be, and to send him to us. We've sent you two trunks full of expensive gifts in the company of this ship captain, because money alone may not be enough to set the boy free. Present these gifts to the bey who rules over the city. If it's necessary to offer him money on top of the gifts, don't hesitate; you are so authorized. In other words, make sure the boy returns. We look forward to a favorable reply, and, indeed, will accept no other. Salutations."

When the consul finished reading the letter, he felt utterly at a loss. He 5.50 knew of the bey's great love for the boy, and that he'd never let him go. In any event, the consul went to see the bey, as was his usual custom, whether or not he had a favor to ask. He presented himself, and the bey invited him to sit down. They began to chat amiably in their regular way, and the consul asked the bey if he would promise to grant a certain request. If not, the consul said, he wouldn't make the request at all. The bey couldn't imagine that the consul would ask for the boy, so he responded immediately.

"Speak, brother! Far be it from me to deny your request, no matter what it is."

The consul hesitated, and the bey repeated his exhortation.

"Brother, do speak up! Don't you know that your requests will never be denied, even if they're at my own expense?" the bey said, so the consul told him about the letter he had received from the duke.

"He has asked me to send the boy back to his parents," the consul explained. 5.51 "They've sent Your Excellency gifts worthy of your station," he said, as he called for the gifts and had them brought before the bey.

البيك الي تلك الهدايا وتذاهر الغيض والاسف علي وجهه وما عاد كلم القنصر ولا بكلمه واحده انما ترك القنصر وحده ودخل الي حرمه بمفرده لان هل هل امر صعب عليه من جهتين جهت الواحده انه اعطا قرار بانه لا يرد رجاه والثانيه غتت عليه مفارقت ذلك الغلام فلما راء القنصر بان رجاه بان ما سلك وامله خاب فمضي الي بيته وهو في غاية الانحصار والحزن واما البيك بقي باله عند محبه القنصر ليلا يكون انحصر منه لانه ما قبل رجاه.

٥٢،٥

فتاني الايام ارسل فدعاه الي عنده لياخد بخاطره فلما اتي الرسول يدعي القنصر الي عند البيك فافتكر بانه يخلص ذلك الغلام بحيله وهي ان كان للقنصر ولد زغير يسما نكولا وكان البيك يحبه بمحبة والديه وكل مره يمضي الي عند البيك فكان البيك يضمه الي صدره ويقبله ويوهبه مهما طلب منه ولا يرد طلبته وهذا الولد كان فجي فايق لقيش في الغايه فعلمه والده القنصر بان لما نزيد نرجع من عند البيك فامسك انت الغلام المذكور واتقربط فيه ولا ترخيه واذا رادوا ياخدوه من يدك فابكي واتوسل الي البيك بانه يبقيه معك وتتنزهوا جمله ذلك اليوم الي المساء ثم جرسه وقله اياك ترخيه ولو انا امرتك برخيه لا ترخيه.

٥٣،٥

فبعد ما جرسه وعلمه كيف يعمل فمضوا الي عند البيك فلما امتثل القنصر امام البيك فاسترحب فيه واخد بخاطره قايلًا له بان بالي بقي عندك ليلا تكون انحصرت مني لاني ما سلكت رجاك ولو اعرف بانك بتريد تترجاني الغلام لما اعطيتك هذا القرار ولكن الشي صار لا يحصل منك مواخده وكان البيك انحل برمه لما شاهد تلك الهدايا التي جابها له القنصر من طرف والد ذلك الغلام ووالدته الحزينه. اخيرًا استقام القنصر والبيك يتصامروا كعادتهم بعدما شربوا المشروب والقهوه فمر عليهم ساعه من الزمان وابن القنصر المذكور كان يلعب مع ذلك الغلام كعادة الاولاد. اخيرًا نهض القنصر واستازن من البيك حتي يمضي الي بيته.

٥٤،٥

حينٍ نيكولا المذكور مسك يد ذلك الغلام وراد ياخده معه فمنعوه خدام البيك بالملق بانه يرخي يد الغلام فما امكن انه يرخي يد ذلك الغلام بل صار يبكي ويتوسل الي

١٣٤    134

But the bey didn't even glance at them. His face was full of anger and sorrow. He didn't say another word to the consul and stormed off to his harem. He was furious, as this affair had put him in a real predicament. On the one hand, he'd promised not to refuse the consul's request. On the other, the prospect of losing the boy filled him with grief.

Meanwhile, the consul realized that his plea had failed to hit the mark. With his hopes dashed, he returned to his house, despondent. But the bey's thoughts continued to dwell on the consul. He loved him dearly and didn't want to put him in dire straits because the request hadn't been granted.

The next day, the bey sent for the consul so they could patch things up. 5.52 When the messenger came by with the summons, the consul suddenly thought of a trick to save the boy. It went like this. The consul had a young son named Nicholas, and the bey loved him as dearly as his parents did. Whenever he accompanied his father on his visits, the bey would hug and kiss him, and grant him whatever he asked for, never denying him any request.

Now, this Nicholas was a bright, precocious, chatty child, and his father said to him, "When we're about to leave the bey's house, grab hold of the boy and cling to him. Don't let go! If they try to take him away from you, cry and beg the bey to let him stay with you, so that you can spend the rest of the day playing together." And the consul added, "Whatever you do, don't let go of that boy, even if I tell you to!"

Having given his instructions, the consul took his son and went to see the 5.53 bey, who welcomed the consul as soon as he arrived.

"I've been so worried," the bey said soothingly. "I hope I haven't put you in a difficult spot by not accepting your request. If only I'd known that you were going to ask me for the boy, I'd never have made that vow! Ah well, what's done is done. I hope you won't hold it against me."

When the bey saw the gifts the consul had brought him from the boy's father and his poor mother, his own anger subsided, and he and the consul sat chatting in their usual way, having some drinks and coffee. An hour or so passed, while the consul's son played with the young boy, as children do. Finally, the consul rose and asked the bey's permission to take his leave and go home.

At that, Nicholas grasped the boy's hand and began pulling him along. The 5.54 bey's servants tried to stop him, asking him gently to let go of the boy's hand.

البيك بانهم يتركوه ياخد الغلام معه كما كان علمه ابوه اما البيك ما اهتدي علي الحيله فصار يملق الولد نيكولا وارسل جاب له فرسه زغيره حتي يركبها ويمضي مع والده فما كان يقبل الا بالغلام انه يروح معه. حينذٍ انتهره والده القنصر بانه يرخيه فزاد في البكاء والتوسل الي البيك فلما راء البيك عزم الولد فما راد يغيظه لاجل خاطر والده ومحبته فيه فسمحله بانه ياخده ويبقيه عنده الي وقت ما يريد. حينذٍ فرح نيكولا وركد قبل يد البيك والبيك ضمه الي صدره وقلبه واطلقه واذن للغلام بانه يروح معه كمن اوهبه هو فمضوا الغلامين معاً الي بيت القنصر فرحانين ومبتهجين.

٥٥،٥ واستقام ذلك الغلام في بيت القنصر كم يوم والبيك ما فتش عليه كانه سليه فلما راء القنصر بان البيك ما عاد سال عنه فصار عنده معلوم بان البيك اوهبه الي ابنه نيكولا في الحال ارسل احضر قبطان ذلك المركب الذي اتي بالهدايا وامره بانه يكون علي هيبة السفر.

٥٦،٥ ولما كان نصف الليل ارسل الغلام الي المركب وفي حال وصوله سافر المركب والغلام معه وبعد مده من الزمان وصل مكاتيب من الدوك ومن الامير ابو الغلام وشاكرين فضله وفضل ابنه نيكولا الذي بسببه خلص ابنه من اليسر وارسل الامير ابو الغلام دخل تلك المكاتب وسيقه مثل جمه وذاكر في تلك الوثيقه باني اوهبت الي نيكولا ابن قنصر ليميروا الفرنساوي من املاكي وقفاً مابداً الذي مدخوله في كل سنه الف غرش ولا احد يمانعه لا هو ولا لدريته مابداً وهذا خط يدي بيشهد علي قولي والسلام وصار له وكيل في روميه يرسل له في كل سنه الف غرس الي يومنا هذا.

٥٧،٥ وهذه حكاية محبة البيك لذلك القنصر المذكور والذي احكالي هل خبر هو كان في ذلك الزمان ترجمان القنصر وكان واقف علي جليته وهو صادق في قوله لاني سمعته من غيره كما هو مذكور.

٥٨،٥ واستقمنا في بيت القنصر في غاية البسط والانشراح الي يوم من الايام وكان حاكم عيد عند اليسوعيه القاطنين في هذه المدينه فودت اروح احضر القداس عندهم

But he wouldn't, and instead began to cry and plead with the bey to let him take the boy home, just as his father had taught him.

Oblivious to the trick that was being played on him, the bey tried to distract Nicholas by sending for a pony that he could ride alongside his father. But Nicholas refused, insisting that the boy come with them.

"Let go of his hand!" the consul chided his son, who only cried more and kept on pleading. Seeing how determined Nicholas was, the bey decided not to upset him any further, if only for his father's sake and his love for him. So he permitted them to take the boy along and keep him at their house for as long as Nicholas wanted. Delighted, Nicholas ran to kiss the bey's hand, and the bey hugged the boy to his chest and kissed him. Then he let him go and gave permission to the boy to accompany Nicholas, as if he'd been the one to offer in the first place. The two boys happily left together.

The young boy remained at the consul's house for a few days, and the bey 5.55 didn't come looking for him. It was as though he'd reconciled himself to losing him. Concluding that the bey had given the boy to his son Nicholas, the consul sent for the captain who had brought the gifts, and ordered him to make ready to sail.

In the middle of the night, he sent the boy to the ship, which set off as soon 5.56 as he was aboard. Some time later, letters arrived from the duke and the boy's father, the prince. They thanked the consul as well as his son Nicholas, who had facilitated the boy's escape. The prince had included among the letters a document that read as follows:

"I hereby bestow upon Nicholas, son of the French consul Lemaire, one of my own properties, whose income is one thousand piasters per year, which no one may deny him or his offspring, in perpetuity. May this signature testify to my statement."

So Nicholas would receive one thousand piasters from an agent in Rome each year, a practice that continues to this very day.

That's the story of the bey's affection for the French consul. I heard it from 5.57 the man who served as the consul's dragoman at the time, and who knew him intimately. I know that his account was faithful, as I heard the same story from others.

We remained at the consul's home in the utmost comfort and ease. One 5.58 day, when the Jesuits living in Tripoli were celebrating one of their holidays,

لاجل الغفران فلبست حوايجي المكلفه التي كنت ارسلت جبتهم من حلب. حينةٍ
قلي عقلي البس الشاش والقاووق الذي هو زي بلادنا فلما راني القنصر بهل ملبس
انبسط مني كان عجبه ملبسي.

اخيرًا مضية الي دير اليسوعيه وحضرت القدس وبعده خرجت من الدير
وتوجهت الي بيت القنصر ولماكنت في الطريق صادفوني اربعة انجكاريه فلما راوني
وقفوا يفرزوني وصاروا يهزوا روسهم ويشتموني بلغتهم ويهمزوا عليّ كانهم بيريدوا
قتلي فارتعبت منهم ليلا يفتكوا بي فما رايت الا انفرد واحد منهم وغار عليّ كانه
قاتلني وخطف الشاش من علي راسي ومضي مع رفقاه فبقيت انا في القرعه مرعوب
وفزعان ومضيع حواسي ورشدي فلما رايتهم بعدوا عني حينةٍ وعيت علي حالي
وصرت امشي واطلع ورايي ليلا يرجعوا الي فوصلت الي بيت القنصر وانا في هل
حاله مكشوف الراس ومضيع الحواس.

فكان في ذلك الوقت واقف في الباب نيكولا ابن القنصر واخته مركاريتا فلما
راوني في هل حاله فاسرعوا واخبروا ابيهم القنصر فلما سمع القنصر ومعلمي هل خبر
عني فنزلوا الاثنين الي عندي فلما راوني في هل حاله بهت القنصر وصار يسالني
ماذا جري لي ومن هو الذي اخد شاشي فاحكيت الي حضرة القنصر بالذي صار
بالتمام فلما سمع القنصر مني هذا الكلام احتد بالغضب وامر في الحال بان يحضروا
الترجمان امامه فلما حضر الترجمان فامره القنصر بانه يفتش ويري من هو الذي اخد
هل شاش والقاووق من علي راس ضيفنا ويجيبهم في الحال منه ولا يعمل اهمال
فخرج الترجمان من امام القنصر وارسل واحد دعاني وسالني عن المكان الذي شلحوني
فيه فقلته هو قريب الزقاق الذي بجانب دير اليسوعيه.

فتركني ومضي وبعد ساعه دعاني ايضًا لعنده وقلي ليش لبست الشاش والقاووق
لان في هل بلاد ما بيقدر احد يلبس شاش وقاووق غير الباشه المرسل من اسطنبول
من قبل الملك بصفة الجي وما عداه ما احد بيقدر يلف شاش وقاووق والان الذين

I decided to attend their mass to obtain some indulgences. I put on the fine clothes that I'd sent for from Aleppo, and something told me to put on my turban and felt cap, my native dress. The consul was very happy to see me dressed in this way, as my outfit delighted him.

I set off for the Jesuit monastery and attended the mass. On my way back to the consul's house, I encountered four janissaries. When they spotted me, they stopped short, pausing to take a good look. Shaking their heads, they began insulting me in their language, and growled as if they were going to kill me. I was terrified! Suddenly, one of them lunged forward, as though he were about to attack, snatched the turban from my head, and went off with his friends. I stood there, bareheaded and senseless with fright! Once they'd gone off a little way, I collected myself and started walking in the other direction, looking behind me to make sure that they weren't coming back. I arrived at the consul's house in that sorry state, my head bare and my wits scattered.

Nicholas, the consul's son, was standing at the door with his sister, Margarita. When they saw me in that condition, they ran off to tell their father. He and my master came down to see me as soon as they got word. The consul was astonished and demanded to know what had happened. Who had taken my turban? I told him the story from start to finish. The consul was furious and immediately summoned the dragoman.

"Go find the people who snatched the turban and cap off the head of our guest," he ordered the dragoman when he appeared. "And bring them here at once!"

The dragoman set out. Soon after, he sent someone to ask me where I'd been robbed.

"Near the alleyway by the Jesuit monastery."

He left, and a short while later called for me again.

"May I ask why you were wearing a turban and cap?" he inquired. "No one is allowed to wear such things in this country—no one, that is, except the pasha sent from Istanbul to serve as the sultan's ambassador. Yes, only the pasha may wear a turban and cap, and the men who took yours won't return them. Now, I worry that this is going to cause some trouble, and it'll have been your fault. If the consul asks you about the turban, just tell him that it was returned.

5.59

5.60

5.61

اخذوا شاشك ما يمكن انهم يردوه وبخاف ليلا يصدر من هل امرفته وتكون انت سببها. المراد ان سالك القنصرعن الشاش قله وصلني حتي نطفي هذا الشر لان جنود هل بلاد صعبين لانهم ارطاوات يحموا بعضهم البعض وما بيهابو البيك اذا تصدروا للشر .

٦٧،٥  فلما سمعت هل كلام فاتوضيت بالحليب واوعدته باني بقول للقنصر بان وصلني شاشي والقاووق وان امرني حتي البسهم باستعفي منه بقولي له بان في هل بلاد محرج علي لبس الشاش والقاووق ولاجل هل امر بطلب بان من فضلك ان تعفيني من لبسهم ليلا يصدر لي ضرر فاتققت مع الترجمان في هل كلام واستقمت لابس قبقي الي حين ما نزل القنصر للغدا فلما راني سالني انكان جابوا لي الشاش فاجبته نم وصلني فقلي لماذا ما لبسته فاجبته كما صار الكلام مع الترجمان فقال لي روح البسه ولا تخف ما احد بيقدر ياسيك وانت في محلي فقلي هل كلام يتغدا صحبة معلي فلما استعوقني فارسل احد الخدام ودعاني امامه وهو علي المايده فقلي ما بالك ما لبست الشاش فاجبته بلبسه نهار غد فقلي بريد انك تلبسه في هذا الوقت فقلي ايضاً معلي امتثل لقول القنصر باني اروح البسه .

٦٣،٥  نخرت في امري كيف اعمل ان قلته ما وصلني وخفت ليلا يصدر فته بسببي وان قلت وصلني بيقلي لماذا ما بتلبسه فالتزمت اقول الي معلي سرا بانه ما وصلني والقنصر بينتضرمني الجواب فلما راء معلي بان القنصر بيريد يعرف انكان وصلني ام لا فالتزم يحكي له صورة الواقعه فلما سمع القنصر بان الترجمان ما جاب الشاش فارسل احضر الترجمان وهذا الترجمان كان اصله يسير واسلم لجابه القنصرالي عنده لاجل ان يرده الي الايمان فلما حضر الترجمان امامه انتهره وشتمه. اخيراً امره بان يروح الي عند البيك ويقله من طرفي بان يجيب هل جندي ويضربه مايتين كرباج وياخد منه الشاش ويرسلي اياه في الحال.

٦٤،٥  فخرج الترجمان من امامه وهو حيران كيف يعمل ان راح الي عند البيك وبمعرفته في البيك ما بيرد كلام اخوه القنصر يحرض الجندي وبضربه واذا ضربه

That way, we'll nip this in the bud. The soldiers here are a tough lot, you know. They're split up into regiments, and protect each other. They certainly don't fear the bey when they get up to mischief."

As I listened to the dragoman, I didn't let my true feelings show,[80] and promised to tell the consul that I'd gotten the turban and cap back. If he told me to wear them, I'd beg off by saying that wearing them was forbidden in this country, so I'd rather not wear them if he didn't mind, to avoid any trouble. The dragoman and I agreed on this response, and I kept my calpac on until the consul came down for lunch.

5.62

"Did they bring you the turban?" he asked.

"Yes," I replied.

"Why aren't you wearing it?" he asked, and I replied as I'd agreed with the dragoman.

"Go put them on, and don't be afraid," the consul said. "No one will harm you while you're staying with me."

He went in to have lunch with my master, and when I failed to follow them in, he sent one of the servants to summon me to the table.

"What's the matter?" he asked. "Why aren't you wearing the turban?"

"I'll put it on tomorrow."

"I'd like you to put it on now."

"Obey the consul's orders," my master said.

What was I supposed to do? I was afraid that if I told him I hadn't gotten it back, I'd cause a lot of trouble. But if I told him I had gotten it back, he'd ask me why I wasn't wearing it. I was compelled to take my master aside privately and tell him that I hadn't received the turban. Meanwhile, the consul awaited my reply, and when my master realized that the consul demanded an answer, he was forced to explain the circumstances. Hearing that the dragoman hadn't gotten the turban back after all, the consul summoned him. This dragoman had once been a prisoner who'd converted to Islam, and the consul had taken him into his home in order to bring him back to the faith. When the dragoman appeared before him, the consul rebuked him, cursed him, and ordered him to go to the bey.

5.63

"Tell him that I want him to seize that soldier, flog him with a hundred lashes, and take back the turban and send it to me immediately!"

The dragoman left the consul's presence, unsure of what to do. If he went to the bey—who'd never refuse the request of his brother, the consul—the soldier

5.64

بتقوم الارط وبيصير شي لا خبر فيه فما عمل بكلام القنصر بل انما راح الي عند اختياريت الوجاق واحكي لهم بالمجراويه فلما سمعوا ذلك فامروا الي اوضاباشي تلك الارطي بانه يرسل الشاش والقاووق في الحال فطاع امرهم وارسله الي عندهم فسلموه للترجمان.

٦٥،٥ وقالوا له بانه يسلم علي حضرة القنصر من طرفهم وبقله بان اختياريت الوجاق منعوني بان اشتكي الي حضرة البيك علي شي ما يحرس بيكون خاطره طيب نحن منطلع من حقه فرجع الترجمان الي عند القنصر وجاب معه الشاش والقاووق واحكي له بالذي جري وان اوضاباشيت الوجاق منعوه بانه يروح يشتكي لحضره البيك علي شي ما يحرس الشكاوه واهداه السلام من عندهم واخد بخاطره كما اوصوه بانهم بيادبوا ذلك الجندي مثل ما بتريد والسلام. حينذٍ امرني القنصر بان الف الشاش والبسه قدامه ففعلت كما امرني ولبست الشاش لكن قلبي مرعوب من تلك الجنود ليلا يصدفوني لابس الشاش بيروحوني بلاش ولماكت اريد اخرج برات بيت القنصركت اشلح الشاش والبس القلبق.

٦٦،٥ وقصر ليميروا المذكور لما رجعت من دورتي رايته في حلب قنصر واولاده معه فرحت سلمت عليه وعلي ابنه نيكولا المذكور فاسترحب في وعملي اكرام وخبر الخواجكيه في لماكت نازل عنده في طرابلس الغرب وعلي الامور التي جرت لماكت بجاوره صحبة خواجه بول لوكا معلمي.

٦٧،٥ ونرجع في الكلام علي ما كنا في صدده فاستقمنا في مدينة طرابلس الغرب في بيت قنصر ليميروا المذكور مقدار ثلاثين يوم علي اكل وشرب وانشراح طول تلك المده واتفرجنا علي اشيا كثيره لكن عدلنا عن ايضاحها لاجل كثرة الكلام.

٦٨،٥ وبعده راد معلمي يسافر الي مدينة تونس الغرب من البرحتي يتفرج علي تلك الاماكن والاراضي فلما اخبر القنصر بذلك فراح الي عند البيك واخد من يده فومان او بيردي توصاي في معلمي لجميع الحكام الموجودين في طريقنا داخل ارضه وحكمه.

would be summoned and flogged. The soldier's regiment would revolt and it would cause an unspeakable mess!

So he didn't actually follow the consul's orders. Instead, he went to the senior members of the janissary corps and told them the whole story. Upon hearing it, they ordered the soldier's commanding officer to have the turban and cap sent immediately. He followed their orders, and they handed the turban and cap over to the dragoman.

"Please convey our regards to His Excellency the consul, and tell him that     5.65
the senior janissaries insisted that His Highness the bey should not be troubled with something so trivial," they said to the dragoman. "The consul may rest assured that we'll ensure that his rights are respected, and will take care of the matter ourselves."

The dragoman returned to the consul with the turban and cap. He told him what happened, and how the senior janissaries had prevented him from going to complain to the bey about something not worth complaining about.

"They send you their greetings, and assure you that they will discipline the soldier as you've requested."

The consul ordered me to put on the turban in front of him, so I did. But I was afraid that I'd run into those soldiers again while I had it on. They'd surely kill me without giving it a second thought! So, whenever I left the consul's house, I'd always take off the turban and wear the calpac instead.

After I returned from my travels, I saw the consul Lemaire in Aleppo, along     5.66
with his children. I went to see him and his son Nicholas. He welcomed me warmly and treated me most honorably. He told all the *khawājah*s about me, how I had stayed with him in Tripoli, and about the things that had happened while I was traveling in the company of Paul Lucas, my master.

Back to our story. We remained in Tripoli at the consul Lemaire's house     5.67
for thirty days, eating and drinking and enjoying ourselves. We saw many things, but I've decided not to mention them all so as not to make this account too long.

My master decided to journey by land to the city of Tunis next, so that we     5.68
could tour its sites and territories. He told the consul about his plan, then went to see the bey, from whom he received a firman—an order—written in his own hand, recommending my master to all the governors under his jurisdiction whom we might encounter along our route.

٦٩،٥ اخيرًا هيا لنا زواده وافره واحضر لعنده رجل قاطرجي رجل ناس ملاح وامين واوصاه بانه يمشينا علي كيفنا وانه لا يطلع لنا عن خلاف بهما اردنا وتلك البلاد هي امان احمل الذهب وسافرنا من غير خوف. اخيرًا ودعنا القنصر وسافرنا من طرابلس قاصدين بلاد تونس فمشينا في تلك الطرق والفيافي في مدة خمسة ايام ولكن كان سفرنا علي كيفنا وكلما نمر علي ضيعه ندخل ونتفرج علي فلاحينها وعلي نظامها واراضيها وما يشبه ذلك.

٧٠،٥ اخيرًا وصلنا الي مدينة جربه فلما دخلنا المدينه صاروا اهل المدينه يتفرسوا فينا لانهم راونا غريبين الزي ويسالوا عنا لذلك القاطرجي الذي كان معنا فاجابهم القطارجي بان هل رجل حكيم وكان عند بيك طرابلس والان رايح الي مدينه تونس يحكم هناك. اخيرًا استدلينا علي صراية حاكم البلد فدلوا الي تلك الصرايا طلبنا اذن حتي ندخل نواجه حضرة الحاكم فبعدما استازنوا لنا دخلنا امام المذكور فاعطاه معلي ذلك البيردي الذي اعطانا هو البيك.

٧١،٥ فلما قراه وفهم معناه فبش وجهه فينا واسترحب في معلي وكت انا الفقير اترجم بينهم. حينٍ سالني البيك عن معلي ما هو ومن اي مله فاجبته بانه حكيم وهو فرنجي فرنساوي الاصل فسالني ايضًا ما هي حاجته ومجيبه الي هذه البلاد فقلته يا سيدي هذا رجل سايح ويتطلب بعض حشايش الموجوده في هل الاراضي لاجل الحكمه.

٧٢،٥ حينٍ اذن لنا في الجلوس فبعدما جلسنا امر الخدام بان يسقونا المشروب وبعده الضطلي والقهوه كعادة بلادهم. اخيرًا طلب من معلي بانه صاير له وجع معده شديد ومن جراه ما يقدر ياكل وان اكل شي في الحال بيتقاياه فلما احكيت الي معلي في هل الذي قاله لي الحاكم فقله معلي قرعينا انا بركب لك معجون واذا استعملته علي ثلاثة ايام بتقوي معدتك وبتعود تاكل خمس مرات في النهار وما بتشبع فلما سمع الحاكم فرح واستبشر في الشفا وفي الحال امر بان يعطونا منزل مفروش وتعيين ماكل ومشرب واطلقنا فدخلنا الي ذلك المنزول وفي الحال طبخ معلي ذلك المعجون وهو

The bey had ample provisions prepared for us and summoned a muleteer who was trustworthy and of good character. He placed us in his care and ordered him to take us at our preferred pace, and not to protest at any of our requests. These lands were safe enough to transport gold through them, and one could travel without fear.

At last the consul bid us farewell, and we set off from Tripoli, headed for Tunis. We traveled the roads and crossed the deserts for five whole days, but went at our own pace. Each time we passed a village, we'd stop and observe the peasants, the organization of the village, its farmland, and so on and so forth.

Finally, we arrived at the city of Djerba. The people scrutinized us when we entered their city as they could see that we were foreigners. They asked the muleteer about us.

"This man is a doctor who was staying with the bey of Tripoli," he said. "He's on his way to Tunis to treat people there."

We asked for directions to the governor's palace, and they pointed the way for us. When we arrived at the palace, we asked permission to enter and meet His Excellency the governor. We were admitted into his presence, and my master presented the order the bey had given him.

When the governor read it, he smiled broadly and welcomed my master. I served as their interpreter.

"Who is this man?" the governor asked me. "Which community is he from?"

"He's a Frankish doctor, of French origin."

"Why did he come here? What is he looking for?"

"He's a traveler, my lord, searching for certain medicinal herbs found in this country," I explained.

He invited us to sit down, and ordered the servants to bring us something to drink, along with some sweets and coffee, as was the custom there. He told my master that he'd developed a severe stomach pain, which made it difficult for him to eat. Whenever he ate something, he'd immediately vomit. I told my master what the governor had said.

"Not to worry. I'll concoct a paste for you. If you use it for three days it will strengthen your stomach," my master said. "You'll be able to eat five times a day, and still won't feel full!"

The governor was overjoyed to hear that he would soon be cured, and he ordered that we be provided with furnished lodgings, food, and drink, and

مركب من ماء البقدونس وعقده بالسكر وضافه بارع متاقيل لولو مسحون وبعض
اجزاوات ووضعه‪‏١‬ في فنجان صيني وارسله هو.

٧٣.٥ فصار يستعمل منه اول يوم وثاني يوم فاستراحت معدته وصار ياكل طيب
كعادته واحسن فلما راء بانه طاب فارسل دعانا الي عنده واستكثر بخير معلي قوي
كثير واعمل له زايد اكرام لاجل انه طاب من وجع معدته وصار ياكل بقابليه مثل
ما كان ياكل سابقاً وطلب منه ايضاً من هل معجون مرتيان حتي يبقيه
عنده الي وقت الحاجه فاجابه معلي بقوله له تكرم علي الراس والعين انما بينقصني
مقدار خمسين درهم لولو ولوكان مكسراو رفيع فارسل في الحال واحضرله مقدار
من اللولو والدراهم فابي معلي بانه ياخد دراهم انما اخدنا اللولو ومضينا الي محلنا
وطبخنا له ذلك المعجون.

٧٤.٥ اخيراً طلعنا ندور ونتفرج علي تلك المدينه فيوماً ونحن دايرين مرينا علي ساحه
فوجدنا مبني في تلك الساحه ثلاثة تلل عاليات وبناهم شكل قالب السكرمن جماجم
موتي فتعجبنا من هذا المنظر المريع فرعلينا رجل اختيار فسالناه ما هذه التلف وهذه
الجماجم المبنيين في هذه الصوامع‪‏٢‬ فاجابنا لما كانت هل بلد في يد النصاره الصبنيوليين
وحاربوهم المغاربه السماعيليين واخدوا منهم جميع هل بلاد طوعاً وقصراً فلما وصلوا
الي هذه المدينه عصيت عليهم واستقامة في الحصار ثلاثة اشهر فما قدروا يملكوها
الا بواسطة الجوع وكان حلف ذلك الامير الذي اجا لمحاربتها‪‏٣‬ بانه اذا املكها يقتل
جميع اهلها رجال مع نسا والاولاد علي اخرهم ولما اخد البلد امر العسكر بانهم
يفتكوا بهم ولا يعفوا عن احد وبنوا من روس القتلا هل تلل تذكره من جيل الي
جيل وداخلهم جتت المقتولين ودايرهم جماجم القتلا كانها سلب مبنيين بجبصين
حتي بناهم لا ينفك ابداً ويستقيم سنين واعوام فلما سمعنا منه هل خبر المحزن فاسفنا
علي اهل تلك البلاد التي بتسما افريقيه وكانت مشتمله علي ثمانية عشر اسقفيه وخبرها
مشهور في التواريخ.

──────────

١ الأصل: ووضه. ٢ الأصل: الصوايع. ٣ الأصل: لمحابتها.

dismissed us. We went to our quarters and my master set about cooking up the paste. It was made of essence of parsley, thickened with sugar, to which he added four *mithqāl*s of crushed pearls and some other ingredients. He put it into a porcelain cup and sent it to the governor.

After just two days the governor's stomach settled, and he began to eat as well as he ever had. Seeing that he was now cured, the governor sent for us and showered my master with gratitude and treated him most honorably for ridding him of his stomach pain and returning his appetite to its previous state. He asked my master to prepare a jar of the paste to keep for times of need.

"It would be my pleasure, but I'll need fifty dirhams' worth of pearls," my master replied. "They can be broken, or small in size," he added, and the governor immediately sent a quantity of pearls, along with a number of dirhams. My master refused the money, but we took the pearls and returned to our lodgings to prepare the paste for him.

We took to touring the city and seeing the sights. One day, while we were out and about, we happened upon a square. There were three tall towers in the square, each built in the shape of a sugar cake, and made entirely of human skulls.[81] We were astonished by this dreadful sight.

An old man passed by.

"What's the meaning of these towers of skulls?" we asked him.

"When these lands were ruled by the Christians of Spain, Ismāʿīlīs from the Maghreb[82] waged war on them and seized these territories by fair means and foul," he said. "When they reached this city, the inhabitants resisted them, and so were placed under siege for three months. The armies only conquered the town by starving its inhabitants, and the prince who waged the war on the city swore that when he took it, he'd kill every last man, woman, and child. And in fact, when the town fell, he ordered his soldiers to kill everyone and not spare a single soul. They built these towers out of the heads of the dead, as a reminder to later generations. In the towers are the corpses, surrounded by the skulls, which were used like building stones, set in gypsum so that the towers wouldn't come apart and would last for years."[83]

When we heard this sad tale, we felt sorry for the people of that region, which is known as Ifrīqiyah. It comprises eighteen bishoprics, its history well known from the chronicles.

5.73

5.74

٧٥،٥ اخيرًا بعدما تفرجنا علي تلك المدينه فرحنا عند الحاكم واخدنا منه اذن حتي نسافر وودعناه فاعطانا مكتوب الي حاكم مدينة اسفقس توصاي فينا فاخدنا المكتوب منه وسافرنا في تلك الاراضي وفي طريقنا مرينا ايضاً علي قري وضيع ومنها اماكن كثيره خراب وما زلنا سايرين حتي وصلنا الي تلك المدينة المذكوره وهي مدينه عامره مشيدة الاصوار ذات بساتين وانهر ورياض.

٧٦،٥ اخيرًا استدلينا علي صراية الحاكم وبعد الاذن دخلنا الي عنده واعطيناه مكتوب البيك ومكتوب حاكم جربه فلما قراهم فاسترحب فينا واذن لنا بالجلوس وبعده جابوا لنا المشروب والقهوه كالعاده وصار يسال معلمي عن ذلك المعجون الذي اعطيناه الي حاكم جربه هل معه باقي منه شي وكان معلمي ابقي منه جزء في حق فقله نعم عندي موجود واوعده بانه يرسل له منه مرطبان زغير وعند ذلك امر بان يعطونا منزول فنزلنا في ذلك المنزول واسترحنا ذلك اليوم.

٧٧،٥ وتاني يوم خرجنا من المنزول ورحنا الي عند الحاكم واعطيناه ذلك المعجون فانبسط وامر الخدام بانهم يضيفونا ويقفوا في واجنا فاستكترنا بخيره ومضينا ندور في المدينه ونتفرج علي تلك الاماكن القديمه وهي من عمارات المسيحيه الذين كانوا قاطنيين في تلك البلاد من كنايس وديوره ومدارس لكن جميعها خراب وكان معلمي ينسخ من تلك الحجاره بعض كتابات تواريخ التي بتني عن تلك الاماكن واشترينا كثير من المداليات القديمه التي كانت معاملة تلك البلاد فضه ونحاس وغير اشيا قدم ايضاً من كتب اخبار وتواريخ الجراكسه منها عربي ومنها لاتيني وما يشبه ذلك وكل هذا كان بواسطة الحكمه لان معلمي كان يحكم ويطلب من تلك الاوادم الذي يحكمهم هذه الاشيا حتي يفتشوله عليها ويشتريها منهم بسخاء.

٧٨،٥ فاستقمنا في تلك المدينه سبعة ايام وبعده رحنا الي عند الحاكم حتي نودعه ونطلب منه مكتوب توصاي فينا للحكام الذي هن في طريقنا فاجابنا الحاكم بان من بعد خروجكم من هل بلد بقناق بتدخلوا في حكم بيك تونس ومكتوبي ما بينفعكم بشي ولكن لا تخفوا الدرب امان.

After touring the city, we went to see the governor and obtained his permis-    5.75
sion to depart, and bid him farewell. He offered us a letter of introduction to
the governor of Sfax, which we brought with us. On our way, we passed various hamlets and villages, many with ruins, and didn't stop till we reached Sfax,
a prosperous city with lofty fortifications, and with many orchards, streams,
and gardens.

When we entered, we asked for directions to the palace of the governor,    5.76
where we were admitted. We presented him with the letters of the bey and the
governor of Djerba. He read them, welcomed us, and invited us to sit down.
Coffee and other beverages were served, as was the usual custom, and the governor asked my master about the medicinal paste he'd made for the governor
of Djerba.

"Do you have any left over?" he inquired.

My master had kept some of the paste in a container, and promised the
governor that he would send him a small jar of it. The governor ordered his
servants to give us a place to stay, and we rested there that day.

The next day, we went to see the governor and presented him with the    5.77
paste. He was pleased, and ordered the servants to treat us as honored guests
and to put themselves at our service. We thanked him and set off to tour the
city and see its ancient sites, which included the churches, monasteries, and
schools of the Christians who had once lived in those lands. They were all in
ruins, but there were dates inscribed on some of the stones, which provided
information about them. My master copied these down. We bought many
old silver and copper medallions, which had served as currency there, along
with other antiques: history books and chronicles about the Saracens, some in
Arabic and others in Latin, and other such things.

All of this was made possible by my master's medical practice. He would
treat people and ask them to search for such objects, which he'd purchase at a
generous price.

We stayed in Sfax for seven days. We then paid a visit to the governor to bid    5.78
him farewell, and asked him for a letter of introduction to the other governors
who were on our route.

"A day's ride from the city, you'll enter the jurisdiction of the bey of Tunis,
and my letter won't be worth anything to you," he said. "But don't worry—
the road is safe."

٧٩٫٥ اخيرًا ودعناه ومضينا الي محلنا واخذنا زواده الدرب وسافرنا صحبة ذاك القاطرجي الذي اجا معنا من طرابلس الغرب ولا زلنا مسافرين نحو ثمانية ايام وفي طريقنا وجدنا اماكن وعماير خرابه شي كثير ومن الجمله مرينا علي ارض فيها تاثير عماره وراينا اشجار سيتون من حجر وموجود فيهم زيتون من حجر وراينا ايضًا في تلك الارض بطيخ وجبس من حجر فكسرنا واحده منهم فراينا داخلها بزر اصفر من حجر وراينا نهر ناشف فوجدنا بين الحجار سمك من حجر وصفحات حجار مطبوع فيهم شكل سمك فتعجبنا من ذلك المنضر وسالنا ذلك القاطرجي الذي كان معنا عن هل اشيا التي رايناها فاجابنا بان هل مكان كان عامر ومسكون من اناس فغضب الله عليهم وارسل ريح عاصف شديد بهذا المقدار حتي نسف من الرمل وغطي هل قريه التي كانت عامره في هل مكان حتي علي فوقها واستقامة مردومه تحت الرمل سنين عديده ولاجل هذا استحاله اشجارها ونباتاتها الي حجر. ' اخيرًا ارسل الله تعالي ريح عظيم فكشف عنها ذلك الرمل وصار تل عالي وهو تجاهنا واروانا ذلك التل.

٨٠٫٥ اخيرًا اخذنا من ذلك الزيتون والبطيخ ومن الحجاره المطبوع فيها هيئة السمك ثم سافرنا الي ان وصلنا الي مدينة سوسا فلما وصلنا الي تلك المدينه فمنعنا القاطرجي ان ندخل اليها بقوله لنا بان اهل البلد ناس ارديا ارفاض وما بيريدوا يجانسوا لا مسلم سني ولا نصراني ولا يهودي ولا احد من غير ملل من كثرة رفضهم وبغضتهم للغير فالتزمنا نزل برات البلد تحت الصور فبتنا تلك الليله في ذلك المكان.

٨١٫٥ ولما اصبح الصبح هممنا في السفر وارسلنا القاطرجي الي البلد حتي يشتري لنا من الزاد واللحم ما بكفينا في الطريق وبعدما تسوق لنا جميع ما نحتاج استكري من واحد من اولاد البلد دبه حتي يسافر معنا لان كان له دبتين وكل بلد التي ندخلها يستكري دبه وصاحبها حتي يسافر معنا فلما استكري تلك الدبه حمل عليها جميع حوايجنا كما كان يفعل مع الغير يركب الي معلي دبه فاضيه ولي دبه فاضيه ايضًا ودبت التي يستكريها يحمل عليها حوايجنا فلما انتهي في تحميل ذلك دبت الرجل فما هان عليه

---

١ «ولاجل هذا. . .الي حجر» في الهامش.

We said goodbye and went back to our lodgings to gather our provisions   5.79
for the road. We set off, together with the muleteer who'd come with us from
Tripoli. We traveled for about eight days, passing many ruined buildings along
the way and other traces of civilization. We also came upon petrified olive
trees, their olives turned to stone, and petrified watermelons as well. Breaking one open, we found yellow seeds inside, similarly transformed into stone.
We also saw a dried riverbed with petrified fish lying among the river stones,
and the shapes of fish stamped onto the surfaces of rocks. We were amazed by
these sights, and asked the muleteer about them.

"This was once a prosperous place, full of people," the muleteer explained.
"Then one day, God grew angry at the people, and kicked up a great storm that
leveled the town and buried it in sand! After years under all that sand, you see,
all the trees and plants were turned to stone." Pointing to a nearby hill, he continued, "Eventually, God sent a strong wind to blow the sand away, and that's
where that hill came from."

We took some of those olives and watermelons with us, as well as some of   5.80
the rocks with the shapes of fish pressed into them, and set off again, continuing on until we reached Sousse. But the muleteer held us back from entering
the city.

"This town is full of horrible heretics," he said.[84] "They're so hateful that
they won't have anything to do with Sunnis, Christians, Jews, or people of any
other community."

So we had to make camp outside, at the base of the city wall, where we
spent the night.

When morning came, we prepared to depart, and sent the muleteer into   5.81
town to buy provisions and some meat for the road. After he got everything
we needed, he hired a mount from one of the townspeople to travel with us.
The muleteer had two beasts of his own, and in every town we entered he
would hire a third, along with its owner, to travel with us. He loaded all of our
things on the hired beast, as he usually did, freeing his own two mounts for my
master and me to ride. The hired beast would carry our luggage.

Once the muleteer finished loading it up, though, the other man was not
pleased to see that his beast was carrying all of the luggage, while the other
two had no load at all.

بانه يحمل جميع اللبش علي دبته ويبقي دبته فارغات من غير تحميل فاجابه القاطرجي اني ما استكريت دبتك الا لاجل احملها جميع اللبش فصاروا يتشاجروا ويتقاتلوا مع بعضهم بعض.

٨٢،٥ اخيرًا قدم ذلك الرجل الي عند دبته وقلب كل شي الذي محمل عليها وكان من جملة المحمل سندوق وداخل اربعة وعشرين قنينت انبيد طيب الذي قنصر طرابلس كان زودنا فيه لان في دربنا ما بيوجد انبيد ومعلي ما كان يقدر يشرب الماء من غير ان يمزجه بنبيد فلما راء ان ذلك الرجل قلب حمل تلك الدبه علي الارض والسندوق ايضًا فخال له بان تكسرت جميع القناني وعدم النبيد فراع عقله وصرخ بصوت عالي وصار يشتم ذلك الرجل بالتركي والعربي والفرنجي لانه تعلم من لسان التركي لفضة بك وبالعربي كلب وقدم الي عنده ودفشه كاد انه يرميه علي وجهه فما راينا الا ذلك الرجل ركض نحو باب البلد صار يصرح يا جداه الحقوني واحد رومي شتمني وقتلني.

٨٣،٥ فتبادرت العالم وخرجت من باب البلد كانهم جراد زعاف وتوجهوا الي طرفنا فلما القاطرجي راء خروج هل عالم من باب البلد فزع علينا وقال الي معلي اهرب وفوز بنفسك والا قتلوك فهرب معلي وصار يتلجي في عوجات براج الصور فهجموا علينا تلك الاوادم فما راوا غيري فمسكوني ورادوا يفتكوا في فصدهم ذلك الرجل عني بقوله ما هو هذا الذي شتمني.

٨٤،٥ ودفعني وبالجهد حتي انا ارتخيت انا من اياديهم وانا اتوسل الي ذلك الرجل واليهم. اخيرًا طلعوا يتراكدوا ويفتشوا علي معلي. اما هو وجد تغره فنزل وتخبي داخلها وغطي حاله بقش كان موجود في تلك الجوره وستر عليه الستار فما قدروا يقشعوه وفي ذلك الوقت كنت انا والقطارجي نتدخل علي ذلك الرجل وانا اوعدته بان ما نحمل دبته شي وانا اركبها فقط فارغه وايضًا قريته بان اعطيه اتنين ذهب ما عدا كروته فلما سمع في الاتنين ذهب انفك برمه وصار يرجع تلك الاوادم بقوله لهم انا بشتكي عليه في تونس للبيك وبعمل علي حرقه.

"That's why I hired that beast of yours," the muleteer said. "To carry the baggage!" They began to quarrel.

Striding over to his beast, the man took hold of the baggage on its back    5.82
and dumped the whole load on the ground. Among the baggage was a case of twenty-four bottles of good wine, which the consul of Tripoli had given us. There was no wine to be found anywhere along our route, you see, and my master was incapable of drinking water without mixing it with wine. When he saw the man dump the load—including the case—onto the ground, he was sure the bottles had broken and his wine was gone.

Flying into a rage, he began screaming and cursing in Turkish and Arabic and French. He knew how to say "dog" in Turkish and Arabic, having learned the words *köpek* and *kalb*. Striding up to the man, he shoved him so hard that he nearly knocked him down. The next thing we knew, the man had dashed off toward the city gate, shouting to the townspeople, "For the love of the Prophet, help me! A Christian has attacked me!"

A crowd burst through the gate like a swarm of locusts, heading right for    5.83
us. When the muleteer saw them coming, he was terrified something might happen to us.

"Run!" he said to my master. "Save yourself, or they'll kill you!"

Taking to his heels, my master found a place to hide in the nooks and crannies around the rampart towers. When the mob arrived, they found only me standing there, so they seized me, meaning to kill me! But the man whose beast we'd hired pushed them away.

"This isn't the one who cursed me," he said.

I begged and pleaded both with him and them. Eventually he pried me out    5.84
of their hands, and they went off in search of my master. But he'd happened upon a crevice to hide in, covering himself with some straw he'd found, so they never saw him.

Meanwhile, the muleteer and I were pleading with the man we'd hired. I promised him that we wouldn't load up his beast with anything at all. I would ride it myself with no luggage. I also promised him that I'd give him two gold pieces on top of his regular fee. When he heard about the two gold pieces, he became more agreeable. He rounded up everyone and said to them,

"I'll lodge a complaint about him in Tunis with the bey, and I'll have him burned!"

٨٥،٥ اخيراً رجعت العالم عنا فعدنا حملنا لبشنا علي دبة القاطرجي وانا استفقدت السندوق المذكور فرايت ما انكسر منه ولا قنينه بل كلهم صاغ ولا انكب من النبيد شي فبعدما حملنا مشينا بجانب الصور حتي نزا الخواجه فما رانا احد فخرنا في امرنا فهو لما رانا من تحت ذلك القش خرج من تلك الحفره ومشي معنا وهو مرعوب ولون وجهه فصرت اجرعه بقولي له لا تخف رجعت تلك الاوادم وما بقا علينا باس وسندوق النبيد ما سايل ولا انكب من النبيد شي واحكيته بالذي جري في غيابه وكيف بالجهد حتي خلصت من ايديهم ولو ما ذلك الرجل يرجعهم عني لكانوا قتلوني لا محاله وايضاً ولو انهم قشعوك لكانوا قتلوك فشكرنا الله تعالي علي جوده واحسانه الذي خلصنا من ايدي اوليك الارديا الوحوش الضاريه .

٨٦،٥ اخيراً ركبناه ومشينا حتي بعدنا عن البلد حكم ساعتين فنزلنا في ارض مرج اخضر ونبع ماء ونزلنا حوايجنا من علي الدواب حتي نتغدا ونستريح شويه فبعدما تغدينا واسترحنا شويه فمشينا في ذلك البر المقفر الي المساء فما وجدنا لا ضيعه ولا ادي حتي ولا طير فبتنا تلك الليله خلاوي من غير ماوي ولما اصبح علينا الصبح فركبنا وسافرنا ذلك النهار الي المساء وصلنا الي وادي يسمي وادي السباع فراينا جماعات نازلين هناك فنزلنا نحن ايضاً بجانبهم .

٨٧،٥ وكان ذلك الوادي ما احد يقدر يجوزه الي ان يجمع عشرين او ثلاثين زلمه حتي يقدروا يجوزوه فزعاً من السباع فبتنا تلك الليله ايضاً في ذلك المكان الي ان اصبح الصبح نزلنا في ذلك الوادي وكنا في العدد خمسة وعشر نفر للمجموعين من تلك الاراضي والقري ومشينا فيه طول ذلك النهار الي المسا وصلنا الي مكان فسحه كبيره وما يدورها نيران شاعله ليل مع نهار لان كل قفل الذي يدخل داخلها يقطعوا من تلك الاشجار ويلقوها في النار ليلا يدخلوا السباع اليها ويفترسوا الاوادم والدواب فبتنا تلك الليله في تلك الفسحه ونسمع في هل ليل حس السباع تزير ويضربوا دنابهم علي بطونهم والخيل تشخر لانهم بيروا السباع في الليل .

٨٨،٥ الي ان اصبح الصبح فسافرنا في ذلك الوادي الي حكم نصف النهار خرجنا من ذلك الوادي ولا زلنا سايرين الي المساء وصلنا الي ارض صبرة ملح علي ما تمد عينك

With that the crowd broke up, and we put our luggage back on the mule-    5.85
teer's beast. When I inspected the trunk, it turned out that not a single bottle
had broken and none of the wine had spilled.

After we'd loaded everything up, we set off along the wall so we could spot
the *khawājah*. Seeing no one, we stopped, uncertain what to do. He spotted us
from under the straw, came out of the crevice, and joined us. He was terrified
and all the color had drained from his face.

"Don't worry, the crowd's gone; we're safe," I reassured him. "And none of
the wine bottles broke!"

I told him what had happened in his absence and how I'd barely escaped.

"If that man hadn't stopped them, they would have killed me for certain,"
I said. "And you too, if they'd spotted you."

We thanked the good Lord for saving us from that pack of savages.

We mounted and rode for two hours. When we came to a green field with    5.86
a spring, we unloaded the beasts so we could have lunch and rest for a while.
After eating and resting, we set off across that desolate landscape, pressing on
until the evening without seeing any villages or a single person—not even a
bird—and had to spend the night out in the open. In the morning, we mounted
again and rode all day, arriving that evening at a place known as the Valley of
Lions. There were some people encamped there, so we set up camp alongside them.

For fear of the lions, no one dared cross the valley without a company of    5.87
twenty or thirty men. We spent the night there, and set off in the morning
through the valley, accompanied by fifteen people rounded up from some local
villages. After a day's journey, we arrived in the evening at a large clearing.
It was surrounded by fires that remained constantly burning, day and night.
Every convoy that entered the clearing would cut down some trees and throw
them into the fire, to prevent the lions venturing in and killing the people and
their mounts.

We passed the night in the clearing, listening to the sounds of the lions roar-
ing and slapping their tails against their bellies, and of the horses snorting—
because they could see the lions in the darkness.

In the morning, we set off through the valley again, emerging from it at    5.88
midday. We pressed on until evening and came to a plain covered in snow-
white salt as far as the eye could see. We spent the night at the edge of the plain,

والنضر والملح ابيض من الثلج فبتنا تلك الليله بجانبها وتاني يوم دخلنا فيها ما لنا غير درب فصرنا نغطي اوجاهنا بمناديل زرق او بواشي حتي لا تنبهر اعينا من ذلك البياض.

فاستقمنا نمشي في ذلك الملح حكم ثلاث ساعات ونيف الي ان خرجنا منها ٨٩٠٥ واستقمنا سايرين الي ان وصلنا الي قريه تسمي الحمامات وهي عامره وادمها ناس ملاح فدخلنا اليها واستقمنا تلك الليله وثاني يوم ايضًا درنا وتفرجنا وراينا ناس من اهل تونس فانسونا لما عرفوا باننا ماضين الي تونس لعند القنصر فاحكينا لهم علي ذلك الرجل الذي استكرينا دبته من مدينة سوسا وكيف انه جمع علينا تلك الاوادم ورادوا قتلنا فلما سمعوا منا هل كلام نهضوا عليه ورادوا يقتلوه في ارضه بقولهم له يا رافضي يا مستاهل القتل . اخيرًا شفع فيه معلمي واعطاه كري دبته ودشرناه وما عاد يستجر يطلب التنين ذهب الذي كنت اوعدته فيهم.

فاستقمنا ذلك اليوم في تلك القريه وتاني يوم سافرنا قاصدين مدينة تونس فلما ٩٠٠٥ وصلنا الي خان الذي هو بعيد عن تونس سفر ثلاثة ساعات فنزل القفل هناك وما رادوا يدخلوا المدينه التجار الذين هم في القفل علي ضوو النهار لاجل انهم بيريدوا يهربوا من الكمرك بعض بضايع فاستقمنا في الخان.

وكان قريب من الخان قبلوجه اعني ما سخن خارج من الارض فرحت الفقير حتي ٩١٠٥ اتفرج علي تلك القبلوجه فدخلت داخل المكان الذي فيه نابع ذلك الماء السخن فرايت بركه كبيره طولها وعرضها بيجي ماية قدم ويعلوها قبه شامخه وسيعه بتغطي تلك البركه وما يدورها اوادم يستحموا منهم واصل الماء لركبهم ومنهم واصله الي بطونهم ومنهم واصله الي صدورهم وهبلت الماء واصله الي علو القبه وفي ناس يحرسوا التياب ولما الرجل يخرج من الماء بيعطي للذي يحرس ثيابه عثماني.

حينذٍ شلحت ثيابي وجلست حدا واحد من تلك المستحمين ومديت رجلي الواحده ٩٢٠٥ لكي اجس الماء ولما حسيت في سخونه الماء فرت هاربًا وايقنت بان رجلي احترقت من شدة سخونة ذلك الماء الشديد فاخد ذلك الرجل يدعيني الي جانبه ويقلي لماذا هربت اجلس حداي وانا اعلمك كيف تستحم فجلست جنبه فقلي مد رجلك الواحد رويدًا

and the next day began our ride across it. There was no other road. We covered our faces with blue scarves and turban cloths so our eyes wouldn't be dazzled by all that glaring whiteness.

It took about three hours of walking to cross the salt flat. From there we continued on till we came to a village called al-Ḥammāmāt, which was prosperous, and whose inhabitants were people of good character. We entered the village and spent the night there, and the next day went sightseeing. We met some people from Tunis, who treated us kindly when they learned that we were on our way there to visit the consul. We told them about the man from Sousse whose beast we'd hired and how he'd brought all those people together to kill us.    5.89

When they heard this, they rose up against him and were going to kill him on the spot.

"Heretic! You deserve to die!" they shouted.

But my master interceded on his behalf and paid him, and we sent him away. He didn't dare ask for the two gold pieces I'd promised him!

After a day in the village, we left the next morning for Tunis, stopping at a caravansary three hours' journey from the city. The merchants in our caravan didn't want to enter Tunis in broad daylight, as they intended to hide some of their goods from the customs agents. So we stayed at the caravansary.    5.90

There was a *qablūjah* nearby, a place where hot water comes out of the ground. I went off to have a look, and entered the building where the hot spring was located. Inside, I found a large pool, a hundred feet in length and the same in width, covered by a vast, towering dome. All around, people were bathing. Some were in up to their knees and others to their stomachs. Some were in all the way up to their chests. The steam rose as high as the top of the dome. There were people watching over the clothes, and whenever a man came out of the water, he would hand the attendant an *'uthmānī* coin.    5.91

I took off my clothes, sat down beside one of the bathers, and stretched out one of my feet to touch the water. When I felt how hot it was, I jerked back, certain I'd scalded my feet from the intense heat! The bather invited me to sit beside him again.    5.92

"Why did you pull away?" he asked. "Sit here next to me, and I'll show you how to bathe."

I sat beside him.

رويدًا حتى تخضر وبعده مد رجلك الثانيه ايضًا رويدًا رويدًا ففعلت[1] كما شار علي فرأيت ركزت رجلي علي درجه والماء وصل الي خلخال رجلي فاستقمت حصه حتي اخدرت رجلي من ذلك الماء السخن وما عدت احس بسخونته.

٩٣،٥ حينِ قلي ذلك الرجل مد رجليك الي ثاني درجه ففعلت[2] كالاول وبعده نزلت الي ثالث درجه وهلم جرا حتي وصل الماء الي صدري وانا راكز رجلي علي ذلك الدرج.

اخيرًا استقمت في الماء حكم نصف ساعه وما عدت احس بسخونه ذلك الماء انما رايت بيتنسل من جسدي الرطوبات التي كانت مخزنه في اعضاي لان هذا الماء الكبريتي له خواص عظيم لجميع الاسقام والامراض وكثير من الناس الذين فيهم اهات واسقام وجدام وغير اوجاع بيقصدوا هذا الماء ومنهم بيجوا من بلاد بعيده لاجل شفاهم من اسقامهم وذلك الحوض دايمًا ماء وطافح ليل مع نهار والي الان.

٩٤،٥ اخيرًا خرجت من الماء ولبست ثيابي ومضيت الي عند معلمي واحكيت له عن هذا الماء والحوض الكثير النفع فلما سمع مني هل خبر راد يروح يستحم هو ايضًا فلما رحنا ودخلنا الي ذلك المكان وراء ذلك الماء الغالي فقلي كيف قدرت تنزل لهذا الماء.

حينِ احكيته كيفيت النزول اليها كما فعلت انا وغيري من الموجودين فمديده للماء حتي يحسه فواه شي ما بينطاق فعدل عن النزول اليه ورجعنا الي محلنا وهو متعجب كيف بيقدروا ينزلوا الي هذا الماء الشديد السخونه وما يحترقوا.

٩٥،٥ اخيرًا استقمنا في ذلك الخان الي حكم نصف الليل فنهضوا التجار والقاطرجيه وحملوا احمالهم وخرجوا من الخان ونحن ايضًا خرجنا معهم فلما صرنا في الصحرا فنضر معلمي الي النجم فواء بان الوقت نصف الليل فما راد يتبع القفل فبقيت انا واياه في تلك البريه وحدنا والقاطرجي ساق امامه دبه المحل عليها لبشنا ومشي مع القفل وما عرف باننا تاخرنا وانفصلنا من القفل فاستقمنا في ذلك القفر الي ان اصبح الصباح فركبنا خيلنا وسرنا نحو المدينه لكن كان مسيرنا في غير سكه فتهنا عن الطريق.

٩٦،٥ واما القاطرجي لما وصل القفل الي المدينه وما رانا فرجع مردود يفتش علينا ونحن سايرين في غير طريق الي ان وجدنا في الطريق رجل فلاح ماضي الي ضيعته فسالناه

---

١ الأصل: ففعلت.  ٢ الأصل: ففعلت.

"Dip one foot in slowly until it goes numb," he said. "Then dip the second one in slowly."

I did as directed. My foot came to rest on a step, the water up to my ankle. I remained there until the heat made my foot go numb and I could no longer feel it.

The man told me to put my feet on the second step, which I did. Then I went down to the third step, and so on, until the water reached my chest, while my feet remained planted on the steps.

5.93

I stayed in the water for about half an hour and stopped feeling the heat. But I could feel the dampness trapped in my limbs dissipating in the sulfurous water, which had wondrous healing properties for all manner of ailments and illnesses. Many people with leprosy and other afflictions would seek it out, some of them coming from faraway lands for a cure. The pool was always full of water, overflowing day and night. It continues to do so to this very day.

I came out of the water, put on my clothes, and went to see my master. I told him about the water and the pool and its beneficial properties. When he heard about it, he wanted to go bathe there as well. We returned to the building, and when my master saw the boiling water, he asked me how I was able to step into it. I explained the method that I and others used to go in, so he dipped his hand into the water to feel, but found it unbearable! He refused to go in, and we went back to our lodgings, even as he continued to marvel at how people could bathe in such hot water without being scalded.[85]

5.94

We stayed at the caravansary until the middle of the night. When the merchants and drivers got up and packed their loads and left the inn, we followed them. While we were in the desert, my master looked up at the stars and determined that it was midnight, and decided he didn't want to follow the caravan. So the two of us remained alone in the wilderness. Meanwhile, our muleteer had gone ahead with the caravan, his beast carrying all of our baggage. He didn't realize that we'd split off from the caravan and stayed behind. After spending the night in the wasteland, we mounted our horses and rode toward the city. But we took a wrong turn and wandered off the main road.

5.95

Meanwhile, the caravan had arrived at the city, and the muleteer, not seeing us anywhere, had turned back to search for us. But we were on the wrong road. On our way we passed a peasant going to his village and asked him if we were close to Tunis.

5.96

هل اننا قربنا الي مدينة تونس فاجابنا انكم فتوا المدينه وان المدينه بقت علي شمالكم ارجعوا الي ان تروا سكه عريضه فاتبعوها الي ان تصلوا الي المدينه. حينذٍ قلنا له ارجع معنا وارونا السكه ونحن منعطيك اجرتك.

٩٧،٥ فرجع معنا الي ان وصلنا الي تلك السكه فسرنا في ذلك الطريق حكم ساعه فوجدنا القاطرجي ومعه اثنين مغاربه من اهل تونس وكان سبب مجي رجلين معه هو ان القاطرجي اوصل حوايجنا الي بيت القنصر فلما سول عنّا[1] فقال لهم انهم تاخروا وما دخلوا مع القفل فلما سمع القنصر في تاخيرنا ارسل اثنين من قبله بانهم يطلعوا مع القاطرجي ويجيبونا الي محله فلما طلعوا برات المدينه وبعلمهم اننا قريبين منهم فما راوا احد يجدوا في المسير الي ان وصلنا قرب المكان الذي كنا نازلين فيه فما راونا فتير القاطرجي وخاف الا يكون حكمنا عارض فعادوا راجعين فراونا من بعيد فصار القاطرجي يصيح علينا فرينا عليه ووصلنا الي عندهم فسالونا عن سبب تاخيرنا فاحكينا له بالذي صار فينا وكيف اننا تهنا عن الدرب.

٩٨،٥ اخيرًا مشينا جمله الي ان وصلنا الي المدينه ومن هناك رحنا الي بيت القنصر وهو خان كبير وداخل ذلك الخان قاطنين تجار الفرنساويه جميعهم. اخيرًا صعدنا في درج ودخلنا الي بيت القنصر فطلع القنصر المذكور الي لقانا واسترحب في معلمي وسلموا علي بعضهم وكان القنصر وصله مكتوب من قنصر طرابلس في وصول معلمي الي عنده واخبره بانه سايح من سواح سلطان فرنسا ولاجل هذا استقبله باكرام زايد واعطاه اوضته المكلفه لاجل منامته واعطوني انا ايضًا اوضه بعدما نقلوا حوايجنا من الخان الي اوضنا وبعد هنيهه اقبلت التجار الي بيت القنصر يسلموا علي معلمي ويهنوا علي سلامته فاستقمنا ذلك اليوم لملاقات التجار.

٩٩،٥ وثاني يوم راح معلمي يرد السلام كجري عوايدهم وبعد ثلاثة ايام قال القنصر الي معلمي حتي يروح معه يسلم علي البيك الذي هو سلطان تونس فرضي معلمي بذلك. حينذٍ هيوا العرابانه فركب معلمي والقنصر بجانبه وايضًا كام واحد من التجار ركبوا خيلهم والخدام والفقير ركبت معهم وسرنا معًا الي سرايت البيك التي تسما عندهم

---

١ الأصل: عنتا.

"You've passed it," he said. "It's off to the left. Go back the way you came. When you arrive at a wide road, follow it till you reach the city."

"If you come with us and show us the way, we'll pay you," we said to him.

So he led us to the road. After walking for about an hour, we came upon     5.97
the muleteer, along with two Maghrebis from Tunis. They'd come with him because he'd taken our things to the consul's house and was asked where we were.

"They fell behind and didn't arrive with the caravan," he replied.

When the consul heard this, he sent two men with the muleteer to fetch us and bring us to his house. They left the city, assuming we had to be nearby, but didn't see anyone. So they set off in hurry, arrived quickly at the place where we'd lodged, but didn't find us. The muleteer was baffled, and he worried that something had befallen us.

On the way back, they spotted us in the distance and the muleteer began to call out. We responded and headed over to meet them. When they asked about the reason for our delay, we explained what had happened and how we'd wandered off the road.

We rode back to the city together, and headed to the consul's house.[86]     5.98
It was inside a large caravansary, and the French merchants resided there together. We went up the stairs to the consul's residence. He came out to meet us and welcome my master. The two men greeted each other. The consul had received a letter from his opposite number in Tripoli, notifying him about my master's arrival, explaining that he was an envoy sent by the sultan of France. The consul of Tunis welcomed him with great cordiality and made available his own sumptuous bedroom for my master to use. They also gave me a room, and brought our things in from the caravansary to our rooms.

After a little while, the merchants came to the consul's house to greet my master and congratulate him on his safe arrival. We remained there that day to meet with all the merchants.

The next day my master went to pay visits to all of them, as was the custom.     5.99
Three days later, the consul invited my master to come with him and meet the bey of Tunis, who was the ruler of the city. My master agreed, and a carriage was prepared for them. My master climbed in and the consul sat next to him, and a few merchants rode alongside on their horses. I rode with the servants,

بارده وهي بعيده عن المدينه حكم ساعه ونصف فلما وصلنا الي ذلك المكان فرأيت شي يفوق الوصف عن تلك البساتين والخضر وينابيع الماء الجاري في تلك الروضه ورأيت في المواسطه معمر سرايا عامره مشيدت الاركان وقصور عاليه مزغرفت البنا بشبابيك بلور ما يدور تلك القصور .

٥،١٠٠ اخيرًا دخلنا من اول باب الي سرايا بلواوين وبرك ماء طافحه واماكن عامره ثم دخلنا ثاني باب وهي مقر البيك وهي اكبر من الاوليه وعماراتها اشرف واكلف ثم صعدنا في درج عالي من جمر المرمر عريض والصعود فيه قوي سهل. اخيرًا انتهينا الي الصحن المكان مرصوف بجارة الرخام الايض ومعمر فيه اربع قصوره في كل ناحيه قصر معمرينهم لاجل اربعة فصول السنه وكان البيك جالس في قصر الذي هو مخصوص لفصل الربع.

٥،١٠١ حينٍ اخبروا البيك في وصول القنصر الي عنده فامر في دخوله. اخيرًا دخلنا الي ذلك القصر وامتثلنا امام البيك وعمل تمني القنصر وجماعته للبيك فاسترحب فيهم وكلفهم للجلوس وبعد جلوسنا جابوا لنا المشروب والقهوه كالعاده. اخيرًا لحض القنصر الي البيك في قدوم معلمي من السياحه الي بلاده والان اجا معنا حتي يتشرف بروياك. حينٍ نهض معلمي من مكانه وعمل تمني لحضرة البيك فاسترحب فيه البيك وهناه علي سلامته وصار يساله علي بعض اشيا التي راها في سياحته وعن المدن التي مر فيها وكان معلمي يجيبه بجميع ما يساله وترجمان القنصر كان شاطر في نقل الكلام وبصناعة الترجمه في تزريفه الكلام وتفهيمه للبيك في غاية ما يكون.

٥،١٠٢ فانبسط البيك من رد الجوابات التي كان يجاوبه فيها معلمي خصوصًا في شكرانه له عن بلاده وحسنها ونظام الذي راه في سرايته وحسن ترتيبها وانه ما راه في غير ممالك العصماليه مثلها. حينٍ ساله البيك هل عجبتك سرايتنا فاجابه نعم وبالاكثر رقة وجهك المنيره وطبايعك اللطيفه وحسن الفاظك الرقيقه وما يشبه ذلك من الفاظ اللينه العذبه لحضرة بيك مثل هذا.

and we all went together to the bey's palace, which was called Bardo.[87] It was an hour and a half away from the city.

When we arrived, I beheld a sight beyond description: a grand palace surrounded by verdant gardens with springs flowing everywhere. The palace had towering columns and lofty, intricately constructed pavilions, with crystal windows on all sides.

We passed through a first gate into a pavilion with open salons, pools overflowing with water, and other exquisite structures. We then entered a second gate, and passed into the private residence of the bey. This was even larger than the previous one, and its construction even nobler and more opulent. We climbed a tall, graceful set of wide marble stairs, and arrived at the palace courtyard, which was paved with white marble. On each of the four sides of the courtyard a pavilion had been erected. There was one for each of the four seasons of the year. The bey was sitting in the spring pavilion.    5.100

Once he was informed of the consul's arrival, the bey ordered that he be brought in. We entered the pavilion and presented ourselves before him. The consul and his entourage bowed deeply before the bey. He welcomed us and invited us all to sit down. We were brought beverages and coffee, as was customary. The consul briefed the bey on the reasons for my master's journey to his country.    5.101

"He came with us today to have the honor of meeting you," the consul concluded.

My master rose from his place and bowed before His Excellency the bey, who welcomed him and congratulated him on his safe arrival. He asked him about the things he'd seen on his travels and the cities he'd visited, and my master replied to all his questions. The consul's dragoman served as a skillful interpreter, embellishing my master's words and helping the bey understand them perfectly.

The bey was pleased with my master's replies, and particularly the praise of his beautiful country and of the elegant design of his palace. My master said that he'd never seen its equal in any of the other Ottoman kingdoms.    5.102

"My palace pleases you, then?" the bey asked.

"Yes indeed," my master replied, "but no more so than your luminescent face, your genial qualities, and your graceful words," adding other such sweet pleasantries to his praise of His Excellency the bey.

١٠٣،٥ اخيراً من بعد خطاب مستطيل نهض القنصر وطلب اذن من حضرة البيك في الرحيل فاذن له وقال للترجمان بان يقول الي معلمي بانه يبقى يزوره طول ما هو في مدينة تونس الي حين ما يسافر فاجابه معلمي سمعاً وطاعه وهذا لي شرف عظيم فامر حينذٍ البيك بان يسبجوله حصان من خاص خيله حتي يركبه لما يريد يجي الي سرايته فاستكثر بخيره وخرجنا من امامه وتوجهنا الي تونس الي بيت القنصر .

١٠٤،٥ وثاني الايام خرجنا من بيت القنصر صحبة رجل من خدام القنصر حتي نتفرج علي المدينه فاينا تكوينها ونظامهم ما له مثيل ودرنا في تلك الشوارع والاسواق والتجار الجالسين في الدكاكين كانهم اماره من حسن اثوابهم وخطابهم الرقيق واستقبالهم لهم للمقبل اليهم بعز واكرام وكان البعض منهم يكلفونا حتي نجلس عندهم حتي يقفوا في خدمتنا انكان يلزمنا حاجه او غرض حتي يقضوه وما يشبه ذلك من اللطافه والاناسيه . المراد الذي رايناه من اهل تونس ما رايناه في غير بلاد من بلاد المغاربه وفي تلك الدوره كل من سالني عن معلمي اقول له هذا حكيم فشاع خبرنا في مدينة تونس بان هل فرنجي حكيم فصاروا يتهادونا من مكان الي مكان لاجل الحكمه وكان معلمي يحكم ويوصف وصفات وطبب كثير ناس من امراض صعبه شاقه .

١٠٥،٥ فرينا علي خان وكان ذلك الخان لليساره فدخلنا اليه فوجدنا من اليساره ناس كثير وكل من هو في شغل وداخل ذلك الخان كنيسه لليساره ورهبان الكبوجين يقدسوا هناك وايضاً ثلاثة خانات اخر لليساره وكل خان داخله كنيسه ورهبان من الاربع الرهبنات ورحنا الي تلك الخانات ايضاً وتفرجنا فايت عيشة تلك اليسارة هنيه في الغايه خلاف عن عيشة يسارة غير بلاد وهذا كله من حسن حلم البيك .

١٠٦،٥ وكانوا ياخدونا الي بيوت الاكابر حتي نشرف علي مرضاهم ودرنا في غير اماكن ايضاً حتي ما خلينا مكان والا تفرجنا عليه فايت عماره هذه المدينه واسواقها وتكوينها مثل مدينة حلب انما هي اصغر من مدينة حلب وكان كل كام يوم¹ نروح لعند حضرة البيك ولما نصل الي صرايته كان² يرسل من قبله ناس حتي يصعدونا الي قصره لان كان يرانا من خروجنا من باب المدينه فيجلس معلمي عنده حتي يتسامروا وكت الفقير اترجم لهم.

---

١ «يوم» لم ترد في الأصل.    ٢ الأصل: كا.

After a lengthy discussion, the consul rose and asked permission to depart, 5.103
and it was granted. The bey had the dragoman tell my master to come back and
visit him as long as he was in Tunis.

"With pleasure," my master replied. "It would be my great honor."

The bey ordered one of his finest horses to be kept ready for my master,
which he could ride whenever he wanted to visit the palace. My master
thanked him warmly and we headed back to the consul's house in Tunis.

The next day, we went out to see the city in the company of one of the 5.104
consul's servants. Its design and organization seemed to us to have no parallel.
We toured its avenues and souks. The merchants sitting in their shops looked
like princes, such was the elegance of their clothing, their graceful manner
of conversation, and their habit of cordially greeting whoever approached
them. Some insisted that we stop and join their company, putting themselves
at our service and affably offering to help us with anything we needed. All in
all, the people of Tunis seemed to us to be unlike those of any other town in
the Maghreb.

During our time there, whenever someone would ask me about my master
I'd tell them he was a doctor. News of the Frankish doctor spread throughout
Tunis, and everywhere we went people began to seek us out for treatment.
My master would offer treatments and prescribe medicines, and he cured
many people of painful ailments.

We passed by a lodging reserved for prisoners of war. It was full of people, 5.105
each occupied with a particular task, and there was a church where Capuchin
monks held mass. In Tunis, there were three similar lodgings, each with a
church and monks from the four monastic orders.[88] We visited these as well,
and I found that the captives led very pleasant lives, unlike in other places. This
was all thanks to the bey's clemency.

We were taken on visits to the homes of the notables, to treat those who 5.106
were ill. And we toured other places as well, leaving no spot unvisited. The
buildings, souks, and general layout of the city seemed to me like Aleppo,
though Tunis is smaller. Every few days, we would go see His Excellency
the bey. When we arrived, he would have sent people to bring us up to his
pavilion, as he could see us coming from the moment we left the gates of the
city.[89] My master would sit with him and they'd converse, while I translated
for them.

١٠٧،٥ فيوم من ذات الايام سال البيك الي معلي انكان علي باله في الجواهر والحجارة الثمينه فاجابه علي قدر الامكان فحينذٍ دخلنا الي خزنت الملك القديمه واحضر ارواه من تلك الحجاره والجواهر وكان معلي ذومعرفه فصار يثمن له تلك الحجار من قسم ياقوت وزمرد والماص وما يشبه ذلك وانوجد حجار ما هن معروفين عند البيك ولا يعرف اساميهم فصار يسمي له كل حجر بمفردها وخواصها وثمنها فانبسط البيك منه ومن معرفته ولا زالوا جالسين في تلك الخزنه الي المساء.

١٠٨،٥ اخيرًا خرج البيك ومعلي وصعدوا للقصر وفي ذلك الوقت راء البيك من شباك ذلك القصر البادري خارج من باب المدينه. حينذٍ قال لليساره الواقفين امامه روحوا استقبلوا بادريكم وكان هل بادري كل ليلة احديجي الي صراية البيك وينام عند تلك اليساره الذين هم في خدمة البيك حتي ثاني يوم يقدس لهم وذلك باذن البيك وكانوا يستقيموا مع البادري ذلك النهاركله ويرجعوا الي خدمتهم للبيك يوم الثنين باكر فاتعجب معلي من اناسيت هل بيك وحلمه شي ما بيتصدق وهذا الذي رايته من هذا الرجل الشريف بل من هل بيك الزريف الرزين الاصيل وما بعرف كيف اوصفه لكن الذي بيقرا خبره يوصفه كما يجب له الوصف. اخيرًا استازن معلي من حضرة البيك ومضينا الي محلنا.

١٠٩،٥ ويوم اخردعانا رجل من التجار الي بيته لاجل مريض الذي كان عنده فمضينا الي بيت ذلك التاجرفاستقبلنا باكرام وبعد ما شرف معلي علي ذلك المريض فهيا لنا ذلك التاجر فطور مكلف وبعدما فطرنا وشربنا القهوه اخد ذلك الرجل يفرجنا علي سراته فرينا علي ديواخانه فرأينا قفص وداخله وحشين زغار فتفرس معلي في تلك الوحوش فواهم غريبين الزي جميلين المنضر وخلقتهم عجيبه غريبه وكانت خلقتهم علي هذه الصفة وهي كل واحد منهم بقد ارنب زغير واجره طوال مثل رجلين الكركي ويديه قصار تحت حنكه مثل كف بني ادم بخمسة اصابع بياكل فيهم ودنبه طويل مثل دنب سبع مرتفع فوق ظهره وثلتين دنبه ريش ابيض واسود درقلي وعيناه عينين غزال وبوزه بوز خنزير وتوبه توب ايل فوجود فيهم اربع خمس خلق من الوحوش.

One day, the bey asked my master if he was interested in jewels and pre-  5.107
cious gems.

"Yes, absolutely," my master replied.

So he took us into the ancient royal treasury and presented some of his
finest gems and jewels. My master, knowledgeable about gemstones, began to
appraise these stones for the bey, pointing out the rubies, emeralds, diamonds,
and other gems. There were some stones in the treasury with which the bey
was unfamiliar, whose names he didn't know. My master identified each one,
along with its properties and value. The bey was delighted with him and his
expertise, and they remained in the treasury until the evening.

Eventually they emerged and went up to the pavilion. From the window,  5.108
the bey spied a priest walking out of the gates of the city.

"Go on," he told the prisoners of war who were standing before him.
"Receive your priest."

This particular priest would come to the bey's palace every Saturday night
and sleep over with the prisoners who were in the bey's service. The next day,
with the bey's blessing, he would hold mass for them, and the prisoners would
spend all day with the priest, returning to service Monday morning.

My master was astonished at the remarkable civility and clemency of the
bey, which could scarcely be believed. That too was my impression of this
noble man. What a charming, dignified, and decent ruler! My description
does not do him justice, so I leave the reader to infer the best description.

We sought the bey's leave, and returned home.

Another day, a merchant invited us to his house to see a sick man who was  5.109
staying with him. Off we went to the house, where the merchant received us
most honorably. My master examined the invalid, and the merchant had a fine
breakfast prepared for us. We ate, and drank coffee, and the merchant showed
us around his palace. As we passed an outdoor salon, we saw a cage with two
small wild animals. My master scrutinized them, finding them most peculiar
in appearance, yet beautiful to look at. Their form was marvelous and bizarre;
I might describe it as follows:

Each was the size of a small rabbit, with long hind legs like a crane's. The
forepaws, which were beneath the jaw, were short; each resembled a human
palm with five fingers, which they used to eat.[90] A long tail, like a lion's, stood
high over the back, and two-thirds of it was covered in striped white and black
plumage. They had the eyes of a gazelle, the snout of a pig, and the coat of a
deer. All told, they combined the traits of four or five different wild animals!

فلما راهم معلي اتعجب من خلقتهم الغريبه وقال لذلك التاجر بانه قط ما راء زيهم مع ١١٠،٥
انه ساح في الدنيا طول عمره . اخيرًا استمنه بانه يبيعهم له فاجابه التاجر بان هل وحوش
مرسلين من رجل صاحب من اراضي السعيد ولاجل خاطرك بكتب لذلك الرجل
بانه يرسلي منهم كام واحد واذا وصلوني بعطيك ايام بلاش وان كان ماصح منهم انا
بعطيك ايام . حينذٍ ساله معلي هل ينوجد منهم كثير في تلك الاراضي فاجابه نعم لكن
صيدهم قوي صعب لان هل وحش ما بيلحقه احدلا كلب حتي ولا طير ولا خيال لانه
خفيف في سيره اسرع من الطيور انما بيصادوه بحيله وهوان الصيادين بيعرفوا اوكاره
ولما بيخرج من وكره يرعي حتي فيمد الصياد يده الي الوكر الي حد عكسه وبيسد ذلك
الوكرمن داخل واذا رجع ذلك الوحش الي وكره فيمد يده الصياد يمسكه وبهذه الحيله
يمسكوهم . اخيرًا اوعد ذلك التاجر الي معلي بانه بيكتب الي صاحبه حتي يرسله من
تلك الوحوش كام واحد فشكر فضله معلي ومضينا الي محلنا.

وفي تلك الايام وصل الي تونس اثنين بادريه من رهبنة اليسوعيه ونزلوا بيت ١١١،٥
القنصر وهل رهبان بيجواكل سنه مره حتي يشتروا يسرا من صدقات المسيحيه وكان
احدهم كاروز معلم في صناعة الكرز فيوم من الايام استمن القنصر الي ذلك الكاروز
بان يكرز له كرزه تكون ماسره في النفوس فاجابه البادري تكرم لكن بشرط ان كرزتي
تستقيم سبعة ايام في كل يوم ساعتين فرضي القنصر بذلك لانه كان رجل مسيحي
خايف الله ومحب الخير والفضيله.

فابتدي البادري في اول كرزه وكان نهار تنين بعد خلوص القداس اعني قبل ١١٢،٥
الظهر بساعتين دخل للكنيسه واغلق الباب والشبابيك والطوق وطفي القناديل حتي
بقينا في ظلمه عظيمه داخل الكنيسه وبعدما رش علي وجهه اشارة الصليب وكان
فتوح خطابه لنا بان هل وعضيه هي عقليه واننا نغمض اعيننا ونمشي معه بالروح في
جميع اقسام الكرزه ولحقته في جميع الاماكن الذي بيدخل اليها بالروح وبدي يشرح في
اول قسم لما خلق الله العالم والنيران والكواكب والملايكه وجمع الماء الي البحور وجميع
ما خلقه علي وجه الارض والقسم الثاني لما خلق الله ادم وحوا وجعلهم في الفردوس

My master was astonished by their strange appearance, and told the mer-    5.110
chant that he'd never seen such a creature though he'd spent his life traveling
all over the world. He implored the man to sell him the animals.

"These were sent to me by a friend living in Upper Egypt," the merchant
said. "As a favor to you, I'd be happy to write to him and ask if he'd send me
a few more. You can have them for free if I receive them from him; and if he
doesn't have any more to send, I'll give you these."

"Are there many such animals to be found in that region?" my master asked
him.

"Yes, but they're very difficult to catch. It's impossible to chase down these
creatures; no person, not even a dog, bird, or horseman, can do so, as they're
very nimble, swifter than birds. So, they use a particular ruse to hunt them.
The hunters know where their dens are, and when the animals come out to
graze, the hunter reaches into the den and blocks it up on the inside. When an
animal returns to its burrow, the hunter thrusts his hand in and seizes it. That's
how they catch them."[91]

The merchant promised he'd write to his friend and ask him to send a few of
the animals. My master thanked him for this, and we returned home.

One day, two Jesuit priests arrived in Tunis and took up lodging in the con-    5.111
sul's house. These monks would visit once a year to purchase prisoners of war,
using alms collected from the Christians. One of them was a preacher skilled
at giving sermons, and one day the consul begged him to preach a sermon that
would stir people's souls.

"Gladly," the priest replied, "if you let me preach two hours a day for seven
days." The consul agreed, for he was a Christian man who feared God and
loved charity and good works.

The priest began the first sermon on a Monday after mass, two hours before    5.112
noon. He went into the church and closed the door, the windows, and the sky-
light. He blew out the candles. We were engulfed in almost total darkness in
the church. He made the sign of the cross upon his face and began his sermon
by saying that it would exercise our intellects. We were to close our eyes and
accompany him in spirit throughout all the parts of the sermon, following him
to all the places he entered spiritually.

In the first part, he began by recounting how God created the world, the
sun and moon, the stars, and the angels, and how He brought all the water

وسقطة ادم وخروجه من الفردوس ثم حيات سيدنا يسوع المسيح وما يشبه ذلك من اخبار الكتب المقدسه.

اخيرًا صار يشرح لنا اربع عواقب الانسان اعني الموت والدينونه والجحيم والنعيم وفي كل واحده يمشينا معه بالروح الي حين ما نزل معنا الي جهنم وفي كل درجه ومكان من جهنم يسال تلك الانفس ماذا كانت خطيتهم حتي حصلوا في ذلك المكان الجهني يتعدبون بغير رحمه مقطوعين الرجا الي ابد الابدين. اخيرًا اصعدنا معه الي الملكوت وهناك كان يسال ضغمات القديسين وكيف تم خلاصهم حتي حظيوا في هل سعادة الابديه وما يشبه ذلك من الالفاظ الماثره في الانفس وفي هذا كمل خطابه في اليوم السابع وخرجنا من هذه الرياضه كاننا سكاره ومضيعين الرشد والحواس بهذا المقدار حتي كل من يراء حاله كانه في غيبوبه.

والفقير صدف لي يوم وانا ركع في الكنيسه بعد حضوري القداس وانا في هل تامل غبت عن حواسي واستمرت ساهي غايب الي ان حكم وقت الغدا وكانوا فتشوا علي حتي اتغذا فراوني راكع في الكنيسه وشاخص بغير وعي فنبهوني من ذلك الرقاد والبحران الذي كنت فيه.

واخيرًا كل واحد منا بادر للاعتراف وتناول الاسرار المقدسه وفي ذلك الغضون وقع معلمي في مرض شديد وشارف علي الموت وقطعنا الرجا من حياته وفي تلك الليله وانا نايم حدي فراشه وانا في غاية الحزن من جري موت هل رجل وانا غاطس في بحر الافكار كيف يصير فيّ بعد موته وانا في تلك الغربه وما لي ملجا من احد وبعيد عن بلادي حتي مضي نصفه من الليل فسمعت نقر عصاته علي الدفه لان كان انقطع صوته بالكليه فالتزمنا باننا نضع قرب وسادته عصاة وتحتها دفه حتي اذا اراد منا شي ينقر العصاه علي الدفه فنبادر اليه وزي ما يحتاج فلما سمعت انه نقر الدفه نهضة عاجلًا اليه.

فامرني باني اجيب الي قرب فراشه سندوق الحكمه بالذي كان له فلما جبته ووضعته علي كرسي مقابله حيندٍ امرني باني اخرج كيس خرجيته من تحت الوساده

into the seas, and created everything on the face of the Earth. The second part of the sermon addressed how God created Adam and Eve and put them in Paradise, and how Adam fell and was expelled from Paradise. He then moved on to the life of Our Lord Jesus Christ, and other stories from the holy books.

He next explained to us the four final stages of the human being: death, the 5.113 final judgment, hellfire, and Paradise. With each one, we walked with him in spirit, until we descended together to Hell. At each station of Hell, he would ask the souls of those who were there what sins had damned them to this infernal place, mercilessly enslaved and cut off from all hope for eternity.

Later, we rose with him to the Kingdom of Heaven, where he asked the assembly of saints about their salvation. How did they come to enjoy this eternal bliss? The preacher continued in this way, stirring our souls with his words, and concluded his sermon here on the seventh day. We emerged from this retreat feeling giddy, dazed, and disoriented, as if in a trance.

One day, while I was kneeling in the church after mass in a state of contem- 5.114 plation, I fell into a similar kind of stupor and remained insensible until lunchtime! When they came looking for me, they found me kneeling in the church, out cold. They had to wake me from my witless state.[92]

Anyway, at the conclusion of the preacher's sermon, each of us went to 5.115 confession to receive the Holy Communion. It was around that time that my master became gravely ill. He was practically on the brink of death, and we'd lost hope of his recovery. That night, I lay down to sleep beside his bed, feeling a profound sorrow about his looming death. I plunged into the ocean of my own thoughts.

"What will happen to me after he dies?" I fretted. "Here I am, a stranger in a strange land, with no one to turn to, far from home."

After half the night had passed, I heard the sound of his cane rapping the board we'd placed beside his cushion so he could summon us if he needed anything, as his voice was too weak. When I heard him strike the board, I hurried over to see him.

He ordered me to fetch his doctor's trunk and place it beside his bed. I 5.116 brought it over and put it on a chair in front of him. He told me to take his purse from under his pillow and find the key to the trunk. I did what he asked and opened the trunk.

واطّلع منه مفتاح ذلك السندوق ففعلت[١] كما امرني وفتحت السندوق فرأيت في نصف ذلك السندوق سندوق زغير من ابانس[٢] مصفح بصفايح نحاس اصفر وكان مغلق كأنه فرد قطعه وما له مكان للفتح فاراوني حركه وهو بصمار مثل باقيت البصامير الموجوده في السندوق فلما رصيت ذلك البصمار في باهي انفتح السندوق فرأيت داخله سندوق زغير وداخل السندوق خنجور من التحف وله برما من النحاس ايضاً.

حينذٍ امرني بان اجيب كاس وداخله اصبعتين انبيد فلما احضرت الكاس والنبيد ١١٧،٥ فقلي دير البرمه التي في فم الخنجور ففعلت كما قلي وانفتح فم الخنجور فرأيت ثاني سداده من التحف ومغطات بشمع عسلي فاخرجت الجميع فقلي حينذٍ ضع باهمك علي فم الخنجور ونقط من ذلك الماء الذي داخله ثلاثة نقط لا غير. اخيراً امرني بان ارجّع كل شي الي مكانه واغلق السندوق واضع المفتاح داخل كيس خرجيته كما كان فبعدما كمت جميع ما امرني به اخد من يدي الكاس وانا ماسك هامه فشربه وخسل الكاس بقليل من ذلك الخمر وشربه وبعده انتكي ونام وانا رجعت الي فراشي ونمت الي ان اصبح الصباح.

فناداني من غير نقر العصاه فنهضت عاجلاً ووقفت امامه وسالته ماذا تريد قلي ١١٨،٥ جيب لي حوايج حتي اتبدل فاحضرت له الحوايج فنهض من ذاته في الفراش من غير اني اسنده فتعجبت من ذلك كيف انه نهض وصار له قوي قابتديت اشلحه فرأيت ثيابه غرقانه من العرق وبالجهد حتي قدرت اشلحه قيصه فبعدما لبسته ثيابه النضاف فاخد يدي ونزل من عن سريره وجلس علي الكرسي. حينذٍ قلته ماذا تريد قلي غير لي الملاحف واقلب الفرش لانهم تندوا من عرقه الذي نفد الي ثالث فراش.

فعملت كما امرني. اخيراً رجع الي سريره ونام حكم ساعتين وانتبه وامرني باني اجيب ١١٩،٥ له شاكاسة المرقه فرحت الي المطبخ وجبت المرقه والمنديل والمعلقه ودخلت الي عنده حتي اسقيه المرقه فوجدته يتمشا في الاوضه ففرحت فيه ولكن اخدني العجب في قيامه من فراشه بعدما كان حسب من الموتا تلك الليلة المضت وما عرفت بان تلك الثلاثة

---
١ الأصل: ففعلت.  ٢ الأصل: ابلس.

Inside, I found a smaller chest made of ebony and plated with brass. It was closed, and seemed as though it were made of a single piece of wood, with no place to insert a key. My master showed me the mechanism that opened it: There was a rivet that looked like all the others on the chest. When I pressed it with my thumb, the chest popped open. Inside, I found yet another small chest, inside which was a crystal flask with a brass stopper.

My master told me to bring him a glass with two fingers' worth of wine in it, which I did. 5.117

"Turn the stopper in the mouth of the flask," he told me. I did as he said, and the mouth of the flask opened. Inside was another stopper, made of crystal and covered in light-brown wax. I took everything out of the trunk.

"Put your thumb over the mouth of the flask and measure out three drops of the liquid—just three!" he said. He told me to put everything away, close the trunk, and put the key back in his purse.

After I finished doing everything he asked, he took the glass from my hand and I held his head in my hands and helped him drink it. He rinsed the glass with a little more wine and drank that. He lay back down and fell asleep, and I went to my own bed and slept until morning.

The next day, he summoned me without rapping the cane. I got up hurriedly and came and stood before him. 5.118

"What do you need?" I asked.

"Bring me some clothes so I can get dressed," he said.

I brought him some clothes, and he sat up by himself in bed, without my help. I was astonished to see that he'd managed to sit up, and that his strength had returned! I began to strip off his clothes, which were soaked through with sweat. It took some effort to peel off his shirt. After I dressed him in fresh clothes, he took hold of my hand, got out of bed, and sat on the chair.

"What else would you like?" I asked.

"Change my blankets and flip the mattress over." They were soaked through with his sweat, which had seeped down as far as the third mattress.

I did as he asked, and he got back in bed and slept for two hours. When he 5.119 woke, he ordered me to bring him a bowl of broth. I went to the kitchen to fetch some broth, a napkin, and a spoon, and brought it all back to feed him. I found him walking around the room! My delight at this sight was mixed with astonishment. How had he managed to stand up after being on his deathbed

النقط التي شربها هي التي صارة سبب شفاه من ذلك المرض الشديد الذي كان حاصل فيه لكن بعد حين هو احكالي بانه شفني في شربه هل ثلاثة نقط.

فلما سمعت منه هل كلام قلته يا سيدي لماذا ما شربتهم من قبل وكت[1] وفوت علينا وعليك هل مضض والشقا الذي حزرت[2] فيه. حينذٍ اتضحك وقلي واكد لي بكلامه بان لو ما عرفت باني قاربت الموت لماكنت شربتهم لان لي اربعة وعشرين سنه سايح في هل دنيا حتي حضيت في فد حشيشه التي هي الاكسير الذي يتدفع الاعراض من الانسان والامراض.

وقلي انا وقفت علي خبر احد السواح وهو مارخ في كتاب تواريخ دير مار فرنسيس في مدينة بهريز هو انه في عيد ذلك القديس بيعطا غفران كامل للذين بيعترفوا و بيتناولوا الاسرار المقدسه فصدف الي واحد كاهن وهو جالس في كرسي الاعتراف بيعرف فسجد امامه واحد من الشباب بهي المنضر وطلب منه انه يقبل اعترافه وشمه باشارة الصليب وقله اعترف يا ولدي ايش لك من الزمان عن الاعتراف فاجابه ذلك الشب يا ابانا لي ستين سنه ما اعترفت فبهت الكاهن من كلامه وقله ما هذا الهزو اما تعلم بان سر الاعتراف ما بيصير فيه كلام هزو وكذب فاجابه ذلك الشاب لماذا تقلي هل كلام يا ابونا هل اني جاهل ومجنون حتي أكذب عليك وعلي الله تعالي نفسه.

فاجابه الكاهن صدقت يا ابني ولكن كيف بقدر اصدق بان لك ستين سنه ما اعترفت وانت بالاكثر حتي يكون عمرك ثلاثين سنه روح اعترف عند غيري انا ما بقدر اعرفك حتي تصدقني في امرك. اخيراً بعرفك فاجابه ذلك الشاب قوم بنا نصعد الي الدير وهناك بعلمك في امري علي التحقيق فرضي الكاهن وصعدوا معاً الي الدير ودخل ذلك الكاهن الي قلايته وكف ذلك الشاب في الدخول وجلسوا[3] اثنين هم فسال الكاهن لذلك الشاب عن جليت امره بالحق.

فاجابه الشاب ان سالت عني يا ابانا انا ابن هل بلاد ولما خرجت للسياحه كان لي من العمر اربعين سنه واستقمت ستين سنه سايح في بلاد بعيده متطلب حشايش

١ «وكت» في الأصل مطموس. ٢ «حزرت» في الأصل مطموس. ٣ «وجلسوا» في الأصل مطموس.

the night before? I hadn't yet realized that those three drops he'd drunk were the reason for his recovery from that terrible illness. Later, he told me how he'd been cured by those three drops.

"But sir, why didn't you take them earlier?" I asked. "You could have saved   5.120 yourself all that pain and suffering, to say nothing of the rest of us!"

He laughed.

"I wouldn't have taken them had I not known that I was near death," he said. "I spent twenty-four years traveling around the world before I was fortunate enough to acquire a unique plant, the elixir that wards off all ailments and illnesses from human beings."

"I once came upon a story by a traveler," he continued, "which was   5.121 recorded in a chronicle of the Monastery of Saint-François in Paris. On the feast day of that saint, the people who come to confess their sins and receive Holy Communion are granted indulgences. One day, while a priest sat in the confessional, a handsome young man bowed down before him and asked him to hear his confession.

"The priest made the sign of the cross over him and said, 'Confess, my son. How long has it been since your last confession?'

"'Sixty years, Father,' the young man replied. The priest was taken aback.

"'Think you're funny, do you?' he said. 'Don't you know that confession is no place for jesting or lying?'

"'Why would you say that, Father?' the young man said. 'Do you think I'm crazy enough to lie to you, or to God for that matter?'

"'Fair enough, my son,' the priest replied, 'but how can I believe that you   5.122 haven't confessed in sixty years, when you can't be a day older than thirty? Run along and give your confession to someone else. I won't accept it unless you can prove your story is true.'

"'Come with me,' said the young man. 'Let's go up to the monastery and I'll tell you my whole story.'

"The priest agreed and the two of them went up to the monastery. The priest went into his cell and invited the young man in. Sitting there, alone together, the priest asked the young man to tell him the truth of the matter.

"'Father, I was born in this country, and embarked upon my travels when   5.123 I was forty years old. I spent sixty years voyaging in faraway lands, searching for certain plants and drugs described in ancient texts. I found the herb that

وعقاقير التي هي مرسومه في الكتب القديمه فوجدت تلك الحشيشه التي كت طالبها وهي حشيشة الاكسير وبتسما في كتب الفلاسفة اليونانين بيروا فيلوسوفه اعني حجر الفلاسفة ومن هل حشيشه ركبت منها ضرور ولما كمل جربته فرايت فعله كما هو مكتوب في تلك الكتب اعني اذا استعمل الانسان منه حكم حبه تمنع عنه الاعارض والامراض عشر سنين وبتستقيم عافيته كايام شبوبيته.

٥،١٢٤ فصرت استعمل منها في كل عشر سنين حبه واستقمت كما تراني في حال الشبوبيه وهذا الذي غواني وانساني الموت وانا غفلان عن خلاص نفسي والان الله تحنن علي ودق قلبي بنعمته ففقت من هل رقاد السيء وعلمت باني اموت لا محاله لان الله عز اسمه حتم علي الانسان بالموت وان اوليك الفلاسفة الذين استعملوا هل حشيشه ماتوا وهذا كان السبب حتي اني رجعت الي بلادي وطلبت الاعتراف والتوبه قبل الموت.

٥،١٢٥ فلما سمع الكاهن من الشاب هل كلام هل تعجب وقله هل بقي معك من هل اكسير الذي ذكرت عنه الان فاجابه الشاب نعم موجود منه معي فقله الكاهن هل بتريد تعطيني منه جزٍ حتي اجربه واصدق كلامك هل هو صدق ام كذب فقله نكرم واخرج من محفظته علبه فضه واعطي الي الكاهن عشرة حبات وقله اذا استعملت في كل عشر سنين حبه من هذا الحب بتعيش ماية سنه ما عدا عمرك الذي انت حاصل فيه فاخدمهم الكاهن منه وبعده صار يعرفه اعتراف عام وبعده ندمه علي خطاياه واعطاه الحله والقانون واصرفه.

٥،١٢٦ اخيرًا صار يفتكر الكاهن كيف بيقدر يجرب ذلك الحب فخطر في باله بان في الدير موجود كلب هرم كبير في العمر وما بقا له قوي للمشي وكان يجيبوا له في انا قليل من المرقه يلقها وهو جالس. حينذٍ اخد الكاهن حبه من تلك الحبات ودوبها في قليل من المرقه ووضعها امامه فلقها ذلك الكلب كما هو معتاد يلق الامراق وتركه ومضي الي قلايته يقرا فرضه فبعدما انتها من صلاته مضي لينضر الكلب فراه داير في صحن الدير وهو يتنفض ورجعت قواه اليه كالاول. وقيدٍ تحقق الكاهن كلام ذلك الشاب وبعده كتب صورة الواقعه علي قرظار.

I was looking for, the elixir—which the books of Greek philosophers call *bīrū fīlūsūfa*, "the philosopher's stone." I composed a medical powder from this herb, and when I finished testing it, I found that its effect was just as the books described: If a man consumes just a bit of it, he's protected from all ailments and illnesses for ten years, his health remaining sound throughout, just as it was in his youth.

"'I began to take a single pill every ten years, and have remained in the youthful state you see me in today. This is what led me astray. It made me forget about death and pay no heed to my soul's salvation. But now, God has shown mercy on me and touched my heart with His grace. I've awoken from that evil slumber, realizing that I will inevitably die, for God—whose name be praised—has ordained death upon every human being. Indeed, the philosophers who made use of this herb eventually perished. So I have returned to my country and seek to confess my sins and repent before I die.'

5.124

"When the priest heard the young man's words, he was amazed.

5.125

"'The elixir you mentioned,' the priest said. 'Is there any of it left?'

"'Yes,' the young man replied. 'In fact, I have some with me here.'

"'Would you give me a little to try, so I can see if you're telling the truth or not?'

"'Certainly,' the young man said, and brought out a silver box from his satchel, from which he took ten pills. He gave them to the priest.

"'If you take one every ten years, you'll live a hundred years past your present age,' he said.

"The priest took the pills from the young man, and heard his confession. He made him repent for his sins, absolving him and imposing a penitence upon him, then sent him away.

"For a while, the priest pondered how he might test the effect of the pills. He recalled that in the monastery there was a decrepit old dog that didn't have the strength to walk. The monks would bring it a little bit of broth in a dish and it would drink without rising. The priest took a pill, dissolved it in a bit of broth, and put it before the dog, who lapped it up as usual. The priest then returned to his cell to read his breviary.

5.126

"After his prayers, the priest returned to see the dog, and found it running around the courtyard of the monastery, invigorated, its strength restored! Convinced the young man's story was true, he wrote down an account of the whole affair in a notebook.

١٢٧،٥ وفي اخرها ذكر انكان ما بتصدقوني انضروا الي الكلب الهرم كيف انه تعافاء ورجعت قوته اليه وترك ذلك القرظار علي مكبته ومضي وما احد عرف له اثار ولما استفقدوه الرهبان وما راوه استازنوا من الريس وكسروا قفل قلايته ودخلوا فاؤذلك القرظار علي مكبته فلما قروه تعجبوا وبادروا حتي ينضروا ذلك الكلب فراوه كما هو ذاكر عنه. حينذِ شاع هذا الخبر في مدينة بهرز فتبادرة الناس الي الديرحتي ينضروا ذلك الكلب المذكور ثم دونوا هذا الخبر في كتاب تواريخ الدير والشاهد ان معلي كان له من العمر ينوف عن الستين سنه وكنت تراه كانه شاب ابن ثلاثين سنه.

١٢٨،٥ فلنرجع الان عن ما كنا في صدده فتعافاء معلي من ذلك المرض القتال ورجعت عافيته اليه كالاول وصرنا ندور في شوارع المدينه كهادتنا واوقاتاً نذهب الي البارده الي عند البيك المذكور ونتنزه في تلك الرياض والبساتين ولا زال حضرة البيك يعمل الي معلي اكرام ويرويه محبة الي يوم الذي هم معلي في السفر من تونس فدخل لعنده وودعه واستكثر بخيره.

١٢٩،٥ ورجعنا الي محلنا وقبل دخولنا الي بيت القنصر صادفنا ذلك الرجل التاجر الذي كان اوعد الي معلي بانه يرسل له من تلك الوحوش الذي رايناهم في منزله فبعدما سلم عليه بشره بان الوحوش وصلوا الي عنده وهن خمسه ففرح معلي في وصولهم فمضينا معه الي منزله فرايناهم وهم في قفص من عروق النخل. حينذِ راد معلي يعطيه ما اصرفه في اتيانهم الي عنده فما قبل ياخد منه شي بل امر الي احد خدامه بانه ياخدهم الي محلنا فشكر معلي فضله ومضينا الي بيت القنصر فوجدنا ذلك الغلام والقفص في يده وهو في انتظارنا.

١٣٠،٥ فاخرج معلي واعطاه حكم عشرة غروش بخشيش واصرفه وفي الحال ارسل احضر نجار الي عنده واشرله شكل قفص قفص له بيوت ومخاضع حتي ينفردوا عن بعضهم ووضعناهم في ذلك القفص وفي الحال كل واحد رايناهم منهم دخل في مخضع واختفي ووضعنا لهم شي للاكل من قسم لوز وبندق وغير حبوب فصاروا ياكلوا من جميع ما نضعه لهم من غير اللحم وبعدما ياكلوا يكنسوا صحن القفص في ادنابهم ويخرجوا الوسخ

ا الأصل: ونتزه.

"'If you don't believe me, go look at that decrepit dog,' he wrote in conclu-   5.127
sion. 'See how its strength has returned!'

"The priest left the notebook on his desk and vanished without a trace.

"When the monks noticed his absence, they asked the abbot for permission to break open the lock of the priest's cell. They found the notebook on the
desk, read it in amazement, and hurried off to see the dog, who was just as the
priest had described.

"The news of this event spread rapidly through the city of Paris. People
rushed to the monastery to see the dog, and the story was recorded in the
monastery's chronicles."

If you don't believe me, consider this: My own master was over sixty years
old, yet looked a man of thirty![93]

Let me get back to what I was saying earlier. My master recovered from   5.128
his terrible illness, and his good health returned. We began touring the streets
of the city as was our custom, and sometimes went to Bardo to visit the bey.
We would stroll through his gardens and orchards, and His Excellency continued to honor my master and treat him affectionately. Eventually, the day came
when my master decided to leave Tunis. He went to see the bey and bid him
farewell, wishing him all the best.

We set out for our lodgings and, just before arriving at the consul's, hap-   5.129
pened upon the merchant who'd promised my master he'd send away for those
wild animals we'd seen at his house. He greeted my master and gave him the
good news: The animals had arrived, five in all! My master was delighted, and
we went with the merchant to his house and found the creatures in a cage
made of palm branches. My master tried to pay the man for the expenses of
obtaining them but he wouldn't accept any money, and even told one of his
servants to carry them to our house. My master thanked him and returned
to the consul's home. When we got there, we found the servant waiting with
the cage.

My master gave him a tip of about ten piasters, and sent him away. He imme-   5.130
diately sent off for a carpenter and explained that he wanted a cage with separate compartments to keep the animals apart. We put them in the cage and
watched each disappear into its own chamber. We gave them some almonds
and hazelnuts and other nuts to eat. In fact, they ate everything we gave them,
other than meat.

وربلهم الي خارج القفص وكان لهم رويا ومناقب عجيبه في اكلهم ونضافتهم كانوا ياكلوا وهن وقوف وياخدوا بايدهم الحبوب ويضعوها في فهم مثل الاوادم وبعد خلوصهم من الاكل يدخل كل واحد منهم الي مخدعه ويختبي وكا نضع لهم في القفص صوف جز كانوا يكوه ويخرجوا الوسخ منه ويدخلوا فيه مختفيين حتي يدفوا لان اراضيهم حاره جداً وكان ذلك التاجر حرسنا بلا ندعهم يبردوا ونوضع لهم من ذلك الصوف لاجل الدفا.

اخيراً بعدما رتبنا لهم ذلك القفص حينذٍ وكلني معلمي في ذلك القفص والوحوش الذين داخله بان احترس عليهم قوي كثير من البرد ليلا يموتوا وان وصلنا الي بهريز وهم طيبين بينويك منهم خير عظيم لان بواسطتهم بتدخل الي اماكن ما بيقدر غيرك يدخلها. حينذٍ شرت اليه بان نضع لهم جلال من جوخ وجللنا ذلك القفص.

فبعد مدة ايام اتا الي اسكلت تونس مركب انكليزي زغير واسق قح حتي يبيعه في ليكورنا فلما اخد خبره القنصر شار علي معلمي بانه يسافر معه وقال له قرصان الانكليز ما بتاخدك وان اخدوا المركب قرصان الفرنساويه ما عليك منهم باس بما انك فرنساوي ومنسوب الي سلطان فرنسا فاستصوب معلمي كلام القنصر وبعده استكينا مع ذلك القبطان الانكليزي حتي نروح معه الي ليكورنا.

وبعد كام يوم نبه علينا القبطان حتي نرسل حوايجنا الي الاسكله التي هي اسكلت مدينة كرتاجنه المشهوره بالكبر والاتساع وكان علي عليها البحر خربت ولما اتاخدت تلك البلاد من الجراكسه باشروا في بناء مدينة تونس وهي بعيده١ عن تلك الاسكله مقدار ثلاث اواربع ميال. اخيراً نقلنا حوايجنا الي الاسكله وكان القنصر هيا لنا زواده وافره من زاد نبيد وجاج وراس غنم وما يشبه ذلك من ما يلزمنا في سفر البحــر.

١٣١،٥

١٣٢،٥

١٣٣،٥

---

١ الأصل: بعديده.

After they'd eaten, they'd sweep the floor of the cage with their tails, expelling all their waste and refuse. Their appearance and manner of eating and cleaning were striking. They would eat standing upright, picking up the nuts with their hands and putting them in their mouths as humans do. Each would then disappear into its chamber. We placed some pieces of raw wool in the cage, which they would shred into lint, clean, and burrow under for warmth. The lands they come from are very hot, and the merchant had warned us not to let them get cold, and to give them pieces of wool for warmth.

After we'd prepared the cage, my master put me in charge of it and of the animals. He told me to guard it carefully and keep it out of the cold, so the animals wouldn't die. 5.131

"If they're still alive when we get to Paris, you'll be glad to have them," he told me. "They'll open doors for you that never open for anyone." Hearing that, I suggested to him that we cover the cage with a horsecloth, and we did.

A few days later, a small English ship came into the port of Tunis. It was carrying wheat to sell in Livorno. When the consul heard about the ship, he suggested that my master consider sailing aboard it. 5.132

"The English corsairs won't seize it. And if French corsairs do, they won't harm you because you're a Frenchman and have connections to the sultan of France."

My master appreciated the wisdom of the consul's words, so we booked passage with the English captain to go with him to Livorno.

After a few days, the captain gave us notice to send our baggage to the port of Carthage, once famous for its vast size. It was ruined when the sea level rose around it. When this region was seized from the Saracens, they built the city of Tunis, which is three or four miles from the harbor.[94] 5.133

We transported our luggage to the port. In the meantime, the consul had prepared ample provisions for us, including wine, chickens, a sheep, and other necessities for a sea journey.

# الفصل السادس

## في سفرنا الي بلاد الفرنجيه سنه ١٧٠٨

٦.١ فكان خروجنا من مدينة تونس في اول شهر حزيران فنزلنا في ذلك المركب المذكور وبعد يوم سافرنا ولا زلنا مسافرين حتي وصلنا الي جزيرة كورسيكا وهي من معاملة ايطاليا فلما رسي المركب في تلك الاسكله صار القبطان يسال اهل تلك الجزيره هل معهم خبر من مركب قرصان فرنساوي في ذلك البحر الذي هو قريب اليهم فاجابوه نعم في مركب قرصان فرنساوي يصلب في هل دوه وحرسوه ليلا يسافر لان المركب كبير ودخله مايتين عسكري وعشرين طوب من غير البحريه فلما سمع القبطان منهم هذا الخبر صمم النيه بانه يستقيم في تلك الجزيره الي حين ما ياخد خبره بانه مضي من تلك الرقعه.

٦.٢ فاستقمنا ذلك اليوم في تلك الاسكله ونحاكا مع اهل الجزيره من مركبنا وكان سافر معنا ثمانية انفار من اليساره من الذين اشتروهم اوليك الباديره المذكورين وكان واحد منهم اختيار وهو من اهل الجزيره واستقام في اليسر عشرين سنه فهذا صار يسال عن حرمته واولاده هل هن طيبين.

٦.٣ فاتوا بهم فلما امتثلوا امامه وراء حرمته واولاده وهن طيبين فصار يبكي من شدة فرحه وايضا حرمته واولاده يبكوا. اخيرا توسلوا اليه بانه يخرج من المركب ويعمل الكرنتينا[١] في بلده اعني يدخل الي مكان الذي يستقيم فيه الوارد من بلاد الشرق او الغرب اربعين يوم وبعد تلك المده يبخروه وبيدعوه يدخل الي المدينه فما راد

---

١ الأصل: الكرتينا.

# Chapter Six

## Our Journey to the Lands of the Franks in the Year 1708

We left Tunis at the beginning of June. We boarded the ship and set sail the next day, making for the island of Corsica, which was ruled by Italy. The ship dropped anchor in the harbor, and the captain asked the locals if they'd heard anything about a French corsair in nearby waters. 6.1

"Yes," they replied. "There is indeed one cruising in the area," and they advised him not to set sail because the ship was large, with twenty cannons and two hundred armed men on board, not counting the sailors. So the captain decided to remain on the island until he received word that the pirates had left the area.

We spent the day in the harbor, chatting with the islanders aboard our ship. Traveling with us were eight prisoners whose ransom had been paid by the Jesuit priests. One of them was an old Corsican man who'd been held prisoner for twenty years. He inquired after his wife and children, asking the local people whether they were still alive. 6.2

They were brought to him. When the man saw his wife and children alive and well with his own eyes, he began to cry tears of joy. His wife and children also wept, and begged him to come down from the ship and go into quarantine, a place where travelers would remain for forty days, whether coming from the east or the west. After that period, they would be fumigated and allowed to enter the city. 6.3

But the old man didn't want to leave the ship.

يخرج انما قلهم انا بروح الي ليكورنا وبقضي بعض مسالح ثم بجي الي عندكم عن قريب فصاروا عياله يتوسلوا الينا حتي نلزمه في الخروج فما امكن انه يسمع لاحد بل استقام في المركب لسوحظه.

٦،٤ فاستقمنا ذلك النهار الي حين غروب الشمس في تلك الاسكله وفي ذلك الوقت خرج ريح من البر مناسب للسفر فلما رااء ذلك الريح القبطان قال في باله بان في بيني وبين ليكورنا مسافة ستين ميل واذا سافرت بطي اسكت ليكورنا في هذا الليل وبخلص من هل مركب القرصان ففعل كما دبره عقله وامر النوتيه بانهم يسحبوا المراسي ويفتحوا القلوع ويسافروا فعملوا كما امرهم وسافر المركب في ذلك الريح الي ان قطعنا مسافة ثلاثين ميل.

٦،٥ وفي ذلك الوقت حدث في البحر غلينه عظيمه وسكت الريح وفرغت القلوع من الهوا واستقام مركبنا واقف كانه مرسي في الاسكله فلما راء القبطان هذه المصيبه خاف وارتعب وصار يامر جماعته بانهم يصلوا ويطلبوا من الله تعالي بانه يرسل لهم قليلًا من الريح حتي يجوزوا تلك المسافة التي بقيت فما استجاب الله دعاهم لاجل امر يريده.

٦،٦ فاستقمنا تلك الليله ومركبنا واقف بغير سير الي ان شق الفجر فامر القبطان الي احد النوتيه بانه يصعد الي علو الصاري وينضر هل يرا مركب في البحر فصعد ذلك النوتي وانحدر وقال بانه راء سواده من ناحيت الغرب فظنوا بان هل سواده هي جبل من جبال بلاد ايطاليا فما اقنع القبطان من ذلك بل ارسل يازنجي المركب الي علو الصاري حتي يحقق الامر هل ان السواده جبل ام مركب فصعد اليازنجي الي علو ذلك الصاري وكان ذلك الوقت اصبح الصباح وانحدر وقال للقبطان بانه راء مركب كبير وهو موجه الي طرفنا وكان ذلك المركب رانا قبل ما نحن نراه.

٦،٧ حينٍ اخذ القبطان الدربين وطلع فراء المركب جايي علينا بسير شديد بواسطة الكريكات وكان معه ستة وثلاثين كريك اعني مقداف ومايتين شب الذين بيقدفوا فاتطر القبطان بانه يضع مقاديف وكان موجود عنده ستة مقاديف فصار ذلك الوقت بيتوسل الي الذين في المركب بانهم يقدفوا ودار المركب الي ناحيت الجزيره التي خرجنا منها تلك الليله فصرنا جميعنا نتعاون ونقدم حتي نهرب من ذلك المركب واوليك ايضاً يجدوا في المسير الينا.

"I just need to go to Livorno to take care of a few matters," he said. "I'll return home soon enough."

His family begged us to force him off the ship but he wouldn't listen to anyone. It was his misfortune to remain on board.

We spent the day in the harbor. At sunset, a favorable offshore breeze rose up. When the captain felt it, he said to himself, "There's sixty miles between me and Livorno. If I set sail now, we'll reach the harbor by morning and escape the corsair."

6.4

Putting this plan into action, he ordered the sailors to weigh anchor, unfurl the sails, and shove off. They did as he ordered, and the ship sailed with those favorable winds for thirty miles.

Then a dead calm settled over the sea and the winds died. The sails went limp, and the ship stood as still as though it were anchored in a harbor. In the face of this disaster, the captain was terrified. He told his men to pray, asking God Most High to send even a little bit of wind to help us cross the remaining distance. Alas, this was not what God had willed.

6.5

The ship remained motionless all night. At dawn, the captain ordered one of the sailors to climb to the top of the mast to see if he could spot any ships. The sailor mounted the mast, then descended, reporting that he'd spied something dark in the west—one of the mountains of Italy perhaps? The captain wasn't convinced, so he sent the first mate up the mast to investigate. Was it a mountain or a ship?

6.6

The first mate climbed to the top of the mast. In the meantime, morning had broken. He climbed down and told the captain he'd seen a large ship headed in our direction. What's more, they'd spotted us before we'd seen them!

The captain took the spyglass and trained it on the ship being rowed swiftly toward us. It had thirty-six blades—that is, oars—rowed by two hundred young men. Our captain was forced to put our own six oars into the water, and begged the passengers to start rowing! Then he turned the ship back toward the island we'd sailed from the night before. We all started working together, rowing to escape the other ship while they too threw themselves into their pursuit of us.

6.7

٨،٦ وفي قليل من الزمان قربوا الينا فلما راء القبطان بانهم قربوا الينا امر النوتيه بان ينزلوا قايق المركب الي البحر وربطوا القايق في منخار المركب ونزل[1] اليازجي ومعه اربعه من النوتيه حتي يقدفوا ويسحبوا المركب الي قدام ولكن كانت نيت القبطان غيرشي وهي ان كان عنده اربع سناديق مرجان الذي كان تسوقهم من اماكن الذي يخرج منهم اعني من بحرهم المرجان وهو في قاع البحر كانه سجار مغروزه في الرمل ومعه ايضاً مبلغ من الريال وفي ذلك الوقت ونحن مشغولين في القدم والهربه نزل تلك الاربع سناديق المرجان وذلك المبلغ من غروش الريال الي القايق من غير احد منا يعرف بذلك.

٩،٦ وبعد هنيهه قرب الينا ذلك المركب القرصان وضرب طوب فمرت الكله من فوق الصاري ولما رانا ما سلمنا ونحن مجدين في الهربه ضرب ثاني طوب فمرت الكله حكم نصف الصاري فما سلمنا والقبطان يجرعنا ويحثنا علي الهربه. حينذٍ ضرب ثالث طوب فمرت الكله من فوق روسنا فسقطنا جميعنا علي اوجاهنا من رعبتنا من عزم ضوضة تلك الكله التي لو تصيبنا لما ابقت منا احد. حينذٍ نهضنا جميعنا وانتهرنا القبطان والزمناه بانه يسلم وركبت منّا ناس ونزلوا البيرق وهذه علامه حتي يكف عن الضرب فلما نزلنا البيرق صرح ذلك القرصان بالبوق قايلاً مينا بالفراسه مينا اعني اعطوا طاعه للفرانسا اعطوا.

١٠،٦ حينذٍ لفينا القلوع وفي ذلك المحل لما راء اليازجي الذي هو في القايق كما ذكرنا بان القبطان تسلّم وما بقا رجا للخلاص قطع حبل المربوط فيه القايق وانهزم راجعاً الي تلك الجزيره[2] والله سلمه وفاز اما مركب القرصان ما دار باله الي ذلك القايق بل نزل قايقه الكبير الي البحر ونزل فيه خمسين شب معددين من تلك العسكر حتي يجوا يضبطوا مركبنا.

١١،٦ وكنت الفقير واقف علي حفت المركب بتفرج وكان بجانبي ذلك اليسير الذي مر ذكره وهو من اهل جزيرة كورسيكا الذي راء عياله هناك من بعد عشرين سنه وابا انه ينزل الي عندهم كما مر الكلام عنه سابقاً فهذا رايت في يده كرمشتون من المعامله

---

After a short while, the other ship drew close, and our captain ordered the    6.8
sailors to drop the ship's rowboat into the water. They tied it to the bow of the
ship, and the first mate jumped in along with four sailors to row ahead, helping
to pull the ship along.

But the captain actually had a different plan in mind. He had four trunks of
coral, which he'd bought from locales where it's harvested from the sea. Coral
grows on the seafloor, just like trees planted in sand. He also had a quantity of
gold *riyāl* coins. While we were busy trying to escape, he put the four trunks of
coral and the coins into the rowboat without anyone noticing.

After a short while, the corsair drew up alongside us and fired a cannon. The    6.9
cannonball flew just over the mast. We kept up our efforts to escape, refusing
to surrender, so the pirates fired a second cannon. This time, the cannonball
passed overhead at half the height of the mast. Still we wouldn't surrender,
and the captain was urging us to make good our escape. Then they fired a third
cannon, and the cannonball passed right over our heads. At the sound of it,
we all hit the deck in terror. Had it struck its target, none of us would have
been spared!

We got to our feet and shouted at the captain, and forced him to surrender.
A few of us hurried to lower our flag, which was the sign to cease fire. As soon
as the flag came down, the corsairs called out with their bullhorn:

"*Maina* to France, *maina!*" which means: "Surrender to France,
surrender!"[95]

We lowered the sails. Meanwhile, the first mate—who was in the rowboat,    6.10
as I mentioned—saw that the captain had surrendered. There was no longer
any hope of being saved, so he cut the rope tying the rowboat to the ship, and
fled in the direction of Corsica. God would see to his safe return.

As for the corsair, it paid no mind to the rowboat. Instead, it lowered its
own large rowboat into the water and fifty armed men jumped in to come over
and seize our ship.

I stood watching from the side of the ship. Beside me was that Corsican pris-    6.11
oner I mentioned earlier, who saw his family after twenty years and refused to

ورايد يرميه في البحر فخطفت الكمر من يده وقلته لماذا بتريد ترميه في البحر فاجابني دعني
ارميه ولا ياخذوه هل قوم الذي اقتنيته من كدي وتعبي في مدة عشرين سنه فقلته
دعه عندي لعل الله سجانه وتعالي يخلصه من ايدي هولاي ومضيت ووضعته
داخل خرج الذي كان فيه الة مطبخ الطريق مثل طنجره ومقليه وبعض صحون ومعالق
وما يشبه ذلك من الت الطبخ الذي كان معنا في سفرنا في الطريق.

١٢.٦ وايضاً في ذلك المحل باقيت اليسراء اعطوا الي معلمي كيس خرجياتهم حتي
يوضعهم في سندوقه بعلمهم انه فرنساوي ما بيشلوه اوليك القرصان.[١] حينذِ
وصل ذلك القايق المرسل من مركب القرصان الي مركبنا فنهضوا في الحال وهجموا علينا
كانهم دياب خاطفه ونزلوا جميعنا في ذلك القايق والذين كانوا في القايق اعني الجنود
استقاموا في المركب والنوتيه اخذونا الي مركب القرصان فلما صعدنا الي المركب فراء
معلمي قبطان ذلك المركب فعرفه وكان اسمه قبطان برمون والقبطان عرف معلمي
فتعانقوا وسلموا علي بعضهم سلام الموده والمحبه.

١٣.٦ فسال القبطان الي معلمي من اين انت جايي وكيف انك نزلت في هل مركب
فاجابه معلمي اني كنت في مدينة تونس والقنصر شار علي باني انزل في هل مركب
خوفاً من قرصان الانكليز ليلا يشلحوني فقله ما عملت الا عين الصواب وبعده قال
الي معلمي بريد ارسل اجيب حوايجك الي هل مركب ليلا يضيع لك شي فقبل معلمي
وشكر فضله. حينذِ امرني باني اروح مع القايق الي ذلك المركب واجمع جميع حوايجنا
ونزلهم في القايق.

١٤.٦ فلما نزلت في القايق امر القبطان للنوتيه بانهم يجيبوا حوايجنا وحوايج جميع اليساره
ولا يخلوا شي من تلك الحوايج فصنعوا كما امرهم ورحنا الي المركب وقبل كل شي نزلت
حوايجنا الي القايق وبعده نزلوا حوايج اليساره وذهبنا الي المركب واصعدوا حوايجنا
وحوايج اوليك اليساره ووضعوهم في كامرة القبطان ونزلوا نوتيت ذلك المركب
وسجانوهم في العنبر.

---

leave the ship and join them. In his hand was a waist purse stuffed with money. He was about to throw it into the sea, but I snatched it from his hand.

"Why do you want to throw it away?" I asked.

"Let me do it!" he pleaded. "I'd rather throw it away than let these people steal what I've toiled for the past twenty years!"

"Why don't you leave it with me?" I said. "Perhaps God Almighty will keep it from falling into their hands."

I went and placed it inside a sack that contained a pot, a frying pan, some plates and spoons, and other cooking supplies we'd brought with us.

Meanwhile, the other prisoners gave my master their own traveling sacks 6.12 to place in his trunk, as they knew he was a Frenchman; the corsairs surely wouldn't rob him. When the rowboat arrived at our ship, the corsairs boarded and pounced on us like rapacious wolves! They brought us down into their dinghy, and the armed men who had come over stayed aboard our vessel while the sailors took us to the pirate ship.

As soon as we'd climbed aboard, my master spotted the pirate captain, and recognized him! His name was Capitaine Brémond, and he also recognized my master. They embraced and exchanged affectionate greetings.

"Where have you come from, and why are you traveling with this ship?" the 6.13 captain asked.

"I was in Tunis, and the consul advised I sail with it," my master replied. "He was afraid that the English privateers would rob me."

"You did just the right thing," the corsair captain replied. "Let me have your bags brought over to my ship so nothing is lost."

My master thanked him and ordered me to return to the ship, gather our things, and load them into the dinghy.

The captain told the sailors to fetch our things along with those of the pris- 6.14 oners, and not to leave anything behind. They did as he ordered. We went to the ship and our baggage was brought down first, then the prisoners' baggage. When we returned to the pirate ship, all the bags were brought on board and put in the captain's chambers. Then they brought the other ship's sailors over and confined them in the hold.

١٥،٦ واستقام مركب القرصان يصلب في تلك الدوه الي ثاني يوم وكان ثاني خميس من
عيد الجسد وكان في المركب بادري فقدس لنا ذلك اليوم قداس وبعد حضورنا القداس
ففطرنا وبعده امر القبطان بان يخرجوا حوايجنا وحوايج اليساره امامه ففتح سناديقهم
وقفهم¹ وكتب كل الموجود. اخيرًا احضروا حوايجنا امامه فصار ياخد الذي بيريده
من حوايجنا وهوكان معنا بندقيه باريع نملات بفرد جقمق وجوز طبنجيلات ايضاً
كل واحده باريع نملات وجقمق وبندقيه. نملتين وجقمق وسيف اسكي شام قوي
ثمين وباقيت عدد مثل بنيار وسيخ فرنجي مكلف. المراد اخد الكل.

١٦،٦ وفتح حوايجي اخد الذي راده ومن جملتهم اخد شاشي باطراف التون بقوله لي لا
حاجه لك في الشاش وانت ماضي الي بلاد الفرنجيه وراء في سندوق معلي يكاس
داخلهم دراهم وكام دسدة طرابيش تونسليات فاستدل من ذلك بان يكاس الخرجيه
والطرابيش لليساره فاخدهم. حيندٍ اشتد معلي بالغضب والتفت الي القبطان بقوله
له هل تريد تشلحني وتاخد حوايجي اما تعلم باني انا مرسل من قبل سلطان فرنسا للسياحه
واخرج اروّاه الفرمان الذي اعطاه له الملك المذكور توصاي فيه الي جميع القناصر
الذين قاطنين في بلاد الشرق فاجابه القبطان انا سلطان في مركبي وبما اني رايتك في
مركب عدو فلي ما اشلحك امضي ضع فرمانك في الماء واشرب ميته.

١٧،٦ في ذلك الوقت شهد عليه ثاني قبطان ومدبرين المركب فما انخش من كلامه
القبطان وضبط الجميع فتركه معلي يعمل الذي بيريده الي حين ما يصلوا الي ليكورنه
فاستقمنا ذلك اليوم وثاني يوم من باكر دخلنا الي اسكلة ليكورنا ولما رسي المركب
في الاسكله وبعد قليل دخل ذلك القايق الذي كان هرب بسناديق المرجان وغروش
الريال من امام مركب برمون مركب القرصان واعطاه خبركيف انه هرب باثمن ما في المركب
فلما راه القبطان فصعب عليه قوي كثير لكن ايش يفيد طار الطير من يده.

١٨،٦ اخيرًا امر القبطان بان ينزلوا قبطان الانكليزي وطايفته الي القايق ومضوا بهم
الي دار الكرتينا فبعدما القوم في ذلك المكان رجع القايق الي المركب فبعده اخرج

---

¹ الأصل: وقفهم.

The corsair continued to cruise the area until the next day. It was the second    6.15
Thursday after the Feast of Corpus Christi, so the priest on board held a mass
for us. Following the mass, we had breakfast, and the captain gave the order to
have our luggage placed before him along with the prisoners' bags.

He opened the prisoners' trunks and baskets and made a list of their contents. When they brought our bags to him, he began to take whatever he
wanted! We had a four-shot rifle with a single hammer, and a pair of pistols,
each also with four shots and a single hammer. There was a two-shot rifle with
a single hammer, a very valuable old damascened sword, a dagger, an expensive Frankish rapier, and other weapons too. The pirate took everything.

Then he opened my bags and took what he wished, including my turban    6.16
with the gold stitching on its borders!

"You won't need a turban in the Frankish lands," he sneered.

Fishing through my master's trunk, he found some sacks full of silver coins
and a packet of Tunisian fezzes. He deduced from the sacks and the fezzes that
they belonged to the prisoners, and took them as well. My master was enraged.
He drew himself up before the corsair captain.

"Are you going to strip me of all my luggage? Perhaps you're not aware that
I've been sent on this voyage by the sultan of France!" he said, taking out his
royal edict of appointment, which recommended him to all the French consuls
residing in the eastern lands.

"On my ship, I am sultan!" the pirate replied. "And seeing as how I found
you aboard an enemy ship, why shouldn't I rob you? Go soak your edict and
suck on it."[96]

The other captain and the officers from our ship testified to the truth of    6.17
what my master said, but the corsair captain paid no mind, seizing everything.
So my master let him do as he wished, biding his time until the ship reached
Livorno.

Early the next day, we entered Livorno's harbor and dropped anchor. A little
while later, the rowboat that had fled the corsair Brémond—with the trunks of
coral and *riyāls*—arrived at the harbor. Brémond got word that it had managed
to escape with the most valuable merchandise on the ship! When the corsair
saw it, he was furious, but what could he do? The bird had flown the coop.

The corsair captain gave an order to have the English captain and his people    6.18
put into the rowboat and taken to the quarantine house. The rowboat dropped

القبطان حوايجنا من غير الذي اخدهم سابقاً ونزلوهم في القايق ونزلت انا ومعلي ايضاً في القايق ورحنا الي دار الكرنتينا فنزلنا هناك واعطونا اوضه وهومكان شرح وما يدوره قناه عريض وداخل القناه ماء البحر والمكان كانه جزيره.

١٩،٦ فاستقمنا ذلك اليوم وثاني يوم من باكركب معلي مكتوب وارسله الي قنصر الفرنساويه في مدينة ليكورنه الذي هو بمقام ايلجي مرسل من قبل سلطان فرنسا فلما وصله المكتوب سال عنه اهل صراته من هو هذا الرجل فكان القبطان سبق واخبر الي حواشي القنصر بان هذا الرجل من الفشارين الذين بيدوروا في الدنيا اذا اشتكي الي حضرة القنصر لا تسمعوه لانه كذاب ومعه فرمان براني تقليد فاجابوا الي حضرة القنصر بكلام الذي انورد اليهم من القبطان فصدق كلامهم القنصر فا رد جواب. اما معلي اصطبر ذلك اليوم فما جا له جواب من القنصر فتاني يوم كتب ايضاً مكتوب وارسله الي القنصر فما التفت القنصر ايضاً الي ثاني مكتوب وبقينا ذلك النهار ايضاً وما جانا جواب.

٢٠،٦ وفي ذلك النهار كنت الفقير بتمشا قريب من منزلنا فرايت من بعد ذلك اليسير الذي خطفت من يده الكمر وهو بيتمشي ايضاً نخطر في بالي ذلك الكمر فمضيت ومديت يدي لذلك الخرج الذي كنت وضعت فيه الكمر فرايت الكمر كما وضعته بين الطنجره والصون فاخرجته من ذلك الخرج وخرجت الي خارج وصرت اروية هو من بعد واناديه فلما قرب لعندي ونضر الكمر انطرح علي الارض علي وجهه وما بقا له عزم بانه يقوم من فرحه.

٢١،٦ حيند مضيت الي عنده ومسكت بيده فنهض وصار يبوس ايدي ويشكرني فقلته يا اخي اشكر الله تعالي الذي اعمام عن كرك اما نضرت كيف انهم فتشوا حوايجنا والخرج الذي كان موضوع فيه الكمر وما قشعوه وهذا صار عنايه من ربنا لحسنة اعيالك. اخيراً راد يفتح ذلك الكمر حتي يعطيني منه جزء فما قبلت اخد منه شي واطلقه.

them off and returned to the ship. Then the corsair brought out our things—besides what he had taken for himself—and had them loaded into the rowboat. My master and I got in, and off we went to the quarantine house, where we were given a room. The place was open to the elements and surrounded by a wide canal filled with seawater, like an island.

We spent the day there. Early the next morning, my master wrote a letter and sent it to the French consul in Livorno, who served as an ambassador, representing the sultan of France. When the letter arrived, the consul made some inquiries about the identity of its sender.

"Who is this fellow?" he asked the people in his palace. But the corsair captain had already spoken to the consul's entourage, telling them that my master was one of those people who traveled around the world, pretending to be someone they weren't.

"If he complains to His Honor the consul, don't listen to him," the captain said. "He's a liar with a counterfeit edict from the king."

They told the consul what they'd heard from the captain and he believed them, so didn't bother responding to the letter. Meanwhile, my master waited patiently all day for the consul's reply, which didn't come. The next day, he wrote to him again, and again the consul paid the letter no mind. Another day passed without a response.

I spent the day strolling about near our lodgings. As I walked, I spotted, some distance away, the prisoner whose waist purse I had snatched while on the ship! He was also out for a stroll. Reminded of the waist purse, I went to rummage through the sack in which I'd placed it. There it was, where I'd left it, between the pot and the plates. I took it out of the sack and went outside again, waving at the man and calling out to him. When he approached me and saw the purse, he sank to the ground in happiness, unable to stand back up.

I walked over to him and clasped his hand to help him up, and he rose, kissing my hand and thanking me.

"Brother, you should thank God Most High, who kept the pirates from spotting your purse," I said. "Did you see how they searched our luggage, including the sack where it was hidden? Somehow they didn't see this! God showed mercy on your family."

The man began to open the purse to give me some of what was in it, but I refused to take anything from him, and sent him on his way.

6.19

6.20

6.21

٢٢،٦ اخيرًا مضي النهار وما جا لمعلي جواب فانحصر في الغايه وقلي نهار غدي بتنضر الذي بده يسير في القبطان وجماعته ولما كان باكر يوم ثالث باكركتب مكتوب وارسله الي القنصر وامره بامرقاطع من قبل سلطان فرنسا بانه يقوم يجي الي النزريت ويسمع دعوته علي قبطان برمون وكتب له بعض اشارات من السلطنه حتي يعرفه بانه مرسول من قبل الملك.

٢٣،٦ فما فات مقدار ساعه والا رايت خارج من باب المدينه جمهور عظيم وكان القنصر راكب عرابانته ومعه حواشيه وجميع تجار الفرنساويه فدخلوا جميعهم داخل النزريت قاطع القناه فطلع الي ملاقاته قبطان النزريت واستقبله واحضرله كرسي والي باقيت التجار ايضًا كراسي فجلسوا جميعهم وجميع خدامهم وقوف امامهم شالحين برانيتهم بغاية الاحتشام. حينذٍ امرحضرة القنصر الي قبطان النزريت بانه يدعي خواجه بول لوكا الفرنساي الذي هو وقيدٍ في النزريت امامه فامرالقبطان الي الذي هو موكل حراسة الاوادم الذين خرجوا من مركب قبطان برمون ويدعي خواجه بول لوكا امام حضرة القنصر.

٢٤،٦ فاجا الينا ذلك الحارس وكلف معلي حتي يمضي يواجه حضرة القنصرفنهض معلي ولبس فروته واخد الفرمان معه وقلي الحقني فمشينا معًا الي مقابلة القنصرفلما امتثل امامه وكان اول كلامه له لا يحصل منك مواخده يا سيدي القنصر[١] في تكليف الخاطر في مجيك الي عندي كان بيكفي ترسل احقرخدامك حتي يقضي هل دعوه التي بيني وبين قبطان برمون ودعوت الملك الله يحفظه التي بتخص الي سيادته تلك بتلزمك بانك تقضيها وترد جوابها الي سيادته فاجابه القنصر ما هي دعوتك وما الذي بتندعي علي قبطان برمون.

٢٥،٦ فقله اولاً نهبني واخد امتعتي وانا التقيت رجل فرنساوي ولما قلته باني مرسل من قبل سلطان فرنساء ومعي منه فرمان فاجابني بقوله لي انا سلطان في مركبي وفرمان الذي معك انا ما بعمل فيه روح انقعه واشرب ميته والي في هذا شهود مدبرين

---

The day passed and still no response arrived for my master, who was now  6.22
furious.

"Just you wait," he said. "You'll see what happens to that captain and his
crew tomorrow."

On the morning of the third day, my master wrote another letter to the
consul, issuing him a direct order on behalf of the king of France to come
to the quarantine house and hear his complaint about Capitaine Brémond.
He included some royal formulas in his letter to prove to the consul that he
was indeed an envoy of the king.

Less than an hour had passed when I saw a large gathering of people emerg-  6.23
ing from the city gates. It was the consul in his carriage, accompanied by his
entourage and all the French merchants. They entered the lazaretto, crossing
the canal.[97] The captain of the lazaretto came out to meet the consul, welcom-
ing him and bringing out chairs for him and his company of merchants. They sat
down while their servants stood before them, their hats removed in deference.

His Honor the consul then ordered the captain to summon *khawājah* Paul
Lucas, the Frenchman, who was presently in the lazaretto. The captain, in
turn, ordered the man responsible for guarding those who'd come from Capitaine Brémond's ship to summon *khawājah* Paul Lucas to appear before His
Honor the consul.

The guard came to see us and issued the invitation. My master rose, put on  6.24
his fur pelt, and brought along his royal edict.

"Follow me," he said.

We walked out together to meet the consul.

When he appeared before the consul, the first thing he said was, "My lord, I
hope this visit does not represent an onerous imposition. It would have sufficed
for you to send your lowliest servant to attend to my suit against Capitaine
Brémond. But since it also now concerns His Majesty the king, God preserve
him, you must adjudicate it yourself and inform His Majesty of your decision."

"What is the nature of your suit, and your charge against Capitaine Brémond?" the consul asked.

"In the first place, he robbed me of my property, even though he recog-  6.25
nized that I was a Frenchman," my master replied. "When I told him that I
was an envoy of the sultan of France and that I had a royal edict of appointment, he said to me, 'On my ship, I'm the sultan, and I don't recognize your

المركب واخرج الفرمان من عبه وارواه الي القنصر فامر القنصر في احد الفرمان حتي يقراه فمدوا من تلك الناحيه قصبه وراسها مشقوق فدخلوا الفرمان في شق تلك القصبه ونخزوا الفرمان واعطوه الي حضرة القنصر .

٢٦،٦ فلما اخذه وقراه نهض من علي الكرسي وكشف الي معلي البرنيطه وصار ياخد بخاطره بقوله لا تواخدني بلغوني عنك خلاف ما انت فيه وامر في الحال الي تباعه بانهم يمضوا الي الاسكله ويحضروا القبطان وجماعته الي النزاريت فمضوا وامروا القبطان من قبل القنصر بانه يمضي هو وجماعته الي النزاريت فلما وصل الي عندنا وامتثل هو وجماعته امام القنصر فساله القنصر هل لفض ما قاله عنه بول لوكا كما ذكرنا فنكر .

٢٧،٦ حينذٍ التفت معلي الي الشهود فما قدروا ينكروا لان صار ذلك في حضور اهل المركب . حينذٍ شهدوا بالحق كما لفض القبطان كلمه بكلمه وبعدما شهدوا واثبت شهادتهم القنصر امر بان يحبسوا القبطان[1] في النزاريت واصرف جماعته الي مركبهم وابقي الدعوه الي ثاني يوم وودع معلي وانصرف الي بيته ونحن رجعنا الي منزولنا وثاني يوم اجا القنصر صحبة جماعته والتجار مثل اول يوم وعقدوا ديوان وارسل القنصر واحضر القبطان امامه وامر بان يجيبوا من المركب جميع الحوايج التي اختلسها من معلي الي النزاريت امامه فلما احضروهم ارسل كلف الي معلي بانه يحضر وياخد حوايجه التي كان اخدها القبطان منه في المركب فلما حضر معلي امام القنصر وذلك الجمهور نهض القنصر ومن معه علي الاقدام ثم قال لمعلي القنصر انضر هل ناقص من حوايجك شي .

٢٨،٦ فامرني معلي بان اتسلم الحوايج التي لنا فبعدما تسلمتهم فردًا فردًا بعدتهم قال معلي ناقصني اربع كياس داخلهم معامله وكيس احمر داخله مايتين وعشرين مداليه اعني فلوس قدم وداخل الكيس خاتم فضه بحجر سليماني وستة دوجينات طرابيش تونسليات فامر القنصر الي القبطان بانه يمضي الي مركبه ويجيب الكياس الذي اخدهم

---
١ الأصل: القبطا.

letter. Go soak it and suck on it!'" My master added, "The ship's officers are my witnesses."

He took the edict from his cloak and held it out to the consul, who ordered it to be brought over to him so that he could read it. His men held out toward my master a length of cane with a slit in its end. They pulled the edict out through the slit and fumigated it before giving it to the consul.

Upon reading the edict, the consul bounded up from his chair, removed his hat, and began apologizing to my master.

"Please forgive me!" he cried. "They told me you were someone else!"

He ordered his attendants to go to the harbor immediately and to bring the captain and his company to the lazaretto. Shortly thereafter, the captain and his men arrived and presented themselves before the consul, who asked the captain if he'd indeed said what Paul Lucas claimed. The captain denied it.

My master turned to the witnesses, who couldn't deny what he'd said. After all, this had all transpired in the presence of those on board. They reported what the captain had said, word for word, and once their testimony had been verified, the consul ordered that the captain be imprisoned in the lazaretto, and sent the crew back to their ship. The trial was set for the next day. The consul then bid my master farewell and went off to his house. We too went to our lodgings.

The following day, the consul returned with his attendants and the merchants, as he had the previous day, and they established a tribunal. The consul summoned Capitaine Brémond, and issued an order to have all of my master's things brought from the ship to the lazaretto. The luggage was brought over, and the consul invited my master to come forward and recover the property the captain had seized from him on the ship.

When my master appeared before the consul and the assembly, everyone got to their feet.

"Is it all there?" the consul asked. "Look and see."

My master instructed me to take delivery of our property. I went through every last object, one by one. When I was finished, he spoke up again.

"I'm missing four pouches of money and a red pouch with two hundred and twenty antique coins," my master said. "There's also a silver ring with a seal of Solomon, and six dozen Tunisian fezzes."[98]

6.26

6.27

6.28

من سندوق معلي والطرابيش ايضاً فاحتج القبطان بان الكياس ما هن له بل انهم كياس اليسراء فاجابه القنصر هل كانوا موجودين في حوايج اليسراء فاجابه القبطان انا رايتهم في سندوق بول لوكاء فانتهره القنصر وقله ما هولك بان تعرف لمن هن اليس اخدتهم من سندوق هل رجل امضي واسرع واتي بهم الي هاهنا.

٢٩،٦ فمضي القبطان الي مركبه وجاب الكياس والطرابيش ما عدا كيس المداليا المذكور فطلب معلي كيس المذكور من القبطان فاجابه القبطان هذا الذي اخدته من سندوقك ما ريت غير هذه الكياس فالتفت معلي وقال للقنصر بان هل كيس المداليات مدون في كسريت تونس وهو مخصص لحضرة الملك لان في كل سياحتي ما رايت مثلهم وبريد بل بسمح للقبطان بان ياخد جميع حوايجي ويرد لي الكيس المذكور.

٣٠،٦ وهذه كانت مكيده من معلي لاجل نكايت القبطان والكيس الذي دكره صحيح وداخله خاتم لكن المداليات كان اودعهم عند قنصر تونس وباقيت اشيا التي جناها من بلاد الغرب في دورته وهكذا كان يفعله في كل مدينة التي موجود فيها قنصر كان يودع عنده من مداليات وكتب وتجاره مصوره ومن تجاره ثمينه وما يشبه ذلك ويدونهم في الكنسلريه وياخد ورقة وصولهم من القنصر حتي يبقي يرسلهم الي مرسيليا ومن هناك ياخدهم معه الي بهريز.

٣١،٦ فلما سمع القنصر من معلي هل كلام تاكد عنده وجود هل كيس فامر ثاني مره للقبطان بانه يروح الي المركب وينقب علي هذا الكيس[1] فاجابه القبطان بقوله له بطلب من فضلك بانك تامر ناس من قبلك يروحوا معي يفتشوا المركب مكان مكان لعلهم يروه لاني انا ما رايته ولا لي علم فيه. حينذٍ القنصر استمن معلي بانه يروح الي المركب وارسل معه الكنسلير واثنين من تباعه حتي يفتشوا كامرة القبطان وسندوقه وسناديق باقيت اهل المركب لعلهم يروه.

---

The consul ordered the captain to go to the ship and bring the pouches he'd taken from my master's trunk, as well as the fezzes. The captain argued that the pouches didn't belong to my master, but rather to the captives.

"Did you find them in the captives' baggage?" the consul asked.

"I saw them in Paul Lucas's trunk," the captain replied.

"So how could you know who they belonged to?" the consul scolded him. "Didn't you take them from this man's trunk? Go get them and bring them here at once!"

The captain went to his ship and brought the pouches of money and the     6.29
hats, but not the pouch of antique coins. My master demanded the last pouch.

"This is all I took from your trunk," the captain said. "I saw only these pouches."

My master turned to the consul.

"The pouch with the antique coins was registered in the chancery of Tunis, and was specifically acquired for His Majesty the king," he said. "In all my travels, I never saw the like of those coins. I'd allow Capitaine Brémond to take all of my things if he only returned that pouch to me."

This was a trick by my master meant to vex the captain! The pouch he'd     6.30
described was real enough, and did in fact contain a ring, but the coins had been left with the consul of Tunis along with other things we'd brought with us from the tour in the East. This was my master's regular practice in every city with a French consul: He'd entrust to his care all of the coins, books, engraved stones, precious gems, and other such things, registering them with the chancery. The consul would issue him a receipt and send everything to Marseille, where my master would pick them up and take them on to Paris.

On hearing my master's offer, the consul was convinced that there was a     6.31
pouch after all. He ordered the captain to return to the ship and search for it.

"I beg you, sir," the captain implored. "Send some of your men with me and tell them to search the ship from top to bottom. They might find that pouch, but I've never laid eyes on it or heard of it!"

The consul kindly asked my master to go to the ship, sending the chancellor with him along with two of his attendants to search the captain's chamber and trunk, as well as the trunks of everyone else on the ship, in hopes of finding the pouch.

٣٢،٦ فمضي معلمي صحبة المذكورين الي المركب وفتشوا كامرة القبطان فراوا الكيس المذكور وداخله الخاتم فجمعوا امام القنصر والكيس في يدهم فلما راه القنصر التفت الي القبطان وقال له ها ان الكيس انوجد بعلامته اين اخفيت المداليات التي هنه الي سلطان فرنسا هل بتقدر تتكرهم فصار القبطان يقسم ويندر علي حاله بالقتل ان كان له خبر او جلية اثر من هل مداليات لخار القنصر في هل دعوه وما عاد يعرف كيف يعمل.

٣٣،٦ فشاروا عليه حينذٍ التجار بانه يرسل ويحضر اهل المركب جميعهم ويفحصهم لعل يبين اثار هل مداليات فامتثل القنصر كلامهم وامر باحضار اهل المركب جميعهم حتي النوتيه فلما حضروا امام القنصر فصار يسالهم واحد بعد واحد هل لهم علم في هل مداليات فانكروا جميعهم فغضب القنصر وامر بحبس جميعهم وتهدد البعض المقربين الي اوضه القبطان بالعداب فلما ظهروا انما المداليات فلما سمعوا النوتيه في الحبس صاروا يقولوا ما احد منا له دنب انما الدنب للسنتينيله اعني حارس كامرة القبطان وخزنة البارود كان يسمح لرفقاته حتي ينشلوا من حوايج اليساره.

٣٤،٦ فلما سمعوا منهم هل كلام اخبروا القنصر بالذي قالوه النوتيه فاحضرهم امامه وسالهم فاحكالوا بالذي صار والخيانه من حارس كامرة القبضان. حينذٍ احضر الحارس امامه وساله هل انه اغتلس شي من كامرت القبطان فنكر وحلف بانه ما اغتلس شي. حينذٍ شهدوا عليه النوتيه فلما شهدوا حكم عليه القنصر بالشنق ان ما جاب المداليات وامر في مسكه ودارواكفه وساقوه للشنق.

٣٥،٦ فلما راء معلمي بان هل مكيده الة الي القتل وان الرجل بري لخاف ليلا القنصر يفرط فيه ويطالب في دمه فقال للقنصر لا تعجل في الحكم ابقي هل رجل في الحبس الي حين ما نفحص وننقب¹ علي باقيت اهل المركب لعلنا ناخد خبرهم. اخيرًا افعل ما بدا لك فابقاه في السجن ولاجل ان القنصر كان فزعان ليلا يجيله عتب وتويخ من الوزير فامر في حبس الجميع وارسل الي اغة المينا وامره بانه يرفع دفت المركب ويرتسم عليه

---

¹ الأصل: نقب.

Off they went to the ship, and upon searching the captain's chamber, they found the pouch with the ring. All then returned to the consul with the sack in hand.

"The pouch has been found," the consul cried, turning to the captain. "Now, where have you hidden the coins meant for the sultan of France? Or do you deny seeing them too?"

The captain began pleading and swearing on his life that he had no knowledge of the coins, nor any idea of their whereabouts. The consul was stymied, and felt at a loss about how to proceed.

The merchants advised him to summon the company of the pirate ship and question them. Might that, perhaps, shed light on the coins? On their advice, the consul summoned all who had been on board, including the seamen. When they assembled before him, the consul asked them one by one if they had any knowledge of the coins. All denied it. Furious, the consul ordered that they be imprisoned, and threatened to torture all who had had access to the captain's cabin if they didn't produce the coins! Threatened with imprisonment, the sailors began to talk among themselves.

"None of us have done anything wrong!" they said to each other. "It's all the fault of the sentinel," meaning the man in charge of guarding the captain's chamber and the gunpowder storeroom. "He used to let his friends pilfer the prisoners' belongings."

When the consul's men heard what the sailors were saying, they reported it to the consul, who brought the sailors before him and asked them to explain themselves. They told him what must have happened: It was surely the captain's guard who had acted treacherously. So the consul summoned the guard and asked him if he'd stolen anything from the captain's chambers. The guard denied it, swearing that he hadn't taken anything. But the sailors testified against him, and the consul sentenced him to hang if he didn't produce the coins. The man was seized, bound, and marched to the gallows.

Realizing that it was now a matter of life and death, my master began to fear that his stratagem would drive the consul to execute an innocent man.

"Let's not rush to judgment," he said to the consul. "Leave this man in prison until we can question the rest of the ship's company. Perhaps they know something. In the end you'll do as you see fit."

Afraid that he'd provoke a complaint and a rebuke from the minister, the consul kept the man in custody, and had everyone else sent to prison as well.

6.32

6.33

6.34

6.35

الي حين ما يبعثله امر من عنده واخذ الكيس وختمه بحضور الجميع وقال الي معلمي
بانه بيرسل الكيس وصورة الدعوه الي الوزير وكيف ما امر الوزير منفعل وبقيوا اهل
المركب والقبطان في النزاريت.

٣٦،٦ حينٍ مضي القنصر وجماعته والتجار الي محلهم ونحن رجعنا الي مكاننا وانفضت
الدعوه علي هذا المنوال واستقمنا في النزاريت الي كملت العشرين يوم وبعده اجا
الحكيم باشي الي النزاريت ودعانا امامه وتقرس فينا واحد واحد فواحد ليلا يكون احدنا فيه
مرض وبعدما احدق احدنا جميعنا فامرنا بان كل واحد منا يدق في يده تحت ابطاته[١]
ويدق علي جوالبه. اخيراً بخرونا واطلقونا.

٣٧،٦ فمضينا الي المدينه ولما دخلنا في باب المدينه حضروا جماعة الحاكم وفتشوا حوايجنا
ليلا يكون معنا تتن او ملح او عرق لان هل ثلاثة عليهم ميري وكل من هو بينهم[٢]
شي بيرسلوه الي الكريك لا محاله ويضبطوا التتن الذي معه فالفقير كان معي اربعين
ربطة تتن قوي طيب من تونس وقبل بليله بلغني خبر بان الذي بيهرب تتن بيضعوه
في الكريك والذي بيضهره بياخذوا منه ميري علي كل رطل حلبي اربع غروش وهذا
جا عليه حتي لا احد ينقل تتن معه الي تلك البلاد لانهم بيرسلوا يجيبوا تتن من غير
بلاد علي كيس الميري يقف في يدهم كل ثلاثة اربعة ارطال بغرش وهن بيبيعوه كل
رطل باربع غروش والملح كذلك.

٣٨،٦ فلما سمعت هل خبر حرت في امري كيف اعمل فافتكرت في اني كيف اهرب ذلك
التتن الذي معي وما افتكرت في الخطر الذي بيعقبه ففتقت الفراش الذي كان معنا
وكيت الصوف الذي فيه وصرت اشق الربطات التتن وامدهم داخل الفراش واضع
فوقهم وتحتهم من ذلك الصوف واخيراً خيطت الفراش وجعلت فيه البصامير كما
كان في السابق فبقي من التتن خمسة ربطات فاسخيت فيهم ان اعطيهم الي حارسنا
الذي كان في خدمتنا تلك المده فلج في بالي فكر وهو اني فتحت سندوق الذي
فيه قناني النبيد واخرجت القناني من السندق والكتيت الذي هو تحت القناني

١ الأصل: باطاه. ٢ «بينهم» في الأصل مطموس.

Then he called for the harbormaster, telling him to remove the ship's rudder, sequester the vessel, and await further instructions. He also took the pouch and sealed it in everyone's presence, telling my master that he would send the pouch and the trial proceedings to the minister, and then do whatever the minister ordered. Meanwhile, the ship's passengers and the captain were to remain in the lazaretto.

The consul, his attendants, and the merchants left. We too returned to our lodgings, and the trial was concluded. We stayed at the lazaretto until the end of the twenty-day quarantine. The chief doctor came to the lazaretto and summoned all of us before him. He examined us each individually to make sure that none of us was afflicted with any disease. After scrutinizing us, he told each of us to strike our armpits and groin with our hands.[99] Then they fumigated us and let us go.   6.36

We went into the city. After we passed through the gates, the governor's men appeared and searched through our things to make sure we had no tobacco, salt, or arak, for those things were assessed import duties. Anyone caught smuggling them would be sent to do hard labor in the galleys, and have his tobacco confiscated.   6.37

I had forty packs of good strong tobacco with me from Tunis. The night before, I'd learned that anyone who smuggled tobacco would be sent to the galleys, and that those who declared it would have to pay a tax of four piasters on each Aleppan *raṭl*. They'd instituted this practice to prevent people from bringing in tobacco from elsewhere; instead, the government would import it from other countries, to benefit the treasury. They'd pay just one piaster for three or four *raṭl*s, and sell each *raṭl* for four piasters. The same went for salt.

When I heard about this, I didn't know what to do! I began to think of a way to smuggle the tobacco without worrying about the dangers involved. I slit open the mattress we had brought with us, ripped out the wool inside, and began stuffing the packs of tobacco into the mattress, placing wool above and below the packs. Then I sewed up the mattress and reattached the buttons. There were five packs of tobacco left. I couldn't bring myself to give them to the guard who was in our service at that time. Then an idea came to me. I opened our trunk with the bottles of wine in it, and took the bottles out as   6.38

وشقيت تلك الربطات ووضعتهم تحت ذلك الكتيت ورجعت القناني كما كانوا وقفلت السندوق.

٣٩.٦ فلما دنوا منا جماعة الحاكم وفتشوا حوايجنا وكان الفراش ملفوف في بساط ومربوط بحبل ففكوا الحبل ورفعوا البساط فراوا فراش ومخده زغيره وما راو غير شي تركه وقالوا لي افتح هل سندوق ففتحت لهم السندوق فراوا فيه قناني النبيد فتركه فتركوه ايضاً وكانوا فتشوا باقيت حوايجنا وخراجنا فما راوا شي فاذنوا لنا بان نرفع حوايجنا ونذهب فلملنا حوايجنا للحمالين ومضينا الي بيت رجل فرنساوي متزوج في ليكورنا وكان صاحب معلمي.

٤٠.٦ فلما دخلنا الي بيته فاستقبلنا بغاية الاكرام وفي الحال امر خدامه فنقلوا حوايجنا الي اعلا المكان وهيا الي معلمي اوضه مفروشه بتخت مكلف وكراسي وما يشبه ذلك مما يخص من الاوض المكلفات واعطوني انا ايضاً اوضه ودخلوا حوايجنا الي تلك الاوضه. حينذٍ خرجت حرمت ذلك الرجل واسترجت فينا وهنت معلمي علي سلامته ووصوله الي بلاد المسيحيه بالسلامه فبعدما سلموا علي بعضهم دخل معلمي وغير حوايج السفر ولبس غير ثياب كاسم بلادنا وبعده حضر الحلاق حلق الي معلمي فامره بان يحلقلي انا ايضاً.

٤١.٦ فجلست علي الكرسي وبعدما خسل وجهي ودقني اخد الموس ومره علي دقني وفي مرته الموس اخد نصف شواربي فلما حسيت بانه حلق نصف شواربي صرخت فيه صوت حتي ارعبته فوقف الحلاق وبهت وقلي ما بالك انا ما جرحتك قلته يا ليتك كنت جرحتي ولا كنت حلقت شواربي اما بتعرف اولاد الشرق ما يحلقوا شواربهم متلكم. اخيراً غصب عني تركه يحلق نصف الاخر لان في تلك البلاد يحلقوا لحام وشواربهم جميعهم حتي الكهنه ما عدا بادريت الكبوجين.

٤٢.٦ فاستقمنا ذلك اليوم في بيت ذلك الرجل بغاية العز والاكرام وكانوا بعض من التجار يجوا عند معلمي حتي يهنوه بالسلامه وكانوا يترجوه في قطان برمون المذكور بانه يسامحه ولا يدع دعوته تتصل الي الوزير فكان هل دعوه ما بقت في يدي لانها تسجلت عليه في حضوركم وحضور القنصر فبقت في يد الوزير فتحت امره هذا شي ما بيتم في

well as the lint padding at the bottom. I took the packs of tobacco, put them under the padding, and replaced the bottles. Then I locked the trunk.

The governor's men approached to search our things. The mattress was wrapped in a carpet and tied up with a rope. They untied it and removed the carpet, finding the mattress and a small pillow inside, but nothing else. So they left it alone. 6.39

"Open this trunk," they said to me.

I did as they asked. Inside were the bottles of wine, which they left alone as well. They searched the rest of our baggage and purses, but didn't find a thing, so they permitted us to pick up our belongings and go. We handed our bags over to some porters and made our way to the home of a Frenchman who had married in Livorno, and who was a friend of my master's.

He welcomed us warmly when we arrived at his house and told his servants to take our things upstairs. For my master, they prepared a room with a fine bed, chairs, and furnishings of the sort found in luxurious quarters. They gave me my own room and put the luggage there as well. 6.40

The man's wife came and welcomed us and congratulated my master on his safe arrival in Christian lands. The greetings out of the way, my master went up to change out of his traveling clothes and put on something that wasn't the clothing of my country. A barber showed up to give my master a shave, and my master told him to shave me as well.

I sat in the chair and he washed my face and beard. Then he took the razor and ran it over my beard, and in so doing took off half my mustache. When I realized what he'd done, I shouted out, and he got a fright. 6.41

"What's the matter?" the barber cried in confusion. "I didn't cut you!"

"If only you'd cut me instead of shaving off my mustache!" I replied. "Don't you know that we men from the East don't shave our mustaches as you do?"

I reluctantly allowed him to shave off the second half. In that country, every man shaved his beard and mustache, even the priests, except the Capuchins.

We spent the rest of the day at the man's home and were treated most hospitably. Some of the merchants came by to see my master and congratulate him on his safe return. They begged him to forgive Capitaine Brémond, and to prevent the suit from reaching the minister's desk. 6.42

"It's out of my hands," my master told them. "I filed my suit against him in your presence, and in the presence of the consul. Now it's up to the minister. There's nothing anyone here can do about it, so there's no need to get involved."

هل بلد لا تتعبوا خاطركم فاستقاموا ثلاثة ايام وفي كل يوم يجبوا ويترجبوا فيه . اخيرًا بعد الثلاثة ايام وبالجهد حتي اعطاهم قرار بانه يسامحه فشكروا فضله ومضوا الي عند القنصر واحكوله بان خواجه بول لوكا سمح عن القبطان وهو يبرد جواب للوزير .

٤٣،٦ حينذٍ القنصرهيا وليمه وارسل كاخيته حتي كلف معلي في ثاني يوم يمضي معلي الي بيت القنصر ويتغدي عنده فرضي معلي بذلك وثاني يوم ايضاً القنصر كاخيته وكلف معلي بالرواح فمضي معه الي صرايت القنصرفلما تواجهوا وسلموا علي بعضهم حينذٍ القنصرسال الي معلي هل له اراده في اطلاق القبطان وطايفته من السجن فاجابه معلي كما لخاطرك وخاطر التجار انا بحمل هل دنب علي حالي اطلقهم يروحوا في حال سبيلهم .

٤٤،٦ فشكر فضله القنصر وارسل في الحال واحضر القبطان وطايفته امامه وقال للقبطان اشكر فضل هل خواجه ولو ما يسمح عنك لكنت استقمت في السجن انت وطايفتك الي حين ما يجي جواب من حضرة الوزير او في ارسالك الي عنده او في ضبط مركبك ومالك حتي يتادب غيرك لانك عوض ما تعمل اكرام لفرمان السلطان وللذي حامله عملت لهم حقاره وحقارتك هذه اتصلت الي صاحب الفرمان اعني به حضرة الملك . حينذٍ ارتمي القبطان علي معلي وقبله واستبري منه ذمه وتصالحوا . اخيرًا جلسوا علي المايده جميعاً وشربوا بسر بعضهم البعض بغاية الفرح والسرور ومضي كل منهم في حال سبيله .

٤٥،٦ وبعد ذلك اليوم خرجت انا الفقير ادور في شوارع المدينه وانا باهت بشوفتي[1] شي قط ما شفته لان اول بلد الذي دخلتها من بلاد المسيحيه ولما رايت النسا في الدكاكين ببيعوا ويبشتروا كانهم رجال ويتمشوا في الطرق مكشوفين الوجوه من غير ستار فصرت كاني قاشع منام وفي ذلك الوقت مريت في شارع من شوارع المدينه فسمعت واحد ببناديني بلسان العربي فالتفت فرايت رجل داخل دكان قهوه فدنوت الي عنده فقال لي السلامه في ابن بلادي ادخل لعندي حتي اشم ريحت بلادي .

---

١ الأصل : بشوفي .

For three days, the merchants continued to come by and plead with him. Finally, after the third day and much strenuous supplication, he promised them that he'd pardon the captain. They thanked him for his benevolence and went to tell the consul that *khawājah* Paul Lucas had pardoned the captain, asking him to notify the minister.

The consul made preparations for a banquet and sent his steward to invite my master to his house the following day for lunch. My master accepted, and the following day the consul dispatched his steward again to accompany my master to the palace. They greeted each other and the consul asked my master if he'd consented to have the captain and his crew released from prison. 6.43

"For your own sake and the sake of the merchants, I'll bear the brunt of this matter myself," my master replied. "Let them go."

The consul thanked him for his benevolence and immediately sent for the captain and his crew. 6.44

"You must thank this *khawājah*," he ordered the captain, "for had he not pardoned you, you'd have stayed in prison along with your gang until I received a response from His Excellency the minister, ordering me to send you to him—or to have your ship and property impounded in order to make an example of you! Instead of honoring the king's letter and its bearer, you treated them both with contempt; a contempt that extends to the source of the letter, meaning of course His Majesty the king!"

The captain threw himself before my master in gratitude. Then he kissed him and begged for forgiveness, and they were reconciled. Sitting at the table together, they drank happily to each other's health, and went their separate ways.

The following day, I went out to stroll the streets of the city. I was utterly stupefied, never having encountered such sights before. It was the first city I'd visited in Christian lands. I saw women in shops, selling and buying goods as though they were men. They strolled down the streets with their faces unveiled. I felt as though I were dreaming. 6.45

As I was walking down one street, someone suddenly called out to me in Arabic. I turned around and saw a man in a coffeehouse. I walked over to him.[100]

"Ho there, countryman!" he said. "Come inside and give me a whiff of home!"

٤٦،٦ فلما دخلت صار يسلم علي بلسان العربي فرديت عليه السلام وسالته من تكون
يا اخي ومن اي بلاد انت فاجابني انا حلبي من طايفة الموارنه فقلتله وانا ايضاً حلبي .
حينِذٍ تعانقنا وتصافحنا وامرني بالجلوس عنده وبعدما ضيفني سقاني قهوه وجاب لي
غليون تتن وجلسنا نتسامر مع بعضنا وصار بيني وبينه عشره وكنت كل يوم ازوره
واساله عن طقوس تلك البلاد فكان يحكيلي عن جميع امورهم الدارجه عندهم.

٤٧،٦ ويوم اخر وانا بتمشي علي حافة البحر وجدت رجل لابس لبس بلادنا فدق وسالني
عن بلدي فاجبته انا حلبي فاسترحب في قوي كثير فقلتله لعلك بتعرفي قلي حقاً ما
بعرفك من تكون الا بما انك ابن بلادنا استانست فيك. حينِذٍ قلي امضي معي يا اخي
حتي نتمشا واحكيلك بالذي جري علي واصابني من البلا.

٤٨،٦ فان سالت عني انا رجل من مدينة دمشق الشام من طايفة السريان وكاتوليكي
الايمان ابن الكنيسه فطايفة السريان الهراتقه كانوا يضطهدوني حتي انهم سلبوا
نصف مالي فلما رايت ما عاد يمكنني باني استقيم في الشام فاخترعت حيله وهي ان
استوفيت الذي لي واوفيت الذي علي من غير ان احد يعرف واودعت اثاثي وداري
تحت يد واحد من قرايبني وبينت علي حالي باني اخد عيالي واروح اقدس وكان
لي من العيال حرمتي وثلاثة اولاد' بنتين وصبي فمضيت صحبة المقادسه وقدست
ورجعت من البحر مع مركب الي مدينة صيدا.

٤٩،٦ فاستقمت مدة ايام في صيدا بستنا مركب حتي اسافر الي بلاد المسيحيه وكانت
نيتي اروح اسكن مدينة روميه انا وعيالي وفي تلك الايام وصل الي اسكلت صيدا
مركب فرنساوي مسافر الي ازمير فقلت في بالي باني اسافر مع ذلك المركب واتسوق
من ازمير بضاعه تكون خرج بلاد المسيحيه لان كان معي مبلغ من الدراهم فصممت
النيه علي هذا المنوال وسافرت مع ذلك المركب وبعد قليل من الايام وصلنا الي ازمير
وبعد وصولنا بكام يوم صرت اسال عن بضاعة التي هي مسالكه في بلاد الفرنجيه
فاتفق ان رجل ناس ملاح شار علي بان اتسوق بضاعة البجم مثل جيت اصبهاني

<hr/>

١ الأصل: اولا.

I obliged, and the fellow continued to greet me with salutations in Arabic, which I returned.

"Who might you be, brother?" I asked. "Which country are you from?"

"I'm from Aleppo," he responded. "A Maronite."

"I'm from Aleppo too!"

We embraced and shook hands, and he invited me to sit with him. He treated me as an honored guest, served me some coffee, and brought me a pipe to smoke. We chatted away. We soon became fast friends and I'd visit him every day to quiz him about the country's customs and to learn about their ways.

One day, I was out for a stroll by the seaside and came upon a man wearing my native dress. He stopped and asked me where I was from.

"I'm from Aleppo," I said, and he greeted me with great warmth and affection.

"Have we met?" I asked.

"To be honest, I have no idea who you are, but I like the look of anyone from my part of the world," he said. "Let's walk together, brother, and I'll tell you about my troubles."

"I'm from Damascus myself," he continued. "I'm a churchgoing Syriac Catholic. Heretic Syriacs persecuted me and stole half of my property. Once I realized I couldn't stay in Damascus any longer, I came up with a plan. I paid off my debts and collected all the money that was owed to me, without anyone suspecting anything. I left my donkey and my house with one of my relatives to take care of, and pretended I was taking my family on a pilgrimage to Jerusalem. With my wife and three children—two girls and a boy—I set off in the company of some other pilgrims and made the pilgrimage. Then I returned by ship to Sidon.

"I stayed in Sidon for a few days, waiting for a ship bound for Christian lands. My plan, you see, was to take my family to Rome. Soon enough, a French ship bound for Izmir appeared in Sidon harbor. 'You should take that ship and buy some goods in Izmir,' I told myself, as I had a certain sum of money with me—'goods that people in Christendom will want to buy,' so I made up my mind to travel with that ship.

6.46

6.47

6.48

6.49

وراوند وخريسانه وما يشبه ذلك من البضايع التي هي خرج هل بلاد.

٦.٥٠ فبعدما كملت مسواقي اشتريت كام طنفسه عجمية من شغل خريسان غاليات الثمن وايضاً كام قنطار شمع عسلي حتي اخده معي الي روميه لاجل الكنايس وكان جملة قيمة المسواق ينوف عن خمسة الف غرش وابقيت معي مقدار الف غرش دهب بندقي لاجل الخرجيه واستقمت في مدينة ازمير برهت ايام الي ما تهيا مركب مسافر الي مرسيليا وكان مركب كبير وموسوق من تجار ازمير . حينذٍ استكريت مع ذلك المركب واوسقت فيه جميع البضاعه التي تسوقتها من ازمير وبعد كام يوم سافر المركب قاصد مينة مرسيليا.

٦.٥١ ولما وصلنا قرب جزيره مالتا فراء القبطان مركب من بعد فخاف[1] ليلا يكون قرصان انكليز دخل الي مينة مالتا فاستقمنا هناك مرسيين عشرة ايام خوفاً من ذلك القرصان وبعد هل مده اخد خبر قبطاننا بان ذلك المركب مضي الي طرف الشرق والبحر نصف من القرصان فجزم علي السفر وكان خروجنا من مالتا بالليل وكان الريح معنا فلما اصبح علينا الصباح فراينا مركب مقابلنا من مراكب الجنتجيه باربعين طوب ومركبنا بعشرين طوب .

٦.٥٢ حينذٍ تهيوا الاثنين للجنك وصاروا يضربوا علي بعضهم المدافع وفي ذلك الوقت نزلت انا وعيالي للعنبر ونحن في غاية الخوف والفزع خصوصاً حرمتي واولادها وناهيك عن حرمه التي التقت في جنك مثل هذا فايسنا من الحيوة وصارت الام تبكي علي اولادها والاولاد يبكوا علي امهم وانا بقيت مثل الضايع عن رشده وحواسه . اخيراً فلما راء ذلك القبطان بان مركبنا ما عمال بيسلم فصار يضرب صايب وقتل من مركبنا وانجرح ناس كثير وانكسر صاريه الواحد وبقا علي حال التلف وما عاد يمكنه يقاوم ذلك المركب بوجه من الوجوه فسلم حاله لذلك الجنكي.

٦.٥٣ اخيراً اخدونا ومضوا بنا الي ليكورنا واخرجونا من ذلك المركب وارمونا في دار النزريت[2] وضبطوا جميع مالنا ما عدا سندوق حرمتي ما سطعوه بما انه سندوق

---

١ الأصل: نخام. ٢ الأصل: النزيت.

"We arrived in Izmir after a few days, and I started looking into what sort of merchandise would sell well in Frankish lands. An honest man advised me to deal in Persian products, like Isfahani printed textiles, rhubarb, wormseed, and other commodities from that part of the world.

"After completing my purchases, I bought a few expensive Persian carpets 6.50 made in Khorasan, as well as a few *qinṭār*s of beeswax to bring to Rome, for the churches. The total value of all the goods was more than five thousand piasters. I had a thousand Venetian gold piasters left over for travel expenses.

"I stayed in Izmir for a few days until a ship was ready to sail to Marseille. It was a large vessel loaded with the merchandise of Izmir's traders. I paid for passage and brought aboard all the goods I'd bought. A few days later we set sail for the port of Marseille.

"When we neared the island of Malta, the captain saw a ship in the dis- 6.51 tance. He feared that English pirates might have entered the port. We remained anchored in place for ten days for fear of the pirates. Finally, the captain received word that their ship had sailed east and that the sea was free of pirates, and he decided to sail on. We left Malta by night with a favorable wind. But when morning broke, we saw before us a warship with forty cannons! Ours was equipped with only twenty.

"The two ships made ready for battle and began to fire their cannons! I took 6.52 my family down to the ship's hold. We were absolutely terrified—especially my wife and children. Can you imagine? A man's wife caught in a battle like that! We lost all hope. The mother began to cry over her children and the children cried over their mother. And I was near senseless with fright.

"When the captain of the other ship saw that we weren't going to surrender, he began to fire upon us directly. Many on board were killed or injured. One of our masts shattered and was completely ruined. Our captain could no longer put up any sort of resistance to the bombardment, so we surrendered to the warship.

"They seized us and brought us here, to Livorno. We were marched off the 6.53 ship and taken to the lazaretto and our property was confiscated. Everything, that is, except for my wife's trunk, which they didn't touch because it belonged to a woman. Mercifully, they returned it to her. Inside the trunk was her purse,

حرمه عملوا معها رحمه واعطوها اياه وكان موجود في السندوق كيس خرجيتها داخله
مقدار ماية غرش ومساغها بيساوي خمسماية غرش وهذه التي تبقت من دراهمنا
والان منعيش منها والاولاد حطيتهم في كارات والحرمه جالسه في البيت مند ثلاثه
اشهر ما خرجت الي المدينه لاجل انها ما بتقدر تخرج من غير غطا وستار وانا عجزت
عنها لكن بطلب من فضلك بما انك ابن بلادنا لعلها تسمع منك وتخرج تتنزه هوا وترفع
هل وهم عنها.

٥٤،٦ فاجبته تكرم اينا وقت الذي بتريده بمضي معك فقلي غدي نهار احد وانا بستناك
في الكنيسه ومنزوح معاً للبيت لعلها بتخرج معنا الي برات المدينه حتي تتنزه شويه
فاستقمنا علي هذا الراي الي ثاني يوم وبعدما حضرنا القداس الالهي مضيت معه
الي بيته فلما دخلت رايت موضوع ستار وهي من داخله فسلمت عليها فردت عليّ
السلام من داخل الستار وما رادة تحضر امامي فقلت لها ما هذا الجنون اخرجي
وانضري جميع النسا دايرين¹ من غير ستار ولا احد بينضر الي احد وهذه بلاد
مسيحيه والحجاب منها مرفوع.

٥٥،٦ وبعد كلام كثير ما امكن انها تاني بالخروج من غير ستار. اخيراً قلت لها هل
عندك خمار قالت نعم قلت تغطي بالخمار واخرجي معنا فامتثلت لقولي واخرجت
من سندوقها بدله مكلفه وخمار زلف وبعدما لبست بدلتها فغطت بذلك الخمار
وخرجت معنا هي واولادها الي ان خرجنا من باب المدينه.

٥٦،٦ وفي ذلك الوقت كان كثير من الناس والنسا خارجين بيتمشوا خارج البلد فلما
راوا هذه الحرمه مغطايه صار كلّ منهم يجي الي طرفنا ويماطي هامه لينضر وجهها
ويسالونا لماذا هل حرمه مغطايه فحرنا كيف نرد جواب لتلك الاوادم وخصوصاً
للنسا وصارة علينا لم من رجال ونسا شي كثير فما عاد يمكننا اننا نمشي في
ذلك الطريق فما عاد وسعنا الا اننا نحيد عن ذلك الطريق والتجينا في كهف جبل
قريب من البحر.

---

¹ الأصل: دارين.

containing the sum of a hundred piasters, and her jewelry, which was worth five hundred piasters. That was all the money we had to live on, so I put the children to work in different trades.

"My wife, though, hasn't left the house for the past three months. She can't bear to go out without a wrap or a veil,[101] and I've given up trying to persuade her. Could I prevail upon you to speak to her, seeing as how you're one of our countrymen? If she hears it from you, maybe she'll put aside her funny ideas and come out of the house for some fresh air."

"I'd be happy to," I replied. "I'll come by whenever you like."                    6.54

"Tomorrow is Sunday," he said. "I'll wait for you at the church and we can go to my house. Perhaps she'll come with us for a walk outside the city."

We agreed on the plan, and the next day, after attending mass, we went to his house. Once inside, I saw that his wife had hidden herself behind a curtain. I greeted her and she responded from behind the curtain, refusing to come out while I was there.

"What's all this foolishness?" I demanded. "Come out and see for yourself! All the women walk around without veils, and no one cares. This is a Christian country, and no one can make you wear one."[102]

Even after a lot of back and forth, she still refused to go out without a veil.    6.55
So I asked her if she had a *khimār* instead.[103]

"Yes," she replied.

"Put it on and come out with us."

She agreed, and took out a fine dress and an embroidered *khimār* from her trunk. She put the dress on, wore the *khimār* covering, and joined us and her children for a walk outside the city gates.

At that hour, there were plenty of men and women heading out for a stroll    6.56
outside the city. When they spotted this woman all covered up, every last one of them came up to us, craning their neck to catch a glimpse of her face, and asking us why she was covered. We were at a loss as to how to respond—especially to the women! The crowd of men and women that gathered around us grew so large that we couldn't stay on that path any longer. We had to veer off and take refuge in a hillside cave near the sea.

٥٧،٦ فلما انتهينا الي ذلك المكان وغبنا عن نضر الناس حينذٍ التفت الي تلك الحرمه وقلت لها انكان بتريدي اني امشي معكم ارفعي هذا الغطا عن هامك وامشي بري النسا السايرات وما احد يلتفت اليك فابت وما رادت انها ترفع الغطا فلما رايت انها استقامة علي عزمها فتركتهم ومضيت راجعًا الي المدينه وما عرفت كيف صار فيهم ومن هذا قد تبين لي بان نسا بلادنا ما بيقدروا يسلكوا نسا تلك البلاد لاجل انهم ربوا في الخبا.

٥٨،٦ ويوم اخر وانا جالس عند صاحبي القهواتي الحلبي المذكور فدخل الي عنده واحد شب بهي المنضر طويل القامه ولايح عليه اثارات النعمه والاحتشام فبعد ما شرب قهوه خرج من عنده وراح في حال سبيله لكني قوي حيته بزياده لحسن منضره واحتشامه فسالت ذلك القهواتي من يكون ذلك الشاب فقلي هذا ابن الميته وحكايته غريه وصار يحكيلي عن خبره.

٥٩،٦ هو ان ابو هل شاب رجل تاجر وكثير الغنا فتزوج بنت رجل تاجر ايضًا فلما تكلم معها اعطاها خاتم الماس بيساوي خمسماية غرس كما بيفعلوا في رتبة الكليل انهم بيعطوا خاتم الرجل الي الامراه وخاتم الامراه الي الرجل وبعدما انتها الكليل مضيت مع جمله من اهلها الي بيت عريسها واستقامة عنده مده من الزمان فصارت تسمن كل يوم عن يوم حتي سمنت غاية السمن فيوم من ذات الايام نضر رجلها الي يدها فاء الخاتم غارز في اصبعتها من عظم سمنها فراد يخرج ذلك الخاتم من اصبعها ليلا يولها فا امكنه ان يخرجه.

٦٠،٦ فارسل واحضر السايغ الي عنده وامره بانه يكسر الخاتم ويخرجه من اصبعها فلما بلغها الخبر بان جاء السايغ حتي يكسر الخاتم ويخرجه من اصبعها فا قبلت ومضت الي عند رجلها وتوسلت اليه بانه لا يسمح لذلك السايغ بانه يكسر الخاتم وان الخاتم ما بياسيها وهي مبسوطه منه فصار يقلها رجلها انا امرت السايغ بانه يسيغه من جديد فاجابته انكان بتحب خاطري ابقي هل هل خاتم في اصبعي ولو مت فيه وكان رجلها

Once we were safely in the cave and out of sight, I turned to the woman.      6.57

"If you want me to keep walking with you, then take that veil off your head!" I said. "Dress like other women do, and no one will glance twice at you."

She refused. So, faced with her stubborn determination, I left them and returned to the city. I don't know what became of them. It became clear to me, from this experience, that women from back home could never learn to behave as women do in this country, as they've been raised never to show themselves to strangers.

One day, while I was visiting with my friend, the Aleppan coffee man, a      6.58 young fellow came in. He was tall and handsome, clearly prosperous, but modest and humble nonetheless. After having some coffee, he went on his way. I took a strong liking to the young man, drawn as I was to his fine appearance and good manners. I asked the coffee man who he was.

"He's the Dead Woman's Son, and his story is a strange one," he replied, and began to recount it to me.

"The boy's father was a merchant, and a wealthy one at that. He married the      6.59 daughter of another merchant, and gave her a diamond wedding ring worth five hundred piasters. According to the marriage traditions in these parts, the husband and wife exchange rings. After the wedding ceremony, the woman moved into her new husband's house along with a group of her relatives. There she lived, and with each passing day she began to grow plump, until eventually she'd become enormously rotund.

"One day, the man looked at his wife's hand and saw she'd grown so fat that her ring had sunk deeply into the flesh of her finger. He tried to remove the ring so that it wouldn't hurt her, but was unable to pry it loose.

"He sent for a jeweler and ordered him to break the ring and take it off her      6.60 finger. When the wife learned that the jeweler had arrived to break the ring, she wouldn't consent! Instead, she went to her husband and begged him not to allow the jeweler to break the ring, insisting that it didn't bother her and that she was very happy with it.

"'But I've told the jeweler to refashion it for you after he takes it off,' her husband explained.

"'If you love me, leave the ring on my finger,' she said, 'even if I die wearing it.'

يحبها في غاية المحبه فما راد يندق خاطرها فأصرف الصايغ وبقي الخاتم في اصبعها مده من الزمان.

٦١.٦ فيوم من الايام وهي جالسه فما راوها الا انها غشيت وغابة عن حواسها وبعد ساعتين ماتت وكان في تلك الايام صاير في البلد موت فجأ كثير فلما تحققوا موتها جنزوها وشلحوها ثيابها ورادوا يخرجوا الخاتم من اصبعها فما قدروا. حينذٍ شاوروا رجلها حتي يقطعوا اصبعها ويخرجوا الخاتم فاتدكر كلامها بان لا تخرج هل خاتم من يدي ولو مت فيه فمنعهم بان لا يخرجوه ابقوه في يدها. اخيراً كفنوها ووضعوها في سندوق ونزلوا السندوق في الخشخاشه بجاري عوايدهم ومضوا.

٦٢.٦ وكان واحد من الذين حضروا تكفينها وراء بان الخاتم بقي في يدها فكمن تلك الليله في حوش المقبره الي ان صار نصف الليل فتح باب الخشخاشه ونزل الي تحت وكان مستحضر معه شمعه وقداحه وكبريته فبعدما شعل الشمعه وركزها في الارض فكشف غطا السندوق ومديده داخل الكفن واخرج يدها اليمين التي فيها الخاتم وسابق علمه بان الخاتم ما يخرج فاستل سكينته وقطع الاصبعه الموجود فيها الخاتم فلما خرج الدم فاقة الميته من غشوتها وصاحة بصوت عالي فين انا فلما سمع صوتها ذلك الرجل ارتاع ليلا تعرفه فابقي الشمعه والسكين وهرب.

٦٣.٦ فلما استفاقة الحرمه علي حالها وراءت ذاتها موضوعه في سندوق ومكنه وهي موضوعه في الخشخاشه بين الموته فصارت تعيط وتولول حتي من شدة صراخها فاق قندلفت الكنيسه وبادر الي الخشخاشه حتي ينضر من هو الذي بيعيط ويولول فراء طابقة الخشخاشه مرفوعه وداخل المكان شمعوله مشعوله فاندهل ذلك القندلفت من ذلك المنضر وتلك الصوات الخارجه من بين الموتي فمضي سرعاً ونبه الريس والرهبان واحكالهم بالذي راءة وسمعه داخل الخشخاشه.

٦٤.٦ فاتوا جميعهم حتي ينضروا الذي صاير في ذلك المكان فراوا كما احكي لهم القندلفت فارتاعوا جميعهم من هذا الامر المفزع المرعب وصاروا يسجعوا البعض منهم بان احدهم ينزل ويكشف لهم الخبر فما احد صار له جرعه بالنزول غير

"Her husband loved her very much and didn't want to go against her wishes, so he sent the jeweler away, and the ring remained on her finger for a good long while.

"One day, while she was seated, she suddenly lost consciousness and was dead within two hours. There had been many sudden deaths of that kind in the country in those days. Once her death was confirmed, they held a funeral service, and removed her clothes. But they couldn't pull the ring off her finger. They consulted her husband about whether to cut her finger off. He remembered her words—'Don't take this ring off my finger, even if I die wearing it'—so he forbade them to remove it: 'Leave it on her hand.'  **6.61**

"In the end they draped her in a burial shroud and put her into a casket. Then they placed it in a mortuary house, as was their custom, and left.

"Now, one of the people who'd attended the woman's shrouding noticed that the ring had remained on her hand. So he spent that night hiding in a thicket within the cemetery. At midnight, he opened the door of the mortuary house and went inside. The man had brought along a candle, a flint, and some matches. He lit the candle, placed it upright on the ground, and removed the lid of the coffin. He reached under the shroud and pulled out her right hand, which had the ring. Knowing in advance that the ring wouldn't just slide off, he pulled out a knife and started to cut off the finger with the ring.  **6.62**

"As soon as the blood began gushing out, the dead woman regained consciousness!

"'Where am I?' she screamed.

"When the man heard her, he was terror-struck. What if she recognized him? So he left the candle and knife behind and fled.

"The woman came to her senses and realized she was in a coffin, shrouded, and lying among the dead in a mortuary house. She began to howl and wail, and woke the sacristan of the church with her screams. He rushed over to the mortuary house to find out who was making all the noise. The door was open and there was a lit candle inside! Baffled at this and at the sounds that were coming from the corpses below, he ran off to wake the abbot and the monks, and told them what he'd seen and heard.  **6.63**

"Everyone rushed to see what was happening in that place. It was just as the sacristan had described. Terrified by the dreadful scene, they began to urge one another to go down into the mortuary house to find out what was going on. The only one courageous enough was the sacristan.  **6.64**

ذلك القندلفت فقال للريس صلّي عليّ يا ابانا انا بنزل فباركه الريس وبعده شدوه بحبل ونزلوه الي اسفل المكان فلما انحدر الي الاسفل فاء تلك الشمعه مشعوله قرب ذلك السندوق الذي فيه تلك الحرمه التي قامت من الموت وهي لا زال تعيط وتبكي.

٦٥،٦ فدنا من السندوق وهو مرتجف ومرعوب. حينٍ سجع ذاته وقال من تكون يا ايها المايت فاجابته تلك الامراه من داخل السندوق انا فلانه حرمة فلان الحقني كرامة الله واخرجني لاني قاربت الموت. حينٍ دنا منها واخرجها من السندق والدم شارر من يدها والسكين بقرب من السندوق فاعتجب ذلك الراهب وما امكنه يعرف بالذي جري لهذه الحرمه.

٦٦،٦ اخيرًا اخرجوها من تلك الخشخاشه وتفرسوا فيها فعرفوها انها فلانه التي جزوها باليوم الماضي فسالوها من الذي جرح يدها فاجابتهم ما بعرف الا ان فقت من رقادي ورايت اني في سندوق ويدي مجروحه والدم خارج منها فلما تفرسوا في يدها وجدوا اصبعها الواحد مقطوع نصف قطع والخاتم عالق بخنصرها. حينٍ عرفوا بانها ما ماتت انما الدم حقن علي قلبها[١] وغشاها ولما قطعوا اصبعها خرج الدم الحاقن علي قلبها ففاقت وكان سبب حياتها ذلك الخاتم. حينٍ ارسلوا خبروا بعلها واقربا فاتوا واخذوها الي بيتها وهي بغاية العافيه وبعد هل مصيبه التي دهمتها جابت ثلاثة اولاد اثنين دكوره وبنت وهذا الشاب الذي رايته الان هو واحد من الثلاثه.

٦٧،٦ ويوم اخر وانا بتمشا في شوارع المدينه فرايت عسكر ماشي كانه متهيي للسفر وكل واحد منهم مسلح بعده كامله وصايرين بلكات وكل بلك ماشي وحده بطبله ونفيره وقطبانه اعني بلك باشيه فسالت فاجابني بان في كل راس شهر يجتمع العسكر في فلان ساحه وهي مكان متتسع لاجل تعليم العسكر لما بيكون في الحرب فمضيت انا الفقير الي تلك الساحه ووقفت في مكان عالي مع جملة اناس

---

"'Pray for me, Father,' he said to the abbot. 'I'll go down.'

"The abbot blessed him. After securing him with a rope, they lowered him into the pit. When he reached the bottom, he saw the lit candle beside the coffin that held the woman who'd risen from the dead. She was still weeping and wailing.

"He approached the coffin, shaking with fear. Steeling himself, he cried out, 'Who are you, O dead body?' 6.65

"The woman identified herself and repeated her plea. 'For God's sake, help me out of here! If you don't, I'll die!'

"The monk went over to her and pulled her out of the coffin. The blood was streaming from her hand and there was a knife beside the coffin. He was astonished by this, and unable to comprehend what had happened to the woman.

"When she was finally brought out of the mortuary house and the people 6.66 got a good look at her, they recognized her as the woman they'd buried the day before.

"'Who cut your hand?'

"'All I remember,' she said, 'is waking up and finding myself in a coffin, bleeding from this cut on my hand!'

"Upon examining her hand, they determined that one of her fingers was half cut off and that the ring was still attached to her little finger. That's when they realized she hadn't, in fact, died at all. Instead, her heart had been congested with blood, which made her lose consciousness. Then, when her finger was cut, the blood began flowing again and she woke up. The ring was what had saved her!

"They sent word to her husband and her relatives, who came and took her home, now the very picture of health. Following this calamity, the woman went on to have three children—two boys and a girl.

"The young man you just saw here was one of the three," the coffee man said.[104]

Another day, as I was strolling through the streets of the city, I saw a troop 6.67 of soldiers marching by, as though preparing to set off on a journey. Each soldier was carrying a full complement of weapons. The soldiers were organized into companies, each marching to the sound of its own fife and drum, and led by its own captain.

"Who are these soldiers?" I asked someone.

فرايت في راس تلك الساحه مكان عالي وجالس رجل عليه القدر والقيمه بثياب فاخره وهو صاري عسكر .

٦٨،٦ وكل واحد من البلكات فيمر من امامه واذا راء واحد من العسكر عدته ما هي نضيفه او ناقص شي منها بيامر في تعديده اعني بيضربوه مايه كرباج علي لواياه امامه حتي يعتبر غيره وبعد مرور البلكات امامه يصطفوا البلكات امام بعضهم حتي تزاحم ما بيزل قدم عن قدم حتي تكامل الصفوف وهي اثني عشر صف وكل ستة منهم مفروقه عن ستة الاخر بشي قليل وفي ذلك الوقت دقت طبول الستة بلكات المتقدمين قدام وبواسطة نقرة الطبول بتدل للجنود بانهم يرفعوا دفكهم بيد الواحده اليمين الي فوق .

٦٩،٦ ثم غيروا النقره وهي بتدل بان كل واحد يكي الدفكه علي كفه وكانه ماسك نيشان وكت تزاحم جميعهم ماسكين تفنكهم فود مسك ما بيزل الواحد عن الاخر شي كانهم كلهم كواحد واذا نضرت الي اقدامهم فتراء اقدامهم ايضاً ما بيزل القدم عن القدم محط شعيره فنقرت الطبول غير تلك النقره فانداروا جميعهم علي جنب اليمين فتغيره النقره فانداروا علي جنب الشمال ورجعوا سوا وهن ماسكين نيشان ومنهيين للضرب . اخيراً بوقوا بالنفير ودقت جميع الطبول وهذه علامة بانهم يفرغوا تفنكهم علي ذلك الاصلوب الذين كانوا منظومين فيه كما دكرنا .

٧٠،٦ حينذٍ تغيرت نقرت الطبول وصوطة البلوك باشيه فما رايت الا دخلت الستة بلكات المتاخره ما بين الذين كانوا قدام وفي لحظه واحده انبدلوا وصارت المتقدمين وراء والذين كانوا ورا صاروا قدام وفعلوا فعل الاولين والاولين بركوا علي ركبهم حتي يدكوا تفنكهم الي حينما يكونوا اوليك فرغوا تفنكهم والحكي ما هو مثل النضر وما يمكني ان اقدر اشرح وادون الحركات التي رايتها في هذا التعليم الذي ما هو موجود في بلاد الشرقيه ولا له ذكر .

٧١،٦ ويوم اخر رايت ايضاً تلك الجنود ماشيين علي منوال الاول فتبعتهم الي ان وصلوا الي تلك الساحه فاستطفوا ما يدور الساحه ورايت في الوسط بارك رجل علي ركبته ومكتف اليدين الي قدام وماسك برنيته بيديه والجلاد واقف فوق راسه

He explained that at the beginning of each month, the troops would gather in a certain square. It was a large, open space, used for the purpose of drilling soldiers for war. I headed to the square and joined a group of others at an elevated spot. I saw, at one end of the square, an impressive-looking man splendidly dressed, and seated upon a dais. He was the commander-in-chief.

Each company passed before the commander. Whenever he saw a soldier carrying a piece of equipment that wasn't clean, or if anything was missing, the commander would order that the man be given a hundred lashes on his buttocks, as an example to the others. After the companies passed inspection, they lined up in formation, one after the other. They marched in unison, without a single foot out of place! Twelve ranks formed, the first company of six separated slightly from the second. The drums of the six forward companies began to beat, and the rhythm indicated that the troops were to raise their muskets high with their right hands.   6.68

Then the beat changed, signaling that they were to raise their muskets and tuck them against their shoulders, as though aiming at a target. They moved as one, holding their weapons in precisely the same way. Their feet, too, were perfectly aligned, not deviating in their symmetry by a hair's breadth. The rhythm of the drums changed, and the soldiers turned to the right. It changed again, and they swung to the left. Then they took up their original stance, with their muskets aimed and ready to fire. Finally, the trumpet blew and all of the drums beat, which was the signal that they were to unload their muskets, which they did in the highly organized fashion I've described.   6.69

The beat changed again and the company commanders cried out. Suddenly, the rear companies marched straight ahead, moving between the ranks of the forward companies. In an instant, they had switched places, and the second group performed the same actions as the first. Meanwhile, the first group knelt to load their muskets as the other group discharged theirs.   6.70

Alas, words don't do justice to this display: I simply can't explain or give an accurate account of the maneuvers I saw during that drill! Nothing like it exists in the East; it's simply unheard of.

Another day, I saw the soldiers marching down the same street, so I followed them to the square. They lined up all around it. In the middle was a man on his knees with his hands shackled in front of him, holding his hat.   6.71

الفصل السادس

وفي يده وثيقه وهي السجل الذي تسجل علي ذلك الرجل فلما كمت البلكات واسطفوا جميعهم حينٍ بدي الجلاد يقرا السجل وهو ان هذا الرجل خان قايده وهرب وكان مستحق الشنق.

لكن صار له مرحمه من الرجاوات التي صارت فحكم عليه بانه يستقيم ماسور في الكريك ثلاثة سناوات ولكي ينعرف من الجميع بان خاين امرت الشريعه بان شرم انفه وتختم جبهته ومسدغيه[1] بختم السلطان محي بالنار فبعدما كمل قراة السجل شرم منخاره وختم جبهته ومسدغيه بذلك الختم الحديد المحي بالنار . اخيراً مروا من امامه جميع الجنود وصاروا يعطوه احسان ثم تسلمه قبطان مركب الكريك وانفضة الجميع علي هذا النسق وكمن راح في حال سبيله.

ويوم اخرصعدت للقلعه مع رجل صاحب وكان هل رجل من تولى[2] القلعه فاخد يفرجني علي كل اماكن القلعه مكان بمكان وفرجني علي تلك الطواب الممسوحين كانهم مرايا من عظم نظافتهم وموضوع علي تقب الذخير ورقه من رصاص ومربوطه في الطوب وفوق الرباط ختم والمجله وبكراتها سريعين الحركه حتي اذا سحبها ولد زغير بتنسحب معه باهون ما تكون.

اخيراً نزلني الي مكان الجباخانه وهي مبنيه باربع صالات تصليب وكل صاله مصفوف فيها صنف من العدد من الجانبين مركوزين علي جناكل من خشب رفيع من الارض الي علو المكان من تفنك وطبنجيليات وسيوف بحدين وسياخ وحراب وغير من العدد وصالت الواحد زروفه سد بولاد وزروفه داوديات اعني ضفر وخود بولاد وتراس ايضاً بولاد حتي رايت زروفه سد بولاد مصنوعين لاجل النسا لهم بزاز مقبيه بيقولوا في زمان المتقدم ايام عبادين الاصنام كانت النسا تخرج للحرب وراءيت[3] داخل ذلك المكان اثني عشر رجل لاجل مسح السلاح بالزيت ليلا يعتريه الصدا وكلما خلص جانب من المسح بيبدوا في الاخر حتي يخلصوا الجميع بيرجعوا من اول وجديد الي اول صاله وهم جراء وهل اثنا عشر رجل لهم علايف ويستقيوا دايماً في ذلك المكان ولما يموت منهم واحد يجيبوا غيره.

<hr>

١ الأصل: مستدغيه. ٢ الأصل: تول. ٣ الأصل: واراءيت.

The executioner stood by, in possession of a document that registered the charges against the man. When the companies finished lining up, the executioner began reading out the register. The man had deceived his commanding officer and had fled, and so deserved to be hanged.

Following some appeals for mercy, however, his sentence had been commuted to three years of labor in the galleys. And so that all would know that he was a traitor, the law ordered that he should have his nostrils slashed, and his forehead and temples branded with the king's seal. After he finished reading the register, the executioner slashed the man's nose and branded him with a burning iron. Then all the soldiers passed before him and offered their sympathy before he was handed over to the captain of the galley. They then all dispersed and went their own way.

6.72

Another day, I climbed up to the citadel with a friend, who served as one of its caretakers. He showed me the various parts of the building one by one. We saw cannons that had been polished so they shone like mirrors. There was a sheet of lead covering each cannon's touchhole, which was tied fast and covered with a seal.[105] Each cannon's carriage moved so swiftly on its wheels that a small child could have easily pulled it along.

6.73

My friend then took me down to the arsenal, which consisted of four rooms in a cruciform arrangement. Each room contained a different type of weapon. These were arranged along two sides of the room and placed on thin wooden hooks, lining the walls from floor to ceiling. There were muskets, pistols, double-edged swords, rapiers, bayonets, and other types of weapon. In one of the rooms, there was steel-plate armor, chainmail, steel helmets, and steel shields. I even saw steel-plate armor made specifically for women, with space for their breasts. It is reported that in ancient times, in the days of idol worship, women used to fight in battle.

6.74

In the arsenal, I saw twelve men at work, polishing the weapons with oil so that they wouldn't rust. When they finished with one set, they'd begin another, continuing in this way until they finished polishing them all. Then they'd go back to the first room and start all over again. These twelve men had all they needed in that place, which was where they lived. When one died, he was replaced with someone else.

٦،٧٥ حينذٍ خطر في بالي قلعت حلب الذي ما لها شبيه في ساير مدن الدنيا لكن طوابها مطمورين أكثرهم في الارض وعجلاتهم مكسره والصدا مغطيهم واذا دخلت برج الجباخانه ترا التراب مزبق بتغطس الرجل فيه وجميع تلك العدد والصلاحات اكلهم الصدا ومطروحين علي بعضهم من هل قدر اجيال التي مره عليهم من غير مسح ولا تزبيت حتي انهم نقلوا بالكليه وما عدا لهم نفع وكل هذا جايه من قلة الاعتنا فيهم وكلامنا هذا ما هو هجو في القلعه والجباخانه لكن في الذين[1] متوكلين علي تلك الخزاين الملوكيه.

٦،٧٦ اخيرًا اصعدني فوق صور المدينه فرايت معمر فوق بدن الصور عزوليات مبنيين من جمر وكل واحده لها طاقه بترمي منهم علي البر ومنهم علي البحر وبين كل واحده لواحده مسافة ماية قدم فسالت ذلك الرجل ما هذه الصومعات فاجابني بان هولاي الصومعات للحراس وهو ان كل بلك من الجنود الذين هم قاطنين في المدينه في كل ليله عليه الحراسه وكل واحد منهم بيدخل الي صومعه وبيستقيم في الحراسه اربع ساعات ثم يجيي غيره الي مكانه وبعد انقضا الساعات المذكوره يمضي ذلك الجندي ويجيي غيره وهلم جرا الي ان يصبح الصباح.

٦،٧٧ وكل صومعه معلق فيها جرس وفي كل ساعه بيدق الاولي جرسه ولما بيسمع الثاني بيدق ايضاً جرسه والثالث كذلك الي ان يدور دور الصور كله وهذا جا لعينه تنبيه للجنود حتي لا يرقدوا[2] واذا مراوضاباشيتهم وراء واحد منهم نايم بينبهه وبيضربه كم ضربه بالصوت الذي بيده حتي يطير نومه وهذا النظام جا عليه خوفًا من العدو لي لا يكمن في الليل وفي فتوح باب البلد يهجم ويدخل ويملك المدينه.

٦،٧٨ وليلة الواحده كت الفقير وذلك الرجل الشامي السرياني الذي مرذكره كّا نتمشا علي حافة البحر برات باب المدينه فاستقمنا الي غروب الشمس فصار يقلي ذلك الرجل قيم رجلك واسرع بنا ليلا يسكر الباب فجدينا بالمسير الي ان وصلنا مقابل باب المدينه فرايت مقدار خمسين جندي متسلحين ودايرين تفنكهم علي خارج الباب كنهم بيريدوا يقوصوا فلما رايتهم فزعت ورجعت قهقرًا فقلي ذلك الرجل ما بالك

---

١ الأصل: اللذين.  ٢ الأصل: لا يرقدا.

I thought back to the citadel of Aleppo, which has no equal in the whole world. But its cannons are buried in the ground, their carriages broken and rusty. When you enter the arsenal tower, you wade ankle-deep in dust. The weapons are strewn in a heap and left to rust, unoiled and unpolished, for generations. As a result, they've degenerated completely and are useless, all because no one has cared for them! My point is not to criticize the citadel or the arsenal, but those who are responsible for maintaining the royal treasuries. 6.75

We climbed to the top of the city's ramparts, where I saw some small masonry structures, each with a window. Some faced the land and others looked out to sea, a hundred paces separating one from the next. 6.76

"What are these?" I asked the man.

"Turrets for the guards."

Each company of soldiers stationed in the city had to stand watch every night. A soldier would go into a turret and remain on watch there for four hours. Then someone would come relieve him. After the next soldier's watch was complete, he too would be relieved, and so on and so forth, till morning.

Inside every turret hung a bell. Every hour on the hour, the guard in the first turret would ring his bell. Upon hearing it, the guard in the second turret would ring his, followed by the third, and so on, until the ringing made a circle of the city walls. The purpose of this practice was to keep the soldiers from falling asleep. If their commanding officer passed by and saw one of them sleeping, he'd wake him up and give him a few lashes with his whip to rouse him. This system was put in place to prevent an enemy from hiding outside the walls at night and attacking the city when the gates were opened in the morning. 6.77

One evening, I was walking by the seashore beyond the gates of the city with that Syriac man from Damascus I mentioned earlier. We stayed out until sunset. 6.78

"Shake a leg!" he cried. "We need to get back before they close the gates!"

We hurried back to the city. Upon our arrival, I saw about fifty armed soldiers, pointing their muskets out the gates, looking as though they were about to fire. I was afraid, and began to retreat in panic.

"What's the matter?" my friend asked. "Go on in, don't be afraid. I'll explain."

We went past the soldiers into the city. Once inside, I asked him why they had been standing there with their muskets.

راجع ادخل لا تخف سوف احكيك السبب فدخلنا من بين تلك الجنود للمدينه . حينئذٍ سألته عن سبب وقوف هل جنود متسلحين ومسكهم هل تفنك فاجابني هذه عاده قديمه عندهم هو وانهم في فتوح باب البلد وتسكيره يقفوا الجنود مثل ما رايت خوفًا ليلا يكون العدو مكمن وهذا هو السبب .

٧٩،٦ وفي تلك الايام ظهر خبر غريب عجيب عن رجل يهودي من اكابر اليهود الذين قاطنين في ليكورنه وهو انه اتفق بان الكران دوك الذي يسما دوك تسكانه الذي هو مالك تلك البلاد وهو قاطن في مدينة فوينسا احتاج دينة دراهم لاجل وفا علايف العسكر وغير مصاريف فالجته الضروره بانه يستدين من احد اكابر بلاده مقدار من المال فلما استشار مدبرين ملكه ممن يستقرد هل مال فاجابوه بان في مدينة ليكورنا رجل يهودي ذو ثروة عظيمه ارسل احظره امامك وهو بيعطيك مهما احتجت من المال .

٨٠،٦ فرضي الدوك بهذا القول وارسل فاحضره امامه فلما امتثل امامه استقبله باكرام واذن له بالجلوس فبعدما انسه وجانسه قله لزمني ثمانين كيس من الدراهم بريد انك تقرضني هي الي حين ما اجمع المال من مملكتي بوفيك اياها فاجابه ذلك الخبيس الماكر سمعًا وطاعه العبد وما ملكت يداه الي سيده وولي نعمته فشكره الدوك وامر كاتب الديوان بان يكتب له وسيقه بهذا المبلغ . حينئذٍ نهض ذلك اليهودي وارتمي علي اقدام الدوك قايلًا ما هذا يا سيدي ما هذا العبد بياخد من استاده وثيقه المال مالك وانا عبدك فاجابه الدوك انا ما بريد اغدر احد من رعيتي وان كان ما بتريد تاخد الوثيقه انا ايضًا ما بريد استدين منك امضي بسلام .

٨١،٦ حينئذٍ اليهودي افتكر في حيله شيطانيه قط ما اشمعت فاجابه اليهودي انا عندي معلوم يا سيدي بان الاسداد ما يحل منيت عبده ولاجل هذا بريد من سيادتك بان تبيعني شي الذي هو تحت تصرفك بهذا المبلغ فقبل البيك وساله ما هو هذا الشي الذي انت طالبه فاجابه ذلك اليهودي الخبيث قايلًا يعني الشمس بهذا المبلغ وكل سنه بعطيك ثمانين كيس واكتب علي وسيقه بحسن قبولي باني ملزوم باعطا هذا المبلغ . وقتيذٍ بهت الدوك وضن بان الرجل مجنون ومضيع رشده .

"It's an old tradition of theirs," he replied. "Whenever the gates of the city are opened or closed, the soldiers line up as you saw them, just in case there is an enemy lying in ambush. That's why."

A peculiar story was recounted about one of the notable Jews of Livorno in those days. It so happened that the Grand Duke—who was known as the Duke of Tuscany, who ruled those lands, and who resided in the city of Florence—was in need of a loan. He had to pay the salaries of his soldiers and some other expenses, and found himself in the position of needing to borrow money from some town notable. The duke consulted the officials in his kingdom to find out whom he might ask for a loan. 6.79

"There's a Jewish gentleman in the city of Livorno with a vast fortune," they replied. "Summon him, and he'll provide you with whatever you need."

The duke took their advice and ordered the man to be brought before him. When he appeared, the duke welcomed him cordially and invited him to sit down. After exchanging some pleasantries, the duke got to the point. 6.80

"I need eighty sacks of silver," he said.[106] "I'd like you to loan me the silver till I can collect some taxes from the kingdom and pay you back."

"Happily," said the sly swindler. "What's mine is yours, my lord! I am at your service."

The duke thanked him and ordered the secretary of the chancery to draft a document guaranteeing full repayment. The Jew threw himself at the duke's feet.

"What is this, my lord? How could a servant accept such a document from his master? The money is yours, just as I am your servant!"

"I have no wish to cheat any of my subjects," said the duke. "If you won't accept the guarantee, then I won't take a loan from you. Go in peace."

The Jew then came up with a devilish scheme, the likes of which had never been heard of before. 6.81

"Sire, I know all too well that a master is surely not obliged to fulfill the wish of his servant," the Jew began. "Which is why I might suggest that your lordship sell me some property you are free to dispose of, for this very sum."

The duke agreed, and asked him what he had in mind.

"Sell me the sun for this price, and I'll give you eighty sacks of silver each year," the duplicitous Jew replied. "You may draft a document stating that I've consented to provide you with this sum on that condition."

The duke was baffled, and believed that the man must have lost his mind.

فأجابه الدوك وقله يا قليل العقل كيف بتريد ابيعك شي ما بملكه هل ان الشمس ٦،٨٢
بتباع وبتنشري فأجابه اليهودي صدقت يا سيدي بما قلت ولكن اسمح لعبدك بهذا
ودع الناس تضحك عليّ. حينئذ مدبرين الملك الذي كانوا حاضرين قالوا للدوك
اعطيه طلبته ودعه انه يضبط الشمس فلما سمع الدوك من المدبرين هل كلام
رضي بمقالهم وراد يعرف نهاية هل امر الغريب فأمر كاتب الديوان بان يكتب لذلك
اليهودي فرمان ويصرفه بالشمس ويكتب عليه وسيقه بانه ملزوم يعطي في كل سنه
المال الميري ثمانين كيس من الدراهم التي هي اربعين الف اسكوت اعني غرش فكتب
له الفرمان وكتب عليه الوثيقه كما ذكرنا واصرفوه.

وما اهتدى الدوك ولا مدبرين بلاطه خباثة ذلك اليهودي بل استقلوا بعقله ٦،٨٣
وهزوا به فمضي ذلك اليهودي الى بلدته اعني مدينة ليكورنا وفي حال وصوله مضي
الى المحكمه وسجل فرمانه وبعد ثلاثة ايام ارسل واحضر الى عنده صاحبين الاراضي
التي ينزرع فيها القمح وباقية الحبوب وقرى لهم الفرمان العاطيه هو حضرة الدوك
بانه صرفه في الشمس وقلهم بان ما زرعكم الا بواسطة الشمس ولاجل هذا
بريد منكم بان تعطوني في كل سنه هل قدر ميري وان ما قبلتوا انا بزرع تلك الاراضي
وبعطي ميريها لحضرة الدوك فخاروا في امرهم اوليك الرجال.

اخيرًا التزموا بانهم يكتبوله وسيقه بذلك المبلغ الذي طلبه منهم وبعده ٦،٨٤
ارسل واحضر اصحاب البساتين واتفق معهم وكتب عليهم وسيقه واصرفهم
وبعده احضر القصارين والسباغين والى كل من هو مفتقر للشمس وكتب علي
كل منهم وسيقه فشاع الخبر في المدينه بالذي فعله ذلك اليهودي بموجب فرمان
من يد الدوك.

حينئذ اجتمعت اكابر واعيان البلده واحضروا لعندهم القضاه والاساقفه واهل ٦،٨٥
الاكليرس وضربوا ديوان واتفقوا جميعهم بان هذا الامر ما يجوز لان الله سبحانه
اشرف شمسه علي الاخيار والاشرار وما احد بيقدر بيتصرف بعطية الله لعبيده
فاتفقوا جميعهم علي هذا الراي وكتبوا عرض محضر ودونوا خطوط ايادي بانهم ما

"Fool! How am I supposed to sell you something I don't own?" he asked. **6.82**
"Can the sun be bought and sold?"

"You're right, my lord," the Jew replied. "But indulge me, even if everyone has a laugh at my expense."

The duke's officials, who were present at the meeting, turned to him and said, "Sire, give him what he asks, and let's see him try to take hold of the sun!"

The duke took the advice of his officials, as he wanted to see where this strange matter would lead. He ordered the secretary of the chancery to draft an edict giving the Jew free disposal of the sun, as well as a document requiring him to provide eighty sacks of silver to the treasury each year—equivalent to forty thousand ecus, or piasters. The secretary drafted the two documents for the Jew, who was then sent on his way.

Neither the duke nor the officials of his court caught on to the Jew's cun- **6.83**
ning scheme. Instead they mocked him, underestimating his intelligence. The Jew, meanwhile, returned to his home in Livorno, and immediately registered the duke's edict at the courthouse. Three days later, he summoned all of the landowners who grew wheat and other grains on their properties, and read them the edict that His Excellency the duke had given him, which granted him authority over the sun.

"Your crops depend on the sun," the Jew said. "Therefore, I ask that you pay me such and such an amount in tax each year. If you refuse, I'll farm the lands myself and pay the tax to His Excellency the duke."

At a loss as to what to do, the men felt compelled to draft a document agree- **6.84**
ing to pay what he demanded. The Jew then summoned the orchard owners and came to an agreement with them. He drafted a document and sent them away. He did the same with the launderers and the dyers, and everyone else whose livelihood depended upon the sun. The news of the Jew's actions—authorized by nothing less than an edict from the duke himself—spread throughout the city.

The notables of Livorno convened and held a council, to which they sum- **6.85**
moned the city's judges, bishops, and clergy. They all agreed that this whole affair was unacceptable. After all, God made His sun shine down upon the virtuous and the wicked alike, and no one had the right to administer the gift God had given to His servants! Unanimously agreed on this position, they drew up a petition testifying to their refusal of the duke's order. Everyone signed the

بيقبلوا ما امر به حضرة الدوك وانتخبوا من ذلك الجمهور كام واحد من اكابر البلد وارسلوهم الي عند حضرة الدوك.

٦،٨٦ فلما وصلوا وامتثلوا امام الدوك وعملوا التمني الواجب عليهم لحضرته ثم اعطوه العرض محضر الذي مدون فيه اكثر من مايتين[1] اسم من اسافقه وكهنه وروسا ديوره وداكرين له بان حضرة مولانا وولي نعمتنا قد انغش من رجل يهودي عدو ديانتنا وانه في هل امر بيدخل له مال عظيم ينوف عن ثلاثماية كيس وذكروله صورة الواقعه كيف انه رتب علي كل من هوكاره مفتقر الي شمس يعطي ميري هل قدر فلما قراء الدوك العرض محضر غضب غضب شديد وانتبه علي خطيته كيف انه سلم لهل ماكر سيف يضرب به رعيته.

٦،٨٧ وفي الحال ركب من عنده قايد من قواد بلاطه وامره بانه يسرع ويحضر امامه ذلك اليهودي المكار فمضي ذلك القايد وفي قليل من الزمان احضره فلما امتثل امام الدوك فقله هكذا بتغشني[2] وبترميني في الخطاء يا خاين الله والسلطان واخد منه الفرمان وجميع التمسكات التي كتبهم علي رعيته وامر بشنقه وضبط ماله ونادي عليه الجلاد هذه جزات من يغش الملوك.

٦،٨٨ وفي تلك الايام ايضاً صدر امر غريب من رجل يهودي وهو ان هذا الرجل في ايام حداثته طلب انه يتنصر ويعتمد فبعدما ابقوه ثلاثة سناوات في التجربه وفحصوه فحص بليغ فراوه ثابت علي عزمه وما اتزعزع ابداً. حيند امر الاسقف للقوري بان يعمده ويعرفه ويعطيه الاسرار المقدسه وبعده فاستقام ذلك الرجل في الامانه وكل يوم عن يوم يزيد في العباده حتي انه دخل للرهبنه واستقام مدة سنين في العباده وحسن السيره. حيند استحق انهم يلبسوه الاسكيم الرهباني المقدس وبعده قليل من الزمان رسموه كاهن وكان الجميع يشهدوا بحسن سيرته فاستقام مدة سنين كاهناً مهذباً ورعاً في غاية ما يكون.

petition, and they elected a few distinguished members of their assembly to
visit the duke.

The representatives went to the duke and presented themselves before His
Excellency, greeting him with the salutations befitting his station. They presented their petition, which contained over two hundred signatures. These
included the names of bishops, priests, and the abbots of monasteries. The
petition read: "His Excellency, our master and gracious benefactor, has been
cheated by a Jew, an enemy of our religion. By means of this swindle, he has
laid hands on an immense fortune surpassing three hundred sacks of silver."
They explained how the man had imposed a certain tax upon every person
whose livelihood depended on the sun.

Once the duke read the petition, he became furious, realizing the mistake
he'd made. How could he have given this swindler a sword with which to smite
his subjects?

The duke summoned one of his court officers and ordered him to bring the
deceitful Jew before him as quickly as possible. The officer left, and soon after
returned with the man in tow.

"You've deceived me and led me astray, you traitor to God and king!" said
the duke to the Jew when the latter appeared before him. He took the edict
back from him and seized all of the debt contracts he'd drawn up against the
duke's subjects. Summoning the executioner, he ordered the Jew to be hanged
and his properties confiscated.

Such is the punishment of those who swindle kings![107]

Another strange affair involving a Jewish man occurred back then. In his
youth, he had sought to convert to Christianity and be baptized. After having
spent three years completing his novitiate, during which time he was subjected
to a profound examination, he was determined to be firm and unwavering in
his conviction. So the bishop ordered the priest to baptize him, to hear his
confession, and to administer Holy Communion. Following his conversion,
the man remained faithful to his decision, growing more pious with each passing day, even electing to join a monastic order. For several years, he devoted
himself to piety and virtuous conduct, so it seemed only fitting that he would
eventually be vested in the sacred habit of the monk. Shortly thereafter, he was
ordained as a priest, and recognized by all for his good deeds. He spent many
years as a deeply virtuous and pious priest.

6.86

6.87

6.88

فاتفق ليله من الليالي ان العسس١ دايرين في شوارع المدينه لاجل الحراسه فمروا ٦،٨٩
من تحت شبابيك ذلك الدير الموجود فيه ذاك الكاهن اليهودي الذي مر ذكره فراوا
خارج من بعض الشبابيك دخان عظيم ولميع نار فضنوا بان تلك القلايه احترقت
فمضت منهم ناس عاجلاً وطرقوا باب الدير طرقاً متيناً الي ان انتبه الخادم واسرع وفتح
الباب فقالوا له الجنود اسرع واطفي النار التي حرقت احد قلالي الدير وها نحنا اتينا
حتي نعلمك فمضي ذلك الخادم ونبه الريس والرهبان واخبرهم بحريق القلايه فداروا
علي القلالي الي ان وصلوا الي قلايه ذلك الكاهن اليهودي فراوا الدخنه خارجه من
شقوق الباب فنتجوا بان القلايه والراهب احترقوا معاً.

فامر الريس الرهبان بانهم يخلعوا الباب ويدخلوا عاجلاً ليلا يحترق الراهب فعملوا ٦،٩٠
كما امرهم ودخلوا داخل القلايه فوجدوا ذلك الكاهن التعيس ناكت فراش القش اعني
النفل الذي يضعوه تحت الفرش بجاري عوايدهم والنار لاهبه منه وداخل النار
موضوع الصلبوت حتي يحترق لكن النار ما اثرت في الصلبوت وهو باقي علي صحته
فرفعوا ذلك المصلوب من النار وقبلوه والتفوا الي ذلك المنكوت حظه وسالوه لماذا
فعل هل فعل فاجابهم وهو مرغي ومزبد قايلاً بريد احرق صليبكم الذي تعبدوه لاني
انا يهودي عدو الصليب.

فهبت الريس وباقيت الرهبان من جسارة هذا الشقي المتكود الحظ. حينئذٍ امر ٦،٩١
الريس بان يمسكوه ويضعوه في الحبس وثاني الايام اعلموا فيه الاسقف فامر باتيانه
فاحضروه امامه فساله حضرة الاسقف هل فعل هل شي بوعي كامل ام حكمه
عارض ماخوليا وجنون وقال هذا حتي يختبره فاجابه ذلك اللعين بانه هو يهودي
عدو الصليب ولاجل هذا اردت اني احرقه. حينئذٍ ارسله الاسقف الي عند حاكم
المدينه واعلمه بخبره فلما امتثل امام الحاكم وقري صورة خبره فارسله الي بيت الشريعه
اعني المحكمه فلما فحصوا خبره سجلوا عليه بانه يحرق حياً وهو لاجل فعله هذا.

---

One night, while the city guards were patrolling the streets, they passed    6.89
beneath the windows of the monastery where the Jewish priest lived. They
saw clouds of smoke billowing from one of the windows, as well as the flicker
of fire, and suspected that the cell was in flames. Some of them rushed up to
the monastery and pounded on the door until a servant woke up and hurried
over to open it.

"We're here to tell you that one of the cells is on fire!" they exclaimed.
"Go and put it out, quickly!"

The servant went off to wake the abbot and monks, and told them about the
burning cell. They made a round of all the cells until they reached the Jewish
priest's room. Smoke was pouring from the spaces around the door. They
assumed that both the cell and the monk were on fire.

The abbot ordered the monks to pull the door off its hinges and rush inside    6.90
to help the monk. They obeyed and entered the cell. They discovered that the
wretched priest had emptied out the mattress that was under the bed of its
clover hay stuffing, which was what they usually used. Flames leapt from the
hay, and a crucifix lay in the center of the fire! And yet the flames had had no
effect on the crucifix, which remained untarnished. The monks yanked it from
the fire and kissed it. Then they turned to the unfortunate man and asked him
why he'd done what he'd done.

"I wanted to burn the crucifix you worship, since I'm a Jew and an enemy of
the cross!" he spat at them, foaming at the mouth in his rage.

The abbot and the monks were baffled by the insolence of this wretched,    6.91
miserable man. The abbot ordered him to be seized and kept in confinement.
The next day, they told the bishop what had happened, and he demanded
that the man be brought to him. His Holiness the bishop asked the man if
he had performed this act while of sound mind, or if he'd been seized by a
bout of melancholy or madness. He asked him this question to determine the
man's intentions.

"I'm a Jew, and an enemy of the cross," the cursed man replied. "That's why
I tried to burn it."

The bishop sent the man to the governor of the city and explained what
had taken place. When he appeared before the governor and the details of
his case were read out, the governor sent him to the tribunal—that is, the
courthouse. His case was examined and he was sentenced to be burned alive
for his crime.

٩٢،٦ فبعدما سجلوا عليه بالحرق مضوا به الي عند الحاكم ليقضي عليه بما امرت الشريعه فالحاكم لما راء بان تسجل عليه الحريق بالنار فما راد ان يميته بهذه الموته الصعبه لان كان قلبه رقيق وما يمكنه بانه يخالف الشريعه خوفاً من العوام فارسله الي مدينة فوينسا الي عند حضرة الدوك حتي يفعل فيه ما يشا وخلص حاله بهل وسيله فلما احضروه امام حضرة الدوك وقري السجل المسجل عليه في الحال امر بحرقه فاحترق جسده في الدنيا واحترقت نفسه في جهنم وبيس المسير .

٩٣،٦ ويوم اخر وكان صباحيت السبت فرايت نسا ورجال من اهل حارتنا متهيين لان يمضوا الي زياره كنيسة مريم العدرا التي هي في جبل الاسود وذلك الجبل قريب من المدينه حكم ثلاثة اميال وكانوا احكولي عن شرف هل كنيسه التي هي علي اسم مريم العذري وكثره العجايب الموجوده فيها فاشتهيت اني اروح ازور هل كنيسه فاستازنت من معلي حتي امضي ازور هل كنيسه فاعطاني اذن بذلك. حينذٍ الست صاحبت البيت ارسلت معي احد خدامهم حتي يرافقني في الطريق واعطتني بنيطه من خوص بقد طبق تنسيف ومع كبرها وزنها مقدار وقيه وقالت لي لما بتصعد للجبل البسها[1] حتي تمنع عنك حرارة الشمس لان الوقت كان حار وهو في اواخر شهر اب.

٩٤،٦ فمضينا انا وذلك الغلام الي ان وصلنا الي ديل الي ذلك الجبل فرايت كثير من الناس صاعدين من نسا ورجال وكثير منهم صاعدين حفاه علي ذلك الصخر الاسود الذي هو واحد من السكاكين وبعضهم صاعدين علي ركبهم بورع عظيم وهن موجهين طلباتهم الي مريم العذري صاحبة العجايب وغيرهم سايرين بروس محنيه طالبين شفاعتها.

٩٥،٦ المراد انتهينا الي قمت الجبل الذي يدعا جبل الاسود وتحت ذلك الجبل البحر بتدق مياه في ذلك الجبل ورايت كنيسه عاليت الاركان بعماره مكلفه ومبني بجانبها دير رهبان متسع. اخيراً دخلنا للكنيسه وفي ذلك الوقت بدي قداس علي مديح العذري الذي فيه ايقونتها وتلك القونه لها ثلاثة استارات مكلفات في ثلث القداس الواحد بيسحبوا اول ستار وفي ثاني ثلث بيسحبوا ثاني ستار وفي ثلث الاخير بيسحبوا ثلث

---

١ الأصل: ابلسها.

Following the sentencing, he was taken before the governor to have the sentence carried out. But the governor was a tenderhearted man, and hesitated as he did not want to put the offender to such a cruel death. He was wary of the people's response should he controvert the law, so he sent the Jew to Florence to appear before His Excellency the duke. That way, he would let the duke make the final decision, sparing himself from doing so. When they brought the man before His Excellency the duke and read out his sentence, the duke immediately ordered him to be burned. And thus, his body burned in this world and his soul burned in Hell. What a terrible fate! **6.92**

One Saturday morning, I saw some women and men of our neighborhood preparing to visit the Church of the Virgin Mary, which stood on the Black Mountain,[108] about three miles from the city. I'd heard about this noble church, which was named for the Virgin Mary, and about all the miracles that had taken place there. I very much wished to visit it, so I asked my master for permission to go, and he consented. The mistress of the house ordered one of her servants to accompany me on the route. She also gave me a hat made of palm leaves to wear. It was as large as a sieve and yet, despite its size, weighed less than half a pound. **6.93**

"Wear it as you climb the mountain, and it will protect from the heat of the sun," she told me. It was August at the time, and the weather was hot.

The servant and I set off and soon arrived at the foot of the mountain. I saw many people, both men and women, climbing up the mountain. Some were barefoot, treading upon the black rocks, which were sharper than knives! Others, demonstrating their deep piety, climbed the slope on their knees, as they addressed their requests to the Virgin Mary, worker of miracles. Others walked with their heads bowed, asking for her intercession. **6.94**

We finally arrived at the summit of the Black Mountain. From it one could see the sea below, crashing against the mountainside. Before me stood a splendidly built church with tall columns, alongside a large monastery. We entered the church just as a mass was beginning, in praise of the Virgin of the icon. This icon was covered by three lavish screens. During the first third of the mass, they would draw the first screen back. During the second third, they would remove the second screen, and during the final third, the last one. The icon of the Virgin Mary would then be fully revealed, and the people would receive her blessings. This took place every Saturday, year round. **6.95**

ستار . حينذٍ بتبان ايقونة مريم العذري وبيتاركوا منها الشعب وهذا بيفعلوه كل نهار سبت علي مدار السنه فبعدما حضرنا القداس وتباركنا من ذلك الهيكل فاخذني ذلك الغلام وصار يدوريني في الكنيسه ويروني العجايب التي فعلتها مريم العذري مع الذين استغاثوا بها في وقت الضروره[1] والخطر الذين كانوا حاصلين فيه وكل عجيبه لها تمثال وكاتبين تحتها صورة العجيبه المفعوله في ذلك الانسان.

٩٦،٦ منهم كان مسافرٍ في البحر وانكسر المركب فيهم فاستغاس بمريم العذري الساكنه في جبل الاسود فنجته من الغريق بواسطة حوت يسمي البرفيل حمله حتي القاه في البر فقدم لكنيسه مركب زغير من فضه وتحته حوت من فضه ومنهم من وقع من سلم عالي جدًا فاستغاث فيها فنجي وما سايل فعلق في الكنيسه سلم من فضه وكتب تحته صورة العجيبه المفعوله معه من مريم العذري وهلم جراء من العجايب المشحونه في تلك الكنيسه شي بيفوق العدد حتمنت لو استقيم ثلاثة ايام لما قدرت احصي تلك العجايب المعلقه في تلك الكنيسه.

٩٧،٦ ومنهم عجيبه التي جرت في بلاد النسا وهي انه في قلعه من قلاع بلاد النسا ودخلها جملت جنود وقايدهم بيحرسوا تلك القلعه فاتفق تنين من الجنود ترابطوا في بعضهم بانهم يهربوا ليلاً من القلعه من غير اذن القايد فلما هربوا وبعد يوم بلغ خبرهم للقايد بانهم هربوا فاحتد بالغضب وحلف يمين بان اذا مسكهم بشنق الاثنين وارسل كم واحد من الجنود الحدق بان ينقبوا عليهم ويعملوا كل جهدهم ويحصلوهم من اي مكان كان فطلعوا اوليك الجنود يفتشوا ويسالوا عنهم فبعد يومين قبضوا عليهم وساقوهم امام القايد فلما راهم فاحتد بغضب وحشي وامر في شنق الاثنين.

٩٨،٦ فصار الواحد منهم يتوسل الي القايد بقوله له بان ارحمني يا سيدي انا ليس لي دنب انما رفيقي خونني فابتدي الاخري يقول للقايد بان ما له دنب كمثل قول الاولي فاحتار القايد ما بينهم منوا منهم مستحق الشنق. حينذٍ قال لهم انا بربي قرعه والذي بتقع عليه بشنقته فلما ربي القرعه وقعت علي واحد منهم فامر القايد بحبسه الي الغد لان الوقت كان ممسي فطرحوه في السجن.

---

١ الأصل: الضروه.

After attending mass and receiving the benediction at the altar, I was taken around the church by the servant who'd come with me to the mountain. He showed me the miracles the Virgin Mary had performed for those who had sought her help in times of need or peril. Each miracle was represented by a statue and a written account placed beneath it.

Among these miracles was one about a man who'd been shipwrecked while traveling at sea. He called out for the help of the Virgin Mary of the Black Mountain, and she saved him by sending him a fish called a dolphin, which carried him to safety and cast him onto dry land. In gratitude, the man gave the church a small ship made of silver, beneath which was a fish, also made of silver. Another miracle regarded a man who'd fallen from a tall ladder. He too called out for the Virgin's help, and escaped unharmed. He offered the church a silver ladder, writing beneath it a description of the miracle performed for him by the Virgin Mary. The church was packed with countless miracles of this kind. It seemed to me that if I spent three days there, I still wouldn't be able to count all of the miraculous stories hanging in that church!

6.96

One of the miracles had taken place in Habsburg lands, where there was a castle guarded by a company of soldiers and their commander. It came to pass that two soldiers hatched a plan to flee the castle by night, without the permission of their commanding officer. The next day, when the officer learned of their flight, he flew into a rage, and swore he'd hang the both of them if they were found. He dispatched a few sharp-eyed soldiers to search for them, and ordered them to do whatever was necessary to bring the runaways back. The soldiers set out in pursuit, asking around if anyone had seen them. Two days later, they caught the deserters and brought them back before the officer who, in a wild fit of rage, ordered them both to be hanged.

6.97

One of the men began to plead for his life. "Have mercy on me, my lord," he cried. "I'm not to blame! My friend got me into this mess!"

6.98

The other man joined in with the same pleas, claiming that he wasn't to blame. The officer was unsure of what to do. Which of the two deserved to be hanged?

"We'll cast lots," he said to the men. "Whoever draws the short stick will hang."

So the officer cast lots and one of the men drew the short stick. The officer ordered him held until the morning, as the hour had grown late, and he was cast into prison.

٦.٩٩ بمجلس وهو يبكي ويندب حاله وهو في تلك الحالة المحزنه فدخل الي عنده رفيقه الذي كان معه لما هربوا فصار يعزيه ويتوجع لمصيبته وكان في السجن ايقونه مريم العذري معلقه فصار يقله يا اخي التجي الي مريم العذري الساكنه في جبل الاسود وهي بتنجيك لان ما احد استجار فيها وخاب. حينذٍ سجد ذلك الرجل امام ايقونة ام الرحمه وهو يبكي بدموع حاره ويطلب منها النجاه الليل كله الي حين ما اصبح الصباح فامر وقيدٍ القايد باتيان ذلك الرجل امامه وامر الجلاد بانه يشنقه في الحال.

٦.١٠٠ فتسلمه الجلاد ومضي به الي المشنقه وخبرق الحبل في عنقه واصعده علي السلم المركوز بجانب المشنقه ودفعه من علي السلم حتي يشنق فصرخ ذلك الرجل بصوت عال وقال يا مريم العذري الساكنه في جبل الاسود نجيني في الحال انقطع الحبل فيه وانطرح علي الارض وهو حي فامر القايد بان يجيبوا غير حبل بيكون متين فشربكوا الحبل في عنقه ايضاً واصعدوه علي السلم وفسه الجلاد كما فعل في الاول وكان ذلك الرجل قوية امانته في مريم العذري التي خلصته في الاول فصرخ ايضاً بصوت عال وقال يا مريم العذري الساكنه في جبل الاسود نجيني.

٦.١٠١ فانقطع الحبل ايضاً وانطرح ذلك الرجل علي الارض وهو حي فغضب القايد وامر بانهم يرموا حبل من كان كثير الطوق فلما كمل فقال ذلك الجاهل الغبي القليل الامانه في مريم العذري هل اغاثتك بتقطع هل حبل ايضاً وما كان اعتقد بان مريم العذري اظهرت هذه العجيبه بقطع الحبل مرتين فبعد ما اصعدوه ايضاً علي السلم وهو مسطمن بامانه متينه في ام الرحمه فلما دفشه الجلاد فصاح باعلي صوته واستغاث في ام العجايب التي هي ساكنه في جبل الاسود في الحال تقطع ذلك الحبل المتين اربًا اربًا خلاف عن المرتين.

٦.١٠٢ فلما راوا الحاضرين تلك المعجزه فصرخوا بصوت واحد قايلين كف يا قايد عن ضلالك وامن في عجايب مريم العذري الظاهره تجاه عينيك. حينذٍ امن ذلك القايد بهذه العجيبه وندم علي سو فعله وقلة ايمانه ودعا ذلك الرجل الجندي وضمه الي صدره واستبره منه دمه وعلا منزلته عنده وقله من الان وصاعد تكون معتوق من الجنديه

The man fell to weeping and cursing his fate. By and by, the friend he'd fled    6.99
with came and joined him, doing what he could to distract him and alleviate
his suffering. In the prison cell hung an icon of the Virgin Mary.

"Don't be afraid, brother," the condemned man's friend said to him. "Turn
to the Virgin Mary of the Black Mountain, and she'll save you. No one who
seeks her protection is ever disappointed."

So the prisoner knelt before the icon of the Mother of Mercy, hot tears
streaming down his face, and begged her all night long to save him. When
dawn broke, the officer summoned the prisoner and ordered the executioner
to hang him immediately.

The executioner led the man to the gallows, dropped the noose around his    6.100
neck, and sent him up the ladder that lay against the side of the gallows. Then
he pushed him off the ladder.

"Virgin Mary of the Black Mountain, save me!" the man cried. At that
instant, the rope snapped and he fell to the ground, very much alive.

The officer ordered a stouter rope to be brought. Again they put a noose
around the man's neck and made him climb the ladder, and the executioner
kicked him off. But the man's faith in the Virgin Mary was strong, and as she
had saved him before, so he again cried out as he fell, "Virgin Mary of the Black
Mountain, save me!"

Again the rope snapped, and the man tumbled to the ground. Exasperated,    6.101
the commanding officer ordered them to use a very strong rope made of linen.

Soon the preparations were complete. "Let's see if your prayers help you
now," said the witless fool of an officer, who didn't believe in the power of the
Virgin and wouldn't admit that she had worked a miracle by breaking the rope
twice. Meanwhile, the condemned man, confident in his faith, had climbed to
the top of the ladder. When the executioner pushed him, he cried out at the
top of his lungs, seeking succor from the wonder-working Virgin of the Black
Mountain. Just like that, the strong rope snapped—and this time it had been
cut to pieces!

"Can't you see it, sir?" the assembled men shouted, after witnessing this    6.102
miracle. "Have faith in the miracles of the Virgin Mary taking place before your
very eyes!"

The officer accepted the miracle and repented of his cruelty and lack of
faith. He summoned the condemned soldier, embraced him, and pardoned
him. The soldier rose in his esteem.

وتكون عندي باعز مقام اما ذلك الرجل قال للقايد دعني امضي واخدم ما تبقا من حياتي الي تلك التي خلصتني ثلاث مرات من الهلاك وصنعت معي هل عجيبة الباهره فلما سمع القايد منه هل كلام فقله افعل ما بدا لك واخرج واعطاه خرجيه وافه وزواده ايضاً واطلقه فمضي ذلك الرجل الي جبل الاسود وشكر فضل مريم العذري ودخل وترهب في ديرها الي ان قضا حياته١ في ذلك الدير بالصوم والصلاه والتعبد الي هذه الست السيده.

٦،١٠٣ فاتفق من بعد رجوعي من تلك البلاد الي حلب احكيت امام جماعات مسيحيه خبر عجايب هل ست السيده التي هي في جبل الاسود المذكور وبينت لهم بان ما احد استغاث في مريم العذري الساكنه في جبل الاسود وخاب من طلبته واحكيت لهم علي تلك العجايب التي رايتها معلقه في كنيستها كما ذكرنا فما فات مده من الزمان والا جاني رجل من تلك الجماعه الذي كت احكيت لهم خبر عجايب مريم العذري.

٦،١٠٤ وقال لي يا اخي كت سمعت منك خبر عجايب مريم العذري الساكنه في جبل الاسود وكان لي مدة سنين واقع في بليه عظيمه وما قدرت اخلص منها فلما استغثت كما دكرت لنا وندرت لها ندر في الحال صار لي من ذلك الديق فرج عظيم والان اتيتك بالندر واخرج واعطاني اثني عشر دهب بندقي حتي ارسلهم الي كنيستها فاخدت منه تلك الدهبات وقلته اتبعني ومضيت به الي عند رجل تاجر فرنساوي يسما خواجه جيلون٢ الذي كان يتاجر الي بلاد ليكورنا واتوسلت اليه بانه يرسل هذا الندر ليد شريكه حتي يرسله الي كنيسة مريم العدري التي هي في جبل الاسود فقبل الرجل وسر الدهبات في قرظار وكتب عليهم امانه الي مريم العذري في جبل الاسود فاستكثرنا خيره ومضينا.

٦،١٠٥ وبعد قليل من الزمان جاني واحد اخر وفي يده عشرة دهب بندقي ايضاً ندر لتلك الكنيسه وكانت خلصته الست السيده لما استغاث بها من تهمه باطله التي

---

١ الأصل: حاته.   ٢ «يسما خواجه جيلون» في الهامش.

"From now on, you're exempt from conscription," the officer told him, "and you have a place of honor with me!"

But the man had another wish.

"Give me leave to spend the rest of my life serving her, as she saved me three times from death, and performed this great miracle for my sake!"

Hearing this, the officer consented and sent him off with a tidy sum of money and ample provisions for his journey. The man traveled to the Black Mountain and gave thanks to the Virgin Mary. He then joined the monastery there and became a monk, spending the rest of his days engaged in fasting and prayer and devotion to Our Lady.

When I returned to Aleppo after my own travels, it so happened that I was 6.103 speaking to some groups of Christians and told them the story of the miracles of Our Lady of the Black Mountain. I explained to them that no one who'd ever sought her help had been refused, and described the testimonies to all the miracles I'd seen in the church, as I recounted earlier. Well, not long afterward, a man from one of those groups I'd spoken to came to see me.

"Brother, I heard you speak about the miracles of the Virgin Mary of the 6.104 Black Mountain," he said. "For several years, I'd been having some serious troubles and could find no way out. But then I followed your advice: I asked the Virgin Mary for help and pledged a votive offering. The next thing I knew, I was saved."

"And here's my votive offering to the Virgin," he continued. He handed me twelve gold Venetian ducats and asked me to send them to the church.

"Follow me," I said, taking the coins. We went off to see a French merchant named *khawājah* Guillon, who had business interests in Livorno. I implored him to send the votive offering to his business partner there, and to ask him to forward it to the Church of the Virgin Mary of the Black Mountain. The man agreed, and he placed the coins in an envelope and wrote on it: "Deposit in trust for the Virgin Mary of the Black Mountain." We thanked him for his kindness and left.

Soon thereafter, another man came to me with twelve Venetian gold 6.105 ducats, which he had vowed to give to the church. Our Lady had aided him when he asked her to deliver him from a false accusation that would have ruined his life.

كانت بتسير سبب خراب بيته والفقير الكاتب هذا الخبر من بعد خمسين سنه التي مرت كان فقد لي شي بيساوي الف وماية غرش وبعد ان مر عليه مقدار اربعين يوم فاقد وقطعت الايأس منه وايقنت في خراب الديار فيوم من الايام خطر في بالي باني استغيث في مريم العذري جبل الاسود في تلك الليله نفسها مضي الذي اخذ تلك الاخيده واعترف الي رجل كاهن في ذلك الذي اختلسه مني والكاهن وقف واسطه رجل متقرب اليّ وبشرني الي وجود ذلك المفقود مني من غير اني اعرف الذي اخذه وبعد يوم جاب لي هو وما نقص منه شي ابدًا فشكرت احسان مريم العذري صاحبت العجايب.

٦.١٠٦ والان نخبر عن ما سمعته من ناس صادقين عن وجود هل ايقونة الشريفه وتأسيس هل كنيسه هو انه كان رجل راعي في ذلك الجبل فمر يوم من الايام في ناحيه من الجبل فوجد بين السخوره ايقونة مريم العذري المذكوره فلما تاملها ذلك الراعي فراها جميله في غاية الجمال فرفعها من بين تلك الصخوره وعلقها في شجر من تلك الاشجار الموجوده في ذلك المكان ولما حان وقت ارتحاله من الجبل قال في باله باخد قونه معي الي البلد وبعطيها الي الاسقف لعله يوهبني شي من الاحسان.

٦.١٠٧ فلما كان المساء اخذ تلك الايقونه ومضي الي عند الاسقف واعطاه هي فلما تفرس فيها حضرة الاسقف راها نادره من النوادر تصوير معلم ماهر . حيندٍ ساله الاسقف منين له هذه القونة الجميله فاجابه باني رايتها في جبل الاسود مريمه بين الصخور فجبتها الي حضرتك فشكره واعطاه احسان واصرفه فمضا ذلك الجريان.

٦.١٠٨ وتاني يوم ساق الغنم امامه ومضي الي ذلك الجبل يرعا غنه كعادته ولما مر في ذلك المكان فراء تلك الايقونه نفسها مريمه بين الصخور كما وجدها في الاول فاعتجب فعاد اخذها ومضي بها الي عند الاسقف فلا راها الاسقف في يده بهت وساله فين وجدت هل قونه فاجابه رايتها في ذلك المكان الذي رايتها فيه نهار امس بين الصخور فتعجب الاسقف وارسل تلميده يروح يشرف في قلايته يرا هل تلك الايقونه موجوده

As for me—writing this account fifty years later—I too once lost something, worth 1,100 piasters. After it had been missing for forty days, I lost all hope of recovering it and felt certain I was on the brink of ruin. One day, it occurred to me to ask the help of the Virgin Mary of the Black Mountain. That very night, the person who had taken my property went to see a priest and confessed to his crime! With the help of a close friend of mine who acted as an intermediary, the priest shared the good news that the lost item had been found, without letting me know who had taken it. My friend brought it to me the next day. Nothing was missing! I gave thanks to the Virgin Mary, Mother of Miracles, for her beneficence.

Let me now recount what I heard from some trustworthy people about that noble icon and the founding of the church. There was once a shepherd who lived on that mountain. One day, as he was walking along the mountainside, he came upon that very icon of the Virgin Mary hidden among some boulders. The shepherd stared at it and was struck by its magnificence. He lifted it from its spot among the boulders and hung it from a tree. 6.106

Later, when the time came for him to leave the mountain, he said to himself, "I'm going to bring this icon into town and give it to the bishop. Maybe he'll give me something for it."

In the evening, he went to see the bishop and gave him the icon. Studying it carefully, His Holiness the bishop recognized it as a rare masterwork, the product of an expert artist. 6.107

"Where did you find this beautiful icon?" the bishop asked the shepherd.

"I spotted it on the Black Mountain, discarded among the rocks, so I brought it to Your Holiness."

The bishop thanked him, gave him a few coins, and sent him off. And that was that.

The next day, the shepherd took his sheep up the mountain, as usual. When he passed by the same spot, he saw very same icon of Mary, lying among the boulders where he'd found it the first time! Amazed, he picked it up and took it to the bishop. 6.108

"And where did you find that icon?" the confused bishop asked when he saw it.

"It was in the same place I found it yesterday, among the rocks," the shepherd replied.

في مكان الذي علقها فيه فرجع التليد وقال بانه ما راها فزاد في العجب واحسن لذلك الراعي واصرفه وعلق تلك الايقونه في قلايته في مكانها الاول.

فرثالث يوم الراعي في ذلك المكان فاء تلك الايقونه في ذلك المكان الذي راها فيه في الاول فاندوخ ذلك الرجل وقال في باله بما انه سادج بان واحد بينشلها من عند الاسقف ويرميها في هذا المكان فعاد اخدها ايضاً ومضي الي عند الاسقف وقله بضن يا سيدنا بان احد من خدامك بينشلها ويضعها في ذلك المكان فعند ذلك نهض الاسقف الي قلايته فما راها فاتكد عنده بان هذه عجيبه من مريم العذري وانها بتريد بان يكون لها مقام في ذلك الجبل.

في الحال ارسل وامرجميع الخوارنه والكهنه وروسا الديوره وكل اهل الاكليرس بانهم يجتمعوا جميعهم في دار الاسقفيه وهن لابسين حلل الكهنوت والشماسه بالشموع والمباخر ويخرجوا بزياح عام محتفل في الغايه ولماكان الغد فاجتمعوا الجميع كما امرهم حضرة الاسقف بذلك الزياح المذكور ولما كملوا حيندٍ رفع الاسقف علي هامه تلك الايقونه بغاية العز والاحترام ومضوا بها الي ذلك الجبل واحضروا الراعي وسالوه عن المكان الذي وجدها فيه فارواهم ذلك المكان فتقدم الاسقف واشرعن بنا الكنيسه في ذلك المكان. حيندٍ احضروا البنايين الفعاله وباشروا في عمارة تلك الكنيسه وعمروا هيكل خصوصي لايقونة مريم العذري.

ومن ذلك الزمان والي الان لم تزل هذه الام الحنونه تفعل عجايب باهره لكل من التجي اليها وطلب منها بامانه ينال مراده وهذا الذي رايته وسمعته عن هل ست السيده الساكنه في جبل الاسود وخبرها مشهور في كل اقليم المسيحيه حتي اذا فات مركب من تحت كنيستها من اي ملة كان ما يمكن الا انه يعطي طاعة لهذه الست السيده ويضرب مدافع اشاره طاعته لها وان فات وما عطا طاعه لا بد ما يحكمه انكيس وعطب وهذا عرفوه بالتجربه والذي ما يصدقني فيسال للذين راحوا الي تلك الاماكن عن حقيقة هذا الخبر.

The bishop was astonished, and sent his disciple to go and check whether the icon was still in his chambers, where he'd hung it. The disciple returned and reported that it had vanished. The bishop grew even more bewildered, gave the shepherd a token of his thanks, and dismissed him. He hung the icon in his cell once again, in the very same spot.

On the third day, the shepherd passed the same place and saw the icon yet again. Stunned, the simpleminded shepherd told himself that someone must surely be stealing the icon from the bishop's room and discarding it here. So he picked it up and hurried back to see the bishop.    **6.109**

"My lord, one of your servants must be stealing the icon and leaving it in that spot!" he said. The bishop raced up to his room and saw that the icon was missing again. Finally, it dawned on him that this was a miracle worked by the Virgin Mary, who wanted a shrine on that mountain.

The bishop immediately summoned all the curates and priests, the abbots of all the monasteries, and the rest of the clergy, ordering them to gather at the bishopric. Wearing their ceremonial vestments, with the deacons carrying candles and censers, they were all to march in a jubilant, festive procession. The next day, they convened as His Holiness had requested, and once all were present, the bishop raised the icon above his head in a gesture of deep respect and veneration, and the procession set off for the mountain.    **6.110**

They summoned the shepherd and asked him about the exact spot where he had found the icon, and he led them there. The bishop then came forward and indicated where the church was to be built. Skilled builders were summoned, and they set about constructing the church, which included a chapel dedicated to the icon of the Virgin Mary.

From that moment until the present day, the Mother of Mercy has continued to work her dazzling miracles. All who seek refuge with her and make their requests faithfully obtain what they ask for.    **6.111**

This is what I saw and heard about Our Lady of the Black Mountain.[109] Her story is so renowned throughout Christendom that whenever a ship sails past the church, regardless of which nation it belongs to, it signals its submission to Our Lady by firing its cannons. Any ship that fails to do so is inevitably beset by misfortune and ruin, as experience has taught. And anyone who doesn't believe that my story is true should ask others who have been there themselves.

وبعده وقعت انا الفقير في مرض وهو البرديه والسخونه واستقمت في ذلك المرض ٦،١١٢ اسبوعين وفي تلك الغضون جانا خبر من جينوا بان وصل الي عندهم ثلاثة كليرات من كليرات سلطان فرنسا جايين من مسينا ومعهم بنات الاماره الذين كانوا راحوا الي مسينا حتي يزوروا اميره من بنات ملوك الفرنساويه فلما سمع معلمي هذا الخبر فرح فرحاً شديد وفي الحين هم في السفر الي جينوا حتي يلحق هل كليرات ويروح معهم الي مرسيليا من غير فزع القرصان.

وبعدما الخواجه هيا شغله للسفر فقلي انت مريض ما يمكنك تروح معي استقيم انته ٦،١١٣ في هل مكان الي حين ما تستريح¹ وانا بستناك في مرسيليا فلما سمعت منه هل كلام فصار عندي حزن شديد وانا في تلك الغربه وفي ذلك المرض. حينذٍ توسلت الي الام الحنونه مريم العذري وفي ذلك الوقت اجا لعندنا رجل اختيار فيلاسوف حتي يودع معلمي فلما راني وانا في تلك الحال وكان يعرفني لما كنت اروح مع معلمي الي عنده فسالني ما بالك وما الذي جرالك فحكيته علي مرضي وان معلمي بيريد يسافر ويبقيني هاهنا فقلي لا تخف انشا الله بتسافر مع معلمك الليله في الاربع ساعات تعال لعندي للبيت بريدك.

ومضي وانا اصطبرت الي ان صارت الاربع ساعات فمضيت الي عنده فرايته في ٦،١١٤ استنضاري. حينذٍ سالني في اينا وقت بتجيك البرديه فقلته بتمسكني في التاسع ساعه وبتستقيم الي وقت الظهر ثم بتجيني السخونه وبتستقيم الي غروب الشمس وبعده بستريح. حينذٍ اخرج من خزانته قنينه بلور وفرغ منها في قنينه زغيره من ذلك الماء المستقطر مقدار ثلاثين درهم واعطاني ايها وقلي اشرب ثلثها عند النوم وثلث الثاني اشربه في محل ما تتيك² البرديه وثلث الثالث اشربه ايضاً عند النوم وان عاد في طول عمرك جتك البرديه ابقا اعتب عليّ ففعلت كما امرني فقطعت عني البرديه ولا عدت رايتها الي الان الذي كنت في سن الخمسة وسبعين سنه وهذا نلته من احسان مريم العذري الذي استغثت³ اليها في ذلك الوقت الذي كنت فيه مريض.

---

١ الأصل: تسريح. ٢ الأصل: تيك. ٣ الأصل: استغث.

Following my own visit to the Black Mountain, I fell ill. For two weeks I  6.112
was overcome with chills and fevers. It was during that time that we received
word from Genoa that three galleys belonging to the French realm had arrived
from Messina. Aboard the galleys were some princesses who had gone to
Messina to pay a visit to another princess, herself the daughter of one of the
members of the French royalty. My master was overjoyed to receive this news,
and decided then and there to travel to Genoa to meet up with the galleys.
From there, he could travel with them to Marseille without fear of encounter-
ing any pirates.

"You're ill," the *khawājah* said to me as he prepared to travel. "You can't  6.113
come with me. Stay here and rest, and I'll wait for you in Marseille."

When I heard these words, I felt miserable. Being so far from home and in
my sorry state, I turned to the Mother of Mercy, the Virgin Mary, beseeching
her to help me. Just then, an old philosopher came by to bid my master farewell. My master and I used to visit him, so he knew who I was.

"What's the matter with you?" he asked when he saw me.

I told him about my illness, and how my master was going to leave me
behind when he left.

"Don't worry. God willing, you'll go with him," he replied, adding, "Come
by my house this evening at four o'clock. I need to see you."

He left, and I waited patiently until four o'clock then headed to his house,  6.114
where I found him waiting for me.

"When do you get the chills?" he asked.

"They begin at nine o'clock in the morning and continue until noon," I
said. "Then I have a fever until sunset. Only after that do I experience some
relief."

He took a crystal flask out of his cabinet and poured a thirty-dirham measure of distilled water into a small bottle.

"Drink a third of this before you go to sleep," he said, handing me the bottle.
"Drink the second third when you get the chills, and the last third before you
go back to sleep. And if you ever have the chills again, you can blame me."

I did as he instructed, and my chills went away. I'm now seventy-five years
old and haven't felt a chill since, all thanks to the beneficence of the Virgin
Mary, whom I called upon when I was ill.

١١٥،٦ وبعد يوم سافرنا من ليكورنا مع شختور وما فارقنا البر فزعًا من القرصان فلما وصلنا الي اسكلت جينوا فخرجنا من ذلك الشختور وحملنا حوايجنا ودخلنا للمدينه الي ان وصلنا الي استريه فودنا ندخل فما راد صاحب الاستريه انه يدخلنا الي حين ما منجيب له ورقة من بيت الحاكم وهذه عندهم عاده طريفه بامرحاكم البلد بالا احد ياوي غريب عنده من غيران يجيب له ورقة من عند الحاكم وهذه لاجل ان يعرف الحاكم ايش قدر موجود من الغربا في مدينته حرصًا ليلا يدخل عدو الي مدينته ويكمن.

١١٦،٦ المراد رحنا الي بيت الحاكم انا ومعلمي فلما دخلنا فرايت رجل جالس في اوضه وهو مخصص لهذا الامرفقط فسالنا انت من اي بلاد فاخبره معلمي بانه فرنساوي الاصل وعني انه رجل شرقي فعاد سالنا ايش هو سبب مجيكم الي هذه البلاد والي اين انتم مسافرين فرد عليه معلمي عن مجينا ورواحنا الي فرنسا. حينذِ كتب لنا طسكره وارخها واعطنا هي فرحنا الي الاستريه واعطينا الطسكره الي صاحب الاستريه. حينذِ دخلوا حوايجنا واعطونا اوض فاستقمنا هناك نستنا الكليرات حتي نسافر معهم وبعد دخولنا بثلاثة ايام فعاد صاحب الاستريه طلب منا بان نروح نغير الطسكره من عند ذلك الرجل الذي اعطانا اول طسكره فالتزمنا نروح نغير تلك التسكره وناخد منه طسكره غيرها بتاريخها.

١١٧،٦ المراد استقمنا في جينوا خمسة عشر يوم وفي تلك الايام كنت اروح اتفرج في المدينه علي تلك العماير المكلفه والصرايات المشيده التي كلها معمره من حجر رخام ابيض وزرت تلك الكنايس العامره فيوم مريت في مكان من ارزق البلد فرايت بعض بيوت خرابانات دكًا دكًا فاعتجبت لما رايت تلك البيوت المشيده المكلفه كلها خراب فسالت عن سبب خراب هذه البيوت.

١١٨،٦ فاجابوني علي سوالي بان سلطان فرنسا كان له الجي في هذه المدينه لاجل ان يبقي نامه عليها كعاده الملوك الذين يرسلوا الجيه من قبلهم لمثل هذه الامريات لاجل حمايتهم لهم من الاعدا ولكن بما ان اهل تلك الامريه جبابره وبلقوها بجينوا الجباره فكانوا يزدروا بذلك الايلجي وما يعملوا له اكرام الواجب له ولا للذي ارسله وكان

The next day, we departed Livorno in a small sailboat. Fearing pirates, the   6.115
boat didn't stray far from land. We arrived at the port of Genoa, disembarked,
and took our baggage with us into the city. We arrived at an inn, but when
we tried to enter, the innkeeper refused to let us in until we brought him a
document from the governor's palace. This was one of their peculiar customs.
By order of the governor, no one was allowed to host a foreigner without permission from the authorities. This was so that the governor knew how many
foreigners were in the city at any given time, and no potential enemies could
infiltrate it.

My master and I went to see the governor. When we arrived, we found a   6.116
man seated in his own room, whose sole occupation was to deal with such
cases.

"Which country are you from?" he asked. My master explained that he was
a Frenchman and that I was from the East.

"What's your purpose in coming to this country? And what's your
destination?"

My master recounted the reasons for our arrival in Genoa and our
intended departure to France. The man wrote out a document of safe conduct, dated it, and handed it over. We took it to the inn and presented it to
the innkeeper. We were finally allowed to bring in our things, and they gave
us rooms. We remained there, waiting till we could leave on the galleys. Three
days later, the innkeeper asked us to renew our travel papers with the man
who had issued us the first document, so we were compelled to return to get
a new, freshly dated document.

We spent fifteen days in Genoa, which I spent touring the city and seeing   6.117
all those magnificent buildings and lofty palaces built out of white marble,
and visiting its splendid churches. One day, as I was walking down an alleyway, I saw some houses in ruins. Surprised by this sight, I asked some people
how these sumptuous dwellings had fallen to pieces, and they told me
the story.

It so happened that the sultan of France once had an ambassador in this   6.118
city, representing his illustrious name. It is the custom of kings to send their
ambassadors to principalities such as these to offer them protection against
their enemies. But the people of this principality are proud—hence its nick-
name, Genoa the Proud. They looked down on this ambassador and didn't

المذكور صابر على هذه الاهانه لانه كان رجل خايف الله وما يريد بان يصدر على يده او بغضه لكن الحياء يورت الخنات.

٦.١١٩ فاتفق يوم من الايام بان خدام الايجي المذكور وجدوا مطروش نجس على باب الصرايا وعلى علامة سلطان فرنسا التي هي معلقه فوق الباب فمضوا واحكوا لحضرة الايجي بالذي راوه فلما سمع الايجي هذا الخبر وتحققه بالنضر حينٍ اخذته غيرة اسداده لاجل تلك الحقاره التي فعلوها اهالي جينوا الى سلطان فرنسا وله فالتزم من باب الدمه بانه يباين تلك البلد ويرحل فبعد يوم اخذ ما يحتاجه للسفر ونزل في جكتريه وسافر الى مرسيليا من حيث ما احد عرف سبب مضيه الى فرنسا فلما وصل الى مرسيليا في الحال ركب في عربانه هو واثنين من خواصه وسافر الى ان وصل الى مدينة بهريز.

٦.١٢٠ وبعدما قابل الوزير واحكى له بالمجراويه فدخل به امام حضرة الملك ليوز الرابع عشر من هل اسم فلما امتثل امام حضرة الملك قدم له عرض حال بالذي جري عليه في مدينة جينوا وعلى تلك الحقاره التي فعلوها اهل تلك البلد وقلة احترامهم لحضرة سلطان فرنسا فلما قري الملك ذلك العرض حال فغضب غضباً شديد وفي الحال امر فاحضر ساري العسكر امامه واعطاه فرمان بان ياخد معه اربعين كليرا وجمله مراكب بجنودها ويمضي الى مدينة جينوا ويري عليها البنبات والمدافع ويخربها دكاً دكاً ولا يبقي حجر على حجر ولو قتلت جميع اهاليها.

٦.١٢١ فمضي ذلك الساري عسكر وفعل كما امره حضرة الملك فلما وصل الى مدينة جينوا امر قباطين المراكب بانهم يرسيوا¹ بعيد عن الاسكله وامر بان الكليرات يرسيوا بقرب المدينة من غير جانب حتى لا بتسلط عليهم مدافع من قلعة المدينه وكل هذا واهل جينوا ما معهم خبر سبب مجيهم ولا خطر في بالهم بانهم يريدوا يخربوا المدينه فما حسوا ودريوا الا وتراكمت عليهم البنبوات كانها جمرات نار نازله من السما على تلك الاماكن تخربها دكاً دكاً فحاروا في امرهم خوفاً عظيم ليلا تقتل اوادمهم وعيالهم تحت ذلك الردم.

---

١ الأصل: يرسلوا.

see fit to treat him with the respect he deserved, nor indeed the king who sent him. Now, the ambassador endured this affront patiently because he was a God-fearing man who didn't wish to cause any trouble or animosity. But modesty only invites treachery.

One day, the ambassador's servants found the door of his residence stained    6.119 with filth, as well as the insignia of the French king that hung above it. They told His Excellency the ambassador what they'd seen, and he went to verify their report with his own eyes. Thereupon he was seized by a desire to avenge the honor of his sovereign against the Genoese for this act of vulgarity. He felt honor bound to leave the city, so the very next day he gathered what he needed, boarded a ship, and sailed to Marseille without anyone being the wiser. From Marseille, he and two of his officers traveled by coach to Paris.

The ambassador went directly to see the king's minister and told him the    6.120 entire story. The minister took him to see His Majesty King Louis XIV. The ambassador submitted a report of what had taken place in Genoa to the king, recounting the vulgar insult proffered by the city's people and their disrespect for His Majesty the king of France. After reading the ambassador's report, the king grew very angry. He immediately summoned the commander-in-chief and issued an edict ordering him to take forty galleys along with a number of troop ships and sail to Genoa. He was to bomb it to pieces, leaving not a single stone standing, even if every last resident perished.

The commander-in-chief set off as His Majesty had ordered. When he was    6.121 outside Genoa, he ordered the captains of the troop ships to drop their anchors far from the harbor, and instructed the galleys to anchor closer to the city and on the other side, so as not to fall prey to the citadel's cannons. Genoa's inhabitants, in the meantime, didn't know why the French had arrived, and it didn't occur to them that they intended to destroy the city. At least, not until the bombs began raining down on them like a shower of embers falling from the sky, landing on buildings and leaving them in ruins. The people were stunned, and feared that they and their families would perish beneath the bombardment.

حينذٍ خرج الدوك ومعه اكابر المدينه والاسقف والكهنه ومضوا في البحر الي ١٢٢،٦
عند ساري العسكر وارتموا عليه بان يكف عن ضرب البونبات ليلا تقتل اهل البلد
فاجابهم القايد بقوله بان سيدي سلطان فنسا امرني باني اخرب هل مدينه
ولا ابقي حجر علي حجر وانكان بتخافوا علي اهل المدينه والعيال امروم بان يخرجوا
ويبعدوا عن المدينه ليلا يقتلوا جميعهم وانا ما يمكني اخالف امر سيدي الذي هو
سلطان فنسا اني اخرب هل مدينة دكًا دكًا. حينذٍ توسلوا اليه بان يعطيهم مهل
الي حين ما يمضوا الي عند الملك لعله انه يعفي عنهم فقبل عدرهم القايد وامر بان يكفوا
عن الضرب الي حين ما يجي امر من حضرة الملك ونحن لكم بالاستندار.

حينذٍ الدوك انتخب عشرين رجلاً من كبرات واشراف جينوا وارسلهم بالهدايا ١٢٣،٦
الي مدينة بهريز الي عند سلطان فنسا فلما وصلوا تواجهوا مع حضرة الوزير
وتوسلوا اليه بان ياخد لهم اذن من الملك حتي يدخلوا يقابلوه فقبل الوزير طلبتهم
واستاذن لهم بالدخول فلما امتثلوا امام حضرة الملك في الحال ارتموا علي اقدامه
متضرعين بانه يعفي عن مدينتهم واهلها لانهم حصلوا في غاية الديق من قبل غضبه
عليهم فحن الملك عليهم وعفا عن دنبهم واعطاهم الامان وامر الوزير بانه يضيفهم
ويعمل لهم اكرام ففعل الوزير مثل ما امره حضرة الملك وهيا لهم وليمه عظيمه
وفرجهم علي جميع الاماكن والمتنزهات الموجوده في سراية الملك التي ما لها مثيل في
ساير الدنيا.

فبعدما تفرجوا واكلوا الضيافه وهموا في الرحيل فسالهم الوزير وكان ملقن من ١٢٤،٦
حضرة الملك قايلاً لهم هل عجبكم نظام ومحاسن سراية سيدي الملك هل انكم
انبسطوا وانشرح خاطركم فاجابوه نعم يا سيدنا راينا كل شي كامل النظام والحسن
الزايد بالتمام ولكن فد شي ناقص وهو كبرات جينوا مرتميين علي اقدام سلطان فنسا
وكان هذا صادر من عظم تجبرهم وكبريام الذي جرا[١] الي الموت كان اهين عليهم
من ذلك الدل والانكسار الذي فعلوه غرمًا عنهم. اخيرًا وبخهم الوزير علي هل

---

١ «الجرا» في الأصل مطموس.

The doge of Genoa went to the seashore accompanied by the city's nota-  6.122
bles, the bishop, and the priests. Flinging themselves before the French commander, they begged him to stop bombing the city, lest all of its inhabitants
be killed.

"My lord the sultan of France has ordered me to destroy this city, and to not
leave a single stone standing," the commander said. "If you're worried about
the people of the city and their families, order them to leave the city and stay
well away so they don't perish. Far be it from me to disobey an order from the
sultan of France to reduce this city to ruins."

They begged him to hold off, to give them an opportunity to visit the king
and seek a pardon. The commander consented, and ordered the bombardment to cease pending further orders from His Majesty the king.

"We will await your return," he told the Genoese.

The doge selected twenty of Genoa's nobles and sent them to Paris with  6.123
gifts for the sultan of France. They went immediately to meet with His Excellency the minister and begged him to ask the king to receive them. The minister consented to their request, and asked permission for them to enter. When
they appeared before His Majesty the king, they threw themselves at his feet,
imploring him to pardon their city and its people, as his fury had placed them
in grave peril!

The king took pity, pardoned them for their infraction, and granted clemency. He ordered the minister to welcome them as guests and treat them honorably. This the minister did. He prepared a grand reception for them and took
them on a tour of all the buildings and gardens in the king's palace, which has
no equal in the entire world.

Once the Genoese had finished their tour and partaken of the food that  6.124
was offered them, they prepared to depart. At that moment, the minister—
instructed by the king—turned to them and asked,

"Are you pleased with the order and beauty of His Majesty's palace? I trust
you are now happy and content?"

"My lord, we found the palace to be exquisitely composed and surpassing
all in perfection," they replied. "In fact, the only thing to detract from it all was
the sight of the notables of Genoa throwing themselves at the feet of the king
of France!"

They spoke these words proudly and arrogantly, for they'd found the prospect of death easier to bear than the act of humiliation and contrition they

كلام المملوا بمعرفه وكبريا ومدح لهم حلم وحنيت الملك واصرفهم نجلين نادمين علي قولهم هذا.

فسافروا من بهريز ولا زالوا سايرين حتي انهم وصلوا الي مدينت جينوا ١٢٥،٦ واعطوا للقايد الفرمان الذي اخدوه من حضرة الملك بانه يرفع الحصار عنهم ويعود راجعًا ولكن لاجل ذلك الكلام الذي تكلموه فارسل الوزير وريد من البر ومعه مكتوب للقايد ومامره بانك لا ترحل حتي تاخد منهم جميع كلف المراكب والكليرات وعلايف العسكر وما يشبه ذلك من المصاريف. حينذٍ ارسل القايد الي الدوك يطلب منه مصاريف المراكب كما ذكرنا التي بتجمع هل قدر من المال وما رحل حتي اخدها علي موجب حسابه بالتمام وعاد راجعًا الي فرنسا واخبر حضرة الملك بالذي فعله بالتمام.

were forced to carry out against their will. The minister scolded them harshly for their haughty and insolent rejoinder, and praised the wisdom and mercy of the king. Disgraced and remorseful, they were promptly dismissed.

The nobles left Paris and traveled directly back to Genoa. They presented the French commander with the order they'd received from His Majesty the king. He was to lift the siege and return to France. However, because of the insulting words the nobles had spoken, the king's minister had also dispatched a messenger by land, carrying a letter for the commander.   6.125

"Do not depart without making them pay for the cost of sending our ships and galleys, the soldiers' salaries, and all other associated expenses," the letter read.

The commander sent a message to the doge asking for a specified sum to cover the expenses of his fleet, and refused to leave until he'd received the full amount. He then returned to France and gave a full report to His Majesty the king.

# الفصل السابع[1]

## في سفـرنا الي بلاد فرنسا

فبعد كام يوم رحلنا مع تلك الكليرات الفرنساويه قاصدين مدينة مرسيليا وكانوا ١.٧
نزلونا في كلريت[2] الاولي الكبيتانه التي راكب فيها بنات الاماره المذكورات وصار
الي معلمي هناك اكرام زايد بما انه معلوم السلطنه فلما نزلت في تلك الكليره فرايت
شي قط ما نضرته وهي في الطول بتنوف عن ماية دراع وفي اولها مكان عالي
وفيه اوضة القبطان وخارج الاوضه مكان كمثل الديواخانه وله شبابيك علي البحر
وخزانات من الطرفين ومدهن بدهانات مكلفه جميله ويعلوا اوضة القبطان سطح
ويعلوه فنكبير من البلور الصافي وهو يعلو قامه واسفل اوضة القبطان موضوع
مدفعين اغلاض طوال وكل واحد وله شباك علي البحر .

فدخلت اوضة القبطان فرايتها كانها قصر ملوكي وشفتها كله مرايا نجف ٢.٧
ومصفوف باريع جوانبها من العدد الملوكيه بتلمع مثل الفضه ومدهنه بدهانات
فضيه ذهبيه شي يبهج الناظر اليه وفي اخر الكليره موضوع ايضاً طوبين غلاض
ولهم شباكين علي البحر ويعلوا ذلك المكان سطح كبير علي عرض الكليره وجموع فيه
الجنود وتحته المطبخ والوجاق من حديد وفرن زغير من حديد لاجل الخبز الطري كل
يوم ودايراوضة القبطان والديواخانه سناديق للزرع بعض حشايش منشان السلطه
وفي العنبر موجود جاج وحمام وفراريج وغنم لاجل الذبيحه الطريه في كل يوم. المراد
كل شي منظوم ومرتب في غاية ما يكون.

---

١ لم يرد رقم لهذا الفصل في الأصل.   ٢ الأصل: كلريت.

# Chapter Seven

## Our Voyage to France

We eventually left Genoa aboard the French galleys, headed for Marseille.    7.1
We were given space on the captain's ship along with the princesses, and my
master was treated with great honor due to his royal connections.

The galley was like nothing I'd ever seen before. It was over a hundred
cubits in length. Aft there was an elevated area where the captain's cabin was
situated.[110] Outside his cabin was a space resembling an outdoor salon, with
windows overlooking the sea and tables on both sides, all exquisitely painted
in beautiful colors. Above the captain's cabin was a deck, over which hung
a large crystal lantern. There were two heavy cannons beneath the captain's
cabin, each with its own porthole facing out to sea.

I ventured into the captain's cabin. It was like a royal palace! Its ceiling was    7.2
covered with crystal mirrors. Arranged along all four walls were weapons fit
for a king, gleaming like silver. The room was painted in dazzling silvery and
golden hues. At the stern of the galley were two more stout cannons, each with
portholes looking out to sea. Above the cannons sat a large deck as wide as
the ship itself, which was where the soldiers were gathered. The kitchen was
belowdecks and contained an iron stove and a small iron oven, which was used
for baking fresh bread each day. All around the captain's cabin and the outdoor
salon were planters full of herbs, for salad. In the hold, there were chickens,
pigeons, pullets, and sheep, to provide fresh meat every day. Everything was
laid out in perfect order.

٣.٧ ولما تقرست في وسط الكليره رايت في كل جانب منها اثني عشر خوان وبين كل خوان وخوان بعد مقدار دراعين وكل خوان داخله ستة انفس من المجرمين بالزلوطه يقدفوا في الكريكات من الجانبين وفي الممشي الذي هو ما بين تلك الخوانات ناس من الجنود وفي يد كل واحد صوت من اعصاب البقر واذا راوا واحد من السته الذين يقدفوا قصر من التعب او من كسل فالجندي الذي في يده الصوت بيضرب السته علي ظهورهم بذلك الصوت حتي يان مكان الضرب ضرب ازرق من عزم الضرب. المراد رويتهم بتحزن وكانهم داخل جهنم والشياطين بتجلدهم وبتعدبهم.

٤.٧ فلما رايت هل منضر المحزن فالتفت الي خوري الكليره الذي كان واقفا بجانبي وقلتله ما هذه القساوه يا ابانا من ناس مسيحيين هل يجوز هذا فاجابني الخوري قايلاً ما بواخدك لاجل انك غريب وما بتعرف هذه الامور وان سالتني يا ابني عن هولاي القوم اجبتك بان كل واحد منهم كان مستاهل القتل لاجل فعله ولكن الشرعة صنعة معهم رحمه لاجل حجج التي بيفهموها فحكموا علي كل واحد منهم علي قدر دنبه منهم انه يستقيم في الكليره ثلاثة سنوات ومنهم خمسة سناوات ومنهم بيستقيم مابد للممات وهذا صاير موعضه للغير حتي لا يرتكبوا هل فواحش والدنوب الظاهره الغير مخفيه فلما سمعت هل كلام من ذلك الخوري فاقتنعت وشبهت حالي باني في الملكوت واوليك في جهنم اجارنا الله من ذلك.

٥.٧ وبعد كام يوم دخلنا الي مينة مرسيليا وفي حال دخولنا انضربت المدافع من القلعتين الذين هن في بوغاز الاسكله لان دخول المراكب من ذلك البوغاز ما بين قلعتين حصينتين ولما يصل المركب الي ذلك البوغاز يلف قلاعه ويسحبوه القيق الي داخل البوغاز حتي يدخل للاسكله وريطوه في البر لان هذه الاسكله هي داخل المدينه والبحر داخلها ومكنها متسع ووسيع في الغايه وجميع المراكب والكليرات داخلها وتلك القلعتين التي هم في البوغاز لهم جنزير حديد غليظ وفي غياب الشمس بيسحبوا ذلك الجنزير من قلعت الواحده بواسطة دولاب حتي انه بيتساوي مع ما البحر حتي ان قايق زغير ما يمكنه ان يدخل او يخرج من ذلك البوغاز ولما بيصبح الصباح بيرخوا ذلك الجنزير في البحر وبيعود بيسلك الدرب للداخلين والخارجين.

When I explored the central part of the galley, I found twelve benches on       7.3
each side, separated from each other by a space of two cubits. On each bench
sat six convicts, completely naked, who operated the ship's oars. Patrolling the
aisle between the two sets of benches were soldiers carrying bull-pizzle whips.
If a soldier saw one of the rowers slowing down out of fatigue or laziness, he'd
strike all six rowers across their backs with his whip, leaving them covered in
blue bruises. It was truly a sorry sight, a living hell where they were flogged
and tortured by demons.

When I saw this awful spectacle, I turned to the ship's priest, standing next       7.4
to me.

"Father, how can Christians treat men so cruelly? Why is that allowed?"

"I don't blame you for being ignorant of these matters, since you're a foreigner," the priest replied. "But since you ask, my son, let me tell you that each
of these men deserved to be put to death for his crime. But the law decreed,
for one reason or another, that they should be treated with mercy. So each was
sentenced to serve in the galleys for a specified length of time, depending on
the seriousness of the offense. Some will spend three years here, others five,
and others will serve a life sentence. They've become an example to others, a
warning not to commit such heinous and manifestly flagrant crimes."

I was persuaded by the priest's response, and realized that my own life was
a heavenly paradise compared to that hellish existence. May God protect us
from such an awful fate!

A few days later, we entered the harbor of Marseille to the sound of can-       7.5
nons from the two citadels that stood at the mouth of the harbor. Entering
the harbor required passing through the straits between the two fortified citadels. As a ship approached, it would lower its sails, and dinghies would tow it
through the straits and into the harbor to be tied to a mooring. The reason for
this was that the harbor was within the city, which is to say that the sea flowed
into the city itself. It was absolutely enormous, and could accommodate all the
ships as well as the galleys. A thick iron chain lay across the straits, extending
from one fortress to the other. After sunset, the chain would be stretched taut
by means of a wheel mechanism located in one of the fortresses. Once it was
pulled up to the surface of the water, even a little dinghy wouldn't be able to
pass through the straits. When morning came, the chain was loosened and it
would sink into the sea, opening the way again to maritime traffic.

٦.٧ ورايت صانعين حركه في تلك الاسكله لاجل تنظيفها وهي رايت قايق كبير متسع وداخله دولاب كبير متسع وداخله اتنين من المجرمين بيديروا هل دولاب برجليهم وبايديهم وهن داخل الدولاب لانهم بيدوسوا علي درجات وبيصعدوا من درجه الي درجه وهن باقين في مكانهم ولما بيندار الدولاب بيضهر جاروفين حديد واحد بينحدر الي الاسفل يجرف الطين وبيصعد بيفرغ ذلك الوحل والطين في غير قايق وبعده بينحدر الثاني يجرف وبيصعد وبيفرغ الي فوق وبيفرغ في القايق المذكور ولهم حركه لما بيصعد الجاروف بيفرغ من غير ان احد يمسه وهم جراء علي مدد ايام السنه.

٧.٧ وبعده لما خرجوا من الكليره تلك الاميرات صنعوا لهم الاي محتفل ودخلوهم الي صرايت الكمندات اعني حاكم المدينه بزفه عظيمه وباكرام زايد بما انهم بنات ملوك واستقامة الوليمه ثمانية ايام وما ابقوا شي من المقترحات الا واحدروهم امامهم ومن الجمله كان في الكليره غلام ابن امير من امرات السلطنه وكان فعل شي مستحق فيه القتل علي موجب الشريعه فعاد صار له رجاوات من الاماره اصحاب والده فا امكن انهم يعفوا عنه الا ان حكموا عليه بانه يستقيم في الكليره الي الممات مابد فهذا الغلام كان حسن الصوره وكان فايق في صناعة الرقس وفريد في بلاد فرنسا في هل صناعه والخفيه ما مثله مسيل.

٨.٧ فافتكر حاكم المدينه بانه يحضره حتي يرقص امام الاميرات فارسل جمله من الجنود الي قبطان الكليره الذي هو موجود فيها وامره بانه يطلق هل غلام من قيوده وياتي به فلما حضر الغلام امام بنات الاماره ثم عمل التمني اللايق لهم وكت الفقير موجود في ذلك المحفل لما دخل. حينذٍ امره الحاكم بانه يرقص امامهم ويروي ما كان عنده من صناعة الرقس فابتدي ذلك الغلام يرقص علي الات النغم الموسيقيه حتي فتك وبهّت جميع الحاضرين فبعدما خلص وانتهي من رقصه فبادر امام تلك بنات الاماره وطلب منهم بدموع سخينه بانهم يامروا بانهم في طلقه بما انهم بنات ملوك ولهم استطاعه بذلك فاجابته واحده منهم وهي الاكبر قايلة اطلب يا غلام مهما اردت واشتهيت فيكون

I saw that they'd fashioned a sort of machine to dredge the harbor. It was a    7.6
large, broad dinghy that held a great wheel. Two convicts were put to work,
turning the wheel with their hands and feet by climbing rungs inside it. In
this way, they remained in the same place while the wheel turned around
them. As it turned, it would cause two iron scoops to emerge from the water.
One scoop would go down to the seabed and dredge up the sediment, then rise
to the surface and empty it into another dinghy. Then the next scoop would
descend, dredge up some more mud, and rise to empty it. It was all mecha-
nized, such that the scoop would come to the surface and empty its contents
without anyone having to touch it. It operated every day of the year.

When the princesses disembarked from the galley, a festive parade was held    7.7
in their honor. They were taken to the palace of the commandant—that is, the
governor of the city—accompanied by a grand, honorable procession befitting
their station as the daughters of royalty. The reception lasted for eight days,
and all manner of entertainments were brought before them.

The entertainment included a young man who'd been on board the galley.
He was the son of a prince, and had once committed a crime worthy of a death
sentence. Some other princes, who were friends of his father, tried to arrange
a pardon for him but were unsuccessful. They did manage to have his punishment reduced to a life sentence of labor on the galleys. Now, this young man
was handsome, and a superb dancer. In all of France, his skill and agility had
no equal.

It occurred to the governor of Marseille to have the young man dance for    7.8
the princesses. He sent a group of soldiers to meet the captain of the galley,
ordering him to free the man and bring him to the palace. I happened to be
at the party when the young man entered and presented himself before the
princesses, greeting them with due deference. The governor then ordered him
to dance and to put all of his skills on display. And so, accompanied by musical
instruments, the young man began to dance, revealing a ravishing mastery of
the craft. All the spectators were stunned. When he was finished, he rushed
up to the princesses and, with hot tears streaming down his face, pleaded with
them to use their royal authority to set him free.

"Whatever you desire will be granted, young man, except your freedom,"
said the eldest princess. "This is your legal punishment, and we have no power
to annul it. Go in peace."

لك ما عدا اطلاقك هذا حكم الشريعه عليك. ما لنا استطاعه تبطيله امضي بسلام نخاب امله وقطع الايس ومضي باكياً حزناً وكل الحاضرين حزنوا لمصابه هذا.

٩،٧ فلنرجع الان ما كنا في صدده وفي دخولنا الي مرسيليا دخلنا في استريه قسما بقي بهريز اعني بهريز الصغيره فاستقبلتنا صاحبة الاستريه باكرام زايد وهيت لنا اوضتين مفروشات اعني كاملات من جميع اللوازم السكنه فبعد ساعتين اردت اقضي حاجة الطبيعه فنزلت افتش علي الادب خانه فسالتني واحده من الخدامات قالت لي ماذا تريد فسالتها علي مطلوبي السابق فاجابتني اصعد الي فوق بتجد مطلوبك.

١٠،٧ فصعدت ثانياً وصرت افتش وافتح الابواب فما رايت المكان الذي انا طالبه فعاودت ونزلت وسالت الخدامه بانها ترويني المكان وما عاد لي صبر فقالت لي مطلوبك داخل اوضتك تحت التخت فصعدت ايضاً ودخلت الي تلك الاوضه ورفعت الجرجف الذي هو فوق التخت فرايت جلاسه كبيره. حينذٍ تبين لي بان ما لهم جشمات فما لي داب الا اني خرجت من الاستريه وسرت اسال مين بينزاح الي خارج المدينه فدلوني فلما خرجت ودخلت ما بين البساتين فرايت لي مكان ستره وقضيت حاجة الطبيعه ورجعت الي الاستريه.

١١،٧ حينذٍ استخبرت عن هل امر الغريب الي رجل حلبي الذي رايته هناك فاجبني بان هل مدينه ما لها جشمات لان ارضها قريبه للماء ولاجل هل سبب ما بيقدروا يحفروا في الارض وبيقضوا حاجة الطبيعه كل واحد في اوضته كما رايت في الجلاسه وفي الليل بيكبوها من الشباك علي الزقاق والسواديه بيخرجوا حكم السلام بيلموا ذلك النجس ولكن كل حاره من حارات المدينه جاري في وسطها ساقيه ما مدوم هو نازل من علو المكان وفي هذا الماء كل واحد بيشطف قبال بابه ذلك الوخم.

١٢،٧ وفي نصف المدينه مكان فسحه ما بين باب روميه وباب بهريز يسما الكورس ومن الجانبين مغروز اشجار وبين شجر وشجر خوان من حجر وجاري في اسفلهم ساقيت ماء

Hopeless and dejected, he left in tears, and everyone present felt sorry for him.

Let's return to our story. Once we entered Marseille, we checked into an 7.9
inn called Petit Paris, which means "Little Paris." The mistress of the inn welcomed us most cordially and prepared two furnished rooms for us, decked out with all the necessities. A couple of hours later, I felt the need to answer the call of nature. I went downstairs to search for a toilet.

"What are you looking for?" one of the servant girls asked me, and I told her. "You'll find it upstairs," she replied.

I returned upstairs, and began hunting for the toilet, opening one door after 7.10
another. No luck! I went back downstairs and asked the servant girl to show me the toilet herself, as I was unable to hold it any longer.

"What you want is in your room, under the bed," she replied.

I went back upstairs to my room and lifted the blanket that covered my bed and saw a large chamber pot. It then dawned on me that they had no latrines! I had no choice but to leave the inn right away.

Once outside, I began asking people about the quickest way out of the city, and they gave me directions. Once I'd made my way to the orchards on the outskirts of the city, I found a secluded spot and did my business. Then I went back to the inn.

Puzzled about the mystery of the chamber pot, I asked a man from Aleppo 7.11
(whom I'd met at the inn) for an explanation.

"There are no latrines in this city because it is close to the sea, which makes it difficult to dig in the ground," he replied. "So each person answers the call of nature in his own room, just as you saw, in a chamber pot. At night, they empty it out the window into the streets, and the garbage collectors come early in the morning to pick up all the filth. The city streets all have central gutters. Water is constantly running through them, flowing down from a high point in the city. Each person also cleans the feces off his doorstep using that water."

In the middle of the city, there was an open space between the Gate of 7.12
Rome and the Gate of Paris, which was called Le Cours. Trees were planted at either end, with a bench set between each two trees. A canal of running water flowed there, day and night. The notables of the city, as well as many ordinary folk, strolled along the wide path that ran through the center. It was a delightful place, a sort of garden, shaded from the sun by the trees.

ماشيه دايمًا ليل ونهار والممشي الذي هو في الوسط طويل متسع يتمشوا فيه اكابر المدينه وكثير من الشعب وهو مكان شرح كمثل روضه وفي تلك الاشجار تمنع اشراق الشمس عن ذلك المكان وفي مكان اخر بيسما بيت البلد وهو متسع عالي الاركان وهذا بتجمع فيه جميع التجار والدلالين وهناك بتصير البازارات والبيع والشراء من قبل الدهر بساعتين الي الدهر وبعد الظهر بساعتين الي ان يحكم العصر ويعلوا هذا المكان بيت القنصر وهناك القنصر يقضي دعاوي التجار كمثل شاه بندر.

٧،١٣ وفي مكان اخر يسما بيت المتاجره يعتني في امور تجار الهند وتجار الشرق كانه حاكم علي كل من يتاجر الي هذه الاقليمين وما احد بيقدر يدخل للمتاجره وبيصير تاجر الا باذن اهل هذا المكان حتي يفحصوا عنه ويكفلوه من غير تجار اقويا الي حد مبلغ من المال وبعده يعطوه اذن انه يتاجر في بلاد الذي بيريدها ودلالين البندر مكفلين من الغير ايضًا وبيشتروا هل وظيفه بثلاثة الاف غرش ضمان لان كل اشغال التجار في يدهم وبيستلموا اموالهم بما انهم امنا والتجار بتركن اليهم في جميع بيعهم وشراهم كانهم صاحبين المال ما احد بيتعارضهم في شي ابدًا وهذا الذي رايته من نظام تجار فرنسا وكتبته.

٧،١٤ وكنت ادور في مدينة مرسيليا اتفرج وازور الكنايس والديوره فيوم من الايام دلوني علي مغارة مريم المجدليه حيث كانت ساكنه هي واخيها العازر لما انفوهم اليهود من مدينة اورشليم ووضعوهم في قارب بغير قلوع ولا دفه وتركوا القارب في البحر تايه فحفظهم ربنا من الغريق واتي بهم القارب الي مدينة مرسيليا وكانت اهاليها في تلك الايام عبادين اصنام فلما دخلوا المدينه تاوو في مغاره وصاروا يشحدوا وياكلوا وصدر منهم عجايب شتي حتي ان امنت اهل المدينه علي يدهم من كثره العجايب التي صنعوها واخيرًا وصلوا الرسل الي تلك البلد وعمدوا اهاليها جميعهم وخبرهم مستطيل. اخيرًا مضيت زرت تلك المغاره المقدسه التي هي في جانب الثاني من الاسكله وقريه من مخازن المرلوس والذي راح الي تلك المدينه بيعرف ذلك المكان.

There was another place called the Hôtel de Ville, a large building with tall columns. That's where all the merchants and brokers would meet and conduct their business, buying and selling from ten o'clock in the morning till noon, and then again from two o'clock till the late afternoon. The consul's residence was upstairs. From there, the consul would oversee the affairs of the merchants, acting as a sort of overseer.

There was another place called the chamber of commerce, where the consul 7.13 supervised the affairs of the merchants of India and the East. He served as a sort of judge over all who traded in the two regions. In order to conduct business or become a merchant, one had to receive permission from these people. They'd look into a person's background and secure a guarantee of a certain sum of money from other reputable merchants before allowing the new person to do business in the lands of his choosing. Similarly, the brokers in the port had to be endorsed by others. They purchased the right to this occupation with a security deposit of three thousand piasters, since they handled all the merchants' goods, after all. They took possession of their merchandise on the strength of their own integrity. The merchants relied upon them in all their commercial dealings, allowing them to act as though they were the proprietors themselves. No one ever stood in their way. This is what I saw of the commercial system in France, which I duly record here.

I wandered the city of Marseille, taking in the sights and visiting churches 7.14 and monasteries. One day, I followed directions to the Cave of Mary Magdalene, where she had lived with her brother Lazarus when they were cast out of Jerusalem by the Jews. They had been put in a boat without mast or rudder and left to float out to sea. Our Lord saved them from drowning and brought the boat to Marseille, whose inhabitants at that time worshipped idols.

Mary and her brother went into the city and took refuge in a cave. They were reduced to begging for food. Over time, however, they performed so many miracles that the people of the city began to have faith, all thanks to them. Eventually, the apostles arrived there and baptized the people. The whole story is too long to tell here.[111]

Anyway, I went to visit that holy cave, which was on the opposite side of the harbor, close to the merling storehouses.[112] Anyone who has visited the city has heard of this place.

١٥.٧ وايضاً زرت كنيسه العذري حارت مرسيليا[1] وهي مبنيه علي راس جبل التي بتسما في لسان الفرنساوي مادامه دكاردي ولها عجايب شتي فلما صعدت لذلك الجبل مع جملت ناس من اهل مرسيليا ورعين متعبدين لمريم العذري فرايت في ديل الجبل بيت مبني وله شباك وداخله يسوع جاتي علي ركبتيه يبصلي بيعني عن صلاته في بستان الزيتون وهو مصنوع بهية انسان تام عرقان ومنزعج كما بيدكرعنه الانجيل المقدس والنظر اليه يحزن وهذا جا لعينه لاجل التامل في الام يسوع فلما صعدت الي اعلاه فوجدت بيت اخر وداخله يسوع مربوط في العامود والشرط في اياديهم المقارع والسياط كانهم بيجلدوه واعلاه بيت اخرداخله يسوع والشرط بيلبسوه كليل الشوك واعلاه ايضاً بيت وفيه محملين يسوع خشبة الصليب .

١٦.٧ ويعلوه بيت وهو الاخير وفيه مطروح السيد المسيح علي خشبة الصليب والجلادين واضعين البصامير علي تقوب يديه ورجليه والمطرقه في يد واحد منهم كانه بيدق المصامير الغليظه في اطراف السيد المسيح وهو بغاية القساوه وحدا ذلك الجندي ولد حامل زبيل البصامير وكل هذا مصنوع بصناعه كامله بهذا المقدار حتي ان الناظر اليه يراكانه كان حاظر في تلك الاماكن التي كمت فيها هل خمس اسرار الالام المذكوره. المراد لما الانسان بيمر علي هل خمس الاماكن الالام وقبل وصوله الي الكنيسه بيصير له خشوع عظيم وندامه كامله. اخيراً صعدت الي تلك الكنيسه وهي في مكان عالي في قمة الجبل وبتشرف علي البحر مسيرة ثلاث اميال ومن هناك بيشرفوا علي المراكب الوارده الي مينتهم والحراس دايماً موجودين هناك بيرقبوا ذلك البحر ليلا ياتيهم العدو .

١٧.٧ فبعد ما دخلت الكنيسه وحضرت القداس الشريف فعاوت راجعاً الي الاستريه وقبل وصولي الي هناك صدفت رجل تاجر من تجار مرسيليا فرايته وقف وصار يتفرس فيَّ وسالني اما انت فلان من مدينة حلب فاجبته نعم فقال لي اما بتعرفني فتفرست فيه وعرفته وهو انه كان معلمي في ايام حداثتي يسمي خواجه زنباو . حينٍ

---

١ الأصل: مرسيليا.

I also visited the Church of the Virgin Mary of Marseille. It stood on the  7.15
summit of a mountain called "Madame de Garde" in French. It was associated
with many miracles. I climbed up the mountain with a group of pious people
from Marseille, all devotees of the Virgin Mary. At the foot of the mountain,
I came upon a chapel with a window. Inside was a statue of Jesus on his knees,
praying.[113] It was a representation of the scene of Jesus praying in the Garden of
Olives.[114] He was fashioned to look like he was covered in sweat and anguished,
just as the Holy Bible describes him—a picture of sorrow. The scene was placed
there to encourage people to contemplate the suffering of Jesus.

Climbing a little higher, I came across another chapel. In this one, there
was a Jesus tied to a pillar, and soldiers carrying switches of thorns and whips,
looking as though they were about to flog him. Beyond that was another
chapel with a Jesus and some soldiers placing a crown of thorns upon his head.
Higher up was yet another house, in which Jesus was being made to carry the
wooden cross.

In the final chapel, farther up, Our Lord the Messiah lay upon the cross  7.16
as the executioners pounded nails into his hands and feet. The hammer in
the hand of one of the cruel executioners seemed poised to strike the heavy
nails into the limbs of the Messiah. A boy stood beside the soldier, carrying a
basket of nails. All of this was fashioned so perfectly that the onlooker felt he
was present in the very places where these five sorrowful mysteries occurred.
Passing by these five painful stations before coming to the church, a person felt
a profound sense of humility and remorse.

I finally arrived at the church. It was perched high up on the summit of the
mountain, with a view that extended three miles out to sea. Sentinels surveyed
ships entering the port of Marseille from that spot, always on the lookout for
enemy vessels coming across the sea.

I entered the church, attended its holy mass, and headed back to the inn.  7.17
On the way, I came upon a merchant from Marseille.

"Aren't you that fellow from Aleppo?" he asked, studying me carefully.

"Yes."

"Don't you recognize me?"

As I looked more closely, I did indeed recognize him! It was *khawājah* Rimbaud, who had been my master when I was a boy. We greeted each other, and
he asked me how I'd come to Marseille. I related my whole story and explained

سلمت عليه وسلم عليّ وسالني كيف كان قدومي الي مرسيليا فحكيت له بمجراويتي من اولها الي اخرها واعلمته في معلي الذي انا ماضي معه الي مدينة بهريز فلما سمع مني هل كلام خاف عليّ وامرني بالمضي معه الي بيته.

١٨،٧ ولما دخلت امر خدامته بانها تجيب لي فتور فبعدما كنا فتورنا حيند طلبت منه اذن حتي امضي الي الاستريه فمنعني عن المضي وقلي استقيم عندي في بيتي انا بسخا فيك ارسلك مع رجل ما هو معروف فاجبته بطلب من فضلك بانك تستخبر عنه لان لي شوق عظيم ان امضي معه الي بهريز حسبما وعدني بانه يصنع معي من الخير فامتثل لكلامي وارسل رجل من تباعه حتي يكلفه الي عنده لكي يتغدا عنده.

١٩،٧ فلما اتي معلي واتواجها فقله خواجه رنباو المذكور اعلم هل غلام انا ربيته لما كنت في مدينة حلب والان رايته هاهنا فبريد ابقيه عندي دايماً فاجابه معلي واخبره عن وظيفته بما انه سايح من سواح سلطان فرنسا وانه مامور من حضرة الوزير بونشطرين وزير الشرق بان اجيب معي رجل من بلاد الشرق يكون يعرف يقرا بلسان العربي لاجل انه يكون موكل علي خزانة كتب العربيه التي هي للملك واكد له بان بينوب هل غلام خير عظيم فلما سمع خواجه رنباو منه هل كلام اقنع ورضي باني امضي معه وبعدما تغدينا ومضي معلي الي محله حيند قلي خواجه رنباو امضي معه وانكان ما كل معك وعده انا بعطيك مكتوب الي واحد من اصحابي الذي هو في بهريز بان يبقي نظره عليك اذا لزمك امر من الامور وهو بيرسلك الي عندي. اخيراً استكترت بخيره ومضيت.

٢٠،٧ وبعده صار كل واحد من تجار حلب الذي كانوا يعرفوني الي عندهم ويعملوا لي اكرام اولهم خواجه بازان وخواجه سيمون وخواجه بنفاي وخواجه روس وخواجه سمطان وهذا كان اعز اصحابي في حلب وكانوا ينزهوني في بساتينهم ويفرجوني علي بعض مفترجات ويعزموني الي بيوتهم ويعملوا لي اكرام بمحبه زايده.

that I was headed to Paris with my master. At this news, *khawājah* Rimbaud became very concerned on my behalf. He asked me to accompany him to his house.

When we arrived, he ordered his servant girl to bring us some breakfast. We ate together, and I then asked permission to return to the inn. But he refused. 7.18

"Why don't you stay here, at my house?" he asked. "I think too much of you to let you go off with some stranger!"

"Would you do me the honor of inquiring about this man? I have my heart set on going to Paris with him," I replied. "He's promised to do right by me."

*Khawājah* Rimbaud consented, and dispatched one of his attendants to invite my master over for lunch.

He arrived soon thereafter, and the two men stood face to face. 7.19

"Would you believe that I raised this young man when I was in Aleppo, and now here he is!" *khawājah* Rimbaud said. "I'd like him to stay here with me."

My master introduced himself and explained that he was one of the king's travelers.

"I've been ordered by His Excellency Minister Pontchartrain, Minister of the Orient, to bring back a man from the Orient who can read Arabic," my master said. "He'll be put in charge of the king's library of Arabic books, and I promise he'll be rewarded handsomely."

*Khawājah* Rimbaud was persuaded by this, and consented to have me go with my master to Paris. However, after they finished lunch and my master left for the inn, *khawājah* Rimbaud spoke to me privately.

"Go with him, but in the event that he does not keep his promise, I will give you a letter addressed to one of my friends in Paris," he said. "It will ask him to keep an eye on you, in case you need anything. And he can send you back to me, if need be."

I thanked him for his kindness and left.

I began to receive invitations from all the merchants of Aleppo who knew me. All of them treated me honorably: *khawājah* Bazan, *khawājah* Simon, *khawājah* Bonifay, *khawājah* Roux, and *khawājah* Samatan, who was my dearest friend in Aleppo.[115] They all would take me for strolls through their orchards and show me various interesting things. They invited me to their homes and treated me with great affection and generosity. 7.20

وبعدما استقمنا في مدينه مرسيليا عشرة ايام وكان معلي في تلك المده تسلم من بيت المتاجرة جميع الذي كان ارسله من بلاد الشرق علي يد القناصر كما ذكرنا وهو سبعت سناديق محزومين ولاجل لا احد من الكمارك الذين في الطريق يقدر يفتحهم حتي يكمرك عليها اخد وسيقه من كمرك مرسيليا بانهم خالصين من الكمرك وجعلوا علي كل سندوق منهم ختم الملك برصاص فلما تم الامر يسلم تلك السناديق مع باقيت امتعه محزومات الي القاطرجي الذي يسافر الي بهريز حتي يودعهم في الكمرك والقاطرجيه في تلك البلاد يحملوا الاقواد علي عربانه طويله بيصفوا الاقواد اعلاها وبتسحبها ستة روس من الخيل القادرين فبعدما سلمهم تلك السناديق واللبش الذي كان معنا وما بقا عندنا شي له نقله غير ثيابنا وقفص الوحوش المذكور وكان يبقي فيه اثنين والثلاثه ماتوا في الطريق .

We spent ten days in Marseille, during which my master went to the cham-  7.21
ber of commerce to pick up all the baggage he'd sent from the East through
the consulates. There were seven locked trunks in all. In order to avoid having
the trunks opened by a customs agent along the way, my master obtained a
certificate from the customhouse of Marseille, stating that no duty was owed
on these goods. They also placed a lead seal bearing the royal insignia on each
trunk. With that done, my master handed over the trunks, along with the rest
of his property—which was all locked up—to the carriage man, who would
travel with them to Paris and deposit them at the customhouse.

In that country, carriage men would transport passengers in long carriages.
The people would sit on top of the carriage, which was pulled by six strong
horses. My master gave the trunks and our other baggage to the carriage man,
and we were left with nothing cumbersome besides our clothes and the cage
with the animals. Two were left, as three had died along the way.

# الفصل الثامن [1]

## في سفرنا من بروينسه الي بلاد
## فرنسا ومدينة بهريس

٨،١ فخرجنا من مدينة مرسيليا في شهر ادار سنة ١٧٠٩ واول مدينة التي دخلناها كانت مدينة ازاي وهي مدينه جميلة العماير والاركان وهل مدينه كان احد ملوك فرنساء اوهبها الي قدس سيدنا الپاپا من پاپاوات القدم لما ذلك الحبر زار سلطان فرنسا وهي الي الان تحت تصرف كل بابت الذي يجلس علي الكرسي الرسولي وهل مدينه مخصوصه بالشريعه لان كل المحاكم والشرايع بيقدوا منها حل المشاكل الشرعيه وبعد يوم خرجنا من تلك المدينه وسرنا في الطريق وجزنا علي مدن وقري شتي وفي طريقنا فكا نتغدا في استريه ونتعشي ونرقد في غيرها علي مدا الطريق بغاية العز والاكرام.

٨،٢ ولا زلنا سايرين الي ان وصلنا الي مدينة ليون فدخلنا في بعض الاستريات وهناك استقمنا خمسة ايام وفي هل مده كت ادور في المدينه واتفرج وهي مدينه عامره متسعة عاليت الاسوار [2] ومشيدة الاركان مكان عماير مكلفه وصرايات عامره وكنايس فاخره ونهر عظيم خارج من داخل المدينه وموجود في هذه المدينه جميع الصنايع وخصوصاً صنعة الحرير والقماشات الفاخره الثمينه من قسم الدياج الملون المحرر بالوان القصب والاتون الذي دراعه بعشرة غروش وغيره من التحف الثمينه وهناك بيسكبوا الجلوخة لاجل تبصيت تبل الاتون وغير صنايع هي الموجوده في ساير البلاد وهذه المدينة العظيمه بالتقريب قدر مدينة حلب بالوسع والكبر.

---

١ لم يرد رقم لهذا الفصل في الأصل.    ٢ الأصل: الاسيوار.

# Chapter Eight

## Our Journey from Provence to France and the City of Paris[116]

We departed the city of Marseille in March of 1708.[117] The first city we encoun-    **8.1**
tered on our way was Āzāy, a city of beautiful buildings and columns.[118]
A French king had given this city to one of the ancient popes during a visit
by His Holiness. Today, it falls under the jurisdiction of whoever sits upon the
Apostolic Throne. The city is known for jurisprudence, and all the courthouses
and tribunals follow its rulings with respect to legal matters.

A day later, we left that city and headed out, passing various cities and villages along the way. While on the road, we would have lunch at one inn, then
have dinner and spend the night at a different inn. As a result, the entire voyage
passed quite gloriously.

When we arrived in the city of Lyon, we checked in to one of its inns and    **8.2**
stayed there five days. I spent that time touring the city and seeing the sights.
It is a large, populous city with high walls and tall columns, elegant buildings,
opulent palaces, magnificent churches, and a great river flowing through it.
Every trade is plied in Lyon. Foremost is the production of silk and other luxurious fabrics, such as silk brocade embroidered with silver and gold thread—
which costs ten piasters per cubit—and other costly luxuries. This is also where
they cast the wheels used to spin gold thread. The city has various other indus-
tries also found in other countries. This impressive city is about the same size
as Aleppo.

٣،٨ وداخل هل مدينة كنيسه عظيمه تسما كنيسة ماري يوحنا فرحت زرتها وبعدما زرت هياكلها انتهيت الي مكان داخل الكنيسه فوجدت ساعه عاليه من البولاد المسقي علوها قامه ومدة يد وبعلوها قبه من النحاس الاصفر وبعلوا القبه ديك من النحاس وتحت القبه ملايكه وكل واحد قدامه ناقوس وكل ناقوس حداه ..... [1] وهي باربعة وجوه وجه الاول سوري اعني طويل وقليل عرض وله عقرب من حديد بيدور في كل ساعه دور علي موجب دقايق الساعه وهو داير وفي دوره بيطول علي طول الداير ولما بيصل الي الوسط بيقصر من ذاته علي قدر الداير الذيق وهو فرد شقفة حديد حتي ان الناظر بيندهل من هل حركه.

٤،٨ وثاني وجه بيدور العقرب في كل اربعة وعشرين ساعه دور ووجه الثالث بيدور العقرب في كل سنه دور وهناك بينبيك عن مطبوخ تلك السنه وفرق اعيادها واصيامها وانعكاس شمسها وقمرها وما يشبه ذلك من امور الافلاك ورابع وجه بيدور العقرب كل مايه سنه وبينبي عن اشيا التي بتفهمه المعلمين المدققين في امور الفلك وايضًا في طاقه كل يوم بيضهر ذلك القديس الذي عيده واسمه اعلاه.

٥،٨ ولما بتنتهي الساعه بيروف الديك الذي هو اعلا القبه وبيصرخ ثلاثة مرات ما بيفرق عن صياح الديك ابدًا وبعد صياحه ثلاث مرات بيتيدوا الملايكه الذين هم تحت القبه بيدقوا النواقيز التي قبالهم شبه نغم موسيقيه وبعد خلوصهم بتظهر مريم العذري راكه وبيظهر ملاك جبرايل امامها بيهديها السلام وفي تلك الدقيقه بيظهر اعلامهم الروح القدس بشكل[2] حمامه بيضا يبرق عليهم وبعد خلوص هذه الحركات جميعها بتدق الساعه.

٦،٨ والذي ذكرناه جميعه بيتم في كل ساعه ليل مع نهار وما بينقص منه شي ابدًا من وقت ما انشغلت هل ساعه والي الان من غير ان احد يديرها وذكروا السواح بان ما وجدوا لها مثيل في ساير اقاليم الدنيا ولاجل هذا حكوا اعين الذي اشتغلها

---

١ من «وتحت القبه...» إلى «حداه...» في هامش الصفحة وآخر الجملة مطموس في الأصل. ٢ «بشكل» مطموس في الأصل.

There was a large church there, the Church of Saint-Jean, which I went to    8.3
see. After visiting its altar, I walked around inside the church and came upon a
tall clock made of hardened steel.[119] It was the height of a man with his arm outstretched, and was topped by a brass dome. Sitting on top of the dome was a
brass rooster. Below the dome were angels, with church bells in front of them,
and beside each church bell was a . . . .[120] The clock had four faces. The first
face was solemn—that is, long and thin. It had an iron clock hand, which made
a complete rotation once every hour, marking each minute. As it turned, the
clock's hand would lengthen or shorten according to the radius of the clockface. When it reached the middle, for instance, the hand would shorten, all on
its own, to the narrower dimensions of the clockface. It was made of a single
piece of iron. It was an astonishing sight to see!

On the second face, the clock hand made a complete rotation every twenty-    8.4
four hours. The third face's clock hand made a full rotation once a year, displaying the almanac for the year—that is, the feasts and fasts, the opposition
of the solar and lunar eclipses, and other such astronomical matters. On the
fourth face, the clock hand rotated once every hundred years, announcing
such things as only scholars with a specialized understanding of astrology
could grasp. And on each saint's day, the saint would appear in a little window,
their names inscribed above them.

Upon the hour, the rooster on top of the dome would flap its wings and    8.5
crow three times, just like a real rooster. Then the angels beneath the dome
would strike the church bells in front of them in a way that resembled a musical melody. A kneeling Virgin Mary would emerge alongside the angel Gabriel,
who saluted her, followed by the Holy Spirit, which circled above them in
the shape of a white dove. When all these movements were done, the clock
would strike.

From the moment this clock was set in motion to the present day, this has    8.6
all taken place every hour, day and night, without missing a stroke, and without a person making it run. The travelers all said they'd never seen anything
like it in the whole world. That's why the man who fashioned the clock was
blinded after he completed it. His eyes were filled with kohl so that he would
never create another clock, ensuring that this one would remain unique.

وحضي بالعماء حتي لا يعود يشتغل غيرها وتبقا فريده في الدنيا هذا ما رايته وعاينته في هل ساعة العجيبه واتفرجت علي اشيا كثيره في هذه المدينه وما كتبتها لاجل الاقتصار.

٧،٨ وبعد خلوص الخمسة ايام سافرنا وجزنا علي ضيع وقصبات واستريات شتي في الطريق وكل ليله ننام في استريه في غاية العز والانشراح وكل شي موجود لخدمتنا وماواتنا علي غاية ما يكون ولا زلنا سايرين الي ان وصلنا الي جسر عالي عظيم البناء يسما جسر الروح القدس وله بابين وفي كل باب قبجي من طرف السلطنه لاجل لخص الداخلين والخارجين وهو اول مدخل بلاد فرنسا الجوانيه.

٨،٨ فبعد الفحص خرجنا من الجسر وفي قرب الجسر ضيعه كبيره عامره فدخلنا الي استريه حتي نتاوا١ تلك الليله فانوجد من المسافرين اثني عشر رجل فينا. حيندٍ سالتنا صاحبت الاستريه هل تريدوا تجلسوا علي فرد مايده اجابوها نعم فقالت لهم ماذا تريدوا ان تكون عشاتكم فاجابها واحد وقال لها عشينا طيب فاجابته تكرم ومضت وارسلت لنا في الحال مع خدامتها فراغ انبيد وصارت تسقينا واحد بعد الاخرحتي شربنا جميعا.

٩،٨ وبعده هيرت المايده بجميع لوازمها من سيتات ومناديل انضاف وملاقيط ومعالق فضه وخبز كماج طري وبعده قدمت لنا في صحن كبير جاجه هنديه واثني عشر فروج مشويين في سيخ الكبير وصحنين فركصاده من اجناح الفراريج وقطع لحم وصحنين سلطة كبوس فجلسنا علي المايده ناكل واثنتين من الخدامات في ايديهم الكاسات يسقونا من الخمر الطيب الي حين ما انتهينا من العشا رفعوا تلك الصحون وجابوا قطعت جبنه فرنساويه وستين زيتون وستين تفاح فروطه وبعده غسلوا ايدينا ورفعوا ما كان علي المايده وجابوا جقق كبير صيني فرنجي ملان من الماء وحوله داخل الماء ستة قداح وتقيليتين انبيد حتي الذي بيريد يشرب يتناول بيده ويشرب علي كيفه.

١٠،٨ اخيرًا لما حان اوان الرقاد كلفونا باننا نمضي كل منا الي سريره وفي ذلك الوقت حضرت صاحبت الاستريه وفتحت خزانه كبيره وداخلها من الملاحف البيض النظاف بقدر

---

١ الأصل: نتتاو.

This is what I witnessed with respect to that wonderful clock. I saw many other things in Lyon, but for the sake of brevity I have not recorded them here.

After five days in Lyon, we set off again, passing many villages and towns and inns, stopping each night to sleep at a different inn, and enjoying the heights of esteem and comfort. Every service and accommodation was made available to us. We pressed on, and eventually arrived at a grand, towering bridge called the Bridge of the Holy Spirit.[121] It had two gates. At each stood a royal guard, who inspected the passengers entering and leaving. This was the first entry point to the interior of France.

8.7

After the inspection, we left the bridge behind us and arrived at a large, prosperous village nearby, where we checked in at an inn to spend the night. There were twelve men in our traveling party.

8.8

"Would you like to have dinner together?" the mistress of the inn asked.

"Yes," all replied.

"And what might you like your dinner to be?" she asked.

"Something delicious," one of our companions responded.

"Right away."

She disappeared and sent one of her servant girls to us with a pitcher of wine. She poured a glass for each of us in turn, and we all had a drink.

The table was set with all the necessities: plates, clean napkins, silver forks and spoons, and soft bread. She then placed a large platter before us with a turkey and twelve grilled chickens on a large skewer. There were two plates of chicken wing fricassée as well as pieces of beef, and two plates of lettuce salad. We sat at the table to eat, and two servant girls appeared with cups in their hands, and continued to fill our glasses with good wine throughout dinner. Afterward, they cleared all the plates away and brought out some French cheese, two plates of olives, and two plates of apples. Following dinner, we all washed our hands and they cleared the table. They brought out a large basin of Frankish porcelain filled with water. Around the edges of the basin, sitting in the water, were six glasses and two carafes of wine.[122] Whoever wished to have a drink could pour some wine for himself at his leisure.

8.9

When it was time to sleep, we were invited to repair to our beds. The mistress of the inn opened a large cupboard containing about two hundred clean

8.10

مايتين من تلك الملاحف وامرت الخدامات بان ياخدوا لكل منا ملحفتين لاجل فراشه ويضعوهم من فوق واسفل ما بين اللحاف والفرش الثلاثه الموضوعين علي السرير فبعدما كملوا ما امرتهم به مضوا الي محلهم. حينئذٍ كل واحد منا انتكي في سريره وفي تلك الفرش الناعمه وجنب السرير موجود متكا وقباله ايقونه للصلوه اذا راد يصلي وموضوع علي الوساده تخفيفه من الكتان الابيض. اخيراً رقدنا جميعنا بغاية الهنا الي ان اصبح الصباح نهضنا من فرشنا ومضينا حضرنا القداس الالهي ورجعنا الي الاستريه.

وقتيذٍ قدمت لنا الفتور وهو قطعه من الجبن وخبز كماج طري وفراغ انبيد فبعدما فطرنا فسالنا صاحبة المكان ما الذي يجب ان نعطيها حق اكلنا ومنامتنا فطلبت اربعة غروش بيلق كل واحد منا ثلث غروش فاستكثرنا طلبتها واعطوها ثلاثة غروش فرضيت واستكثرت بخيرنا ومضينا في دربنا وسفرنا وان سالني سايل هل في كل سفرنا في تلك البلاد التي مرينا فيها وجدنا رخص مثل هذا كلا لان بلاد بروينسا مغليه خلاف عن بلاد فرنسا لانها بلاد مرخصه وغلاتها وافره خصوصاً في برها وديعها.

ومن هناك دخلنا الي اراضي بركونيا وهي كثيرة الاثمار والكروم وعلي ما نقلوا لي بان اربعة ايام طول واربعة ايام عرض كلها مغروسه كروم عنب ويلقبوها بنبع النبيد الذي ما له مثيل في كل بلاد فرنسا وهو شبه نبيد الجردي الذي في بلاد لبنان. المراد لا زلنا سايرين حتي وصلنا الي مدينة بهريس وكان وصولنا الي هذه المدينة العظيمه حكم نصف عشي.

فلما شرفنا علي هذه المدينه فرايت امامي فسحه كبيره ممتده علي ما يمد النظر وتلك الفسحه الشاسعه مملوه اضويه كانها شعله. حينئذٍ سالت معلي ما هذه الاضويه وهذه الشعله فاجابني بان هذه مدينة بهريس لان هذه المدينه ما لها صور بعجب النظر اليها فلما دخلنا المدينه ونحن سايرين في ازقتها وشوارعها العراض المتسعات فرايت جميع الدكاكين من علي الجانبين في كل دكان شمعتين وثلاثه ومعلق بين كل عشرين ثلاثين قدم فنر بلور وداخله شمعه طويله شاعله.

وناهيك عن مدينة بهريس وسعها وكبرها وعدد بيوتها شيي ما بينحصي وكل باب بيت وجانبه دكان صاحب البيت وفي داخل الدكان كخانه كل صنف بصنفه من

white sheets. She ordered the servant girls to take two sheets for each man's bed and lay them on top of each other between the blanket and mattress, so that there were three layers on the bed. They did as she asked then retired to their own rooms. Each of us got into his bed and stretched out on a soft mattress. Beside each bed was a cushion set before an icon, in case one wished to pray, and a white linen nightcap lay on the pillow. We all fell into peaceful slumber and slept till morning. We rose from our beds, headed out to attend mass, and returned to the inn.

Soon after, breakfast arrived. There was cheese, soft bread, and a pitcher of    8.11
wine. We finished breakfast and asked the mistress of the place what we owed her for room and board. She asked for four piasters in all, charging each man a third of a piaster. They protested that her price was too high, and offered her three piasters instead. She accepted, thanked us kindly, and we set off.

If you were to ask me if we'd encountered such reasonable prices throughout our travels, I'd have to say certainly not! The lands of Provence were expensive, unlike the lands of France, which were cheap due to the abundance of its harvests, particularly in the countryside and the villages.[123]

We passed into the region of Bourgogne, a land rich in fruits and vines.    8.12
According to what I was told, it was a four-day journey from one end of the region to the other—in both length and width—and all of it was covered with grapevines. Bourgogne was known as "the fount of wine," and produced the finest wine in all of France, similar to the wine of the Jurd district in Lebanon. From there, we pressed on to Paris, arriving at that magnificent city in the evening.

As we approached the city, I saw a vast expanse extending as far as the eye    8.13
could see, so crowded with lights that it shone as bright as day.

"What's that great blaze of lights?" I asked my master.

He told me it was the city of Paris, which had no walls to hide it from view. As we entered the city and traveled down its little lanes and broad avenues, I saw that all of the shops on either side of the street were lit by two or three candles. Every twenty or thirty feet there hung a glass lantern with a tall candle burning inside.

How marvelous Paris was, in all its immensity! There were countless houses.    8.14
Next to each one was the shop belonging to the master of the house, with his workshop inside. Every trade was represented, and every shop was grouped

جميع الكارات ومنها بيصعد الي منزله الذي هو اول طبقه لان بيوتهم معمره من خمسة طبقات وكل طبقه بتعلوا الاخره بخمسة او ستة درجات‹ واذا انتهيت الي ثاني طبقه بترا صفه وباب واذا دخلت ذلك الباب ترا مكان داخله اوض وساله ومطبخ سكنت عليه والاوض لها شبابيك بكار بيشرفوا علي الزقاق واذا صعدت الي الثلاثه والرابعه والخامسه فترى جميعهم علي نسق الذي دكرناه واما الفنزرات هن مرتين علي كيس المدينه بيقدموا شمع لاهل تلك الحاره حتي يشعلوهم في محلهم وكل فنزر له خزانه في مصمره في الحيط وعلي كل واحد من ولاد الحاره انه يشعل الشماع المذكوره شهر تمام.

١٥،٨ وايضاً بحسب امر الحاكم بان كل صاحب بيت ملزوم بانه كل يوم باكر يكنس قبال باب بيته وبعد الشمس بساعه بيدور الشوباصي الذي هو موكل من قبل الحاكم علي هذا الامر وكل بيت الذي ما هو مكنس قبال باب بيته بيكتب عليه غرش والغرش بيلزم للذي موكل في التكنيس من اجير او اجيره او صاحب البيت نفسه والزبالات التي بتتكوم في الزقات لها اوادم بيلموها ويضعوها في سندوق موضوع فوق عرابانه ويكبوها برات المدينه حتي ترا بعد الشمس بساعه جميع صقاقات مدينة بهريس مكنسه نضيفه خاليه من كل وسخ وزباله بالكليه هذا اول نظام التي رايته في مدينت بهريس العامره.

١٦،٨ ونرجع ما كنا في صدده انه بعد دخولنا الي المدينه استقمنا مقدار نصف ساعه ماشيين الي ان وصلنا الي بيت رجل وهو من اصحاب معلي فنزلنا عنده لان بلد معلي بعيده عن مدينة بهريس سفر اربعة ايام تسما راون فاستقبلنا ذلك الرجل بغاية الاكرام ودخلوا حوايجنا الي داخل وهيوا لنا اوض وفرشات علي غاية المراد.

---

with others in the same trade. From one's own shop, a person could climb up to his house on the second story. All of the houses had five floors, each being five or six steps above the lower one. On the second floor was a threshold and a door, beyond which was the family home, with various bedrooms, a sitting room, and a kitchen. The rooms all had large windows overlooking the street. The third, fourth, and fifth floors all had the same arrangement.

As for the lanterns, they were installed by the city authorities. Candles were distributed to the residents of the quarter, who would place them in their lanterns. Each lantern was equipped with a locker nailed to the wall, and every resident of the quarter was responsible for lighting the candles for a whole month.

Each homeowner is also required, by order of the governor, to sweep in front of his door each morning. An hour after sunrise, the inspector appointed to this task by the governor makes his rounds. Anyone who hasn't swept is fined a piaster, to be paid by the person responsible for sweeping, whether a male or female servant, or indeed the owner of the property. As for the rubbish that piles up in the streets, it's collected by people who put it in a bin atop a wagon, and dump it outside the city. In other words, an hour after sunrise, one finds the streets of Paris cleanly swept and free of dirt and rubbish. This was just the first example of orderliness that I saw in the splendid city of Paris.

8.15

But let's go back to our story. After reaching Paris, we spent half an hour walking to the house of one of my master's friends. We were staying with him because my master's hometown, Rouen, was a four-day journey from Paris. We were welcomed most honorably by the friend, who had our things brought inside and had rooms and fine beds prepared for us.

8.16

# Notes

1    The first five folios of the manuscript are lost. The extant text begins in the middle of an account of the monastery of Saint Elishaʿ, in the Kadisha Valley of northern Lebanon, to which Diyāb and some friends have traveled from Aleppo to join the Maronite monastic order. The first folios may have contained a table of contents, like the one in Ilyās al-Mawṣilī's *Kitāb al-Siyāḥah*, of which Ḥannā Diyāb owned a copy.

2    Fahmé-Thiéry et al. suggest that the steward is Tūmā al-Labbūdī, a member of Diyāb's family who is known to have been at the monastery at the same time and who in 1711 succeeded Jirmānūs Farḥāt as the monastery's superior (Diyāb, *D'Alep à Paris*, 54n1). However, that Tūmā dates his first monastic experience to August 1706 (al-Labbūdī, "Sīrat Al-Ḥibr aṭ-Ṭayyib al-dhikr ʿAbdallāh Qarāʿalī al-Marūnī al-Ḥalabī," 82). Since he became a novice around the same time as Ḥannā Diyāb, he cannot be the steward referred to here.

3    This curious expression may allude to the baggy outer garment that lemon sellers use to hold their wares.

4    This is likely Yūsuf ibn Shāhīn Çelebi, who is listed among the three Aleppans who leave the monastery with Diyāb (see folio 6v). A certain Ilyās ibn Abū Yūsuf Shāhīn from Aleppo (who might be the brother of the abovementioned) is to be found among the students of the Maronite college in Rome in 1711 (Gemayel, *Les échanges culturels entre les Maronites et l'Europe*, 121).

5    *Labneh*, a cheese made of strained yogurt. This word is obscured by a stamp in the manuscript; it may have read *jibneh* (cheese).

6    At this point in the narrative, there is a shift of tense from perfect to imperfect, as Diyāb begins to recount the day-to-day routine of monastic life, rather than the events of a specific day.

7    *Dīwānkhāna* is a term used throughout the Islamicate world, variously denoting an audience hall, sitting room, or guest quarters. Diyāb uses it mostly to refer to outdoor seating areas meant for social gatherings and recreation.

8    The evening and night prayers, respectively.

9    The midday prayer.

10   Jirmānūs Jibrīl Farḥāt (d. 1732) was the abbot during Diyāb's stay at the monastery of Saint Elishaʿ.

11   A reference to the biblical Parable of the Workers in the Vineyard (Matthew 20:1–16).

12   Maronite monks were forbidden to consume animal fat, as they were in general not allowed to eat meat. They were also permitted to travel only in pairs and with the abbot's permission. See "Qawānīn al-Ruhbāniyyah al-Lubnāniyya," 195 and 198. The following sentence is struck out in the manuscript: "I've ordered Brother Mūsā to put you on the mule when you get to Bsharrī, so do so and obey his commands along the route."

13   The term *rās al-nahr* (riverhead) may refer to the source of the Kadisha River, where the monastery of Saint Sergius (Dayr Mār Sarkīs, also known as Dayr Rās al-Nahr) is located. It is a six-mile walk from the monastery where Diyāb was staying.

14   Jirmānūs Farḥāt mentions the harm done to the monastery by the Ḥamādah, a tribe that gained authority under Ottoman rule over the northern area of Lebanon as tax collectors, during their tenure as governors of the Bsharrī district ("Tārīkh Ta'sīs al-Rahbāniyyah al-Lubnāniyyah," 129). Maronite families cooperated with them, but later portrayed them as oppressors as part of an effort to foster ties with the French as a new protecting force (see Winter, "Shiite Emirs and Ottoman Authorities: The Campaign against the Hamadas of Mt Lebanon, 1693–1694," 216ff.).

15   Jirmānūs Farḥāt, in his "Tārīkh Ta'sīs," (128–29), interprets the crowding of Saint Elisha' as a trial for the young order, but in Diyāb's account he appears concerned about the opposite problem: the loss of novices from the monastery.

16   'Abdallāh Qarā'alī (1672–1742), one of the three founders of the Lebanese Maronite order in 1695, was indeed the superior general of the Lebanese Maronite order, but happened to be absent during Diyāb's stay, as he was involved in opening the monastery of Yuḥannā Rashīma. His biographer mentions the superior's return in late 1706, which may be the moment Diyāb is referring to here.

17   Aforementioned in the lost opening folios of the manuscript.

18   Given Rémuzat's hostile reaction to Diyāb's return, it may be that he had advised him not to leave Aleppo to join the monastery in Lebanon. This encounter is likely also described in the lost folios.

19   The prayer to which Diyāb refers is not the Christian morning prayer that he observed at the monastery but rather the Muslim call to prayer at dawn (*ṣalāt al-fajr*), which was preceded by a recitation (*salām*). See Barthélemy, *Dictionnaire*, 354.

20   Diyāb variously refers to Louis XIV as *sulṭān Frānsā* and *malik Frānsā*, which we have rendered as "sultan of France" and "king of France," respectively. While it may be argued that Diyāb uses the words *sulṭān* and *malik* interchangeably, *sulṭān Frānsā* nicely conjures a juxtaposition with the Ottoman sultan. Whether this was consciously intended by Diyāb is impossible to say; nonetheless, we have elected to preserve the distinction between the two words.

21  A monument located to the west of the al-Fayḍ neighborhood, in the western suburbs of Aleppo.

22  A reference to the Royal Library in Paris, which began collecting Arabic, Persian, and Turkish manuscripts in the seventeenth century.

23  This must be one of the many Byzantine "dead cities" of northwestern Syria. Around the village of Sarmadā on Mount Barīshā, about a day's ride north of Kaftīn, are the remains of a Roman temple, several tombs, and a Byzantine monastery, among other sites. See Mattern, *A travers les villes mortes de Haute Syrie. Promenades archéologiques en 1928, 1929, 1931*, 118–19.

24  *Abū kalb* or *ebu kalb* was the name given to a type of Dutch coin (Pamuk, *A Monetary History of the Ottoman Empire*, 99).

25  Bernard Heyberger (introduction to Dyab, *D'Alep à Paris*) points out several intriguing similarities between Ḥannā Diyāb's account of this episode and the tale of Aladdin, which Diyāb would later tell Antoine Galland. The sequence of events is significant: A young person sets off on a voyage with a stranger, someone climbs down into a cave, and a ring and a lamp are discovered in a subterranean setting. Paul Lucas includes a report of these same events in his account of his later travels through Syria (Lucas, *Troisième Voyage*, 109–10). In his *Deuxième Voyage* (164), he describes the trip from Aleppo to Tripoli as having taken place between March 24 and April 6, 1707.

26  According to Lucas's *Deuxième Voyage* (164–85), the stage recounted in this chapter took place between the beginning of April and June 9, 1707. Lucas records that they left Tripoli for Beirut on April 6.

27  Fahmé-Thiéry et al. suggest that this is Gio Battista del Giudice, called Shidyāq Ḥannā al-Muḥāsib in Arabic (Diyāb, *D'Alep à Paris*, 75). He belonged to the well-known Khāzin family. He bore the title of *cavaliere/chevalier* ("knight") by 1701.

28  Christians under Ottoman rule typically wore blue turbans, but certain semiautonomous cities, including Beirut, which at the time was controlled by Maronite notables from the Khāzin clans, had less severe sartorial restrictions. The white turban was usually reserved for Muslims, and the green was the exclusive preserve of those who claimed descent from the Prophet Muḥammad.

29  An *iwān* is a near-universal feature of Islamicate architecture, a three-walled room whose fourth wall opens onto the exterior.

30  The *mīrī* was a tax to be paid on all land owned by the Ottoman sovereign (see Inalcik, *An Economic and Social History of the Ottoman Empire, 1300–1914*, 103–18) which in the seventeenth century the Khāzin family collected in Kisrawān.

31  A *maʿṣarānī* is an artisan who extracts the oil from sesame seeds (Barthélemy, *Dictionnaire*, 533).

32  In this instance, the *thulth* ("third") is probably equivalent to an *akçe*, a silver coin.

33  A *miṣriyyah* ("Egyptian") was a coin of Egyptian origin normally worth one-fortieth of a piaster, or half a piece of silver.

34  The signet ring of the biblical King Solomon is known as the Seal of Solomon. In the legends about Solomon that developed in later Jewish, Christian, and Muslim cultures, the ring was associated with magical powers that allowed Solomon to control demons and speak to animals. In the Arabic-speaking world, the Seal of Solomon is typically represented by a six-pointed star and commonly used as an amulet.

35  Lucas (*Deuxième Voyage*, 180) recounts his wanderings through this area later, after his return from Jerusalem. He mentions visiting a cedar forest planted by the famous prince Fakhr al-Dīn al-Maʿnī, as well as the Druze princes' residence (evidently Dayr al-Qamar), and the village of ʿAbāy (spelled "Abeie"), which he situates in the region of Kisrawān. As used by Diyāb and Lucas, the expression "Druze mountains" means the region between Beirut and Sidon inhabited by Druze clans. It was thus more extensive than the Chouf district of present-day Lebanon.

36  Diyāb refers to these friars as *al-Sakalant*, a reference to the Zoccolanti ("sandal wearers"), a branch of the Franciscan Order of Friars Minor.

37  Lucas recounts that his trip to Jerusalem took place between April 12 and May 6, 1707 (*Deuxième Voyage*, 165–79).

38  According to Lucas, both travelers stayed together in Sidon between June 3 and 9, 1707, before finally embarking on a ship to Cyprus (*Deuxième Voyage*, 179–85).

39  According to Paul Lucas (*Deuxième Voyage*, 185–86), the events recounted in this chapter took place between June 9 and July 9, 1707.

40  This individual was probably Antonio Callimeri, who belonged to a well-known Cypriot family (Diyāb, *D'Alep à Paris*, 87n2). There is no mention of him in Paul Lucas's travelogues.

41  İnalcik, "A Note on the Population of Cyprus," explains that after the Ottoman conquest of the island many Anatolians married Christian women in Cyprus. The Ottomans, for reasons of taxation, did not encourage conversion to Islam.

42  This building is very likely the former Hagia Sophia church of Nicosia, which the Ottomans had turned into the Selimiye Mosque in 1571. Thomas S. R. Boase ("Ecclesiastical Art," 170) mentions a 1948 renovation of the porch that uncovered an undamaged voussoir sculpture under the plaster.

43  This is Diyāb's first encounter during his travels with unveiled women in public, an experience he will have several times, and will continue to remark upon.

44  Jennings, *Christians and Muslims in Ottoman Cyprus and the Mediterranean World, 1571–1640*, 160–61, notes that trading wine in Cyprus was usually permitted.

45    According to Paul Lucas, *Deuxième Voyage*, 186–207, the events recounted in this chapter took place between July 10 and October 27, 1707. The French translation (Diyāb, *D'Alep à Paris*, 95n1), with reference to Martin, "Souvenirs," 472, suggests that Ḥannā Diyāb's dating may be more accurate, as he or Lucas would by then have noticed, as they traveled southward, the rise in the levels of the Nile that took place in Cairo as early as mid-July.

46    Diyāb opposes the notion of *maḥabbah* ("charity") with the *ẓulm* ("oppressive conditions") he encountered in Cyprus and for which he blames the Greek population. After centuries of Venetian rule over the island, the Greeks reestablished dominance over the Latin denominations by confiscating Maronite churches and forcing Maronites to obey the Orthodox authorities.

47    In seventeenth- through nineteenth-century Aleppo, a *qinṭār* might have weighed between 487 and 564 kilograms.

48    Maurice Martin mentions this monument, the Cleopatra obelisk, in his "Souvenirs," 472. Lucas refers to it as *l'aiguille de Cléopâtre* (Cleopatra's needle). Lucas has a drawing of it in his *Troisième Voyage*, 137.

49    Note that there is another place called the Cave of the Slave, encountered later in the travelogue, when Diyāb returns to Aleppo.

50    Until the early nineteenth century, hundreds of these deep underground water reservoirs still existed in Alexandria. They were probably built during the Ptolemaic or early Roman period, and partially rebuilt and restored during the Islamic period (McKenzie, *The Architecture of Alexandria and Egypt, 300 B.C. to A.D. 700*, 220). Lucas mentions them in his *Premier Voyage du Sieur Paul Lucas dans le Levant*, 52.

51    It is unclear where Diyāb may have encountered this kind of astrological lore.

52    According to Lucas, *Premier Voyage*, 53, who calls it a *germe*, this was a small, flat boat that was uncovered and had a single large sail.

53    Rosetta and Damietta, at the western and eastern ends of the Nile Delta, respectively, are each about one hundred miles away from Cairo.

54    This merchant is also mentioned in Lucas, *Deuxième Voyage*, 207.

55    Whereas Diyāb recounts a longer stay in Cairo before the visit south to Fayoum, Lucas reports that they spent a longer time in Cairo on their return north to the Mediterranean (*Deuxième Voyage*, 198–207).

56    The Church of the Virgin of the Pot of Basil (*Qaṣriyyat al-Rīḥān*), as deduced by Fahmé-Thiéry et al. in Diyāb, *D'Alep à Paris*, 106n2, is one of the oldest church foundations in the old city.

57    Matthew 2:13–23. Diyāb must be referring to the crypt below the Abu Serga church (the Church of Saints Sergius and Bacchus), parts of which are dated to the tenth century

Notes

(Davidson and Gitlitz, *Pilgrimage*, 3). It is situated beside the Church of the Virgin of the Pot of Basil.

58 According to one explanation current in the Middle Ages, the famous pyramids of Giza, which stand some seven miles away from Old Cairo, were the granaries built by the patriarch Joseph to save Egypt from famine. Here, though, Diyāb is apparently describing a ruined structure in Old Cairo; cf. the account by the French traveler Antoine Morison, who visited in 1704 (*Relation*, 154).

59 Estrangelo is the oldest form of the Syriac alphabet.

60 The *'ashrāwī* is a dromedary that can survive for ten days at a time without drinking water.

61 Fahmé-Thiéry et al. have identified this figure as Giovanni Battista della Fratta, a controversial healer and missionary who had been living in Fayoum since 1688 (Diyāb, *D'Alep à Paris*, 115n3 and 127nn1–2).

62 While he does not specify their religion, the distinction that Diyāb makes between the peasants and the Copts suggests that the former were either Muslims or practiced a form of religion unfamiliar to Diyāb.

63 A type of reed used in the manufacture of mats.

64 Diyāb may be drawing a distinction here between the areas of Lucas's expertise, such as medicine, that he believed rubbed off on him, and those that did not.

65 Diyāb repeatedly mentions his mother's melancholy and Lucas's successful attempt to treat it.

66 Today, *kazan kebabı* designates a meat dish prepared in a sort of cauldron.

67 This is the ancient obelisk of Begig, which the seventeenth-century British traveler E. W. Pococke describes in detail, noting that it was forty feet tall (*A Description of the East and Some Other Countries*, 59–60).

68 Lucas recounts this adventure differently. See *Deuxième Voyage*, 193.

69 Diyāb calls the vermin *qamal*, usually "lice." His description, however, suggests a different insect.

70 "Tripoli of the West" is the city of Tripoli in present-day Libya, as opposed to the city of the same name in Lebanon.

71 A reference to the War of the Spanish Succession (1701–14), which pitted the Bourbons of France and Spain against the Grand Alliance of the Holy Roman Empire, Great Britain, the Dutch Republic, and the Spanish Habsburgs.

72 According to Lucas's *Deuxième Voyage*, 207–20, this part of the trip took place between October 27, 1707, and June 4, 1708.

73 The Gulf of Sidra is formed by the contours of the northern coast of Libya. It extends over 100 miles inland and is over 250 miles wide.

74  Diyāb appears to be describing a waterspout.

75  *Qaṣb* (usually *qasb*) is a type of dried date.

76  Paul Lucas does not seem to be part of this excursion in Diyāb's account (cf. *Deuxième Voyage*, 208).

77  In his *Deuxième Voyage*, 208, Lucas writes that the passengers ate dates until their arrival in Tripoli on December 10, 1707, after thirty-four days of sea travel.

78  Diyāb uses the cryptic term *al-aḍāt* (elsewhere *al-aḍāwāt*) to refer to an administrative district of the Ottoman Empire known as the Province of the Islands, which comprised most of the islands of the Ottoman-controlled Mediterranean.

79  The spahis (from Turk. *sipāhī*), in the Ottoman Empire, were feudal cavalrymen paid with land grants.

80  The literal meaning of the phrase Diyāb uses here (*twaḍḍayt bi-l-ḥalīb*) is "I performed my ablutions with milk," a colorful expression suggesting that he had to use milk to hide his flushed appearance.

81  The "Tower of Skulls" (*Burj al-ru'ūs*) was built in the mid-sixteenth century. It stood until 1848, when it was torn down by the ruler of Tunis, Aḥmad Bey, and replaced with a memorial.

82  The French translators suggest that Diyāb uses the word "Ismāʿīlīs" to refer to Muslims in general, not just to members of the Ismāʿīlī sect (see Diyāb, *D'Alep à Paris*, 161n2). This seems doubtful, as the term does not appear elsewhere in the travelogue.

83  Diyāb here refers to the catastrophic defeat of the naval forces of the Holy League, led by Philip II of Spain, by the Ottoman fleet at Djerba in May of 1560. Philip's forces had seized and fortified Djerba earlier that year, as part of a strategy to wrest control of the southern Mediterranean coast from the Ottoman navy.

84  The term for "heretics" here (*arfāḍ*, sing. *rāfiḍī*; literally "rejectionists") is a derogatory label used by some Sunnis to designate various Shiite sects.

85  This thermal bath is located in present-day Ḥammām al-Anf, on the way from Tunis to al-Ḥammāmāt, which the two travelers passed through as well. Lucas transliterates the town's name as "Mamelif" and, like Diyāb, describes the healing power of the water (see his *Deuxième Voyage*, 219–20). Contrary to what Diyāb says, however, Lucas claims to have actually taken a bath, albeit with difficulty.

86  According to Lucas, the travelers arrived in Tunis after February 21, 1708 (*Deuxième Voyage*, 219–20).

87  The Bardo was the palace of the Ḥafsid dynasty (1229–1574), which was restored as a royal court by the Murādī beys in the middle of the seventeenth century.

88  The four major monastic orders at this time were the Benedictines, the Carthusians, the Cistercians, and the Cluniacs, but not all of these had a significant presence in North

Africa or the Near East. Diyāb may have had in mind, instead, mendicant orders such as the Dominicans or Franciscans.

89  In spite of the hour and a half it took for Diyāb and Lucas to travel to the palace, the distance between Bardo and the city is only a little over a mile as the crow flies.

90  The animals are jerboas, a desert rodent found across Asia and northern Africa. These animals would come to play an important role in Diyāb's story.

91  In other words, the hunter catches the jerboa by plugging up its burrow so the animal cannot retreat into it any farther than the length of the hunter's arm.

92  On Jesuit devotional practices, see the helpful note in Diyāb, *D'Alep à Paris*, 179n2; see also Heyberger, *Les chrétiens*, 358–70.

93  Paul Lucas was actually only forty-three years old at this time, not sixty, as Diyāb supposed.

94  The harbor to which Diyāb refers here was probably not Carthage but La Goulette, the port of Tunis at the time (see Diyāb, *D'Alep à Paris*, 186n3).

95  As argued by Fahmé-Thiéry et al. (Diyāb, *D'Alep à Paris*, 190n), the word *mīnā* must be Diyāb's transliteration of the Lingua Franca *maina* ("lower away!"), the imperative of *mainar* ("to lower a sail"; cf. the obsolete English "amain"). "The word is Pan-Mediterranean . . . the filiation of meanings is 'to lower'; 'to surrender' (from 'to lower flag or sails in sign of surrender'), as an exclamation of 'mercy!'" (Kahane et al., *Lingua Franca*, 279–82).

96  For Lucas's account of this episode, see *Deuxième Voyage*, 222–24.

97  A lazaretto is another term for a quarantine station.

98  In addition to Seals of Solomon, certain gemstones, including a few varieties of agate, are referred to by the name *sulaymānī*.

99  Swollen lymph nodes in the groin and armpits were a well-known symptom of the bubonic plague.

100  Livorno was the principal port through which coffee was introduced to Europe, beginning in 1632 (Diyāb, *D'Alep à Paris*, 203n2).

101  The term *ghaṭā* refers to a wrap made of silk, cotton, or satin, attaching at the waist with a corded belt, and used by Syrian women to cover their head and back (see Barthélemy, *Dictionnaire*, 578.) A *sitār* is a general term for a veil, screen, or covering.

102  Diyāb uses two different terms (*ḥijāb* and *sitār*) to refer to the veil. The former may designate a specific item of clothing while the latter indicates the more general practice of veiling.

103  A *khimār* is a veil that covers the bottom half of the face but not the eyes.

104  The buried-alive motif was both popular and a source of anxiety in eighteenth-century Europe (Brendnich, "Frau," 200). Diyāb recounts it in the stolen-ring version known

from fifteenth-century Cologne (Bolte, "Die Sage von der erweckten Scheintoten," 356–57), adding a semi-scientific explanation for it.

105  When a cannon was not in use, its touchhole—which provided access to the powder charge—was protected from seawater, debris, and accidental ignition with a lead apron.

106  The term *kīs* may refer, generically, to a sack or purse. In this instance, however, it also designates a specific amount of money, equivalent to five hundred piasters (see Barthélemy, *Dictionnaire*, 735).

107  Addobbati draws parallels between Diyāb's tale and, among others, the novella of the *Three Rings* (*Tre anelli*) from Boccaccio's *Decameron*, which begins with a similar confrontation between a Jewish merchant and a sovereign (*Il mercante*, 834–36).

108  A reference to the Santuario della Madonna di Montenero, in the hills outside Livorno.

109  Diyāb recounts here the well-known foundational story of the Santuario, involving a lowly shepherd finding an icon of Mary between the rocks of the Montenero (see Gagliardi, "'Ave maris Stella': Il santuario mariano di Montenero presso Livorno," 196), to which he adds the popular motif of the returning icon. Ilyās al-Mawṣilī invokes the same motif when describing the founding the Church of the Virgin Mary of Quinche in Ecuador (Matar, *Lands of the Christians*, 65–66); instead of a shepherd, it is a Native American who finds the icon three times in the same place. Diyāb's contemporary, the Aleppan bishop Arsāniyūs ibn Shukrī (ms Gotha arab. 1549, 193r) mentions a reappearing cross in the northern Spanish town of Burgos.

110  Note that Diyāb says that this area (the poop deck) was located at the front of the ship, but in all likelihood it would have been at the rear.

111  The legendary association of Mary Magdalene with the city of Marseille, established as early as the thirteenth century, appears as part of the story of Mary Magdalene (Maryam al-Majdaliyyah as in Diyāb's book, or "al-Majdalāniyyah") in the hagiographic collection that Ḥannā Diyāb owned (*Akhbār*, vol. 3, fol. 51v).

112  The cave is the Grotte de Sainte-Baume, some twenty-five miles outside of Marseille. Merling is a type of fish.

113  Diyāb is describing a "Way of the Cross" (*via crucis*), a series of depictions of the suffering of Jesus Christ on the day of his crucifixion. Worshippers follow the path from one station to the next, contemplating the trials of Jesus as a form of spiritual pilgrimage.

114  A reference to the Garden of Gethsemane, at the base of the Mount of Olives, where Jesus went to pray following the Last Supper.

115  Bonifay, Roux, Samatan, Rémuzat, and Rimbaud were sons of rich and influential merchant families in Marseille, and most were French deputies in Aleppo between 1698 and 1724. For details about them and the others, see Teissier, ed., *Inventaire des archives*

*historiques de la Chambre de Commerce de Marseille*, 182–83, and Diyāb, *D'Alep à Paris*, 248n2.

116 The region of Provence was incorporated into the French realm in 1486, but its cities remained resistant to the Bourbon monarchy through much of the seventeenth century. Diyāb's assumption that Provence was a region separate from France suggests that the process of incorporation remained, to an extent, incomplete.

117 Diyāb makes an error in dating here, recording the year as 1709 rather than 1708. Various events described much later in the text (such as the Great Frost) took place well before March 1709. Lucas gives June 29 as the date of their departure from Genoa and July 1708 as the date of their arrival (*Deuxième Voyage*, 224).

118 Diyāb appears to be conflating two French cities: Aix-en-Provence, a city of jurists; and Avignon, with historic ties to the papacy. The Provençal name of Aix is very similar to Diyāb's "Āzāy." See further Diyāb, *D'Alep à Paris*, 251n1.

119 This is the Astronomical Clock of Lyon, which remains in the Cathédrale Saint-Jean to this day. The presence of an astronomical clock there was documented in the fourteenth century.

120 The sentence beginning "Below the dome . . ." is in the margin of the text. The final word is unreadable.

121 Apparently the Pont Saint-Esprit, which connects Provence with Languedoc, hence "the interior of France." It is, however, approximately 125 miles south of Lyon. It must have been after leaving Avignon, not Lyon, that the travelers crossed the Rhône.

122 Evidently a porcelain *verrière* or *refraichissoire*, a receptacle used to keep bottles and glasses cool.

123 Diyāb's dating implies that the travelers left Provence some time before they stayed at this particular inn. This is another indication that he has confused the order of events.

# Glossary of Names and Terms

Names and terms appear as they do in the translation.

*abū kalb*   name given to the Dutch lion dollar, a coin that circulated in the Ottoman Empire.

*Adana*   a large city in southeastern Anatolia, home to some thirty-five thousand people in the late seventeenth century.

*Afyonkarahisar*   a city in central-west Anatolia, named for a nearby citadel (Turk. *kara hisar*, "dark fortress") and for its cultivation of opium (Turk. *afyon*).

*agha*   "chief" or "master," a title given to Ottoman government officials, mostly those associated with the military.

*alājah*   a luxury fabric made of a mixture of silk and cotton.

*Aleppo*   a city in northern Syria, home to a large community of European merchants during the seventeenth and eighteenth centuries.

*Alexandria*   a major port city on Egypt's Mediterranean coast and home to a large European trading community in Diyāb's time.

*Antep*   modern-day Gaziantep, an important town in southeastern Anatolia.

*Antioch*   a city in what is now Turkey, about fifty-five miles west of Aleppo.

*Arabic Library*   the collection of Arabic manuscripts in the French Royal Library (the *Bibliothèque du Roi*).

*Asyūṭ*   an Egyptian town that was a center for cotton and linen weaving. Linen from Asyūṭ was exported to Europe.

*Bālistān souk*   likely a reference to the oldest section of the Grand Bazaar, known as the Bedesten, built by the Ottoman emperor Mehmed II in 1455.

*Barbary*   a common Western European name for Northwest Africa, designating Morocco and some western Ottoman provinces, including Tripoli and Tunis (see Maghreb).

*barjādāt*   a type of clothing or fabric.

*Bey of Tripoli*   Khalīl Pasha, ruler of the Ottoman province of Tripolitania from 1702 to 1709; deposed and executed by Qaramānlī Aḥmad Bey in 1711.

*Bey of Tunis*  al-Ḥusayn ibn ʿAlī (r. 1705–35), the bey of Tunis and the founder of the Husaynid Dynasty.

*bey*  a Turkish title bestowed on dignitaries of the Ottoman Empire, especially rulers of provinces.

*Beyoğlu*  a quarter in Istanbul, on the European side, north of the Golden Horn; during the period of Diyāb's visit mostly inhabited by Christians and foreign diplomats.

*Bsharrī*  a village in the province of Tripoli adjoining the Qadisha valley, in present-day northern Lebanon.

*Būlāq*  Ottoman Cairo's principal port on the Nile.

*Cairo*  the largest city in the Arabic-speaking lands of the Ottoman Empire, today the capital of Egypt.

*Callimeri, Antonio*  a Cypriot interpreter, protégé of France, and graduate from the Greek college in Rome.

*calpac*  (Ottoman Turkish) a form of headgear covered in sheepskin or fur, in Diyāb's time worn mostly by non-Muslims and Europeans.

*çelebi*  an honorary Ottoman Turkish title given to persons of high status or good education.

*cheramide*  a brick-colored precious stone.

*chevalier*  knight; a French title of nobility conferred during the seventeenth and eighteenth centuries upon members of influential families such as the Khāzin clan of Kisrawān (Lebanon).

*Christofalo*  see *Zamāriyā*.

*Cilician Gates*  a pass through the Taurus Mountains, which has been used for millennia to travel between the lowlands of Cilicia and the Anatolian plateau.

*Damietta*  a port city at the eastern end of the Nile Delta, about one hundred miles from Cairo. Along with Rosetta, it is one of the two principal Nile ports on the Mediterranean Sea.

*de Camps, François*  (1643–1723) French historian, theologian, antiquarian, numismatist, and abbot of Signy.

*diligence*  a large, public, long-distance stagecoach that could carry up to sixteen people. They were common in France and England during the eighteenth and nineteenth centuries.

*dirham*  an Ottoman silver coin and a unit of weight, equivalent to one-tenth of an ounce during the seventeenth century.

*dīwānkhāna*   an audience hall, sitting room, or guest quarters. In Diyāb's use, mostly an outdoor seating area meant for social gatherings and recreation.

*Djerba*   an island off the coast of Tunisia, captured by the Ottomans from the Spaniards in 1560. The island's main town is Houmt Souk, which was called Djerba in Diyāb's time

*ecu*   a French silver coin.

*effendi*   Ottoman title of respect for a member of the civil administration.

*Fagon, Guy-Crescent*   (1638–1718) botanist, physician to Louis XIV, and director of the Royal Gardens at Versailles.

*Farḥāt, Jirmānūs*   (1670–1732) Aleppan Maronite cleric, poet, grammarian, lexicographer, and traveler active in spreading knowledge of Arabic among Christians; he was made bishop of Aleppo in 1725.

*Fayoum*   an Egyptian town located southwest of Cairo in the Fayoum Oasis and linked to the Nile by a canal.

*fils*   a coin whose value varied between eight and eighteen for one *pāra*; known in Ottoman Egypt as a *jadīd*.

*Frank*   (Ar. *franjī*, pl. *franj*) a European (distinct from *fransāwī*, pl. *fransāwiyyah*, "French").

*Frankish*   (Ar. *franjī*) the Mediterranean lingua franca, a hybrid idiom used among seamen, traders, and other travelers. When used as an adjective, equivalent to "European" (e.g., "Frankish lands").

*Galata*   a quarter of Istanbul on the northern shore of the Golden Horn, south of Beyoğlu; today called Karaköy.

*Galland, Antoine*   (1646–1717) a French Orientalist and scholar of classical languages, an expert in numismatics, and a traveler to the Ottoman lands. He contributed to the encyclopedia *Bibliothèque orientale d'Herbelot* and was the first translator of the *Arabian Nights* into a European language.

*Gate of the Janissaries and the al-ʿAzab Gate*   two of the three main gates to the Cairo Citadel, one of the city's main monuments, dating to the Ayyūbid period.

*ghuzzī*   an Ottoman functionary of Egypt; the term derives from *ghuz*, "the Oguz," the Turks claimed as ancestors by the Ottomans.

*Grand Vizier of the Ottoman Empire*   the chief minister of the empire and the second most powerful figure in the political hierarchy.

*Greek (Ar. rūmī, pl. rūm)*   a speaker of Greek, usually of Greek Orthodox (*krīkī*) denomination; sometimes also a Latin Christian; distinct from *yūnānī*, "Ancient Greek."

*Ibn al-Zughbī, Ḥannā* an Aleppan Maronite, and a friend of Diyāb's who accompanies him during his Anatolian journey.

*Ifrīqiyah* a region of North Africa with indistinct borders. Diyāb's usage suggests that he took it to encompass present-day Tunisia and western Libya.

*isbanj* (Turk. *ispenç*, "a fifth") a tax paid by non-Muslims for pasturage, e.g., of swine.

*Iṣṭifān the Damascene* an Armenian who at the end of the seventeenth century opened one of the first coffeehouses in Paris.

*jadīd* see *fils.*

*jakhjūr* (Turk. *chāqshīr*) a type of trousers fastened around the waist with a band, and sewed to light leather boots around the ankle hems.

*janissary* an elite Ottoman infantryman.

*jarq* (Turk. *charkhī*, a five-piaster piece) a coin worth four *'uthmānī*s, or two soldi.

*jūkhadār* (Turk. *chohadar*) originally a lackey, footman, or valet; for Diyāb, an attendant, bureaucrat, or high-ranking embassy official.

*Kaftīn* a village in northern Syria, close to Aleppo and to several ruined Byzantine cities.

*Karanlık Kapı (Gate of Darkness)* a pass in the Nur Mountains of southeastern Anatolia (the Amanus range in Ancient Greek), along the Cilician highway to Syria.

*kazan kebabı* a type of meat dish, cooked in a large pot.

*khan* a caravansary, i.e., a roadside staging post with lodging for travelers and their mounts; also, a warehouse and hostel, often built in the outskirts of cities; for Diyāb, also a market or marketplace, and, in one case, a dormitory for prisoners.

*Khan Abrak* a marketplace in Aleppo, found in the Sūq al-Qaṣābiyyah.

*Khan al-'Asal* a town on the western outskirts of Aleppo.

*Khan al-'Ulabiyyah* a monumental sixteenth-century caravansary near Bizzeh Square in southern Aleppo.

*khāṣṣāt (sing. khāṣṣah)* a type of fine, tightly woven cotton.

*khawājah* an informal honorary title given to foreign or Christian merchants during the Ottoman period; Diyāb's first designation for Paul Lucas, later replaced by *mu'allimī* ("[my] master," "boss,").

*Khāzin family* a Maronite landowning family of Mount Lebanon whose members wielded considerable economic and political power between the sixteenth and nineteenth centuries. Beginning in the seventeenth century, they gained political privileges through close economic collaboration with French authorities, for which some members were awarded the title of chevalier.

*Kız Kulesi (Maiden's Tower)*   a small tower that stands on an island in the Bosphorus, near the coast of Üsküdar. The tower dates to the twelfth century.

*Konya*   a city in central Anatolia.

*Larnaca*   (Ar. Milāḥah) a coastal city in southeastern Cyprus.

*Lemaire*   a family of diplomats originally from Joinville in the province of Champagne; one member, Claude, was French consul in Tripoli and later in Aleppo.

*Livorno*   (Ar. Līkūrnā, from Genoese Ligorna) a coastal town in the Italian province of Tuscany and a commercial center in the early modern period.

*londrin*   a type of lightweight, fulled woolen cloth, made in France and England and exported to the Levant.

*Lucas, Paul*   (1646–1734) traveler, adventurer, and antiquarian in the service of Louis XIV; the son of a Rouen goldsmith and the author of three travelogues covering the period between 1699 and 1717; known during the European Enlightenment for his fanciful reports of distant places.

*Madame d'Orléans*   (1677–1749) Françoise Marie de Bourbon, the youngest daughter of Louis XIV with his mistress the Marquise de Montespan; wife of Philippe II, the Duke of Orléans and Regent of France during the minority of Louis XV.

*Madame de Bourgogne*   (1685–1712) Marie Adélaïde of Savoy, wife of Louis XIV's grandson, Louis le Petit Dauphin, Duke of Burgundy, and mother of Louis XV.

*Madame de Maintenon*   (1635–1719) Françoise d'Aubigné, second wife of Louis XIV.

*Maghreb*   the "West," i.e., the western territories of North Africa, including present-day Morocco, Algeria, Libya, and Tunisia.

*miṣriyyah*   a coin of Egyptian origin normally worth one-fortieth of a piaster, or half a piece of silver.

*Messina*   a city on the northeastern tip of Sicily, just across the narrow strait separating the island from the south of Italy.

*mīrī*   a tax on land owned by the Ottoman sovereign.

*Misis*   a town in southeastern Anatolia, about seventeen miles east of Adana. Also called Mopsuestia.

*mithqāl*　a measurement of weight equivalent to one and a half dirhams; in Diyāb's time, around four and a half grams.

*Monseigneur the Dauphin*　(1661–1711) Louis le Grand Dauphin, son of Louis XIV and heir to the French throne, father of Philip V of Spain, and grandfather of Louis XV of France.

*Morea*　the region now referred to as the Peloponnese.

*Mouski quarter*　a district in central Cairo, in the seventeenth and eighteenth centuries home to many European consuls and merchants (and thus also called the Frankish quarter), as well as several Jewish families.

*mujaddarah*　an ancient Near Eastern dish composed of lentils, rice or bulgur, spices, and onions. It remains a staple of many local cuisines, especially in the Levant.

*L'Opéra*　the Paris Opera (known at this time as the Académie Royale de Musique) was housed in the Théâtre du Palais-Royal on the rue Saint-Honoré from 1673 to 1763.

*pāra*　a silver Ottoman coin first issued in the early eighteenth century.

*Paulo Çelebi*　see *Zamāriyā*.

*Peloponnese*　see *Morea*.

*piaster*　see *qirsh*.

*Pontchartrain*　Jérôme Phélypeaux (1674–1747), a French politician who served as secretary of state for the Maison du Roi and for the navy under Louis XIV.

*Province of the Islands*　a province comprising all the major islands of the Ottoman Mediterranean, with the exception of Crete; also known as the Eyalet of the Archipelago.

*qabiji*　(Turk. *qapuči*) originally a gatekeeper or porter, then a palace guard or chamberlain, later a senior palace official or eunuch who guarded the sultan's harem; for Diyāb, also a French royal border guard, or a cavalry commander.

*qinṭār*　a measurement of weight equivalent to one hundred *raṭl*s, variable according to time and place; in seventeenth- through nineteenth-century Aleppo, probably between 487 and 564 pounds.

*qirsh*　(piaster) a heavy silver coin worth forty *pāra*s.

*raṭl*　a measurement of weight whose value varied according to time and place; in seventeenth- through nineteenth-century Aleppo, probably between 4.87 and 5.64 pounds.

*rayyis*　chief, captain, boss, superior.

*Rémuzat*   (or Rémusat) a famous merchant family of Marseille with long-lasting ties to cities in the Ottoman Empire. One member, Auguste Rémuzat, was France's deputy consul in Aleppo, and apparently also the young Diyāb's second patron and employer.

*Rimbaud*   a merchant family from Marseille that supplied many deputies or principal merchants of the French nation in Aleppo during Diyāb's lifetime.

*riyāl*   an originally Spanish silver coin (*real*) of considerable value, widely used in Ottoman lands until 1714, when the Ottomans in Tunis banned its use and began to mint their own. Also called *riyāl qurūsh* (*riyal quruş*).

*Rosetta*   a port city at the western end of the Nile Delta, about one hundred miles from Cairo. Along with Damietta, it is one of the two principal Nile ports on the Mediterranean Sea.

*Rūm, Rūmī*   see *Greek.*

*Saint Elishaʿ*   a monastery on the hillside below the village of Bsharrī, and the main residence of the Maronite Lebanese order during the time of Diyāb's stay.

*Saint Geneviève*   the patron saint of Paris, according to the Roman Catholic and Eastern Orthodox rites.

*Samatan*   a French merchant originally from Marseille, prominent in Aleppo between 1698 and 1708.

*sanjaq*   an administrative subdivision of an Ottoman province (Turk. *eyalet* or *beylic*), administered by a *sanjaq bey*.

*Sauron*   a prominent French merchant in Aleppo during the first two decades of the eighteenth century.

*Sfax*   a commercial city on the coast of what is now Tunisia.

*shāhbandar*   an Ottoman term meaning "harbormaster" (literally "king of the port"); in Diyāb's use the main representative of a group of merchants or the manager of a trading port.

*shāhiyyāt*   (Ar., sing. *shāhī*) An Ottoman silver coin.

*shāsh*   a long strip of cloth used to wind a turban.

*soldi*   (It., sing. *soldo*) An Italian silver coin worth half a *jarq* or two ʿ*uthmānī*s.

*Sousse*   a coastal town in what is now Tunisia.

*Sultan Aḥmad*   (1673–1736) the twenty-third Ottoman sultan, known as Aḥmad III.

*thulth*   in Diyāb's use, a coin worth a third of a piaster; also a third of a dinar, or a third of a *pāra*.

*Tripoli*   a city in northern Lebanon, situated on the Mediterranean coast.

*Tripoli (of the West)*   the capital of present-day Libya, situated on the Mediterranean coast.

*Tunis*   the capital of present-day Tunisia, situated on the Mediterranean coast.

*ūqiyyah*   a measurement of weight whose value varied according to time and place. In Diyāb's Aleppo, it was equivalent to one-twelfth of a *raṭl* or one-sixth of an *uqqah* (around seven and a half ounces; see Barthélémy, 905).

*uqqah*   a measurement of weight whose value varied according to time and place; in Diyāb's Aleppo, it was equivalent to four hundred dirhams, half a *raṭl*, or six *ūqiyyah* (about 2.8 pounds).

*Üsküdar*   an ancient city on the Asian side of the Bosphorus, today a district of Istanbul.

*'uthmānī*   another word for *akče*, a silver coin worth a third or a quarter *pāra*.

*Yūsuf Çelebi*   see *Zamāriyā*.

*zolota*   a coin worth thirty *pāra*s, or three-quarters of a piaster (*qirsh*). The name comes from the Polish *złoty*, a currency exported to Ottoman lands during the seventeenth century.

*Zamāriyā*   a French family residing in Aleppo, some of whose members held important diplomatic posts. The head was Pierre Maunier. Diyāb met Maunier's son Christofalo (Christophe) in Paris, where he served as the steward of Cardinal de Noailles. Diyāb knew Christophe's brothers, Paulo Çelebi (Paul) and Yūsuf Çelebi (Joseph), in Aleppo. The oldest brother, known as Zamāriyā, served as syndic of the Holy Land in Istanbul.

*Zūq Mīkāyīl / Zouq Mkayel*   a village in Kisrawān, between Jounieh and Beirut in what is now Lebanon, in Diyāb's time administered by the Khāzin family and inhabited, perhaps exclusively, by Maronites.

*Zuqāq al-Khall*   (Vinegar Alley) a predominantly Christian quarter on the northern edge of Aleppo. In Diyāb's time, it served as a point of entry to the Christian suburbs.

# Bibliography

## Manuscripts

*Bibliothèque nationale de France*
*Voyages de Paul Lucas*, MS 3820. Bibliothèque de l'Arsenal.
"Comte de Pontchartrain (Louis Phélypeaux) to Marquis de Ferriol, French Ambassador to Constantinople," MS franc. Nouv. acq. 801.

*Gotha, Forschungsbibliothek*
Arab. 1548: *Riḥlat Saʿīd Bāshā*
Arab. 1549: *Riḥlat al-Ab Arsāniyūs Shukrī*
Arab. 1550: *Riḥlat al-shammās Ḥannā al-Ṭabīb*

*Syrian Catholic Archdiocese of Aleppo*
Ar 7/25: *Kitāb Mufīd fī ʿilm al-niyyah*

*Université Saint Joseph (USJ), Bibliothèque Orientale*
BO 29: *Kitāb Siyāḥat al-ḥūrī Ilyās al-Mawṣilī*
BO 594–597: *Kitāb Akhbār al-qiddīsīn*
BO 645: *al-Durr al-nafīs fī sīrat al-qiddīs Fransīs*

*Vatican Apostolic Library*
Sbath 108: *Kitāb Siyāḥat al-ḥūrī Ilyās al-Mawṣilī* and *Riḥlat Saʿīd Bāshā*
Sbath 254: [*Kitāb Siyāḥat Ḥannā Diyāb*]

## Works Cited

Abdel-Halim, Mohamed. *Antoine Galland: Sa vie et son oeuvre*. Thèse en lettres, Paris: A. G. Nizet, 1964.
Addobbati, Andrea. "Hanna Dyab, il mercante di storie." *Quaderni Storico* 3 (2016): 830–42.
Al-Asadī, Khayr al-Dīn. *Mawsūʿat Ḥalab al-muqāranah*. Ḥalab: Jāmiʿat Ḥalab, 1981–88.

Bibliography

Barthélemy, Adrien. *Dictionnaire arabe-français: Dialectes de Syrie: Alep, Damas, Liban, Jérusalem*. Paris: Geuthner, 1935.

Bauden, Frédéric and Richard Waller, eds. *Le journal d'Antoine Galland (1646–1715): La Période Parisienne*. Vol. I. Leuven, Belgium: Peeters, 2011.

Blau, Joshua. *On Pseudo-Corrections in Some Semitic Languages*. Jerusalem: The Israel Academy of Sciences and Humanities, 1970.

Boase, Thomas S. R. "Ecclesiastical Art." In *A History of the Crusades*, edited by Kenneth M. Setton, 165–95. Madison, WI: The University of Wisconsin Press, 1977.

Bóka, Éva, and Katalin Vargyas. "Le marquis Charles de Ferriol ambassadeur de France à Constantinople (1699–1703)." *Acta Historica Academiae Scientiarum Hungaricae* 31, nos. 1–2 (1985): 87–112.

Bolte, Johannes. "Die Sage von der erweckten Scheintoten." *Zeitschrift des Vereins für Volkskunde* 20 (1910): 353–81.

Bottigheimer, Ruth B. "East Meets West: Hannā Diyāb and *The Thousand and One Nights*." *Marvels and Tales* 28, no. 2 (2014): 302–24.

Brednich, Rolf Wilhelm. "Frau: Die tote F. kehrt zurück." In *Enzyklopädie des Märchens: Handwörterbuch zur historischen und vergleichenden Erzählforschung*, Vol. 5, edited by Rolf Wilhelm Brednich and Hermann Bausinger, 199–203. Berlin: de Gruyter, 1987.

Chraïbi, Aboubakr. "Galland's 'Ali Baba' and Other Arabic Versions." *Marvels and Tales* 18, no. 2 (2004): 159–69.

Commission des Antiquités. "Note sur Paul Lucas." *Bulletin de la Commission des Antiquités de la Seine-Inférieure* 10, no. 3 (1897): 338–40.

Davidson, Linda Kay, and David M. Gitlitz. *Pilgrimage: From the Ganges to Graceland; An Encyclopedia*. Santa Barbara, CA: ABC-Clio, 2002.

Dew, Nicholas. *Orientalism in Louis XIV's France*. Oxford, UK: Oxford University Press, 2009.

Diyāb, Ḥannā [Hanna Dyâb]. *D'Alep à Paris: Les pérégrinations d'un jeune syrien au temps de Louis XIV; Récit traduit de l'arabe (Syrie) et annoté par Paule Fahmé-Thiéry, Bernard Heyberger et Jérôme Lentin*. Paris: Actes Sud, 2015.

———. *The Man Who Wrote Aladin*. Translated by Paul Lunde. Edinburgh: Harding Simpole, 2020.

———. *Von Aleppo nach Paris: Die Reise eines jungen Syrers bis an den Hof Ludwigs XIV*. Translated by Gennaro Ghirardelli. Berlin: Die Andere Bibliothek, 2016.

Dobie, Madeleine. "Translation in the Contact Zone: Antoine Galland's *Mille et une nuits: Contes arabes*." In *The Arabian Nights in Historical Context: Between East and West*, edited by Saree Makdisi and Felicity Nussbaum, 25–49. Oxford, UK: Oxford University Press, 2008.

٣٠٢ ❦ 302

Dozy, Reinhart P. A. *Supplément aux dictionnaires arabes*. Beirut: Librairie du Liban, 1968.

Duranton, Henri. "Paul Lucas." In *Christian-Muslim Relations: A Bibliographical History*.
Vol. 13 (1700–1800), edited by David Thomas and John Chesworth, 548–55. Leiden,
Netherlands: Brill, 2019.

Fahd, Buṭrus. *Tārīkh al-rahbāniyyah al-lubnāniyah bi-farʿayhā l-ḥalabī wa-l-lubnānī,
1743–1770*. Vol. 4. Jūniyah, Lebanon: Maṭbaʿat Kuraym, 1966.

*EI2* = Bearman, P., Th. Bianquis, C. E. Bosworth, E. van Donzel, and W. P. Heinrichs, eds.
*Encyclopaedia of Islam*. 2nd ed. 13 vols. Leiden, Netherlands: Brill, 1960–2009.

*EI3* = Gaborieau, Marc, Roger Allen, Gudrun Krämer, Kate Fleet, Denis Matringe, John
Abdallah Nawas, and Everett K. Rowson, eds. *Encyclopaedia of Islam, Three*. Leiden,
Netherlands: Brill, 2007–.

Fahmé-Thiéry, Paule. "L'arabe dialectal aleppin dans le récit de voyage de Hanna Dyâb." In
*Arabic Varieties: Far and Wide; Proceedings of the 11th International Conference of AIDA—
Bucharest, 2015*, edited by George Grigore and Gabriel Biţună, 223–30. Bucharest:
Editura Universiţăţii din Bucureşti, 2016.

———. "Ecriture et conscience de soi: Récits de voyage et accès à la modernité chez Bûlus
ez Zaïm et Hanna Dyâb." Presented at the Kiev colloquium "Sous l'oeil de l'Orient:
L'Europe dans les sources arabes," September 22–23, 2015.

Farḥāt, Jirmānūs. "Tārīkh taʾsīs al-rahbāniyyah al-Lubnāniyyah." In *Bidāyāt al-rahbāniyyah
al-Lubnāniyyah*, edited by Jūzīf Qazzī, 111–78.

Gagliardi, Isabella. "'Ave maris Stella': Il santuario mariano di Montenero presso Livorno."
In *Dio, il mare e gli uomini*, edited by Luciano Fanin, E. Ferrarini, and A. Galdi, 185–213.
Verona: Cierre edizioni, 2008.

Galland, Antoine. *De l'origine et du progrès du café*. Paris: Poisson/Lance, 1836.

———. *Les mille et une nuits: Contes arabes*. 3 vols. Edited by Jean-Paul Sermain. Paris:
Éditions Flammarion, 2004.

———. *Le journal d'Antoine Galland (1646–1715)*. Edited by F. Bauden and R. Waller.
Leeuven, Belgium: Peeters, 2011–15.

———. *Voyage à Constantinople (1672–1673)*. Edited by Charles Schefer. Paris: Maisonneuve
et Larose, 2002.

Gemayel, Nasser. *Les échanges culturels entre les Maronites et l'Europe: Du collège Maronite
de Rome (1584) au collège de ʿAyn-Warqa (1789)*. Beirut: L'imprimerie V. & Ph. Gemayel,
1984.

Gerhardt, Mia. *The Art of Story-Telling: A Literary Study of the Thousand and One Nights*.
Leiden, Netherlands: Brill, 1963.

Ghobrial, John-Paul A. "Stories Never Told: The First Arabic History of the New World."
*The Journal of Ottoman Studies* 40 (2012): 259–82.

———. "The Secret Life of Elias of Babylon and the Uses of Global Microhistory." *Past and Present* (2014): 51–93.

———. "The Life and Hard Times of Solomon Negri: An Arabic Teacher in Early Modern Europe." In *The Teaching and Learning of Arabic in Early Modern Europe*, edited by Jan Loop, Alastair Hamilton, and Charles Burnett, 310–31. Leiden, Netherlands: Brill, 2017.

Gibb, H. A. R. *The Travels of Ibn Battuta in Asia and Africa, AD 1325–1354.* 5 vols. Cambridge, UK: Cambridge University Press, 1958.

Göçek, Fatma Müge. *East Encounters West: France and the Ottoman Empire in the Eighteenth Century.* New York: Oxford University Press, 1987.

Görner, Florian. "Das Regulativ der Wahrscheinlichkeit: Zur Funktion literarischer Fiktionalität im 18; Jahrhundert." PhD diss., Universität Köln, 2011.

Gossard, Julia M. "Breaking a Child's Will: Eighteenth-Century Parisian Juvenile Detention Centers." *French Historical Studies* 42, no. 2 (2019): 239–59.

Graf, Georg. *Geschichte der christlichen arabischen Literatur.* Vols. 3 and 4. Vatican City: Biblioteca Apostolica Vaticana, 1949–51.

———. *Verzeichnis arabischer kirchlicher Termini.* Louvain, Belgium: Imprimerie Orientaliste L. Durbecq, 1954.

Hayek, Michel. "Al-Rāhibah Hindiyyah (1720–1798)." *Al-Mashriq* 9 (1965): 525–646, 685–734.

Heyberger, Bernard. *Hindiyya: Mystique et criminelle 1720–1798.* Paris: Aubier, 2001. English translation: *Hindiyya, Mystic and Criminal, 1720–1798.* Translated by Renée Champion. Cambridge, UK: James Clarke, 2013.

———. *Les chrétiens du Proche-Orient au temps de la réforme catholique (Syrie, Liban, Palestine, XVIIe–XVIIIe siècles).* Rome: Ecole française de Rome, 2014.

———. Introduction to Hanna Dyâb: *D'Alep à Paris; Les pérégrinations d'un jeune syrien au temps de Louis XIV; Récit traduit de l'arabe (Syrie) et annoté par Paule Fahmé-Thiéry, Bernard Heyberger et Jérôme Lentin*, 7–47. Paris: Actes Sud, 2015.

Horta, Paulo Lemos. *Marvellous Thieves: Secret Authors of the Arabian Nights.* Cambridge, MA: Harvard University Press, 2017.

———. "Tales of Aladdin and Their Tellers, from Aleppo to Paris." *Words without Borders*, April 16, 2020. Accessed October 7, 2020. https://www.wordswithoutborders.org/dispatches/article/tales-of-aladdin-and-their-tellers-from-aleppo-to-paris-paulo-lemos-horta.

Ibn al-Ṣāyigh, Fatḥallāh Ibn Anṭūn. *Riḥlah ilā bādiyat al-Shām wa-Ṣaḥārā l-ʿIrāq wa-l-ʿajam wa-l-Jazīrah al-ʿArabiyyah.* Edited by ʿAbdallāh Ibrāhīm al-ʿAskar and Muḥammad Khayr Maḥmūd al-Biqāʿī. Beirut: Jadawel, 2012.

Bibliography

İnalcik, Halil. *An Economic and Social History of the Ottoman Empire, 1300–1914.* Vol. 1, 1300–1600. Cambridge, UK: Cambridge University Press, 1994.

———. "A Note on the Population of Cyprus." *Journal for Cypriot Studies* 3, no. 1 (1997): 3–11.

Jennings, Ronald. *Christians and Muslims in Ottoman Cyprus and the Mediterranean World, 1571–1640.* New York: New York University Press, 1992.

Juillien (professor of botany at the Royal Garden). Undated memorandum to Paul Lucas. *Correspondance et papiers de Paul Lucas, voyageur et antiquaire français.* Richelieu Collection, Monnaies et Médailles, carton 1, dossier 27. Bibliothèque Nationale de France, Paris.

Kahane, Henry Romanos, Renée Kahane, and Andreas Tietze. *The Lingua Franca in the Levant: Turkish Nautical Terms of Italian and Greek Origin.* Urbana, IL: University of Illinois University Press, 1958.

Kallas, Elie. "The Aleppo Dialect According to the Travel Accounts of Ibn Ra'd (1656) Ms. Sbath 89 and Ḥanna Dyāb (1764) Ms. Sbath 254." In *De los manuscritos medievales a internet: La presencia del árabe vernáculo en las fuentes escritas,* edited by M. Meouak, P. Sánchez, and Á. Vicente, 221–54. Zaragoza, Spain: Área de Estudios Árabes e Islámicos, 2012.

———. "Gerboise: L'entrée du terme arabe ǧerbū' à la cour de Louis XIV." In *Approaches to the History and Dialectology of Arabic in Honor of Pierre Larcher,* edited by Manuel Sartori, Manuela E. B. Giolfo, and Philippe Cassuto, 342–61. Leiden, Netherlands: Brill, 2017.

Kilpatrick, Hilary, and Gerald J. Toomer. "Niqūlāwus al-Ḥalabī (c. 1611–c. 1661): A Greek Orthodox Syrian Copyist and His Letters to Pococke and Golius." *Lias* 43, no. 1 (2016): 1–159.

Krimsti, Feras. "The Lives and Afterlives of the Library of the Maronite Physician Ḥannā al-Ṭabīb (c. 1702–1775) from Aleppo." *Journal of Islamic Manuscripts* 9 (2018): 190–217.

———. "Arsāniyūs Shukrī al-Ḥakīm's Account of His Journey to France, the Iberian Peninsula, and Italy (1748–1757) from Travel Journal to Edition." *Philological Encounters* 4, nos. 3–4 (2019): 202–44.

Al-Labbūdī, Tūmā. "Sīrat al-ḥibr al-ṭayyib al-dhikr 'Abdallāh Qarā'alī al-Marūnī al-Ḥalabī." In *Bidāyāt al-rahbāniyyah al-Lubnāniyyah,* edited by Jūzīf Qazzī, 75–105.

Larzul, Sylvette. "Further Considerations on Galland's *Mille et une Nuits*: A Study of the Tales Told by Hannâ." *Marvels and Tales* 18, no. 2 (2004): 258–71. Reprinted in *The Arabian Nights in Transnational Perspective,* edited by Ulrich Marzolph, 17–31. Detroit, MI: Wayne State University Press, 2007.

———. "Les Mille et une nuits de Galland; ou, L'acclimatation d'une 'Belle étrangère.'" *Revue de littérature compare* 3 (1995): 312–18.

———. *Les traductions françaises des "Mille et une nuits": Études des versions Galland, Trébutien et Mardrus*. Paris: Harmattan, 1996.

Lentin, Jérôme. "Recherches sur l'histoire de la langue arabe au Proche-Orient à l'époque moderne." PhD diss., Université de la Sorbonne Nouvelle—Paris III, 1997.

———. "Middle Arabic." In *Encyclopedia of Arabic Language and Linguistics*, edited by Lutz Edzard and Rudolf de Jong. Leiden, Netherlands: Brill, 2011. http://dx.doi.org/10.1163/1570-6699_eall_EALL_COM_vol3_0213.

———. "Note sur la langue de Hanna Dyâb." In *D'Alep à Paris: Les pérégrinations d'un jeune syrien au temps de Louis XIV; Récit traduit de l'arabe (Syrie) et annoté par Paule Fahmé-Thiéry, Bernard Heyberger et Jérôme Lentin*, 48–51. Paris: Sindbad/Actes Sud, 2015.

Lucas, Paul. *[Premier] Voyage du Sieur Paul Lucas dans le Levant: Juin 1699–juillet 1703; Présenté par Henri Duranton*. Saint-Étienne, France: Publications de l'Université de Saint-Étienne, 1998.

———. *Deuxième Voyage du Sieur Paul Lucas dans le Levant: Octobre 1704–septembre 1708; Présenté par Henri Duranton*. Saint-Étienne, France: Publications de l'Université de Saint-Étienne, 2002.

———. *Troisième Voyage du Sieur Paul Lucas dans le Levant: Mai 1714–novembre 1717; Présenté par Henri Duranton*. Saint-Étienne, France: Publications de l'Université de Saint-Étienne, 2004.

Luterbacher, Jürg, Daniel Dietrich, Elena Xoplaki, Martin Grosjean, and Heinz Wanner. "European Seasonal and Annual Temperature Variability, Trends, and Extremes since 1500." *Science* 3, no. 5 (2004): 1499–1503.

Madsen, Peter. "'Auf, Auf, ihr Christen': Representing the Clash of Empires, Vienna 1683." In *Empires and World Literature*, edited by Piero Boitani and Irene Montori, 83–95. Milan: Albo Versorio, 2019.

Martin, Maurice. "Souvenirs d'un compagnion de voyage de Paul Lucas en Égypte (1707)." In *Hommages à la mémoire de Serge Sauneron. Tome II: Égypte post-pharaonique, 1927–1976*, edited by Jean Vercoutter, 471–75. Cairo: Institut Français d'archéologie orientale, 1979.

Marzolph, Ulrich. *101 Middle Eastern Tales and Their Impact on Western Oral Tradition*. Detroit, MI: Wayne State University Press, 2020.

———. "The Man Who Made the Nights Immortal: The Tales of the Syrian Maronite Storyteller Ḥannā Diyāb." *Marvels and Tales* 32, no. 1 (2018): 114–29.

Marzolph, Ulrich, with Anne E. Duggan. "Hanna Diyab's Tales, Part II." *Marvels and Tales* 32, no. 2 (2018): 435–56.

Masters, Bruce. *Christians and Jews in the Ottoman Arab World: The Roots of Sectarianism.* Cambridge, UK: Cambridge University Press, 2001.

Matar, Nabil. *In the Lands of the Christians: Arab Travel Writing in the Seventeenth Century.* London: Routledge, 2003.

Mattern, Joseph. *A travers les villes mortes de Haute Syrie: Promenades archéologiques en 1928, 1929, 1931.* Beirut: Imprimerie Catholique, 1933.

Al-Mawṣilī, Ilyās. "Riḥlat awwal sāʾiḥ sharqī ilā Amirkah. [Taḥqīq Anṭūn Rabbāṭ.]" *Al-Mašriq* 8, no. 2 (1905): 821–34, 875–86, 931–42, 974–83, 1022–33, 1080–88, 1118–1028.

May, Georges. *Les "Mille et une nuits" d'Antoine Galland, ou, Le chef-d'oeuvre invisible.* Paris: Presses universitaires de France, 1986.

McKenzie, Judith. *The Architecture of Alexandria and Egypt, 300 B.C. to A.D. 700.* New Haven, CT: Yale University Press, 2007.

Morison, Antoine. *Relation historique d'un voyage nouvellement fait au Mont de Sinaï et à Jerusalem.* Paris: A. Laurent, 1704.

Omont, Henri. *Missions archéologiques françaises en Orient aux XVIIè et XVIIIè siècles: Documents.* Paris: Imprimerie Nationale, 1902.

Ong, Walter J. *Orality and Literacy: The Technologizing of the World.* London: Routledge, 2002.

Ott, Claudia. "From the Coffeehouse into the Manuscript: The Storyteller and His Audience in the Manuscripts of an Arabic Epic." *Oriente Moderno* 22, no. 2 (2003): 443–51.

Özay, Yeliz. "Evliyâ Çelebi's Strange and Wondrous Europe." *Cahiers balkaniques* 41 (2013): 61–69.

Pamuk, Sevket. *A Monetary History of the Ottoman Empire.* Cambridge, UK: Cambridge University Press, 2000.

Patel, Abdulrazzak. *The Arab Nahḍah: The Making of the Intellectual and Humanist Movement.* Edinburgh: Edinburgh University Press, 2013.

Peucker, Brigitte. "The Material Image in Goethe's *Wahlverwandtschaften.*" *The Germanic Review: Literature, Culture, Theory* 74, no. 3 (1999): 195–213.

Pitou, Spire. *The Paris Opéra: An Encyclopedia of Operas, Ballets, Composers, and Performers.* Westport, CN: Greenwood Press, 1983.

Pococke, Richard. *A Description of the East and Some Other Countries.* London: W. Bowyer, 1743.

Qarāʿalī, ʿAbdallāh. "Mudhakkirāt." In *Bidāyāt al-rahbāniyyah al-Lubnāniyyah*, edited by Jūzīf Qazzī, 23–71.

Qarāʿalī, ʿAbdallāh et al. "Qawānīn al-rahbāniyyah al-Lubnāniyyah." In *Bidāyāt al-rahbāniyyah al-Lubnāniyyah*, edited by Jūzīf Qazzī, 179–210.

Qazzī, Jūzīf, ed. *Bidāyāt al-rahbāniyyah al-Lubnāniyyah*. Kaslik, Lebanon: Markaz al-Nashr wa-l-Tawzīʿ, 1988.

Raymond, André. "An Expanding Community: The Christians of Aleppo in the Ottoman Era (Sixteenth–Eighteenth Centuries)." In *Arab Cities in the Ottoman Period*, edited by André Raymond, 83–100. Aldershot, UK: Ashgate, 2002.

Redhouse, James W. A. *Turkish and English Lexicon*. Istanbul: A. H. Boyajian, 1890.

Reynolds, Dwight, ed. *Interpreting the Self: Autobiography in the Arabic Literary Tradition*. Berkeley, CA: University of California Press, 2001.

Russell, Alexander. *The Natural History of Aleppo*. Vol 1. Revised by Patrick Russell. London: G. G. and J. Robinson, 1794.

Sadan, Joseph. "Background, Date and Meaning of the Story of the Alexandrian Lover and the Magic Lamp: A Little-Known Story from Ottoman Times, with a Partial Resemblance to the Story of Aladdin." *Quaderni di Studi Arabi* 19 (2001): 137–92.

Sbath, Paul. *Bibliothèque de manuscrits: Catalogue*. Vol. 1. Cairo: H. Friedrich, 1928.

———. "Les manuscrits orientaux de la bibliothèque du R. P. Paul Sbath (Suite)." *Échos d'Orient* 23 (1924): 339–58.

Schwab, Raymond. *L'auteur des "Mille et une nuits": Vie d'Antoine Galland*. Paris: Mercure de France, 2004.

Seale, Yasmine, trans. *Aladdin: A New Translation*. Edited by Paulo Lemos Horta. New York, NY: Liveright Publishing, 2019.

Stephan, Johannes. "Von der Bezeugung zur Narrativen Vergegenwärtigung: Fokalisierung im Reisebuch des Syrers Ḥanna Dyāb (1764)." *Diegesis* 4, no. 2 (2015).

———. "Spuren fiktionaler Vergegenwärtigung im Osmanischen Aleppo: Narratologische Analysen und Kontextualisierungen des Reisebuchs von Hanna Dyāb (1764)." PhD diss., Universität Bern, 2016.

Teissier, Octave, ed. *Inventaire des archives historiques de la Chambre de Commerce de Marseille*. Marseille: Barlatier-Feissat, 1878.

Thompson, Ian. *The Sun King's Garden: Louis XIV, André le Nôtre and the Creation of the Garden of Versailles*. New York: Bloomsbury, 2006.

Touati, Houari. *Islam et voyage au Moyen Âge: Histoire et anthropologie d'une pratique lettrée*. Paris: Seuil, 2000.

Van Leeuwen, Richard, and Ulrich Marzolph, eds. *The Arabian Nights Encyclopedia*. Santa Barbara, CA: ABC-CLIO, 2004.

Vasari, Giorgio. *The Life of the Artists*. Translated by Julia Conaway Bondanella and Peter Bondanella. Oxford, UK: Oxford University Press, 2008.

Wahrmund, Adolf. *Handwörterbuch der neu-arabischen und deutschen Sprache*. Beirut: Librairie du Liban, 1974.

Warner, Marina. *Stranger Magic: Charmed States and the Arabian Nights*. London: Vintage, 2012.

Winter, Stefan. "Shiite Emirs and Ottoman Authorities: The Campaign against the Hamadas of Mt Lebanon, 1693–1694." In *Archivum Ottomanicum*, edited by György Hazai, 209–45. Wiesbaden, Germany: Harrassowitz, 2000.

Zotenberg, Hermann. "Notice sur quelques manuscrits des *Mille et Une Nuits* et la traduction de Galland." *Notices et extraits des manuscrits de la Bibliothèque nationale et autres bibliothèques* 28 (1887): 167–235.

# Further Reading

The literature on Ḥannā Diyāb's travelogue and its textual environment is still rather scarce. Due to its conspicuous features and history, *The Book of Travels* will always remain connected to at least four fields of scholarship. The first and most important of these involves studies related to the *Arabian Nights* and the orphan stories, which are Ḥannā Diyāb's contribution to world literature. The second involves research on travelers and travelogues during the early modern period. The third involves studies related to historical linguistics of Arabic. Finally, in recent years scholarship has emerged on the mobility and the textual production of Eastern Christians in the early and middle Ottoman periods, which includes Diyāb's book and similar narrative literature. Autobiographical artifacts such as *The Book of Travels* have yet to be included in the vast research on the history of the early modern Ottoman world and its entanglement with Western Europe.

In the 1990s, *The Book of Travels* drew attention from the field of linguistics, notably in Jérôme Lentin's dissertation, "Recherches sur l'histoire de la langue arabe au Proche-Orient à l'époque moderne," and in other studies of his. In the past seven years, Ruth Bottigheimer and Ulrich Marzolph have published important work regarding Ḥannā Diyāb's connection to the *Arabian Nights*. Bernard Heyberger's introduction to the French translation (2015) and some of his other works, as well as John-Paul Ghobrial's research on the traces of Middle Eastern Christians around the globe, have helped place Ḥannā Diyāb's book in the social context of the Christians of the Ottoman Empire and their entangled histories.

Selected works from these research areas that are not already mentioned in the bibliography to this volume are listed below.

## Literary and Cultural History of the Levant in the Early Modern Period

ʿĀnūtī, Usāma. *Al-Ḥarakah al-adabiyyah fī Bilād ash-Shām khilāl al-qarn al-thāmin ʿashar.* Beirut: Manshūrāt al-Jāmiʿa al-Lubnāniyya, 1971.

Dakhlia, Jocelyne. *Lingua franca.* Arles, France: Actes Sud, 2008.

Hanna, Nelly. *In Praise of Books: A Cultural History of Cairo's Middle Class, Sixteenth to the Eighteenth Century.* Syracuse, NY: Syracuse University Press, 2003.

Kilpatrick, Hilary. "From *Literatur* to *Adab*: The Literary Renaissance in Aleppo around 1700." *Journal of Eastern Christian Studies* 58, nos. 3–4 (2006): 195–220.

Masters, Bruce. *The Arabs of the Ottoman Empire, 1516–1918: A Social and Cultural History.* Cambridge, UK: Cambridge University Press, 2013.

Sajdi, Dana. "Decline, Its Discontents and Ottoman Cultural History: By Way of Introduction." In *Ottoman Tulips, Ottoman Coffee: Leisure and Lifestyle in the Eighteenth Century,* edited by Dana Sajdi, 1–40. London: I. B. Tauris, 2007.

———. *The Barber of Damascus: Nouveau Literacy in Eighteenth-Century Ottoman Levant.* Stanford, CA: Stanford University Press, 2013.

Van den Boogert, Maurits. *Aleppo Observed: Ottoman Syria through the Eyes of Two Scottish Doctors, Alexander and Patrick Russell.* Oxford, UK: Oxford University Press, 2010.

## Antoine Galland and the Orphan Stories

Akel, Ibrahim, and William Granara, eds. *The Thousand and One Nights: Sources and Transformations in Literature, Art, and Science.* Leiden, Netherlands: Brill, 2020.

Bauden, Frédéric, and Richard Waller, eds. *Antoine Galland (1646–1715) et son journal: Actes du colloque international organisé à l'Université de Liège (16–18 février 2015) à l'occasion du tricentenaire de sa mort.* Leeuwen, Belgium: Peeters, 2020.

Bottigheimer, Ruth B., and Claudia Ott. "The Case of the Ebony Horse: Part 1." *Gramarye* 5 (2014): 8–20.

Bottigheimer, Ruth B. "The Case of the Ebony Horse: Hannâ Diyâb's Creation of a Third Tradition; Part 2." *Gramarye* 6 (2014): 6–16.

———. "Reading for Fun in Eighteenth-Century Aleppo: The Hanna Dyâb Tales of Galland's *Mille et une nuits.*" *Book History* 22 (2019): 133–60.

Marzolph, Ulrich. "A Scholar in the Making: Antoine Galland's Early Travel Diaries in the Light of Comparative Folk Narrative Research." *Middle Eastern Literatures* 18, no. 3 (2015): 283–300.

# Early Modern Travel Literature

Elger, Ralf. "Arabic Travelogues from the Mashrek 1700–1834: A Preliminary Survey of the Genre's Development." In *Crossing and Passages in Genre and Culture*, edited by Christian Szyska and Friederike Pannewick, 27–40. Wiesbaden, Germany: Reichert, 2003.

———. "Die Reisen eines Reiseberichts: Ibn Baṭṭūṭas Riḥla im Vorderen Orient des 17. und 18. Jahrhunderts." In *Buchkultur im Nahen Osten des 17. und 18. Jahrhunderts*, edited by Tobias Heinzelmann and Henning Sievert, 53–98. Bern: Peter Lang, 2010.

Göçek, Fatma Müge. *East Encounters West: France and the Ottoman Empire in the Eighteenth Century*. New York, NY: Oxford University Press, 1987.

Heyberger, Bernard and Carsten Walbiner, eds. *Les européens vus par les libanais à l'époque ottoman*. Würzburg, Germany: Ergon, 2002.

Kallas, Elie. "Aventures de Hanna Diyab avec Paul Lucas et Antoine Galland (1707–1710)." *Romano-Arabica* 15 (2015): 255–67.

———. *The Travel Accounts of Raʻd to Venice (1656) and Its Aleppo Dialect According to the MS. Sbath 89*. Vatican City: Biblioteca Apostolica Vaticana, 2015.

Kilpatrick, Hilary. "Between Ibn Baṭṭūṭa and al-Ṭahṭāwī: Arabic Travel Accounts of the Early Ottoman Period." *Middle Eastern Literatures* 11, no. 2 (2008): 233–248.

Muhanna, Elias. "Ilyās al-Mawṣilī." In *Essays in Arabic Literary Biography: 1350–1850*, edited by Joseph E. Lowry and Devin J. Stewart, 295–299. Wiesbaden, Germany: Harrassowitz, 2009.

Salmon, Olivier, ed. *Alep dans la littérature de voyage européenne pendant la période ottomane (1516–1918)*. Aleppo: El-Mudarris, 2011.

Walbiner, Carsten-Michael. "Riḥlat ʻRaʻd' min Ḥalab ilā al-Bunduqīya." In *Mélanges en mémoire de Mgr Néophytos Edelby (1920–1995)*, edited by Nagi Edelby and Pierre Masri, 367–83. Beirut: Université St. Joseph, 2005.

Yirmisekiz Çelebī Efendi, Meḥmed. *Le paradis des infidèles: Relation de Yirmisekiz Çelebi Mehmed efendi, ambassadeur ottoman en France sous la Régence*. Paris: François Maspero, 1981.

# Near Eastern Christianities

Ghobrial, John-Paul A. "The Ottoman World of ʻAbdallah Zakher: Shuwayr Bindings in the Arcadian Library." In *The Arcadian Library: Bindings and Provenance*, edited by Giles Mandelbrote and Willem de Bruijn, 193–231. Oxford, UK: Oxford University Press, 2014.

———. "Migration from Within and Without: In the Footsteps of Eastern Christians in the Early Modern World." *Transactions of the Royal Historical Society* 27 (2017): 153–73.

Heyberger, Bernard. "Livres et pratique de la lecture chez les chrétiens (Syrie, Liban) XVIIe–XVIIIe siècles." *Revue des mondes musulmans et de la Méditerranée* 87–88 (1999): 209–23.

Khater, Akram Fouad. *Embracing the Divine: Gender, Passion, and Politics in the Christian Middle East, 1720–1798.* New York, NY: Syracuse University Press, 2011.

Walbiner, Carsten-Michael. "Monastic Reading and Learning in Eighteenth-Century Bilād al-Šām: Some Evidence from the Monastery of al-Šuwayr (Mount Lebanon)." *Arabica* 51, no. 4 (2004): 462–77.

# Index

abbots, xix, §§1.1–2, §§1.5–16, §§1.18–22,
§§1.24–25, §§3.8–9, §5.127, §§6.63–64,
§6.86, §§6.89–91, §6.110, 283n10, 284n12

'Abdallāh (brother of Ḥannā Diyāb), xviii,
xx

'Abdallāh (ibn) Qarā'alī, xix, xxxi, §1.26,
283n2, 284n16

*abū kalb* (coin), §1.36, 285n24

Abyssinia, §4.49

Adam and Eve, §5.112

agarwood, §4.64

agate, §4.59, §4.61, 290n98

*aghā*, xxxviii. *See also* commander; officer

Aix-en-Provence (referred to as Āzāy by
Diyāb), §8.1, 292n118

"Aladdin" (tale), xii, xiv, xvii, xxiii, xxvi,
285n25

Aleppo, xi–xii, xv, xvii–xx, xxii–xxiv, xxvii,
xxix–xxxi, xxxiv, xxxix n4, xxxix n10,
xl n27, xl n33, xli n44, xlii n57, xlii n62,
§1.1, §1.23, §§1.27–29, §§1.31–32, §§1.40–
41, §§2.5–6, §§2.16–17, §2.20, §4.61,
§5.58, §5.66, §5.106, §6.37, §§6.46–47,
§6.75, §6.103, §7.11, §7.17, §§7.19–20,
§8.2, 283n1, 283n4, 284n18, 285n21,
285n25, 287n47, 287n49, 291n115;
Aleppan, xviii–xxi, xxx, xxxii, xxxvii,
xxxix n8, §1.21, §1.37, §3.12, §4.3, §6.58,
283n4, 291n109; Citadel of, §6.75

Alexandria, xvii, xl n32, §3.24, §§4.3–4, §4.6,
§4.12, §4.24, §4.70, §4.80, §5.27, 287n50

"'Alī Bābā and the Forty Thieves" (tale),
xvii, xxiii

ambassadors, xxix–xxx, §5.61, §6.19,
§§6.118–20

anchors, §4.1, §4.3, §5.3, §5.7, §5.14, §5.19,
§5.21, §5.23, §5.25, §5.38, §5.42, §5.46,
§6.1, §§6.4–5, §6.17, §6.51, §6.121

ancient buildings, §3.9; cities, §4.12; coins,
§2.12, §4.30; customs, §5.31; kings,
§1.34, §2.7, §2.11; obelisk, 288n67;
popes, §8.1; ruins, xxi, §4.29; sites,
§4.12, §4.29, §5.77; texts, §5.123; times,
§6.74; treasury, §5.107

animals, xi, xxi, xxvi, §1.35, §4.8, §4.70,
§§4.78–79, §§5.109–10, §§5.129–31,
§7.21, 284n12, 286n34, 290n90, 290n91.
*See also* beasts; birds; camels; chicken;
cows; deer; dogs; donkeys; fish;
gazelles; goats; horses; hyenas; jerboas;
kangaroos; lions; maggots; mice;
mosquitoes; mules; panthers; pigeons;
reptiles; sheep

antiques, §5.77; coins, §§6.28–29

apples, §8.9

Arabic, xli n35; language, xi, xix, xxi–xxiii,
xxvii–xxviii, xxx, xxxii, xxxv–xxxviii,
xl n31, xli n48, §1.33, §3.12, §5.77,
§5.82, §§6.45–46, §7.19, 285n27,
286n34; Levantine (dialect), xxxv–
xxxviii; library, xix, §7.19; Middle,
xxviii, xxxii, xxxvi–xxxvii, xlii n60;

Index

Gate of Paris (in Marseille), §7.12

Gate of Rome (in Marseille), §7.12

Gate of the Janissaries (in Cairo), §4.47

gathering place/space, §§1.7–8

gazelles, §4.8, §4.70, §5.109

gems/gemstones, xi, §2.12, §4.38, §4.60,
§5.107, §6.30, 290n98. See also
diamonds; emeralds; rubies; pearls;
precious stones

Geneviève, Sainte, xxix

Genoa, xvii, §5.46, §6.112, §§6.116–18,
§§6.120–25, §7.1, 292n117

geometry, xx, §4.27, §4.58

George, Saint, §2.6

gerboas. See jerboas

German/Germany, xv, xxxiv

ghuzzī, §4.25, §4.28

Gio Battista del Giudice, 285n27

Giovanni Battista della Fratta, 288n61

goats, §4.2; goatherd, §1.36

God, xxii, xli n42, §1.1, §1.11, §1.17, §1.23,
§1.31, §1.33, §2.18, §3.15, §4.11, §4.65,
§4.73, §4.76, §5.4, §5.7, §5.10, §§5.15–19,
§5.22, §5.36, §5.79, §§5.111–12, §5.121,
§5.124, §6.5, §§6.10–11, §6.21, §6.24,
§6.65, §6.85, §6.87, §6.113, §7.4; God-
fearing, xxx, §6.118

Gospels, Holy Book, §4.28

La Goulette, 290n94

governors, §3.21, §5.68, §5.78; of Bsharrī
district, 284n14; of Djerba, §§5.70–73,
§5.75; of Fayoum, §4.50, §§4.55–58,
§§4.62–69, §4.80; of Genoa, §§6.115–16;
of Livorno, §6.37, §6.39, §§6.91–92; of
Marseille, §§7.7–8; of Paris, §8.15; of
Sfax, §§5.75–78; of Tripoli, xxx, §5.31;
palaces, §4.57, §4.73, §5.70, §5.76, §6.115

grains, §1.5, §3.7, §4.29, §6.83. See also
wheat

grapes, §4.2; grapevines, §8.12. See also
vineyards

Great Frost, the, 292n117

Greek, §3.4, §3.12, §§3.15–16, §3.23, §4.5,
287n46; language, xii, §3.4, §3.11, §3.13,
§3.15; Orthodox, xli n48; philosophers,
§4.9, §5.123; ship, §3.1

Grotte de Sainte-Baume, 291n112

guards, §§1.35–36, §5.10, §5.37, §5.47,
§6.24, §6.34, §6.38, §6.89, §8.7. See also
sentinel; in turrets, §§6.76–77

Guillon, khawājah, §6.104

Gulf of Sidra, xiii, §5.1, 288n73

Hagia Sophia church of Nicosia, 286n42

ham, §3.8. See also pork

Ḥamādah tribe, §1.20, 284n14

al-Ḥammāmāt, §5.89, 289n85

hanging (execution), §6.34, §6.71, §6.87,
§§6.97–99

Ḥannā (chevalier), §2.1

Ḥannā, Father. See Father Ḥannā

Ḥannā ibn Shukrī al-Ṭabīb, xxx, xxxii,
xli n44

harbor, §4.6, §4.13, §§5.21–25, §§5.35–36,
§5.43, §5.46, §5.49, §5.133, §§6.1–2,
§§6.4–5, §6.17, §6.26, §6.49, §6.121,
§§7.5–6, §7.14, 290n94; harbormaster,
§6.35

hard labor (punishment), §6.37, §6.72, §7.7

hardtack, §4.51, §§5.8–10

harems, §§4.63–65, §5.48, §5.51

Harlequin, xii

Heaven, §5.113; heavenly, §7.4

Hebrew, §4.58

Index

orderliness, §8.15

Ottoman xii, xv, xvii, xxv, xxviii, 284n14, 286n44, 289n78; ambassador, xxix–xxx; codices, xxxiii; conquest, 286n41; diplomats, xxx; embassy, xxx; Empire, xi, xviii, xxi, xli n47, 285n24, 285n30, 289n78, 289n79; era, xxxix; fleet, 289n83; kingdoms, §5.102; navy, 289n83; relations, xxx; rule, 284n14, 285n28; sovereign, 285n30; sultan, 284n20; style, §2.6; Turkish, xxxvi–xxxvii

Ottomans, 286n41, 286n42

Palace of Justice, §4.56, §4.58, §4.63

palm tree, §5.11; branches, §5.129; leaves, §6.93

panthers, §1.35, §4.70

Paphos, §4.1

Paradise, §§5.112–13; paradise, §7.4

parchment, §4.31, §4.58

Paris, xi, xiii, xvii, xix–xx, xxii–xxiii, xxvi, xxix–xxxi, xxxiv, xxxvii, xxxix n4, xli n45, xlii n59, §1.33, §1.38, §1.40, §2.20, §5.121, §5.127, §5.131, §6.30, §6.119, §6.123, §6.125, §7.9, §7.12, §§7.17–19, §7.21, §§8.12–16, 283n2, 285n22, 285n25, 285n27, 286n40, 287n45, 287n56, 288n61, 289n82, 290n92, 290n94, 290n95, 290n100, 292n118

Parisian homes, §§8.14–15

Parisian shops, §8.14

pasha, §3.14, §3.22, §5.61

paste, xii, §§5.72–73, §§5.76–77. See also elixir; medicine; ointment

Paul Lucas, xi–xii, xvii, xix–xx, xxii, xxxi, xxxix n7, xl n15, xlii n53, §1.29, §§1.38–39,

§2.1, §2.17, §4.34, §5.66, §6.23, §6.26, §6.28, §6.42, 285n25, 286n39, 286n40, 287n45, 289n76, 290n93

Paul, Saint, §3.19

pearls, xii, §§5.72–73; Precious Pearl, The, xxvii–xxix

peasants, §4.1, §§4.38–44, §4.55, §4.79, §5.69, §5.96, 288n62

Persian carpets, §6.50

Peter, Saint, §3.19

petrification (turn to stone), §5.79

Pharaoh's palace, §4.25

pharaohs, §4.31, §4.39

philosopher's stone, xxiv, §5.123. See also elixir

philosophy, xx, §4.27

physiognomy, §4.27

piaster, §§2.9–11, §2.18, §4.3, §§4.31–32, §4.38, §4.40, §5.13, §5.56, §5.130, §6.37, §6.50, §6.53, §6.59, §6.82, §6.105, §7.13, §8.2, §8.11, §8.15, 286n33, 291n106

pigeon, §7.2

pigs, xiii, §3.6, §4.2, §5.109

pipes (tobacco), §1.32, §3.13, §4.19, §4.64, §6.46

pirates, xiii, §4.82, §6.1, §6.9, §6.12, §§6.14–16, §6.21, §6.33, §6.51, §6.112, §6.115

pistols, §6.15, §6.74

plague, 290n99

Pont Saint-Esprit, 292n121; as Bridge of the Holy Spirit, §8.7

Pontchartrain (Minister of the Orient), §7.19

popes, xxxvii, §8.1

porcelain, §5.72, §8.9, 292n122

pork, §§3.20–21; salted, §3.8. See also ham

# About the NYU Abu Dhabi Institute

The Library of Arabic Literature is supported by a grant from the NYU Abu Dhabi Institute, a major hub of intellectual and creative activity and advanced research. The Institute hosts academic conferences, workshops, lectures, film series, performances, and other public programs directed both to audiences within the UAE and to the worldwide academic and research community. It is a center of the scholarly community for Abu Dhabi, bringing together faculty and researchers from institutions of higher learning throughout the region.

NYU Abu Dhabi, through the NYU Abu Dhabi Institute, is a world-class center of cutting-edge research, scholarship, and cultural activity. The Institute creates singular opportunities for leading researchers from across the arts, humanities, social sciences, sciences, engineering, and the professions to carry out creative scholarship and conduct research on issues of major disciplinary, multidisciplinary, and global significance.

# About the Typefaces

The Arabic body text is set in DecoType Naskh, designed by Thomas Milo and Mirjam Somers, based on an analysis of five centuries of Ottoman manuscript practice. The exceptionally legible result is the first and only typeface in a style that fully implements the principles of script grammar (*qawāʿid al-khaṭṭ*).

The Arabic footnote text is set in DecoType Emiri, drawn by Mirjam Somers, based on the metal typeface in the naskh style that was cut for the 1924 Cairo edition of the Qurʾan.

Both Arabic typefaces in this series are controlled by a dedicated font layout engine. ACE, the Arabic Calligraphic Engine, invented by Peter Somers, Thomas Milo, and Mirjam Somers of DecoType, first operational in 1985, pioneered the principle followed by later smart font layout technologies such as OpenType, which is used for all other typefaces in this series.

The Arabic text was set with WinSoft Tasmeem, a sophisticated user interface for DecoType ACE inside Adobe InDesign. Tasmeem was conceived and created by Thomas Milo (DecoType) and Pascal Rubini (WinSoft) in 2005.

The English text is set in Adobe Text, a new and versatile text typeface family designed by Robert Slimbach for Western (Latin, Greek, Cyrillic) typesetting. Its workhorse qualities make it perfect for a wide variety of applications, especially for longer passages of text where legibility and economy are important. Adobe Text bridges the gap between calligraphic Renaissance types of the 15th and 16th centuries and high-contrast Modern styles of the 18th century, taking many of its design cues from early post-Renaissance Baroque transitional types cut by designers such as Christoffel van Dijck, Nicolaus Kis, and William Caslon. While grounded in classical form, Adobe Text is also a statement of contemporary utilitarian design, well suited to a wide variety of print and on-screen applications.

# Titles Published by the Library of Arabic Literature

For more details on individual titles, visit www.libraryofarabicliterature.org

**Classical Arabic Literature: A Library of Arabic Literature Anthology**
Selected and translated by Geert Jan van Gelder (2012)

**A Treasury of Virtues: Sayings, Sermons, and Teachings of ʿAlī**, by al-Qāḍī
al-Quḍāʿī, with the **One Hundred Proverbs** attributed to al-Jāḥiẓ
Edited and translated by Tahera Qutbuddin (2013)

**The Epistle on Legal Theory**, by al-Shāfiʿī
Edited and translated by Joseph E. Lowry (2013)

**Leg over Leg**, by Aḥmad Fāris al-Shidyāq
Edited and translated by Humphrey Davies (4 volumes; 2013–14)

**Virtues of the Imām Aḥmad ibn Ḥanbal**, by Ibn al-Jawzī
Edited and translated by Michael Cooperson (2 volumes; 2013–15)

**The Epistle of Forgiveness**, by Abū l-ʿAlāʾ al-Maʿarrī
Edited and translated by Geert Jan van Gelder and Gregor Schoeler
(2 volumes; 2013–14)

**The Principles of Sufism**, by ʿĀʾishah al-Bāʿūniyyah
Edited and translated by Th. Emil Homerin (2014)

**The Expeditions: An Early Biography of Muḥammad**, by Maʿmar ibn Rāshid
Edited and translated by Sean W. Anthony (2014)

**Two Arabic Travel Books**
**Accounts of China and India**, by Abū Zayd al-Sīrāfī
Edited and translated by Tim Mackintosh-Smith (2014)
**Mission to the Volga**, by Aḥmad ibn Faḍlān
Edited and translated by James Montgomery (2014)

**Disagreements of the Jurists: A Manual of Islamic Legal Theory**, by al-Qāḍī al-Nuʿmān
Edited and translated by Devin J. Stewart (2015)

**Consorts of the Caliphs: Women and the Court of Baghdad**, by Ibn al-Sāʿī
Edited by Shawkat M. Toorawa and translated by the Editors of the Library of Arabic Literature (2015)

**What ʿĪsā ibn Hishām Told Us**, by Muḥammad al-Muwayliḥī
Edited and translated by Roger Allen (2 volumes; 2015)

**The Life and Times of Abū Tammām**, by Abū Bakr Muḥammad ibn Yaḥyā al-Ṣūlī
Edited and translated by Beatrice Gruendler (2015)

**The Sword of Ambition: Bureaucratic Rivalry in Medieval Egypt**, by ʿUthmān ibn Ibrāhīm al-Nābulusī
Edited and translated by Luke Yarbrough (2016)

**Brains Confounded by the Ode of Abū Shādūf Expounded**, by Yūsuf al-Shirbīnī
Edited and translated by Humphrey Davies (2 volumes; 2016)

**Light in the Heavens: Sayings of the Prophet Muḥammad**, by al-Qāḍī al-Quḍāʿī
Edited and translated by Tahera Qutbuddin (2016)

**Risible Rhymes**, by Muḥammad ibn Maḥfūẓ al-Sanhūrī
Edited and translated by Humphrey Davies (2016)

**A Hundred and One Nights**
Edited and translated by Bruce Fudge (2016)

**The Excellence of the Arabs**, by Ibn Qutaybah
Edited by James E. Montgomery and Peter Webb
Translated by Sarah Bowen Savant and Peter Webb (2017)

**Scents and Flavors: A Syrian Cookbook**
Edited and translated by Charles Perry (2017)

**Arabian Satire: Poetry from 18th-Century Najd**, by Ḥmēdān al-Shwēʿir
Edited and translated by Marcel Kurpershoek (2017)

**In Darfur: An Account of the Sultanate and Its People**, by Muḥammad ibn ʿUmar al-Tūnisī
Edited and translated by Humphrey Davies (2 volumes; 2018)

**War Songs**, by ʿAntarah ibn Shaddād
Edited by James E. Montgomery
Translated by James E. Montgomery with Richard Sieburth (2018)

**Arabian Romantic: Poems on Bedouin Life and Love**, by ʿAbdallāh ibn Sbayyil
Edited and translated by Marcel Kurpershoek (2018)

**Dīwān ʿAntarah ibn Shaddād: A Literary-Historical Study**
By James E. Montgomery (2018)

**Stories of Piety and Prayer: Deliverance Follows Adversity**, by al-Muḥassin ibn ʿAlī al-Tanūkhī
Edited and translated by Julia Bray (2019)

**The Philosopher Responds: An Intellectual Correspondence from the Tenth Century**, by Abū Ḥayyān al-Tawḥīdī and Abū ʿAlī Miskawayh
Edited by Bilal Orfali and Maurice A. Pomerantz
Translated by Sophia Vasalou and James E. Montgomery (2 volumes; 2019)

**Tajrīd sayf al-himmah li-stikhrāj mā fī dhimmat al-dhimmah: A Scholarly Edition of ʿUthmān ibn Ibrāhīm al-Nābulusī's Text**
By Luke Yarbrough (2020)

**The Discourses: Reflections on History, Sufism, Theology, and Literature— Volume One**, by al-Ḥasan al-Yūsī
Edited and translated by Justin Stearns (2020)

**Impostures**, by al-Ḥarīrī
Translated by Michael Cooperson (2020)

**Maqāmāt Abī Zayd al-Sarūjī**, by al-Ḥarīrī
Edited by Michael Cooperson (2020)

**The Yoga Sutras of Patañjali**, by Abū Rayḥān al-Bīrūnī
Edited and translated by Mario Kozah (2020)

**The Book of Charlatans**, by Jamāl al-Dīn ʿAbd al-Raḥīm al-Jawbarī
Edited by Manuela Dengler
Translated by Humphrey Davies (2020)

**A Physician on the Nile**, by ʿAbd al-Laṭīf al-Baghdādī
Edited and translated by Tim Mackintosh-Smith (**2021**)

**The Book of Travels**, by Ḥannā Diyāb
Edited by Johannes Stephan
Translated by Elias Muhanna (**2 volumes; 2021**)

English-only Paperbacks

**Leg over Leg**, by Aḥmad Fāris al-Shidyāq (**2 volumes; 2015**)
**The Expeditions: An Early Biography of Muḥammad**, by Maʿmar ibn Rāshid (**2015**)
**The Epistle on Legal Theory: A Translation of al-Shāfiʿī's** *Risālah*, by al-Shāfiʿī (**2015**)
**The Epistle of Forgiveness**, by Abū l-ʿAlāʾ al-Maʿarrī (**2016**)
**The Principles of Sufism**, by ʿĀʾishah al-Bāʿūniyyah (**2016**)
**A Treasury of Virtues: Sayings, Sermons, and Teachings of ʿAlī**, by al-Qāḍī al-Quḍāʿī, with the **One Hundred Proverbs** attributed to al-Jāḥiẓ (**2016**)
**The Life of Ibn Ḥanbal**, by Ibn al-Jawzī (**2016**)
**Mission to the Volga**, by Ibn Faḍlān (**2017**)
**Accounts of China and India**, by Abū Zayd al-Sīrāfī (**2017**)
**A Hundred and One Nights** (**2017**)
**Consorts of the Caliphs: Women and the Court of Baghdad**, by Ibn al-Sāʿī (**2017**)
**Disagreements of the Jurists: A Manual of Islamic Legal Theory**, by al-Qāḍī al-Nuʿmān (**2017**)
**What ʿĪsā ibn Hishām Told Us**, by Muḥammad al-Muwayliḥī (**2018**)
**War Songs**, by ʿAntarah ibn Shaddād (**2018**)
**The Life and Times of Abū Tammām**, by Abū Bakr Muḥammad ibn Yaḥyā al-Ṣūlī (**2018**)
**The Sword of Ambition**, by ʿUthmān ibn Ibrāhīm al-Nābulusī (**2019**)
**Brains Confounded by the Ode of Abū Shādūf Expounded: Volume One**, by Yūsuf al-Shirbīnī (**2019**)
**Brains Confounded by the Ode of Abū Shādūf Expounded: Volume Two**, by Yūsuf al-Shirbīnī and **Risible Rhymes**, by Muḥammad ibn Maḥfūẓ al-Sanhūrī (**2019**)
**The Excellence of the Arabs**, by Ibn Qutaybah (**2019**)

**Light in the Heavens: Sayings of the Prophet Muḥammad**, by al-Qāḍī al-Quḍāʿī (2019)

**Scents and Flavors: A Syrian Cookbook** (2020)

**Arabian Satire: Poetry from 18th-Century Najd**, by Ḥmēdān al-Shwēʿir (2020)

**In Darfur: An Account of the Sultanate and Its People**, by Muḥammad al-Tūnisī (2020)

**Arabian Romantic**, by ʿAbdallāh ibn Sbayyil (2020)

**The Philosopher Reponds**, by Abū Ḥayyān al-Tawḥīdī and Abū ʿAlī Miskawayh (2021)

# About the Editor

Johannes Stephan earned his Ph.D. at the University of Bern. Currently, he holds a postdoc in the ERC project *Kalīlah and Dimnah*—AnonymClassic at the Freie Universität Berlin, scrutinizing the early Arabic reception (eighth to thirteenth centuries) of the *Book of Kalīlah wa-Dimnah* and elaborating on the concepts of narrative framing and fictionality. His forthcoming monograph, *Vergegenwärtigendes Erzählen: Das Reisebuch (1764) des tausendundeine-Nacht-Erzählers Ḥannā Diyāb im Rahmen einer inklusiven arabischen Literaturgeschichte*, analyzes and contextualizes the literariness of Diyāb's *Book of Travels*.

# About the Translator

**Elias Muhanna** is Associate Professor of Comparative Literature and History at Brown University. He is the author of *The World in a Book: al-Nuwayri and the Islamic Encyclopedic Tradition* and translator of Shihāb al-Dīn al-Nuwayrī's fourteenth-century encyclopedia, *The Ultimate Ambition in the Arts of Erudition.*